Literary Studies in Luke-Acts
Essays in Honor of Joseph B. Tyson

D1193136

Joseph B. Tyson

Literary Studies in Luke-Acts

Essays in Honor of Joseph B. Tyson

edited by
Richard P. Thompson
and
Thomas E. Phillips

MERCER UNIVERSITY PRESS

ISBN 0-86554-563-4   MUP/P185

Literary Studies in Luke-Acts.
Essays in Honor of Joseph B. Tyson.
Copyright ©1998
Mercer University Press, Macon, Georgia 31210-3960 USA

Library of Congress Cataloging-in-Publication Data

Literary studies in Luke-Acts : essays in honor of Joseph B. Tyson /
    edited by Richard P. Thompson and Thomas E. Phillips.
    xviii+374pp. 6x9" (15x23cm.).
    Includes bibliographical references and indexes.
    ISBN 0-86554-563-4 (alk. paper).
    1. Bible. N.T. Luke--Criticism, interpretation, etc.
    2. Bible. N.T. Acts—Criticism, interpretation, etc.
    3. Jews in the New Testament.
    I. Tyson, Joseph B. II. Thompson, Richard P. III. Phillips, Thomas E.
    BS2589.L58   1998
    226.4'06—dc21   98-21502
                                                     CIP

Table of Contents

Part I
Luke and Acts within First-Century Judaism, the New Testament, and Early Christianity

Part II
Lukan Themes, Characters, and Rhetoric

Abbreviations

AB	Anchor Bible
ABD	*Anchor Bible Dictionary*
AJT	*American Journal of Theology*
ANRW	*Aufstieg und Niedergang der römischen Welt*
ASNU	Acta seminarii neotestamentici upsaliensis
ATR	*Anglican Theological Review*
BAGD	Bauer-Arndt-Gingrich-Danker,
	Greek-English Lexicon of the NT, 2nd ed. (1979)
BBB	Bonner biblische Beiträge
BDF	Blass-Debrunner-Funk, *A Greek Grammar of the NT*
Beginnings	*The Beginnings of Christianity*, I: *The Acts of the Apostles*,
	ed. Foakes-Jackson and Lake (1920–1933)
BETL	Bibliotheca ephemeridum theologicarum lovaniensium
BHT	Beiträge zur historischen Theologie
Bib	*Biblica*
BibRev	*Bible Review*
BJS	Brown Judaic Studies
BNTC	Black's N.T. Commentary
BTB	*Biblical Theology Bulletin*
BWANT	Beiträge zur Wissenschaft vom Alten und Neuen Testament
BZ	*Biblische Zeitschrift*
CB	*Cultura bíblica*
CBC	Cambridge Bible Commentary
CBQ	*Catholic Biblical Quarterly*
ConBNT	Coniectanea biblica, New Testament
CrIn	*Critical Inquiry*
CurTM	*Currents in Theology and Mission*
Ebib	*Etudes bibliques*
EKKNT	Evangelisch-katholischer Kommentar zum Neuen Testament
ETL	*Ephemerides theologicae lovanienses*
ETR	*Etudes théologiques et religieuses*
EvQ	*Evangelical Quarterly*
EVV	English versions
ExpTim	*Expository Times*
FRLANT	Forschungen zur Religion und Literatur
	des Alten und Neuen Testaments
GTA	Göttingen theologische Arbeiten
HNTC	Harper's N.T. Commentaries
HTKNT	Herders theologischer Kommentar zum Neuen Testament
HTR	*Harvard Theological Review*

IBS	*Irish Biblical Studies*
ICC	International Critical Commentary
IDB	*Interpreter's Dictionary of the Bible* (1962)
IEJ	*Israel Exploration Journal*
Int	*Interpretation*
ITS	*Indian Theological Journal*
JBL	*Journal of Biblical Literature*
JES	*Journal of Ecumenical Studies*
JETS	*Journal of the Evangelical Theological Society*
JHS	*Journal of Hellenic Studies*
JJS	*Journal of Jewish Studies*
JQR	*Jewish Quarterly Review*
JR	*Journal of Religion*
JSNT	*Journal for the Study of the New Testament*
JSNTSup	Journal for the Study of the New Testament—Supplement Series
JSOTSup	Journal for the Study of the Old Testament—Supplement Series
JSPSup	Journal for the Study of the Pseudepigrapha—Supplement Series
JTS	*Journal of Theological Studies*
KEKNT	Kritisch-exegetischer Kommentar über Neue Testament
LAJP	*Luke-Acts and the Jewish People: Eight Critical Pespectives*, ed. J. B. Tyson (1988)
LCBI	Literary Currents in Biblical Interpretation
LCL	Loeb Classical Library
LD	Lectio divina
LEC	Library of Early Christianity
LS	*Louvain Studies*
LSJ	Liddell-Scott-Jones, *Greek-English Lexicon* (1940)
MNTC	Moffatt NT Commentary
NCB	New Century Bible
NEB	New English Bible
NGS	New Gospel Studies
NIBC	New International Bible Commentary
NICNT	New International Commentary on the New Testament
NIDNTT	*New International Dictionary of New Testament Theology*
NIGTC	New International Greek Testament Commentary
NJB	New Jerusalem Bible
NovT	*Novum Testamentum*
NRSV	New Revised Standard Version
NRT	*La nouvelle revue théologique*
NTD	Das Neue Testament Deutsch
NTS	*New Testament Studies*
OBO	Orbis biblicus et orientalis

OBT	Overtures to Biblical Theology
OTNT	Ökumenischer Taschenbuchkommentar zum Neuen Testament
PerRS	*Perspectives in Religious Studies*
PSTJ	*Perkins School of Theology Journal*
RevExp	*Review and Expositor*
RevistB	*Revista bíblica*
RGG	*Religion in Geschichte und Gegenwart*
RHPR	*Revue d'histoire et de philosophie religieuses*
RSR	*Recherches de science religieuse*
RSV	Revised Standard Version
SBLDS	Society of Biblical Literature Dissertation Series
SBLMS	Society of Biblical Literature Monograph Series
SBLSP	*Society of Biblical Literature Seminar Papers*
SBT	Studies in Biblical Theology
SecCent	*Second Century*
SNTSMS	Society for New Testament Studies Monograph Series
ST	*Studia theologica*
Studies	*Studies in Luke-Acts*, ed. Keck and Martyn (1966)
SUNT	Studien zur Umwelt des Neuen Testaments
SwJT	*Southwestern Journal of Theology*
TDNT	*Theological Dictionary of the New Testament*, ed. Kittel and Friedrich
TLZ	*Theologische Literaturzeitung*
TPINTC	Trinity Press International New Testament Commentary
TS	*Theological Studies*
TToday	*Theology Today*
TZ	*Theologische Zeitschrift*
VC	*Vigiliae christianae*
VT	*Vetus Testamentum*
WBC	Word Biblical Commentary
WTJ	*Westminster Theological Journal*
WUNT	Wissenschaftliche Untersuchungen zum Neuen Testament
ZAW	*Zeitschrift für die alttestamentliche Wissenschaft*
ZNW	*Zeitschrift für die neutestamentliche Wissenschaft*

Foreword

The whole of Joseph Tyson's exemplary career as teacher-scholar, beginning in 1958, has been spent at Southern Methodist University. Ever since my own appointment to the SMU faculty one year later, I have been privileged to count him a good friend as well as a respected colleague in our common field of study. I have therefore welcomed the invitation of the editors to contribute this word of personal appreciation in the form of a foreword to the impressive group of essays they have so ably assembled to honor him.

Joe Tyson's teaching and scholarship have been shaped and energized by three particular interests. First, he has been concerned, as he himself has put it, "to bore a small hole in the wall that separates the N[ew] T[estament] from early church history" (*The New Testament and Early Christianity*, vii). In this regard, he has identified a paper presented in 1966 by our late colleague, Albert C. Outler, as having provided "the germinal idea" from which he developed his commitment to take this particular approach to the study of Christian origins (*A Study of Early Christianity*, vii). Without diminishing the importance of the New Testament for historical work, he has insisted that other Christian writings, especially of the first two centuries, are equally important sources for gaining an understanding of the rise and early development of Christianity; and further, that this entire corpus of Christian literature, in all of its variety, must be set within the still broader context of the political, social, and religious history of the Greco-Roman world.

This is the approach Tyson has followed consistently in the classroom, in his various scholarly publications, and in his widely used college textbook, *A Study of Early Christianity* (1973), of which his later volume, *The New Testament and Early Christianity* (1984), is a significant expansion and revision. In the latter, for example, he identifies the broader boundaries of his study as ca. 336 BCE to 306 CE, and then focuses more particularly on the whole of the first and second centuries CE, not narrowly on some allegedly "New Testament period." Moreover, he devotes almost one-third of that volume to explaining what is involved in the kind of historical inquiry to which he is committed, and to summarizing the historical and religious context of early Christianity. Following this, his presentation continues to be rigorously historical—beginning with a section on Jesus (where apocryphal as well as canonical gospels are in view), and proceeding with two further sections which are devoted, not to specified segments of the New Testament canon, but to developments in Christianity in the historical periods, 30–70 and 70–185 CE, respectively. In these two sections, as throughout, he draws the New Testament writings into his discussion not just because they are canonical, but because they belong to the larger corpus of early Christian literature—noncanonical as well as canonical—which he judges to be important for understanding Christianity as a religious phenomenon of the Greco-Roman world.

Tyson's second great interest has been with Luke-Acts, as the bulk of his scholarly publications attest. Is this because the author of that great two-volume work, which comprises more than one-fourth of the New Testament canon, was also concerned—of course in his own way—with the history of early Christianity, and seems to have been more interested than any other writer represented in the New Testament to locate the church's story within the context of secular events? At least in retrospect, this explanation seems plausible. Tyson's study of Luke began in the 1950s with his doctoral research at New York's Union Theological Seminary, where his dissertation ("The Execution of Jesus: An Investigation into the Background of and Charges at the Trial of Jesus") was completed in 1959. His earliest published work on Acts appeared some twenty years later ("The Problem of Food in Acts: A Study of Literary Patterns with Particular Reference to Acts 6:1-7," 1979). His subsequent monograph on *The Death of Jesus in Luke-Acts* (1986) therefore represents the coalescing of several long-standing interests. In addition, along with the article on Acts, the 1986 monograph discloses an increasing interest in using the methods of literary criticism to supplement the historical-critical procedures he had emphasized in his earlier writings. Meanwhile, within the Society of Biblical Literature he had been instrumental in organizing a program unit on the Book of Acts, over which he presided as chair from 1984 to 1990. His leadership role in furthering the discussion of Luke-Acts is well documented in the scholarly literature, including the essays contributed to this volume.

A third major concern, and one which in recent years has played an especially important role in shaping his teaching and scholarship, has been to reexamine the vexed and extremely critical question of Christianity's relation to Judaism in the first two centuries. One suspects this interest has developed in part from his earlier work on the trial of Jesus and from his various studies of Luke-Acts, although it is surely motivated as well by his strong commitment to fostering genuine and constructive dialogue between Jews and Christians in our own day. His engagement with this topic is evident in a number of scholarly publications devoted to it, including a volume of essays he has edited, *Luke-Acts and the Jewish People: Eight Critical Perspectives* (1988), and his own important monograph on *Images of Judaism in Luke-Acts* (1992). It is evident, no less, in an undergraduate course he regularly teaches on the Holocaust, and in his service as a member of the Committee on Church Relations of the United States Holocaust Memorial Council, of Washington, D.C. The wisdom, informed understanding, and human sensitivity which characterize his contributions to this very timely subject were impressively attested, albeit inadvertently, by one of the students in his course on the Holocaust. Having put a question to him, privately, which assumed that he, like herself, was Jewish, the young woman was quite astonished to discover that in fact he is not.

In addition to his leadership in the Acts group of the international Society of Biblical Literature, Joe Tyson has been president of the Southwest Region, American Academy of Religion (1968–1969), and has held various offices in the Southwest Commission on Religious Studies, including a term as chair of its board of directors (1978–1980) and a term as its president (1983–1984). He has also been entrusted with significant administrative responsibilities at SMU, having been called upon at various times to serve as an assistant dean, chair of the Department of Religious Studies, director of the Center for the Study of Religion in the Greco-Roman World, and president of the Faculty Senate. During 1993–1994 he was the recipient of the John G. Gammie Senior Lectureship Award, bestowed annually by the Southwest Commission on Religious Studies, and on two occasions the SMU student body has given him an Outstanding Professor Award. In addition, and most appropriately, Southern Methodist University honored his contributions both in the classroom and to scholarship by naming him the 1996–1997 University Scholar/Teacher of the Year, an award established by the United Methodist Church.

It is a pleasure now to join with others in further honoring this friend and colleague, with appreciation for what he has already contributed as a teacher-scholar, and in anticipation of many more years of cordial and constructive dialogue with him about the New Testament and early Christianity.

Victor Paul Furnish
University Distinguished Professor of New Testament
Southern Methodist University

Preface

This volume arises from the deep respect which we the coeditors, Dick Thompson and Tom Phillips, have for our "doctor-father," Joseph B. Tyson. Because we have found Joe Tyson to be a patient, courteous, and insightful mentor and scholar, we wish to honor him at his retirement from active teaching with a tribute appropriate to his distinguished career.

As relative newcomers to the scholarly world (Thompson earned his Ph.D. in 1996 and Phillips will receive his Ph.D. in 1998), we were uncertain exactly how to proceed with a project of this scope and caliber. At the earliest stages of this project, the helpful advice of C. Clifton Black and Mikeal Parsons proved invaluable, and we wish to thank them for their early assistance. As we followed their advice, we were able quickly to assemble the group of distinguished scholars represented in this volume. We were pleased, but not surprised, to hear that Joe Tyson is both well respected and well liked by his professional and scholarly colleagues. Many of the contributors to this volume have used the occasion of their respective essays to offer words of praise to Joe Tyson. We believe we speak for all the contributors when we go beyond those individual accolades and say that Joseph B. Tyson is viewed with sincere respect, appreciation, and fondness by all of his colleagues who have contributed to this volume in his honor.

All of the authors represented here, with the exception of his former students Tom Phillips and Dick Thompson, have significant professional ties to Joe Tyson and his scholarly activities. Some contributors are current or former teaching colleagues at SMU; others have collaborated with him on various publishing projects; still others have developed their relationship with him through ongoing scholarly dialogue at professional meetings and conferences like those sponsored by the Society of Biblical Literature and the Southwest Commission on Religious Studies.

The topics addressed in this volume largely correspond to Tyson's scholarly interests, specifically the place of the New Testament in early Christianity, the literary analysis of Luke-Acts, and the issues of Jews and anti-Judaism within those New Testament books. The organization of this volume is explained by the structure of the table of contents; it may be helpful, however, to indicate how the various essays within each section of the *Festschrift* are related.

In part I, the essays deal with various aspects of how the Gospel of Luke and the Acts of the Apostles are related to their literary and theological environment in first-century Judaism and early Christianity. The essays in this section address the religious context of the charges brought against Jesus in his trial before the high priests, the literary relationship between Luke and the other synoptic gospels, the use of Luke in non-canonical early Christian documents, and the historical relationship between the traditions preserved about Paul by the author of Acts and the traditions preserved by Paul himself in his letters.

In part II, the essays employ different forms of literary analysis to investigate various Lukan themes, characters, and rhetorical patterns. The essays in this section address the characters of John Mark and Gamaliel, the themes of conversion and Jerusalem, and the rhetorical patterns in Luke 1–2, in Luke 11, and in Acts 1–2.

In part III, the essays deal with issues regarding Jews and anti-Judaism in the Gospel of Luke and the Acts of the Apostles and with the scholarship that interprets these issues within the Lukan texts. After initial essays, which locate the issues within the context of twentieth-century scholarship and contemporary hermeneutics, the remaining essays address key issues of the current debate over the portraits of the Jews and Judaism in Luke and Acts.

We would not neglect to thank Southern Methodist University for the generosity extended by our alma mater in providing funds to help offset the cost of this project. Special thanks are also due Anthony Baker, a teaching assistant in the Division of Religion at Olivet Nazarene University, for his help in preparing the indexes.

Finally, unless otherwise noted, in these essays, translations of biblical texts are those of the respective authors.

Tom Phillips
Dick Thompson

A Bibliography
of the Writings of Joseph B. Tyson

I. Books

1992 *Images of Judaism in Luke-Acts*. Columbia: University of South Carolina Press.

Editor, with Mikeal C. Parsons. *Cadbury, Knox, and Talbert: American Contributions to the Study of Acts*. Atlanta: Scholars Press.

1988 Editor. *Luke-Acts and the Jewish People: Eight Critical Perspectives*. Minneapolis: Augsburg Publishing House.

1986 *The Death of Jesus in Luke-Acts*. Columbia: University of South Carolina Press.

1985 Editor, with Arthur J. Bellinzoni, Jr. and William O. Walker, Jr. *The Two Source Hypothesis: A Critical Appraisal*. Macon GA: Mercer University Press.

1984 *The New Testament and Early Christianity*. New York: Macmillan Publishing Company.

1978 With Thomas R. W. Longstaff. *Synoptic Abstract*. Wooster OH: Biblical Research Associates.

1973 *A Study of Early Christianity*. New York: Macmillan Publishing Company.

II. Articles

1996 "The Acts of the Apostles." In *The HarperCollins Bible Dictionary*, rev. ed., ed. Paul J. Achtemeier et al., 10-12. San Francisco: HarperCollins.

"The Gospel According to Luke." In *The HarperCollins Bible Dictionary*, rev. ed., 629-31.

1995 "Jews and Judaism in Luke-Acts: Reading as a Godfearer." *New Testament Studies* 41:19-38.

1992 "Authority in Acts." *The Bible Today* 30:279-83.

"John Knox and the Acts of the Apostles." In *Cadbury, Knox, and Talbert: American Contributions to the Study of Acts*, ed. Mikeal C. Parsons and Joseph B. Tyson, 55-80. Atlanta: Scholars Press.

"Torah and Prophets in Luke-Acts: Temporary or Permanent?" In *Society of Biblical Literature Seminar Papers*, ed. Eugene H. Lovering, Jr., 539-48. Atlanta: Scholars Press.

1990 "The Birth Narratives and the Beginning of Luke's Gospel." *Semeia* 52:101-18.

1988 "The Emerging Church and the Problem of Authority in Acts." *Interpretation* 42:132-45.

Editor, "Order in the Synoptic Gospels: Patterns of Agreement within Pericopes." *Second Century* 6 (1987–1988): 65-109.

"The Problem of Jewish Rejection in Acts." In *Luke-Acts and the Jewish People: Eight Critical Perspectives*, ed. Joseph B. Tyson, 124-37. Minneapolis: Augsburg Publishing House.

1987 "Further Thoughts on *The Death of Jesus in Luke-Acts*." *Perkins School of Theology Journal* 40 (April): 48-50.

"The Gentile Mission and the Authority of Scripture in Acts." *New Testament Studies* 33:619-31.

"Scripture, Torah, and Sabbath in Luke-Acts." In *Jesus, the Gospels, and the Church: Essays in Honor of William R. Farmer*, ed. Ed P. Sanders, 89-104. Macon GA: Mercer University Press.

1985 "The Acts of the Apostles." In *Harper's Bible Dictionary*, ed. Paul J. Achtemeier et al., 10-11. San Francisco: Harper and Row.

"The Gospel According to Luke." In *Harper's Bible Dictionary*, 583-85.

"Luke." In *Harper's Bible Dictionary*, 582-83.

"Pentecost." In *Harper's Bible Dictionary*, 769.

"Speaking with Tongues." In *Harper's Bible Dictionary*, 1081-82.

"The Synoptic Problem." In *Harper's Bible Dictionary*, 1009.

"Theophilus." In *Harper's Bible Dictionary*, 1063.

"Tongue." In *Harper's Bible Dictionary*, 1081.

"Tongues as of Fire." In *Harper's Bible Dictionary*, 1082.

"The Two-Source Hypothesis: A Critical Appraisal." In *The Two-Source Hypothesis: A Critical Appraisal*, 437-52.

1984 "The Jewish Public in Luke-Acts." *New Testament Studies* 30:574-83.

1983 "Acts 6:1-7 and Dietary Regulations in Early Christianity." *Perspectives in Religious Studies* 10:145-61.

"The Blindness of the Disciples in Mark." In *The Messianic Secret*, ed. Christopher Tuckett, 35-43. Philadelphia: Fortress Press; London: SPCK (a republication of a 1961 article in the *Journal of Biblical Literature*).

"Conflict as a Literary Theme in the Gospel of Luke." In *New Synoptic Studies*, ed. William R. Farmer, 303-27. Macon GA: Mercer University Press.

1979 "The Problem of Food in Acts: A Study of Literary Patterns with Particular Reference to Acts 6:1-7." In *Society of Biblical Literature Seminar Papers*, ed. Paul J. Achtemeier, 69-85. Missoula MT: Scholars Press.

1978 "Literary Criticism and the Gospels." In *The Relationships among the Gospels: An Interdisciplinary Dialogue*, ed. William O. Walker, Jr., 323-41. San Antonio: Trinity University Press.

"The Opposition to Jesus in the Gospel of Luke." *Perspectives in Religious Studies* 5:144-50.

"Source Criticism of the Gospel of Luke." In *Perspectives on Luke-Acts*, ed. Charles H. Talbert, 24-39. Macon GA: Mercer University Press.

1976 "Paul's Opponents at Philippi." *Perspectives in Religious Studies* 3:82-95.

"Sequential Parallelism in the Synoptic Gospels." *New Testament Studies* 22:276-308.

"The Sources of Luke: A Proposal for the Consultation on the Relationships of the Gospels." In *Society of Biblical Literature Seminar Papers*, ed. George MacRae, 279-86. Missoula MT: Scholars Press.

1973 " 'Works of Law' in Galatians." *Journal of Biblical Literature* 92:423-31.

1968 "Paul's Opponents in Galatia." *Novum Testamentum* 10:241-54.
1961 "The Blindness of the Disciples in Mark." *Journal of Biblical Literature*
80:261-68.
1960 "Jesus and Herod Antipas." *Journal of Biblical Literature* 79:239-46.
1959 "The Lukan Version of the Trial of Jesus." *Novum Testamentum* 3:249-58.

III. Book Reviews

1997 *Jesus' Entry into Jerusalem: In the Context of Lukan Theology and the
Politics of His Day*, by Brent Kinman. *Journal of Biblical Literature*
116:746-47.

1996 *Identitätssuche des syrischen Urchristentums: Mission, Inkulturation and
Pluralität im ältesten Heidenchristentum*, by Andreas Feldtkeller.
Journal of Biblical Literature 115:347-49.

1990 *Early Christianity according to the Traditions in Acts: A Commentary*, by
Gerd Lüdemann. *Perkins School of Theology Journal* 43
(January–April): 30-31.
The Narrative Unity of Luke-Acts: A Literary Interpretation, vol. 2: *The
Acts of the Apostles*, by Robert C. Tannehill. *Perkins School of
Theology Journal* 43 (July–October): 30-31.

1989 *Profit with Delight: The Literary Genre of the Acts of the Apostles*, by
Richard I. Pervo. *Perkins School of Theology Journal* 42
(January–April): 32-33.

1988 *The Early Christians: Their World Mission and Self-Discovery*, by Ben F.
Meyer. *Interpretation* 42:96-97.
The Lukan Voice: Confusion and Irony in the Gospel of Luke, by James M.
Dawsey. *Journal of Biblical Literature* 107:545-46.
Luke-Acts and the Jews: Conflict, Apology, and Conciliation, by Robert L.
Brawley. *The Cumberland Seminarian* 26 (Winter): 104-105.

1987 *The Narrative Unity of Luke-Acts: A Literary Interpretation*, vol. 1: *The
Gospel According to Luke*, by Robert C. Tannehill. *Perkins School of
Theology Journal* 40 (October): 42-43.

1986 *Luke: Artist and Theologian: Luke's Passion Account as Literature*, by
Robert J. Karris. *Perkins School of Theology Journal* 39 (April): 63-64.
The Unity of Luke's Theology: An Analysis of Luke-Acts, by Robert F.
O'Toole. *Perkins School of Theology Journal* 39 (January): 60-61.

1985 *Reading Luke: A Literary and Theological Commentary on the Third
Gospel*, by Charles H. Talbert. *Journal of Biblical Literature* 104:340-
42.

1984 *In Memory of Her: A Feminist Theological Reconstruction of Christian
Origins*, by Elisabeth Schüssler Fiorenza. *Interpretation* 38:106-108.

1981 *Prophecy and History in Luke-Acts*, by David L. Tiede. *Perkins School of
Theology Journal* 34 (Spring): 48-49.

1977 *The Horizontal Line Synopsis of the Gospels*, by Reuben J. Swanson.
Journal of Biblical Literature 96:138-39.

1975 *Literary Interpretations of Biblical Narratives*, ed. by Kenneth R. R. Gros
Louis et al. *Perkins School of Theology Journal* 28 (Summer): 54-55.

1974 *Herod Antipas*, by Harold Hoehner. *Journal of the American Academy of Religion* 42:774-75.

Peter in the New Testament, ed. by Raymond E. Brown et al. *Perkins School of Theology Journal* 27 (Summer): 38-39.

1970 *Saint Paul: A Study in the Development of His Thought*, by Charles Buck and Greer Taylor. *Perkins School of Theology Journal* 23 (Spring): 30-31.

Synopticon, by William R. Farmer. *Perkins School of Theology Journal* 23 (Spring): 26-27.

1967 *The Formation of the New Testament*, by Robert M. Grant. *Perkins School of Theology Journal* 20 (Fall–Winter): 49-50.

1966 *Jesus and the Son of Man*, by A. J. B. Higgins. *Perkins School of Theology Journal* 19 (Spring): 50-51.

1964 *The Justice of God in the Teaching of Jesus*, by J. Arthur Baird. *Perkins School of Theology Journal* 17 (Winter–Spring): 44-45.

Part I

**Luke and Acts
within First-Century Judaism,
the New Testament,
and Early Christianity**

Crucifixion, Qumran,
and the Jewish Interrogation of Jesus

Darrell L. Bock

It is a pleasure to dedicate this essay to Joseph Tyson, who shares my intense interest in Lukan studies. It is also appropriate to write on a topic that directly responds to a question Professor Tyson raised as moderator of a presentation I made at the 1997 Southwestern regional meeting of the Society of Biblical Literature. My essay focused on the historical background to the Jewish leadership's interrogation of Jesus. I had examined Jewish views on the themes of exaltation into the presence of God and blasphemy as a backdrop for the interrogation of Jesus, where there is a clash between his claims of exaltation and the Jewish reading of those claims as blasphemous. During that presentation I cited the *Temple Scroll* as giving evidence that those who engaged in a form of potential political betrayal and slander were subject to crucifixion as a penalty for their crime. Such an act, I argued, if it was tied to criticism of the current Jewish leadership, would be seen as blasphemous on the basis of Exodus 22:27 (22:28 EVV). In referring to the *Temple Scroll*, I argued that the examination scene fit nicely within a Jewish milieu.

In his typical perceptive fashion, Professor Tyson asked whether a document found at Qumran and possessing likely Essene roots could be applied to a setting involving the Jewish leadership, since that leadership was composed mostly of Sadducees and, to a lesser degree, of Pharisees.[1] This essay is an attempt to answer that question more fully than I could in the short time there. I will point to evidence of a pattern of response to these kinds of politically threatening situations within Judaism.

Why should one study a historical question like this in a volume dedicated to the literary study of Luke-Acts? Two reasons suffice. First, Lukan studies on the North American continent have focused increasingly on literary readings of this gospel. Yet even within this narrative world, cultural assumptions may be embedded within the language of the text.

---

[1] For a short history to the background of the makeup of the Jewish leadership and the role of the various sects within Judaism, see Richard A. Horsley and John S. Hanson, *Bandits, Prophets, and Messiahs: Popular Movements at the Time of Jesus* (San Francisco: HarperCollins, 1988) 23-43.

The surfacing of such cultural background may well reveal motives for actions, in terms of customary expectation, that do not need explicit mention because they "come with the territory" of what is mentioned. The Jewish interrogation of Jesus might include such embedded cultural background that helps us appreciate what tensions the scene evokes. This essay shows that such background is indeed present in this scene. Second, though we shall concentrate on Mark's portrayal in this essay, what is said in terms of the cultural background is so basic that this reading would apply to any of the interrogation scenes in the synoptic gospels, including the one in Luke's gospel. Thus, the results of this study provide a better understanding of the Lukan interrogation scene, not merely at a literary level, but also at a cultural one. The conclusion may have historical implications, as well, as the conclusion to this essay notes.

I. The Thesis Stated and the *Temple Scroll*

An examination of blasphemy in Judaism indicates that there is a category of verbal blasphemy, as *m. Sanh.* 7.5 shows. This Mishnaic text indicates that blasphemy involves pronunciation of the divine Name in a way that insults God. However, other Jewish texts suggest that, in addition, there are acts of blasphemy. Such insulting actions reflect intense disrespect toward God, including speech that contains arrogant claims. Such a category is noted by Philo in *Decalogue* 62-63, where those who usurp the unique honor of the Creator are called "demented and miserable men" and are described as those who "venture to blaspheme the Deity."[2] Another relevant Philonic text is *On Dreams* 2.130-31, where a prefect of Egypt who compares himself to one possessing the power of creation is called "evil of an extraordinary nature" and "a man in every respect miserable, [as he] has dared to compare himself to the all-blessed God." He is said to utter blasphemies against the sun, moon, and the rest of the stars, as Philo personifies the elements of the creation in a manner typical of the ancients.

Josephus also notes acts of blasphemy. One striking example occurs in *Antiquities* 10.233-42, where Belshazzar's use of temple utensils in the midst of one of his own parties is seen as an insult to God's presence.

---

[2]This remark regards one of the motives as an attempt to vex the pious, who felt afflicted upon hearing such claims. Section 64 of the *Decalogue* notes that one should not seek to worship one who actually is a brother. The context of the remark is about pagan leaders who make exaggerated, insolent claims about their power.

According to *Antiquities* 6.183, Goliath blasphemes God when he slanders the army of God's people (1 Sam 17). Such disrespect looks back to the legal proscription from Exodus 22:27 with its warning that to attack the leadership whom God has appointed is blasphemous, only now in the Goliath setting the image has been expanded to include God's people as a whole. Another biblical incident in this vein is 2 Kings 18–19 (=Isa 37), where Sennacherib's words against Israel and her God lead the Israelites to tear their garments in reaction to the blasphemous remarks. This event is seen as one of the prototypical examples of blasphemy in the rabbinic material (Tob 1:18; *b. Moed Qatan* 25b; *p. Moed Qatan* 3.83b). When God judges Sennacherib's blasphemous army, justice prevails.

These examples and others like them support the contention that the Jewish leadership's charge of blasphemy against Jesus resulted from their interpretation of two elements within his remarks before the leadership. In the Markan account, Jesus responds to the high priest's question whether he is the Christ, the Son of the Blessed One, with the reply, "I am; and you will see the Son of man seated at the right hand of Power, and coming on the clouds of heaven" (Mark 14:62). First, the claim to sit at God's right hand as Son of man would be seen as an offense against both the uniqueness of God and the sanctity of God's holy presence. Second, the claim to return on the clouds as the judging Son of man gives Jesus a major eschatological role and thus contains an implicit criticism of any person preparing to judge him. The leadership would have perceived such a major criticism of its role as the divinely appointed caretaker of the religious well-being of the nation as a violation of Exodus 22:27. In addition, such a claim would confirm a potentially seditious element in Jesus' view of the leadership, since that claim allowed for the raising of additional political considerations in assessing the penalty due him, especially given his earlier public attack on the Jewish leadership in the temple.

It is here that the evidence of the *Temple Scroll* (11QTemple 64:6-10) at Qumran has potential relevance.[3] This text reads,

---

[3]The potential significance of this text and of the yet to be mentioned 4QpNahum for the assessment of crucifixion in Palestine has long been noted. For the pesher on Nahum, see Y. Yadin, "Pesher Nahum (4QpNahum) Reconsidered," *IEJ* 21 (1971): 1-12. For the *Temple Scroll*, O. Betz, "Probleme des Prozesses Jesu," *ANRW* 25/1: 606-608; "The Temple Scroll and the Trial of Jesus," *SwJT* 30 (1988): 5-8; and "Jesus and the Temple Scroll," in *Jesus and the Dead Sea Scrolls*, ed. James H. Charlesworth (New York:

[7]If a man slanders his [God's] people and delivers his people up to a foreign nation and does evil to his people [8]you shall hang him on the tree [note the allusion to Deut 21:22-23], and he shall die. According to the testimony of two witnesses and the testimony of three witnesses [9]he shall be put to death, and they shall hang him on a tree.

The text notes that someone who threatens to deliver the nation over to foreigners is subject to the death penalty. Sedition also could include "slandering his [God's] people," which is what Jesus' threat of judging the leadership could be interpreted as representing. This sedition, there-fore, is a serious political crime that could be regarded as a capital offense. The *Temple Scroll*, which purports to be additional revelation from Moses, looks to appropriate regulations for the nation and gives a midrash on Deuteronomy 21:22-23, which explains how a capital penalty is to be executed. This Torah text was applied to crucifixion in the first century, as well as to the hanging of those who were executed by other means.[4] We know that crucifixion was practiced in Judea under various Roman prefects and generals: Varus (*War* 2.75 [ca. 3 BCE]), Cumanus (*War* 2.241 [48-52 CE]), Felix (*War* 2.306, 308 [52-ca. 60 CE]), and Titus (*War* 5.289, 449-51 [70 CE]). If such a view of sedition and crucifixion existed among the Sanhedrin, then Jesus' remarks, if seen as blasphe-mous, would be read as worthy of crucifixion on political grounds as well.

But what kind of a situation might lead Jews to remand someone into Roman custody? The threat of sedition could be enough, which in Jesus' case could also be viewed as a political charge against him. My thesis involves three claims. First, Jesus' remarks against his accusers were seen as sedition by the Jewish leadership. Second, that leadership would also perceive such remarks as blasphemy, as a religious and political threat with which they had to deal. Finally, the challenge to them that was inherent within this threat allowed Jesus to be taken before Roman authorities. According to Mark's portrayal, this threat of sedition explains how Jesus ended up before Pilate. It is why a political charge that Jesus claimed to be king could be the basis of Jesus' death as the *titulus* on the

---

Doubleday, 1992) 79-83. The translation in this paper follows that of Betz in "Jesus and the Temple Scroll," 81.

[4]David Halperin, "Crucifixion, the Nahum Pesher, and the Rabbinic Penalty of Strangulation," *JJS* 32 (1981): 32-46.

cross indicates (Mark 15:26). Nothing in the Lukan portrait alters these observations about the background to this scene.

Jesus' rejection of the leadership, along with his earlier challenge of the temple practices, created a situation where Jesus could be charged with undermining the leadership's position and putting the nation at risk. The Jewish leaders represented a respected political body to which the Romans had already committed themselves. If the Jewish leadership could not control the people in conjunction with Rome, then Rome might intervene and take even more direct control. The later events of 70 CE prove that Rome would respond this way, if her oversight was threatened. These later events indicate that the leadership's fears were not without potential merit.

In other words, the exchange of Jesus before the Jewish leadership and their reaction make perfect cultural sense in their first century setting. But Professor Tyson's question still remains before us. To what extent does this Essene text from the *Temple Scroll* reflect the beliefs of other Jews? It is here that evidence from other texts shows that the precedent for such action did exist from within other segments of Judaism. In these parallels are found the elements that allow one to respond positively to the query.

II. Other Possible Examples of Death for Sedition

In fact, evidence does exist that sedition leads to capital punishment. This was the case in major struggles for control of power. The first example involves the rule of Alexander Janneus (103-76 BCE). He hung eight hundred of his enemies from the Pharisees "on trees," because they had asked the Syrian king, Demetrius III, for aid in challenging the rule of this unpopular king (*War* 1.92-97; *Ant.* 13.376-83).[5] When the plot failed in a fierce battle waged near Shechem, the losers were executed in what certainly would have been portrayed by Alexander as execution for sedition.

In fact, the Qumran documents allude to this event, showing that they could comment on events in Israel. 4QpNahum 1:6-8 speaks of "the Lion of Wrath . . . who hangs men alive." In a now well-known essay, Y. Yadin has shown how the discovery of the *Temple Scroll* helps to illumine the meaning of this pesher. He argues that the text is not

---

[5]Betz, "The Temple Scroll and the Trial of Jesus," 6.

negative toward this particular action of the king, but rather is grounded in a pesher development of Deuteronomy 21:22-23.[6] The important point for us is that the pesher shows the potential similarity of views about sedition and crucifixion between a leader who had close ties with the Sadducees in the past and the Essene perspective reflected in the *Temple Scroll*.[7] Even the Qumranians looking at the event from outside the perspectives of the protaganists used the biblical language of hanging to describe the event. As Yadin says, "it is quite clear that, according to the injunctions in our scroll, the הורשׁי החלקות who invited Demetrius to come to Jerusalem and joined him in his war against Israel deserved capital punishment by hanging."[8]

A second example appears in the curious account of Rabbi Shimeon ben Shetach, a Pharisee who lived during the first half of the first century BCE and who is credited with leading a major restoration of the Torah during this period. In a tradition that appears in various locales within Judaism, he supposedly hung eighty witches at Ashkelon (*m. Sanh.* 6.4-5; *y. Sanh.* 23c [=Neusner 6.6]; *Sifre* Deut §221).[9] The relevant portion of the Mishnah reads,

> "All those who are stoned are hanged on a tree," the words of R. Eliezer. And the sages say, "Only the blasphemer and the one who worships an idol are hanged." "As to a man, they hang him facing the people, as to a women, her face is toward the tree," the words of R. Eliezer. And the sages say, "The man is hanged, but the woman is not hanged." Said to them R. Eliezer, "And did not Simeon b. Shatah hang women in Ashkelon?" They said to him, "He hanged eighty women, and they do not judge even two on a single day![10]

The account, if taken straightforwardly, appears to present the execution of witches for blasphemous acts, since blasphemy is the topic of the section of the Mishnah and Talmud where the discussion appears. Interestingly enough, a discussion of Deuteronomy 21:23 also appears in the

---

[6]Yadin, "Pesher Nahum (4QpNahum) Reconsidered," 1-12.

[7]It should be noted in making this point that Yadin leaves open the question whether the later stages of Janneus's rule led the community to come to regard him later as the "wicked priest." See "Pesher Nahum (4Q pNahum) Reconsidered," 12.

[8]Yadin, "Pesher Nahum (4QpNahum) Reconsidered," 12.

[9]For the Palestinian Talmud, see *The Talmud of the Land of Israel*, vol. 31, trans. Jacob Neusner (Chicago: University of Chicago Press, 1984) 180-82.

[10]Translation is from Jacob Neusner, *The Mishnah: A New Translation* (New Haven: Yale University Press, 1988) 595.

context of the presentation by the Mishnah, the Palestinian Talmud, as well as in *Sifre*. Taken in this light, the account simply shows that capital execution could take place for severe religious unfaithfulness, that is, for an act like blasphemy.

However, Martin Hengel has made a strong case for reading the reference to witches metaphorically and polemically for a group of Sadducees who also were friends of Alexander Janneus. These Sadducean friends of Janneus were the objects of an execution of revenge after the Pharisees with the support of Alexandra came back to power after Janneus.[11] If this is the case, then political revenge for "sedition" became a tool for some Pharisees among the Jewish religious leadership. This would mean that Essene, Sadducean, and Pharisaical sects all provide evidence for the use of crucifixion in cases of sedition. Regardless of which view is taken of this second incident, it does show that all three sects had various uses for forms of political and religious execution.

III. Conclusion

There appears to be good historical evidence for reading the position of the *Temple Scroll* at Qumran as reflecting a larger Jewish view about sedition and capital punishment, a view reflected in the actions of those connected both to the Sadducees and the Pharisees. If such a community-wide view existed, then it is quite likely that the Jewish leadership perceived Jesus' challenge of them and his threat to judge them one day as a seditious claim that was worthy of the death penalty. His remarks raised both religious and political questions. Earlier events would have reinforced such questions, namely, his previous attack on the temple's commercial trade within the sacred temple precincts which the priesthood had supported and which served to underwrite the priesthood's authority. The high priest's tearing of his garment shows that Jesus' remarks were seen as blasphemous. In addition, these remarks, along with Jesus' actions, provided a legal ground for taking Jesus before the Roman ruler. The entire scene, therefore, fits well within a Jewish milieu. The appropriateness of the charges against Jesus from a Jewish cultural perspective is all this essay claims to show.

---

[11]Martin Hengel, *Rabbinische Legende und frühpharisäische Geschichte: Shimeon b. Schetach und die achtzig Hexen von Askelon*, Abhandlungen der Heidelberger Akademie der Wissenschaften, Philosophisch-historische Klasse (Heidelberg: Carl Winter Universitätsverlag, 1984).

The background applies to this interrogation scene, whether one is considering the Matthean, Markan, or Lukan accounts. Behind the narrative stand important cultural assumptions that help to explain why certain actions and reactions take place. Sensitive readings, even of a narratological-literary nature, should not ignore such potentially important cultural assumptions embedded in the text. Determining whether the scene reflects an adequate historical summary of the Jewish examination of Jesus would require the careful study of a much larger range of issues, including the authenticity of the remarks at this scene, a question I hope to address fully in a larger, more technical monograph which I am currently completing.

The Present State of the Synoptic Problem

William R. Farmer

Only once before have I undertaken the task of surveying the state of the ongoing discussion of the synoptic problem. That was twenty years ago.[1] The occasion of this *Festschrift* for Joseph Tyson affords me opportunity to take up the task once more.

It was also twenty years ago that Joseph Tyson along with Thomas R. W. Longstaff published *Synoptic Abstract*, which was the first use of computer analysis in the discussion of the synoptic problem.[2] Six years later Tyson was the first to state publicly that the discussion of the synoptic problem had advanced to the point where it was possible to conclude that the view that Mark was the third gospel written and had used the two earlier gospels of Matthew and Luke was now the chief rival of the still dominant two-source hypothesis.[3]

This is not the place to give a complete *Forschungsbericht* of the synoptic problem since Tyson made this observation. But I do wish to share my opinion with the reader that Professor Tyson has made a major contribution to the shaping of the discussion of the synoptic problem in the United States by the role he has played in Lukan studies since the publication of his 1986 book *The Death of Jesus in Luke-Acts.*[4]

In effect what has happened in Lukan studies in the intervening years is that Hans Conzelmann's once highly regarded redactional method has gradually but steadily dropped from view. In the place of studying Luke from the perspective of the two-source hypothesis utilizing redaction criticism as Conzelmann and his followers were then doing, Tyson and others, including Charles Talbert and David Moessner, quietly under the aegis of the annual program meetings of the Society of Biblical Literature, carried through a revolution in Lukan studies. This new perspective,

---

[1]William R. Farmer, "The Present State of the Synoptic Problem" *PSTJ* 32/1 (1978): 1-7.

[2]Joseph B. Tyson and Thomas R. W. Longstaff, *Synoptic Abstract* (Wooster OH: Biblical Research Associates, 1978).

[3]See "The Synoptic Problem," in Joseph B. Tyson, *The New Testament and Early Christianity* (New York: Macmillan, 1984) 148-58.

[4]Joseph B. Tyson, *The Death of Jesus in Luke-Acts* (Columbia: University of South Carolina Press, 1986).

promoted by Tyson and others, studied Luke without any particular reference to Mark and gave increasing attention to its companion volume, the Acts of the Apostles. Meanwhile, such redaction-critical work on Luke as has been done within the program structures of SBL has often proceeded on the assumption of the two-gospel hypothesis, primarily the assumption that Luke used Matthew, not Mark, as his primary source. This brings us directly to our topic: "the present state of the synoptic problem."

The present state of the synoptic problem can best be gauged in the light of brief observations on five important publications appearing between 1990 and 1996. The picture that emerges from a consideration of these five books suggests that only one major task remains to be completed in order to solve the synoptic problem.

The verification of this conclusion requires a more detailed discussion of scholars' work published in three additional books appearing between 1988 and 1990. In effect this report on the present state of the synoptic problem draws selectively upon work by scholars published during the 1988–1996 period. This report is written for the eyes of my colleagues Joseph Tyson and his friends. I think especially of Thomas R. W. Longstaff and William O. Walker, Jr., both participants in the ongoing discussion. Needless to say, this report is written from my own point of view, that of an adherent of the two-gospel hypothesis. This hypothesis, formerly known as the Griesbach hypothesis, suggests that the gospels were probably composed in the sequence Matthew, Luke, Mark, that Luke used Matthew as a source, and that Mark used both Matthew and Luke as sources.

I. Five Important Books on the Synoptic Problem

The first of the five books about which I wish to make brief observations is the 1990 volume *The Interrelations of the Gospels*.[5] This book reports on a 1984 symposium on the gospels held in Jerusalem. Among the participants were Frans Neirynck and Christopher M. Tuckett whose responsibility was to advocate the merits of the two-source hypothesis over two rival hypotheses, the two-gospel hypothesis and the "multiple-stage hypothesis."[6]

---

[5]David L. Dungan, ed., *The Interrelations of the Gospels: A Symposium Led by M.-É. Boismard, William R. Farmer, Frans Neirynck. Jerusalem 1984*, BETL 95 (Leuven: Leuven University Press; Macon GA: Mercer University Press, 1990).

[6]See *The Interrelations of the Gospels* for the detailed defense given for all three of

In an "Agenda for Future Research," the contributors unanimously agreed "that a literary, historical, and theological explanation of the evangelists' compositional activity, giving a coherent and reasonable picture of the whole of each Gospel, is the most important method of argumentation in defense of a source hypothesis."[7] This remarkable agreement among some of the world's leading experts on the synoptic problem represented a significant change in the study of this problem. Traditionally, defenses of one hypothesis over against another had been made on the basis of detailed analyses of one or more texts or on the basis of some particular criterion, for example, whether one gospel is more or less Jewish or Palestinian or both. However, experts were being advised to undertake a more comprehensive approach to the problem. Slowly but surely during the intervening years, this dictum of the 1984 Jerusalem symposium has come to be the guiding criterion in the contemporary study of the synoptic problem.

The second book on which I wish to comment briefly is the volume *Minor Agreements: Symposium Göttingen 1991*.[8] We only note here that this volume was the first to make a serious break with traditional methodology for studying the minor agreements. Instead of considering the minor agreements in relative isolation from their compositional contexts, a proposal was made to study these agreements within their widest possible compositional contexts. In this respect, the 1991 Göttingen symposium stands in methodological continuity with the 1984 Jerusalem symposium. In other respects, much of the argumentation was in the traditional mode of atomistic analysis.

The third book to be considered is a 1995 volume of *The New Interpreter's Bible*. Christopher M. Tuckett's introductory article on "Jesus and the Gospels" includes a discussion of the synoptic problem.[9] Tuckett notes that the contemporary debate has highlighted the "weak and inconclusive nature" of some arguments that have been used to promote the two-source hypothesis. This critique applies especially to some of the more "formal" arguments. For example, in arguing for Markan priority,

---

these hypotheses.

[7]Dungan, *The Interrelations of the Gospels*, 609.

[8]Georg Strecker, ed., *Minor Agreements: Symposium Göttingen 1991* (Göttingen: Vandenhoeck & Ruprecht, 1993). See the volume for detailed defenses made on behalf of rival hypotheses.

[9]Christopher M. Tuckett, "Jesus and the Gospels," in *The New Interpreter's Bible*, vol. 8, ed. Leander E. Keck et al. (Nashville: Abingdon, 1995) 71-86.

Tuckett observes that some scholars appeal to the fact that "nearly all of Mark is paralleled in Matthew or Luke or both." Tuckett continues:

> Yet all this shows is that some literary relationship exists; it does not prove that the only possibility is that Mark's Gospel was the *source* of Matthew and Luke. Similarly, the much discussed appeal to the failure of Matthew and Luke ever (or hardly ever) to agree against Mark in order and wording does not prove that Matthew and Luke independently used Mark as a source; it only shows that Mark is some kind of "middle term" between the other two in any pattern of relationships.[10]

On the basis of this open acknowledgment in a commentary within the mainstream of scholarship, we can now say this about the present state of the synoptic problem: the standard arguments for Markan priority, which were popularized by Streeter seventy-four years ago, have at long last come to be recognized as "weak and inconclusive."

Yet, in a major publication appearing in the same year (1995), a group of highly regarded specialists in gospel studies stated that their research (and therefore their conclusions) rested heavily on the two pillars of Markan priority and the existence of "Q."[11] Then, in an attempt to provide their readers with the scientific basis upon which these two pillars rested, the editors of this volume cited the very arguments (albeit in different words) which Tuckett had already discounted as "weak and inconclusive."[12]

The present state of the synoptic problem, therefore, is characterized by a remarkable lack of consensus among practicing specialists in gospel studies as to the scientific grounds for their work. The ongoing discussion of the synoptic problem has reached a "critical mass" where a "consensus" among *experts* on the synoptic problem (that the Streeterian arguments for Markan priority are no longer persuasive) serves to undermine critical confidence in work based upon that hypothesis. We have already noted that this lack of certainty has led some important Lukan scholars to prescind from the use of the two-source hypothesis.

The fourth book to be considered is Allan J. McNicol's 1996 monograph *Jesus' Directions for the Future*.[13] McNicol was a participant in the

---

[10]Tuckett, "Jesus and the Gospels," 76.

[11]Robert Funk and Roy W. Hoover, *The Five Gospels: The Search for the Authentic Words of Jesus* (New York: Macmillan, 1995) 3.

[12]Funk and Hoover, *The Five Gospels*, 10-11.

[13]Allan J. McNicol, *Jesus' Directions for the Future: A Source and Redaction-History Study of the Use of the Eschatological Traditions in Paul and in the Synoptic Accounts*

1984 Jerusalem symposium, which called for "a literary, historical, and theological explanation of the evangelists' compositional activity, giving a coherent and reasonable picture of the whole of each Gospel."[14] With just this task in mind, McNicol decided to write a monograph on the synoptic apocalypse, beginning with the Pauline parallels and then proceeding to the texts of Matthew, Luke, and Mark (in that order). Although far short of the coherent and reasonable picture of the *whole of each gospel*, for which the Jerusalem symposium called, McNicol's work is a significant step toward providing readers with some idea of how this picture will look when it is completed for each gospel. Meanwhile, in the case of the Gospel of Luke, we already have a compositional analysis which can help provide us with a "coherent and reasonable picture" of the whole of at least this gospel.

This leads us to the final book we wish to consider: *Beyond the Q Impasse: Luke's Use of Matthew*.[15] The importance of this book for understanding the present state of the synoptic problem resides in the fact that it removes the theoretical basis for "Q" by giving a "coherent and reasonable picture" of the whole of Luke assuming a direct use of Matthew by Luke. Until the 1996 publication of this book, no one had ever given a pericope-by-pericope account of how the author of the Gospel of Luke had used the text of the Gospel of Matthew. As a consequence, critical scholars *could* assert that Luke had not used Matthew simply because they had difficulty imagining how Luke could have derived his gospel from Matthew. If Luke did not use Matthew directly, then the non-Markan material which Matthew and Luke had in common must *ipso facto* have been derived from a hypothetical source, that is, "Q." At present, critical confidence in this theoretical basis for "Q" continues to erode to the extent that a "coherent and reasonable account" of Luke's compositional activity can be demonstrated while working from the hypothesis that Luke had direct access to and made use of the text of Matthew.

We see then that the present state of the synoptic problem calls into question the theoretical basis for the existence of "Q." As we have seen,

---

of Jesus' Last Eschatological Discourse, NGS 9 (Macon GA: Mercer University Press, 1996).

[14]See n. 7 above.

[15]Allan J. McNicol, David L. Dungan, and David B. Peabody, eds., *Beyond the Q Impasse: Luke's Use of Matthew: A Demonstration by the Research Team of the International Institute for Gospel Studies* (Philadelphia: Trinity Press International, 1996).

the old Streeterian reasons for belief in Markan priority are no longer regarded as valid. Nonetheless, *most* scholars continue to use the two-source hypothesis as the "best working hypothesis." The reasons given for this continued practice vary, but the most recurring reason is that all major alternatives appear to be fraught with even greater difficulties than those associated with the reigning two-source hypothesis. This popular view, however, is not sustainable, as will be shown later.

However, one difficulty appears seriously to block a shift away from the two-source hypothesis in the direction of its major rival, the two-gospel hypothesis. This difficulty is imagining how one can explain the reasons for Mark's omission of significant portions of the gospels of Matthew and Luke on the assumption that he has derived his gospel largely from those two earlier gospels.

In order to verify the claim that only one major task remains to be completed in order to solve the synoptic problem, we turn now to a detailed examination of three important publications. Our analysis of the first two serves to assure the reader that no new arguments for the priority of Mark have replaced the "weak and inconclusive" arguments given by Streeter. Our analysis of the third shows that the two-source hypothesis is the least satisfactory of all the major hypothesis under consideration today. It also confirms that, until now, those who adhere to the two-gospel hypothesis have failed to explain satisfactorily why Mark omitted what he has omitted from Matthew and Luke, and that for the majority of scholars this failure has served to block a serious consideration of the merits of their hypothesis.

II. The 1988 Commentary by W. D. Davies and Dale C. Allison

The first volume of the new ICC commentary on Matthew by W. D. Davies and Dale C. Allison appeared in 1988.[16] The authors devote thirty-one pages to the issue of "the sources of Matthew," in which they survey the study of the literary relationships among the gospels.[17] Not since Joseph A. Fitzmyer's forty-page defense of Streeter had anyone attempted to accomplish what Davies and Allison attempt, namely, a comprehensive and evenhanded analysis of the main arguments against Markan priority and a defense of the two-source hypothesis.[18]

---

[16]W. D. Davies and Dale C. Allison, *A Critical and Exegetical Commentary on the Gospel according to Saint Matthew*, 3 vols., ICC (Edinburgh: T.&T. Clark, 1988–).

[17]Davies and Allison, *Gospel according to Saint Matthew*, 1:97-127.

[18]Joseph A. Fitzmyer, "The Priority of Mark and the 'Q' Source in Luke," in *Jesus*

Fitzmyer's commentary on Luke attempted to justify his view that Luke used Mark and "Q"; Davies and Allison, in their commentary, attempt to justify their view that Matthew used the same two sources. Unlike Fitzmyer, however, who saw the synoptic problem as a "can of worms" and held to the two-source hypothesis basically because it seemed to be the most useful, Davies and Allison speak confidently of "compelling" reasons for believing in Markan priority.[19]

Like Fitzmyer, Davies and Allison also recognize the difficulty of explaining the minor agreements on the two-source hypothesis. They write:

> The so-called "minor agreements" between Matthew and Luke in the triple tradition are generally admitted to be the most serious obstacles in the way of accepting the viewpoint we have taken in this commentary—for they appear to be *prima facie* evidence for literary contact between Matthew and Luke.[20]

This statement precedes an acknowledgment of the criticisms that have been made of Streeter's attempt to explain these agreements by dividing them into different categories and thus atomizing the evidence. Then follows an extraordinarily candid paragraph which helps explain why so many scholars continue to adhere to the two-source hypothesis even though it has been convincingly falsified in the eyes of a steadily increasing number of critics. The paragraph needs to be cited in full to be appreciated:

> Despite the queries concerning Streeter's approach and conclusions, we have not become convinced that the minor agreements are as devastating to his position as some have made out. Furthermore, *because the reasons for Markan priority are compelling, whatever one infers from the minor agreements will have to be consistent with the priority of Mark.* With this in mind we offer the following observations.[21]

Then follows an analysis of Hans-Herbert Stoldt's compilation of 272 minor agreements, but this analysis is preceded by the observation: "At first glance, Stoldt's listing of the data appears overwhelming."[22] Then comes the statement:

---

and *Man's Hope*, ed. David G. Buttrick, 2 vols. (Pittsburgh: Pittsburgh Theological Seminary, 1970) 1:131-70.

[19]Davies and Allison, *Gospel according to Saint Matthew*, 1:110.

[20]Davies and Allison, *Gospel according to Saint Matthew*, 1:109.

[21]Davies and Allison, *Gospel according to Saint Matthew*, 1:110; emphasis added.

[22]Davies and Allison, *Gospel according to Saint Matthew*, 1:110.

Our conclusion concerning Stoldt's listing of the minor agreements of Matthew and Luke against Mark is this: it is only their sheer number that impresses. When looked at one by one, almost every agreement has an obvious explanation if one assumes that Matthew and Luke independently employed Mark.[23]

But what confidence are we to place in the conclusions of scholars who operate on the principle that "whatever one infers from" a given body of data "will have to be consistent with" the very thing which is at issue in the discussion, in this instance, Markan priority? Only those who agree with the premise of Davies and Allison that there are compelling reasons for Markan priority will be disposed to take seriously their attempt to explain away the minor agreements. So the prior question is this: What are the compelling reasons for Markan priority which dictate that a correct understanding of the minor agreements *must be consistent with that postulate*? One searches in vain for any compelling reason for believing in Markan priority in the seventeen pages Davies and Allison devote to their discussion of Mark. To prove this we will demonstrate this lack of a compelling reason by carefully examining exactly what they have written under five headings: (a) the minor agreements, (b) the Markan additions, (c) inconcinnities, (d) the tendencies of the synoptic tradition, and (e) the argument from order.

A. Minor Agreements

We have already noted that Davies and Allison acknowledge that the minor agreements are an admitted difficulty for the two-source hypothesis. Indeed, the final point Davies and Allison make in their discussion of the minor agreements is very revealing. They write:

> One way of getting around the apparent problem of the minor agreements is to postulate Luke's knowledge of Matthew or Matthew's knowledge of Luke. As proponents of the two-source theory, and for reasons given immediately below, we resist this alternative. We prefer to solve the riddle of the minor agreements by recourse to coincidental editing, oral tradition, and textual corruption.[24]

In other words, after a quarter century of critical reflection on the minor agreements, which has led many scholars to admit that either Luke had access to Matthew, or Luke and Matthew did not copy the text of Mark

---

[23]Davies and Allison, *Gospel according to Saint Matthew*, 1:112.
[24]Davies and Allison, *Gospel according to Saint Matthew*, 1:114.

known to us, Davies and Allison continue to place their trust in the method of Streeter, as a preferable "way of getting around" the "apparent" problem of the minor agreements.

Because of Michael Goulder's determination to press his two-source colleagues on this issue, it is doubtful that Davies' and Allison's recourse to "coincidental editing," "oral tradition," and "textual corruption" will succeed in persuading anyone except those who want to be persuaded. Goulder has taken what Streeter designated as one of his "residual cases," the mocking of Jesus (Matt 26:67-68 ‖ Mark 14:65 ‖ Luke 22:64), and has shown that the agreements of Matthew and Luke against Mark cannot be explained on any of these grounds, but on the contrary, call for the expansion of "Q" to include a passion narrative. This reduces to an absurdity the chief tenant of the two-source hypothesis: that is, that it can most simply account for the synoptic data by offering the dependence of Matthew and Luke on Mark to explain their narrative agreement and the dependence of Matthew and Luke on "Q" to explain their agreement in the non-Markan sayings of Jesus.[25]

There is clearly no compelling reason for Markan priority in Davies' and Allison's treatment of the minor agreements.

B. The Markan additions

Eighteen passages, totaling forty verses, are present in Mark but wholly absent from Matthew and Luke. Only one of these passages (Mark 4:26-29) causes Davies and Allison any problem. Without comment, Davies and Allison pass on Streeter's attempted explanation that, due to a scribal error, neither Matthew nor Luke had this passage in their copies of Mark.

According to the two-gospel hypothesis, these passages present significant agreements of Matthew and Luke against Mark and should be added to the evidence against the two-source hypothesis. Davies and Allison conclude their discussion under this heading with a question which offers an implied critique of the two-gospel hypothesis:

[C]an one seriously envision someone rewriting Matthew and Luke so as to omit the miraculous birth of Jesus, the sermon on the mount, and the resurrection appearances, while, on the other hand, adding the tale of the

---

[25]Michael D. Goulder, *Luke: A New Paradigm*, 2 vols., JSNTSup 20 (Sheffield: JSOT Press, 1989) 1:6-11.

naked young man, a healing miracle in which Jesus has trouble healing, and the remark that Jesus' family thought him mad?[26]

At best, this very misleading, aggregative approach provides a nice rhetorical question, but it is difficult to see in it any "compelling" reason for Markan priority. It does, however, give good reason for critical reluctance to accept the view that Mark is later than Matthew and Luke unless some credible reasons can be offered to explain these Markan omissions.

C. Inconcinnities

Under this heading, Davies and Allison review two passages put forward by G. M. Styler containing "logical flaws" which he thinks are best explained by the hypothesis of Markan priority (Mark 6:17-29 ‖ Matt 14:3-12; Mark 15:6-10 ‖ Matt 27:15-18). Although no mention is made of this fact, Lamar Cope had discussed Styler's treatment of the first pericope and concluded:

> In this case, too, the evidence reverses itself. Matthew's account of the death of John the Baptist, and the context in which it is set, is the more coherent but the more difficult text. One can understand Mark's revision not only by noting his knack for storytelling detail, but also as an attempt to clarify what was for him a confusing passage. The alternative is to argue that Matthew, in "improving and abbreviating" Mark, edited so as to produce a blunder. But since that argument [as demonstrated above] is grammatically unsound, there appears to be compelling reason to believe that here Mark has edited Matthew.[27]

Four years later, Harold Riley discussed Styler's work on both passages.[28] He gave reason to conclude that, in the case of the death of the Baptist, Styler overlooked evidence which indicates that Mark borrowed from Matthew.[29] In the example of "Pilate's Offer to Release a Prisoner," Riley, after closely examining Styler's discussion, concluded that his claim that this passage offers decisive evidence for Markan priority is "difficult to appreciate."[30]

---

[26]Davies and Allison, *Gospel according to Saint Matthew*, 1:109.

[27]Lamar Cope, "The Argument Revolves: The Pivotal Evidence for Marcan Priority Is Reversing Itself," in *New Synoptic Studies: The Cambridge Gospel Conference and Beyond*, ed. William R. Farmer (Macon GA: Mercer University Press, 1983) 150.

[28]Harold Riley, appendix 1, "Styler's Key Passages," in *The Order of the Synoptics: Why Three Synoptic Gospels?* (Macon GA: Mercer University Press, 1987) 100-104.

[29]Riley, "Styler's Key Passages," 100.

[30]Riley, "Styler's Key Passages," 103.

There would appear to be no valid argument, let alone a compelling reason for Markan priority to be found under this heading.

D. The Tendencies of the Synoptic Tradition

In their discussion of this topic, Davies and Allison, interestingly enough, state that those who hold the view that Mark has made use of Matthew and Luke "can summon support from the conclusions of E. P. Sanders's *The Tendencies of the Synoptic Tradition*."[31] Furthermore, the argument for Markan priority which Streeter based on Matthew's supposed tendency to improve Mark's style is, for Davies and Allison, quite unconvincing. Nonetheless, there seem to remain "at least three facts or tendencies which make Mark appear to be earlier than Matthew."[32]

The first of these facts or tendencies concerns the "general direction of early Christology." Davies and Allison list twenty-seven passages where they think Mark makes Jesus more human than Matthew.[33] But this argument is not valid since it has never been established, independent of a source theory, what direction primitive Christology took. A high Son-of-God Christology, according to evidence from Paul's letters, was well entrenched in the church long before the gospels were written.

The second fact or tendency, which makes Mark appear to be earlier than Matthew, involves twelve verses where Mark has a "rare or unusual word" and Matthew has a "common word or phrase." Davies and Allison ask: "How are we to explain this?" and they conclude: "It is not impossible that this question has a satisfactory answer; but what it might be we cannot guess."[34]

It should be noted that the reader is not given the contrary evidence, if there is any, where the reverse may be true. Moreover, it has never been demonstrated by reliable criteria what was usual or unusual for Mark's readers. In fact, such a demonstration would be an almost impossible task. We can be confident only that Mark was reasonably successful in using language that was well understood by his intended readers. There is no argument here, and certainly no "compelling" reason given for Markan priority.

Davies' and Allison's third fact or tendency is a source of great confusion, namely, Semitic words. This topic deserves special attention.

---

[31]Davies and Allison, *Gospel according to Saint Matthew*, 1:104.
[32]Davies and Allison, *Gospel according to Saint Matthew*, 1:104.
[33]Davies and Allison, *Gospel according to Saint Matthew*, 1:104-105.
[34]Davies and Allison, *Gospel according to Saint Matthew*, 1:106.

Davies and Allison cite six Semitic expressions found in Mark but not in Matthew (Streeter's argument #4) and ask how those who deny Markan priority account for these data.[35] A similar and related problem is created by the Greek text for Jesus' question, "My God, my God, why hast thou forsaken me?" In Mark 15:34, this saying conforms to Aramaic orthography whereas in Matthew 27:46, it conforms to Hebrew orthography. It is generally understood that only Matthew's Hebrew "Eli, Eli" makes sense out of the bystander's observation ("This man is calling Elijah."). Mark's Aramaic "Eloi, Eloi" is, therefore, best explained as a change which destroys the point of the observation that Mark repeated. Davies and Allison overlook the relevance of how one would apply Burton's criterion of "clear omission from one document of matter which was in the other, the omission of which destroys the connection," to decide that Mark's text is secondary to Matthew in this instance.[36]

Davies and Allison direct attention away from the problems that these data cause for Markan priority and succeed in creating the illusion that these data really support their view by suggesting that there can be no credible answer to the question why Mark would change Matthew's "Eli, Eli" to "Eloi, Eloi." If Mark was composed in any cosmopolitan center of the Roman empire, we can easily imagine that he would have been able to locate one or more persons who knew a little Aramaic, if he did not himself. The fact that Mark has used Aramaic expressions elsewhere in his gospel indicates that he had an interest in including such expressions in his text. Furthermore, the use of the Aramaic word *Abba* for Father in addressing God, well established in churches acquainted with Paul's letters including the Christian community in Rome, constantly reminded Mark's readers of the importance of Aramaic in the (prayer) life

---

[35]Davies and Allison, *Gospel according to Saint Matthew*, 1:106. Davies and Allison appear to be unaware of comments on these data by David L. Dungan, "Mark: The Abridgment of Matthew and Luke," in *Jesus and Man's Hope*, 1:68, where Dungan draws attention to I. Rabinowitz's article ("Did Jesus Speak Hebrew?" *ZNW* 53 [1962]: 229-38) and observes: "Mark's transliterations are curiously inconsistent with known forms of the alleged Aramaic or Hebrew words he translates."

[36]Cf. William R. Farmer, *The Synoptic Problem: A Critical Analysis* (Dillsboro NC: Western North Carolina [dist. by Mercer University Press], 1976) 227-32, for a comprehensive list of nine canons of criticism to be used in historical-critical work with synoptic texts, including six set forth by Ernest DeWitt Burton, *Some Principles of Literary Criticism and Their Application to the Synoptic Problem* (Chicago: University of Chicago Press, 1904) 198, of which this canon is listed as number three. By omitting the Hebrew, Mark destroys the connection.

of Jesus and the liturgical life of the earliest Christians. The importance attached to Aramaic affords a simple explanation for why Mark would want to archaize the text of his gospel by enriching it with expressions from this sacred language.[37]

No critic would deny that the Gospel of Matthew is both more Jewish and more Palestinian than Mark. So the significance of the highly selective set of data presented by Davies and Allison under this heading is doubly misleading.

In any case, there is no "compelling" reason for Markan priority to be found in their treatment of Semitic usage in the two gospels.[38]

E. The Argument from Order

We come now to the final topic we must treat before we can say that we have dealt with all the arguments cited by Davies and Allison to back up their claim that there are "compelling" reasons for Markan priority. We have attempted to trace their confidence in their reasons for believing in Markan priority back to its presumed source: "the phenomenon of order." Here we hope to find the answer to our bottom-line question: *How is it possible for scholars to write that there are compelling reasons for Markan priority in the demonstrated absence of such reasons and in the face of so much contrary evidence?*

For the first half of the twentieth century, the argument from order was believed to be the main reason for accepting Mark as our earliest gospel. Rudolf Bultmann, in the spring of 1965, upon being informed that B. C. Butler's refutation of Streeter's argument from order was now generally accepted, said: "If the argument from order does not support Markan priority, that would make a great difference to me, because that has always been the main reason why I accepted Markan priority."[39]

---

[37]That some Aramaic expressions used by Mark were no longer understood by many of his readers is clear from the fact that he sometimes translates them (e.g., Mark 3:17; 5:41; 7:11). Mark's translation of the Aramaic word *korban* (Mark 7:11) for the benefit of his readers whereas, when Matt uses a related word elsewhere in his gospel (Matt 27:6), he leaves it untranslated, clearly indicates that at least some of the Greek text of Matt was first used in Greek-speaking circles where Aramaic loanwords in Greek were well understood.

[38]Readers could be misled by the reference to "six Semitic expressions found in Mark but not in Matthew," (Davies and Allison, *Gospel according to Saint Matthew*, 1:106) since, while none of these six expressions is in the parallel texts of Matt, one of the most frequently used expressions, *korban*, in the related form of *korbanas*, is found elsewhere in Matt (27:6). In addition, there are other Aramaic words used in Matt that do not appear in Mark.

[39]This statement was made by Professor Bultmann in a conversation with the author

Davies and Allison begin their discussion of the argument from order by stating Streeter's formulation of it. Then they note that in 1951 Butler demonstrated that the alternating support for Mark's order found in Matthew and Luke requires only that Mark be the middle term. They go on to observe that, according to the two-gospel hypothesis, it is possible to turn Streeter's argument on its head by observing that only someone who was writing after Matthew and Luke and who was attempting to combine these two narratives would have been able both to preserve what order Luke preserved from Matthew and also to follow the order of either Luke or Matthew in those cases where Luke departed from Matthew's order. This, of course, has always been the main argument for Mark being third.

At this point, however, Davies and Allison draw back and state: "It is exceedingly hard to fathom" how this observation (which they do not challenge) can "move us beyond Butler's analysis, according to which the phenomenon of relative order proves by itself only the mediating position of the Second Gospel."[40] It is no less hard for the critic who does not assume Markan priority to "fathom" how Davies and Allison, having come so close to a solution for the synoptic problem's central fact of agreement and disagreement among the synoptic gospels, can fail to see what seems so obvious. We may turn to their own words to illustrate the point. In discussing the text of Matthew, Davies and Allison write:

> The Greek text printed in this commentary is based primarily upon two sources: the twenty-sixth edition of the Nestle-Aland *Novum Testamentum Graece* and the Huck-Greeven *Synopse der drei ersten Evangelien*. Where these two handbooks agree, we have judged their combined testimony to be truly weighty. Indeed, only a very few times . . . have we been moved to dissent from their concurrence. Where (these two sources) do part company, we have indicated this, cited pertinent textual witness, and usually given our reasons for following one authority rather than the other ["order" in the original must be a misprint].[41]

Davies' and Allison's description of their procedure for combining their sources is very similar to the procedure used by the historian

---

about the synoptic problem, which took place in his home in Marburg. In response to the observation that his "earliest strata of the Synoptic tradition" was better represented in the *Sondergut* of Matt and Luke than in Mark and "Q," Professor Bultmann went on to say: "If true, that would be very important to me, because I have always had more confidence in form criticism than in source criticism."

[40]Davies and Allison, *Gospel according to Saint Matthew*, 1:100.

[41]Davies and Allison, *Gospel according to Saint Matthew*, 1:147-48.

Flavius Arrian, a contemporary of the evangelists, when he faced the task of producing a new biography based on two earlier biographical sources.[42] One does not have to proceed as Arrian proceeded, nor as Davies and Allison did, but to do so is understandable. It is not hard to fathom why one would proceed in this manner.

So why have Davies and Allison drawn back from what would appear to be obvious in the case of Mark when they have followed essentially the same procedure? In order to answer this question we must go back to the opening paragraph of their discussion. There we discover a root of the problem. Davies and Allison do not seem to understand the most elementary facts of the debate over the synoptic problem. In this opening paragraph they write:

> Serious study of the literary relationships among the gospels began in the latter half of the eighteenth century, and the time since then has seen an array of theories propounded. But in the twentieth century, the majority of scholars have come to accept one or the other of two fundamental positions. According to most, Mark was a source for both Matthew and Luke. A minority, however, has postulated the primacy of Matthew. In their view, both Mark and Luke knew and used the First Gospel.[43]

At this point Davies and Allison provide a footnote which states: "This is the Griesbach hypothesis."[44] This is the first signal that something is amiss. For while, according to the Griesbach hypothesis, it is indeed true to say that "Mark and Luke knew and used the First Gospel," this is no less true according to the so-called Augustinian hypothesis,[45] as Davies and Allison also noted.[46] From this point forward Davies and Allison proceed as if their only tasks were to explain why Matthew has

---

[42]"Wherever Ptolemy the son of Lagos and Aristoboulos the son of Aristoboulos have both written the same things concerning Alexander the son of Philip, these I have written as being completely true. But those things (they wrote) that were not the same, I chose (from one or the other) those things which seemed to me more believable and at the same time more interesting." This is from Arrian's preface to his account of "The Expedition of Alexander," as translated by David R. Cartlidge and David L. Dungan, *Documents for the Study of the Gospels* (Cleveland: Collins, 1980) 126.

[43]Davies and Allison, *Gospel according to Saint Matthew*, 1:97.

[44]Davies and Allison, *Gospel according to Saint Matthew*, 1:97n.51.

[45]"So-called," because as David Peabody has shown, Augustine himself preferred a hypothesis which envisioned Mark combining themes of Matt and Luke, to the view that Mark wrote second and abbreviated Matt. Cf. David B. Peabody, "Augustine and the Augustinian Hypothesis: A Reexamination of Augustine's Thought in *De consensu evangelistarum*," in *New Synoptic Studies*, 37-64.

[46]Davies and Allison, *Gospel according to Saint Matthew*, 1:97n.50.

changed the order of Mark and to point out the difficulties in explaining why Mark would have changed the order of Matthew. This procedure is effective in arguing against the so-called Augustinian hypothesis, in which Mark is presumed to have been written second and to have used Matthew as his primary source. But this procedure is not a way to test the Griesbach hypothesis since, according to that hypothesis, Mark is third and never faces the order of episodes in Matthew in isolation from the corresponding order of episodes in Luke. Failure to observe this essential difference between these two classic hypotheses is a source of methodological confusion.

For example, in their chart comparing the order of the gospels,[47] Davies and Allison confine themselves to the comparison of the order of Mark and Matthew. According to the view that Mark was third and had *both* Matthew *and* Luke before him, it would be difficult if not impossible to understand Mark's compositional procedure without having Luke on the chart. Davies and Allison conclude exactly that: it is impossible to understand Mark's compositional procedure on the basis of their chart. So from the vantage point of Mark being the third gospel written, it could well be said that Davies and Allison have only rendered the service of showing that one chief rival to the Griesbach hypothesis (that is, that Mark was second and Luke used Mark and Matthew) faces difficulties. These difficulties must be answered by adherents of that view. But Davies and Allison have done more. They have done damage. They have shut out the opportunity for themselves and their readers to view evidence which comes as close as anything to being "compelling" in solving the synoptic problem. One has to see a chart which shows the sequential relationships between all three gospels *together* in order to see the way it is possible to view Mark preserving the order of his sources when they agree and following one source and then the other when they disagree. That is what the word "synopsis" means: to see these three gospels *together*.

III. Frans Neirynck on the Synoptic Problem

At the close of the 1980s, the editors of the *New Jerome Biblical Commentary* nailed Frans Neirynck's article on the "Synoptic Problem" to the masthead of their treatment of the church's gospels.[48] Neirynck

---

[47]Davies and Allison, *Gospel according to Saint Matthew*, 1:100-101.

[48]Frans Neirynck, "Synoptic Problem," in *The New Jerome Biblical Commentary*, ed.

tells his readers that the priority of Mark became the predominant scholarly opinion as a result of "decisive debate in the 1830s to 1860s." Nowhere has this ever been demonstrated. In fact, to the contrary, what can be demonstrated is that nothing critically decisive in favor of Markan priority happened in this period.[49]

In 1866, Hajo Uden Meyboom surveyed this period and noted the growing popularity of the Markan hypothesis, culminating in Holzmann's 1863 work.[50] Meyboom documents the fact that, as of 1866, this development was taking place not primarily because of scholarly debate, but because of philosophical, political, and theological considerations inherent in the discussion. The idea that the shortest gospel must be first was based on the nineteenth-century philosophical idea of development from the simple to the complex. The idea that the grammatically improved texts of Matthew and Luke come after Mark agreed with the nineteenth-century theory of progress.

Theology seems to have played the major role in winning support for the Markan hypothesis. Meyboom traced the development favoring the Markan hypothesis to theological reactions to David Friedrich Strauss in 1835. Meyboom carefully laid bare the logical flaws in Holzmann's work, reviewing the scholarly literature of his time and documenting the fact that the growing popularity of the Markan hypothesis was not supported by the most careful research of the day. Meyboom predicted that, mainly for theological reasons, the popularity of the Markan hypothesis would continue for a long time, but that eventually its scientific inadequacies would become apparent and it would be replaced by a theory or some theories that recognize the secondary character of Mark in relation to Matthew and Luke.

This replacement of the two-source hypothesis is exactly what is happening today, not only among neo-Griesbachians, but also among scholars like Boismard and even among scholars who continue to adhere

---

Raymond E. Brown, Joseph A. Fitzmyer, and Roland E. Murphy (Englewood Cliffs NJ: Prentice Hall, 1990) 587-95.

[49]Cf. David Peabody, "Chapters in the History of the Linguistic Argument for Solving the Synoptic Problem: The Nineteenth Century in Context," in *Jesus, the Gospels, and the Church: Essays in Honor of William R. Farmer*, ed. E. P. Sanders (Macon GA: Mercer University Press, 1987) 47-68.

[50]Hajo Uden Meyboom [Meijboom], *Geschiedenis en critiek der Marcushypothese* (Amsterdam: Kraay, 1866). ET: *A History and Critique of the Origin of the Marcan Hypothesis 1835–1866: A Contemporary Report Rediscovered*, NGS 8 (Macon GA: Mercer University Press, 1992).

to some modified form of the two-source hypothesis, as may be seen in the work of Helmut Koester.[51] Insights like Meyboom's offer one reason why it is imperative for New Testament scholars to undertake in earnest the investigation of the history of their discipline.[52]

In the second paragraph of his article, Neirynck explains the distribution of Mark's content in Matthew and Luke in terms of the two-source hypothesis. Thus, at the outset it is clear that the title "Synoptic Problem" that has been placed at the head of Neirynck's article does not stand for a scientific exposition of the nature of that problem. Rather, Neirynck's article is an exposition of the Markan hypothesis and a rejection of rival hypotheses. Moreover, it proceeds from a particular understanding of the *history* of that problem, an understanding which, as we have just seen, is at best problematic and at worst misleading. Neirynck is willing to admit that the Markan hypothesis "has obvious limitations."[53] If this hypothesis has "obvious limitations," why does Neirynck not give it up? The answer is found in his insistence on disagreeing with his colleagues on the fundamental starting point for a scientific discussion of the problem. To his credit, Neirynck acknowledges the methodological challenge that his opponents addressed to him and publicly states how he would defend himself against this challenge.

The challenge Neirynck faces may be put this way: since the synoptic problem is the problem of explaining the synoptic "fact" of agreement and disagreement between the synoptic gospels—Matthew, Mark, and Luke—it is important to see these three gospels *together*. The point is so obvious to the scientist that it would seem hardly necessary to state it. Yet Neirynck proceeds to divide the synoptic gospels into pairs and, like Davies and Allison, engages in a false abstraction. He discusses his first

[51]Helmut Koester, "History and Development of Mark's Gospel," in *Colloquy on New Testament Studies: A Time for Reappraisal and Fresh Approaches*, ed. Bruce Corley (Macon GA: Mercer University Press, 1983) 35-85. See also David Peabody, "The Late Secondary Redaction of Mark's Gospel and the Griesbach Hypothesis: A Response to Helmut Koester," in *Colloquy on New Testament Studies*, 87-132.

[52]The meeting of specialists on nineteenth-century German universities with Professor Graf Reventlow, 8-10 September 1990, in Latrobe, Pennsylvania, is of special interest in this regard. This conference led to a major conference on gospel studies in the nineteenth century held at the University of the Ruhr, in Bochum, Germany in 1992. See Henning Graf Reventlow and William R. Farmer, eds., *Biblical Studies and the Shifting of Paradigms, 1850–1914*, JSOTSup 192 (Sheffield: Sheffield Academic Press, 1995).

[53]Neirynck, "The Synoptic Problem," 594.

pair, Mark and Matthew, under the heading "Marcan order in Matthew,"[54] and then, unlike Davies and Allison, goes on to discuss his second pair, Mark and Luke, under the heading "Marcan order in Luke."[55] From these headings, it is clear that he stands within an exegetical tradition which no longer places the critic under the obligation of examining all three gospels together in order to explain the phenomenon of their order. In his defense against the arbitrary character of this procedure, which Neirynck acknowledges he has taken over from Lachmann, he writes:

> The objection that the argument from order explains Matthew in relationship to Mark on the one hand, and then Luke in relationship to Mark on the other, but that the relationship among all three remains unexplained is hardly convincing. Mark need not be explained "in relationship to both Matthew and Luke taken together." For it cannot be decided a priori that all three synoptic gospels should be interrelated. A solution of independence between Matthew and Luke is possible.[56]

This defense not only rests on an erroneous premise, but proceeds from a complete misunderstanding of the challenge being addressed to it by the Griesbach (or two-gospel) hypothesis. We will take up the misunderstanding first.

The methodological objection to any arbitrary division of the three synoptic gospels into two disparate pairs does not proceed from a denial of the right to experiment with various categories of evidence. The right to categorize is essential to all scientific work, and has been since the time of Aristotle. But once one has decided to categorize the data, he or she must be consistent and uniform in his or her treatment of *all* the data in *all* the categories. If we divide the synoptic gospels into pairs, we will have *three* pairs: Matthew-Mark, Mark-Luke, and Luke-Matthew. Any analysis of the synoptic data that confines itself to any one or any two, rather than *all three*, of these pairs will be something less than scientifically adequate. So the objection to Lachmann's procedure is not to categorization per se, but to the arbitrary character of its categorization de facto.

Nor do colleagues of Neirynck who challenge his method hold that it can be decided a priori that all three gospels should be interrelated. Rather, they recognize the obligation to demonstrate this fact, as they

---

[54]Neirynck, "The Synoptic Problem," 588.
[55]Neirynck, "The Synoptic Problem," 589.
[56]Neirynck, "The Synoptic Problem," 589.

have sought to do. The healing of the centurion's servant (Matt 8:7-10; Luke 7:6-9), not found in Mark, is only one example of the clear evidence that there is some literary interrelationship between Matthew and Luke that cannot be satisfied by hypothecating their dependence upon Mark. Since there are also agreements like this between Matthew and Mark against Luke and between Luke and Mark against Matthew, it follows that, without additional hypothetical documents, it will not be possible to explain the synoptic "fact" without acknowledging (not a priori, but de facto) a presumed direct literary interrelation between all three synoptic gospels. Thus, Neirynck is mistaken to think that colleagues who oppose him on this point regard it as self-evident that there is an interrelationship between all three synoptic gospels. They only insist that the proper method to follow is to test those arrangements which posit this three-way interrelationship before opening Pandora's box of "hypothetical sources." Having performed this test, Neirynck's critics put before the public the hypothesis they claim can best explain all the data, namely, a sequence of Matthew, Luke, Mark, where the second used the first, and the third used both the first and the second.[57]

We take up now the premise on which Neirynck rests his defense, namely, that "Mark need not be explained in relationship to both Matthew and Luke taken together." This premise follows only if some major hypothetical source (or group of sources) is posited to explain the agreements of Matthew and Luke against Mark. Otherwise, how would Neirynck explain these agreements if there was not some interrelationship between all three—given the corresponding agreements of Matthew and Mark against Luke, and of Matthew and Luke against Mark?

Therefore, to the degree that the existence of "Q" may be questioned, as well as that of other hypothetical documents like Proto-Mark, Proto-Matthew, Proto-Luke, "M," "L," "K," let alone Deutero-Mark, etc., Neirynck's defense as stated in the article rests upon a questionable premise. Because this intrinsically questionable premise is backed up in turn by a misunderstanding, Neirynck's method is left without effective defense and his whole treatment of the synoptic problem is rendered unreliable.

---

[57]Farmer, *The Synoptic Problem*, 191-232. These pages have been reissued in Arthur J. Bellinzoni, Jr., Joseph B. Tyson, and William O. Walker, Jr., eds., *The Two-Source Hypothesis: A Critical Appraisal* (Macon GA: Mercer University Press, 1985) 163-97.

Neirynck's concluding sentence is so modest that it suggests his possible awareness of the difficulties in his defense: "A solution of independence between Matthew and Luke is possible." Even the unlikely oral theory, which Neirynck correctly rejects, is "possible." Of course, Helmut Koester's complex theory of several earlier versions of Mark and a whole host of other solutions that have been propounded over the past two centuries are also possible. The historian can ill afford overly to concern himself or herself with what is merely possible. The question is whether literary independence between Matthew and Luke is probable. The two-source hypothesis requires that, but that is also where the two-source hypothesis runs afoul of the evidence. The total array of agreements of Matthew and Luke against Mark has never been satisfactorily explained by advocates of the two-source hypothesis. Until they are so explained, the two-source hypothesis will not only be judged as having "obvious limitations," but will be judged as less probable than other major alternatives, chiefly (1) Boismard's multiple-source hypothesis, (2) Austin Farrer's hypothesis of Markan priority which acknowledges that Luke knew Matthew and thus dispenses with "Q," and (3) the two-gospel hypothesis which dispenses with Markan priority and "Q," postulating that Luke used Matthew and that Mark used both Matthew and Luke.

The above way of evaluating the two-source hypothesis conforms closely, if not exactly, with the conclusions reached in the volume to be examined next.

IV. The Work of E. P. Sanders and Margaret Davies

In their book *Studying the Synoptic Gospels*, E. P. Sanders and Margaret Davies devote sixty-nine pages to a discussion of the synoptic problem.[58] This book is an advanced-level study guide to the synoptic gospels. While numerous charts and diagrams are used to make the subject understandable, these authors indulge in very little of the oversimplification that characterizes most comparable handbooks. As a consequence, the reader finds the presentation tough going as he or she is skillfully led through a maze of synoptic considerations.

After surveying what they see as the strengths and weaknesses of the two-source hypothesis and the Griesbach hypothesis, Sanders and Davies

---

[58]E. P. Sanders and Margaret Davies, *Studying the Synoptic Gospels* (London and Philadelphia: SCM and Trinity Press International, 1989) 51-119.

conclude that the two-source hypothesis is "unsatisfactory" for three reasons:

(1) The minor agreements are too many and too substantial to be explained away.

(2) There are instances in which Matthew is the middle term, and in which the simplest explanation is that Mark and Luke copied Matthew.

(3) The defense of the two-source hypothesis, by appealing to overlaps between Mark and "Q," is not satisfactory. This defense simply shifts some of the principal problems of the hypothesis to the relationship between Mark and "Q." "Q" then keeps growing to explain numerous agreements of Matthew and Luke against Mark.

The two-source hypothesis then, according to Sanders and Davies, must maintain the independence of Matthew and Luke—against the strong evidence that one knew the other, and the independence of Mark and "Q"—despite the numerous "overlaps." It is not adequate to the task.[59] Sanders and Davies ask:

> If the two-source hypothesis is not fully satisfactory, can we give the nod to the Griesbach [two-gospel] hypothesis? It seems to us mechanically feasible. Mark could have written his entire gospel by conflating Matthew and Luke. In this sense the Griesbach proposal has an advantage over the two-source hypothesis. The latter simply cannot account for all the agreements between Matthew and Luke, and thus must be modified and complicated in numerous ways in order to be maintained at all. But Mark could have done what the Griesbach proposal had him do.[60]

After noting some of the conventional objections raised against the view that Mark was written third, and after noting that these objections do not require a full answer, Sanders and Davies offer some suggestions as to why Mark might have combined Matthew and Luke, including the oft-made suggestion: "Perhaps he wrote to synthesize competing gospels and thus achieve harmony." Yet they finally conclude: "While we agree that we cannot fully recover an ancient author's intention, and thus that we cannot say that Griesbach's Mark is impossible, still it must be granted that, to the modern mind, there is very strong objection to putting Mark third."[61]

---

[59]Sanders and Davies, *Studying the Synoptic Gospels*, 91.
[60]Sanders and Davies, *Studying the Synoptic Gospels*, 92.
[61]Sanders and Davies, *Studying the Synoptic Gospels*, 92.

Without making quite clear whether they themselves strongly object to putting Mark third, and if so why, Sanders and Davies proceed to take up a series of other hypotheses, including Proto-Mark and Deutero-Mark, though focusing on the two most satisfactory, that is, those of Austin Farrer and Boismard. Sanders and Davies conclude that Goulder (representing the Austin Farrer hypothesis) has proven that Luke did know Matthew.[62] Yet Goulder's explanations of the composition of Matthew are not "fully convincing."[63]

As for Boismard's hypothesis, it answers all the data, but is very complicated. "In explaining everything Boismard takes us into the realm of conjecture, where everything is possible."[64] In reference to these two hypotheses, Sanders and Davies write:

> Our own inclination is to accept some of each hypothesis but to avoid the extremes. The evangelists were authors, though perhaps not as inventive as Goulder thinks, but in any case authors rather than only wielders of scissors and paste. On the other hand Boismard is probably on the right track in thinking of different editions and in allowing for criss-cross copying. . . .
>
> Thus we think that Luke knew Matthew (so Goulder, the Griesbachians and others) and that both Luke and Matthew were original authors of some of their sayings material (so especially Goulder). Following Boismard, we think it likely that one or more of the gospels existed in more than one edition, and that the gospels as we have them may have been dependent on more than one proto- or intermediate gospel.[65]

As we can see, Sanders and Davies have no hypothesis of their own. By their own admission, their view is hybrid or eclectic. The merit of their work lies in clearing away much of the conflicting synoptic "underbrush," not in having offered their own viable solution for the synoptic problem, which they do not claim to do. They succeed in clarifying in an original way why the two-source hypothesis is critically "unsatisfactory" and in pointing out the remaining difficulties (no mean achievement) standing in the way of fully accepting any one of the major alternative hypotheses now under consideration. There are, according to Sanders and Davies, three alternatives: the Griesbach hypothesis, Goulder's hypothesis, and Boismard's multiple-source hypothesis.[66]

---

[62]Sanders and Davies, *Studying the Synoptic Gospels*, 96.
[63]Sanders and Davies, *Studying the Synoptic Gospels*, 113.
[64]Sanders and Davies, *Studying the Synoptic Gospels*, 111.
[65]Sanders and Davies, *Studying the Synoptic Gospels*, 112-13.
[66]Sanders and Davies, *Studying the Synoptic Gospels*, 85.

We may offer our own somewhat more detailed and explicit summary of Sanders's and Davies' survey of the present state of the synoptic problem:

(1) The Griesbach (two-gospel) hypothesis is technically possible. Its main advantage over all rival hypotheses is its simple and straightforward explanation of the phenomenon of alternating support of Mark by Matthew and Luke in order of pericopes without appeal to "lost sources."[67] Its main difficulty is providing a comprehensible account of Mark's composition.

(2) The Goulder (Austin Farrer) hypothesis is technically possible. It is superior to the two-source hypothesis because it can explain the agreements of Matthew and Luke against Mark by acknowledging Luke's direct use of Matthew, thus dispensing with any need for "Q." But it cannot explain the phenomenon of order in Mark in relationship to Matthew and Luke as well as the Griesbach hypothesis can. Yet Sanders and Davies prefer Goulder's hypothesis to Griesbach's, presumably because they find it easier to explain how Matthew used Mark and how Luke used Mark and Matthew than to explain how Mark used Matthew and Luke.

(3) The Boismard multiple-source hypothesis is technically possible. It affords an explanation for agreements between Matthew and Luke against Mark and is thus superior to the two-source hypothesis. Yet its complexity makes it less likely than the Goulder (Austin Farrer) hypothesis. No preference is expressed as to the relative satisfactoriness of the Griesbach and the Boismard hypotheses. Both are more satisfactory than the two-source hypothesis for reasons clearly stated, yet both are less satisfactory than the Goulder hypothesis for reasons not clearly stated.[68]

In addition to our summary of Sanders's and Davies' survey, we may also assert that the two-source hypothesis is not technically possible. The main reason for this assertion is the extensive amount of agreement between Matthew and Luke against Mark. These extensive agreements are most simply explained by Luke's use of Matthew, thus paving the way for dispensing with "Q" as well as, in the light of the very significant

---

[67]Sanders and Davies, *Studying the Synoptic Gospels*, 88.

[68]A recent, appreciative study of Goulder's work is Mark S. Goodacre, *Goulder and the Gospels: An Examination of a New Paradigm*, JSNTSup 133 (Sheffield: Sheffield Academic Press, 1996).

agreement of Matthew and Luke against Mark 14:65, the priority of Mark.

Sanders's and Davies' analysis of the ins and outs of the synoptic problem marked a transition in the general discussion. When a major British ecumenical press, SCM, joins with a highly regarded American ecumenical press, Trinity Press International, in the publication of an advanced textbook, and the authors of that textbook clearly designate the reigning hypothesis as "unsatisfactory," it is safe to say that the long-term erosion of critical confidence in that hypothesis is well on its way to approaching a "critical mass," as far as expert opinion is concerned. This scholarly development, which began in 1951 with the decision of Cambridge University Press to publish B. C. Butler's *The Originality of Matthew: A Critique of the Two-Document Hypothesis*, calls into question a so-called "scholarly" consensus held within the guild of New Testament scholarship for almost a century.

One must make a distinction between what the majority of New Testament scholars (most of whom are not experts on the synoptic problem) holds, and what the majority of experts on the synoptic problem holds. The majority of synoptic specialists is coming to realize that the difficulties with the two-source hypothesis are fatal to that hypothesis. Until now, however, they have not been able to agree on an alternative hypothesis.

V. Concluding Comments

If and when advocates of the two-gospel hypothesis are able to provide readers with a literary, historical, and theological explanation of Mark's compositional activity and are able to give a coherent and reasonable picture of the whole of this gospel, the last major task in solving the synoptic problem will have been completed. Of course, there will also be the further need to provide a literary, historical, and theological explanation of Matthew's compositional activity and to give a coherent and reasonable picture of the whole of this gospel before the synoptic problem can be put to final rest. When that need has been filled, we may expect to better understand why Matthew was once, and many would say remains today, the foundational gospel of the church.[69]

---

[69]See Édouard Massaux, *Influence de l'Évangile de saint Matthieu sur la littérature chrétienne avant saint Irénée* (Leuven: Leuven University Press, 1950; [2]1986). ET: *The Influence of the Gospel of Saint Matthew on Christian Literature before Saint Irenaeus*,

Few if any students of Matthew today will deny that it is easier to make sense out of this gospel by studying it on its own terms than by giving compositional weight to the changes the author of Matthew has purportedly made in the text of Mark. Leading specialists in the study of Matthew openly acknowledge that no scholarly consensus has been reached on the purpose or provenance of that gospel. Scholars have reached an impasse in their efforts to settle these fundamental questions. It is not rash to suggest that a breaking of this impasse awaits a solution to the synoptic problem. The question of Matthew's sources is such a fundamental one that, until Matthew's relationship to Mark is settled, we can expect confusion to reign in gospel studies.

In summarizing the present state of the synoptic problem, we can say that, while in fact confusion appears to reign, in principle the synoptic problem may be close to a solution. It is now clear that Luke probably used Matthew. If it can be shown by explaining Mark's omissions from Matthew and Luke that he probably made use of those gospels, this will automatically make Matthew the earliest of the three. Work on Matthew then becomes a matter of understanding how the first gospel was written.

Work on the text of Matthew which assumes its priority is now under way in a research seminar at the University of Dallas. This work started in the fall of 1997 and is scheduled to last between three and five years. Meanwhile, work on Mark by the research team[70] that published *Beyond the Q Impasse*, this time under the editorial leadership of David Peabody, is well under way. Publication of this work, demonstrating how Mark has used Luke and Matthew, including the reasons for Mark's omissions of material from his sources, is scheduled for the fall of 1999.

NGS 5/1, 5/2, 5/3, trans. Norman J. Belval and Suzanne Hecht, ed. Arthur J. Bellinzoni (Macon GA: Mercer University Press, 1990, 1992, 1993).

[70]Thomas R. W. Longstaff has joined this team.

Luke's Sequential Use of the Sayings of Jesus from Matthew's Great Discourses: A Chapter in the Source-Critical Analysis of Luke on the Two-Gospel (Neo-Griesbach) Hypothesis

David B. Peabody

I. Joseph B. Tyson: Mentor, Colleague, and Friend

In 1958, a year before he completed his Ph.D. at Union Theological Seminary in New York, Joseph B. Tyson accepted an appointment in the Department of Religion at Southern Methodist University. Six years later, I matriculated as a first-year undergraduate at the same university. In almost two decades of work, 1964–1983, I earned three degrees from SMU, but, somehow, never had a single class with Professor Tyson. Nevertheless, I count him as one of my mentors in the academic study of religion for reasons I will try to recount below. I owe him many debts of gratitude. I am, therefore, pleased and privileged to contribute to this *Festschrift* in his honor.

The publication dates of the two editions of his textbook (1973, 1984) circumscribe the time I worked most closely with Joe Tyson in Dallas. In 1973, he was serving both as chair of the Department of Religious Studies and as the director of the M.A. program in religion at SMU. He, therefore, sent me my letter of admission to the M.A. program. During 1973–1974, Professor Tyson monitored my progress, served as my academic advisor, and at year's end recommended me for transfer to the Ph.D. program. It is quite possible that I would neither have pursued the Ph.D. nor entered the teaching profession at the postsecondary level, had it not been for that year in the M.A. program with Professor Tyson as its director.

After entering the M.A. program, I joined Professor Tyson, other professors, and graduate students in New Testament as a member of the Southwest Seminar on Gospel Studies. As part of his contributions to this seminar, Professor Tyson shared drafts of his developing article on

"Sequential Parallelism in the Synoptic Gospels"[1] and explored some of the problems of presenting in tabular form the kinds and percentages of verbal agreements between the synoptic gospels.[2] Two or more of these seminar papers helped to lay the methodological groundwork for the research tool Professor Tyson coauthored that was entitled *Synoptic Abstract.*[3]

Taking advantage of the collegiality that developed during meetings of the Southwest Seminar on Gospel Studies and other postdoctoral research seminars in the region at the time, such as the Southwest Seminar on the Development of Early Catholic Christianity and the Southwest Seminar on Biblical Studies, other conferences and colloquia were planned and successfully completed. Among these was the "Colloquy on the Relationships among the Gospels" that convened at Trinity University in San Antonio, Texas, 26-29 May 1977. Professor Tyson served as coconvener of the steering committee for that colloquy, along with Trinity Professor William O. Walker.[4] For the volume of colloquy proceedings, Professor Tyson produced a summary evaluation of a seminar that was held during that colloquy, namely, that on "Literary Criticism and the Gospels."[5]

Another development of the postdoctoral research seminars that met in the Southwest during the 1970s and 1980s was their institutionalization

---

[1]Joseph B. Tyson, "Sequential Parallelism in the Synoptic Gospels," *NTS* 22 (1976): 276-308.

[2]"A Model for a Synoptic Abstract," presented to the Southwest Seminar on Gospel Studies, 14 Mar. 1975; and "Verbal Agreements and Literary Parallelism," presented to the Southwest Seminar on Gospel Studies, 19 Apr. 1975. Other papers by Professor Tyson that I reviewed as a member of this seminar include "Notes on the Possible Source for Luke 7:1-10," presented 18 Oct. 1975; "Geographical Elements in the Gospel of Luke," presented 21 Feb. 1976; and "Criteria for Determining Literary Parallelism in the Synoptic Gospels: An Analysis of Matthew 5-7," n.d. Professor Tyson also presented "The Synoptic Problem" to this seminar on 15 Nov. 1972, but that was prior to my return to graduate study.

[3]Joseph B. Tyson and Thomas R. W. Longstaff, eds., *Synoptic Abstract* (Wooster OH: Biblical Research Associates, 1978). It was also in light of the wise counsel I received from Joe Tyson and other members of this seminar that I was able to shape a paper into my first scholarly publication. David Peabody, "A Pre-Markan Prophetic Sayings Tradition and the Synoptic Problem," *JBL* 97 (1978): 391-409.

[4]William O. Walker, Jr., ed., *The Relationships among the Gospels: An Interdisciplinary Dialogue* (San Antonio: Trinity University Press, 1978). Professor Walker invited me to served as his administrative assistant during that colloquy.

[5]Joseph B. Tyson, "Literary Criticism and the Gospels: The Seminar," in *The Relationships among the Gospels*, 323-41.

in the form of the Center for the Study of Religion in the Greco-Roman World. Professor Tyson was named the center's first director in 1983, and he hired me as his first assistant. Fellows of the center were drawn from a variety of institutions of higher education and a variety of academic disciplines (classics, religious studies, history, and art). During my tenure as assistant to the director (1983–1984), the center retained James M. Robinson as a consultant, and Henry Chadwick, Regius Professor of Divinity at Cambridge University, came to the North Texas region as a center-sponsored distinguished scholar-in-residence. He delivered a public lecture on "St. Augustine: Portrait of a Man," on 20 February 1984.

The responsibilities of the assistant to the director provided many opportunities for continued academic growth. Others from the SMU Graduate Program in Religious Studies, namely Eugene H. Lovering, Jr. (1984–1987) and James S. Bury (1987–1989), also held the position of assistant to the director while Professor Tyson served as director (1983–1989). As part of our duties, Professor Tyson invited Gene Lovering and me to share in the research of his book, *The Death of Jesus in Luke-Acts.*[6] Jim Bury was invited to share in the production of the volume of essays edited by Professor Tyson, entitled *Luke-Acts and the Jewish People: Eight Critical Perspectives.*[7] During my year as his assistant, my relationship with Joe Tyson grew from mentor to colleague to friend, and he has continued to be all of these.

I left my position at the center in the fall of 1984 to accept a position in the Department of Religion at Nebraska Wesleyan University. I have often quoted Professor Tyson's advice to me as I prepared to accept my first full-time teaching position. "David," he said, "if you only read undergraduate papers, your mind will turn to mush." Wise counsel. In those first years of undergraduate teaching, Professor Tyson's *The New Testament and Early Christianity* introduced my students to that intelligible field of inquiry within which the New Testament is most adequately understood.

After I left the Dallas area, Professor Tyson kept me informed and involved in the activities of the center as a corresponding fellow. In the fall of 1984, I returned to Dallas to participate in a center-sponsored

---

[6]Joseph B. Tyson, *The Death of Jesus in Luke-Acts* (Columbia: University of South Carolina Press, 1986).

[7]Joseph B. Tyson, ed., *Luke-Acts and the Jewish People: Eight Critical Perspectives* (Minneapolis: Augsburg, 1988).

colloquy on "Order in the Synoptic Gospels: Patterns of Agreement within Pericopes" that featured the work of Thomas R. W. Longstaff (Colby College) on conflation in Mark. A few years later, Professor Tyson edited papers on this topic for the journal *Second Century*.[8] In the fall of 1985, my own work on the history of nineteenth-century gospel criticism was featured at a similar center-sponsored colloquy, along with work by Professor Bo Reicke of the University of Basel.[9] In the fall of 1986, I participated in a third center-sponsored colloquy that addressed the topic of "New Critical Approaches in Synoptic Studies." Professor Tyson's book, *The Death of Jesus in Luke-Acts*, was one of the featured publications during that colloquy,[10] and I provided a review of the volume edited by Arthur J. Bellinzoni, Joseph B. Tyson, and William O. Walker, Jr., entitled *The Two-Source Hypothesis: A Critical Appraisal.*[11]

In 1987, the center sponsored a colloquy that featured the published form of my doctoral dissertation, *Mark as Composer*, along with a collection of John Bowden's English translation of Martin Hengel's *Studies in the Gospel of Mark*.[12] Joe Tyson provided one of seven reviews of my book during that colloquy which he entitled, "Peabody and Composition Criticism." Few scholars have enjoyed such comprehensive review of a first book. For this I owe much to Joe Tyson and the other

---

[8]Thomas R. W. Longstaff, *Evidence of Conflation in Mark? A Study in the Synoptic Problem* (Missoula MT: Scholars Press, 1977); cf. Joseph B. Tyson, ed., "Order in the Synoptic Gospels: Patterns of Agreement within Pericopes," *SecCent* 6 (1987–1988): 65-109.

[9]David B. Peabody, "Chapters in the History of the Linguistic Argument for Solving the Synoptic Problem: The Nineteenth Century in Context," in *Jesus, the Gospels and the Church: Essays in Honor of William R. Farmer*, ed. E. P. Sanders (Macon GA: Mercer University Press, 1987) 47-68; and Bo Reicke, "From Strauss to Holtzmann and Meijboom: Synoptic Theories Advanced During the Consolidation of Germany, 1830–1870," *NovT* 29 (1987): 1-21.

[10]See also Joseph B. Tyson, "Further Thoughts on The Death of Jesus in Luke-Acts," *PSTJ* 40 (April 1987): 48-50; Daryl Schmidt, "Tyson's Approach to the Literary Death of Jesus," *PSTJ* 40 (April 1987): 33-38; David L. Balch, "Comparing Literary Patterns in Luke and Lucian," *PSTJ* 40 (April 1987): 39-42; and Philip L. Shuler, "Questions of an Holistic Approach to Luke-Acts," *PSTJ* 40 (April 1987): 43-47.

[11]Arthur J. Bellinzoni, Joseph B. Tyson, and William O. Walker, Jr., eds., *The Two-Source Hypothesis: A Critical Appraisal* (Macon GA: Mercer University Press, 1985). See my review of this work entitled "In Retrospect and Prospect," *PSTJ* 40 (April 1987): 9-16.

[12]David B. Peabody, *Mark as Composer*, NGS 1 (Macon GA: Mercer University Press, 1987); and Martin Hengel, *Studies in the Gospel of Mark* (Philadelphia: Fortress, 1985).

scholars who gathered for that colloquy.[13] In March of 1987, the center sponsored a major conference on "Paul and the Legacies of Paul" and, on another occasion, helped bring scholars together to explore the "Social History of the Matthean Community."[14]

While serving as chair of the national SBL Acts group (1984–1990), Joe Tyson simultaneously supported and attended at least five of the eight annual meetings of the unit on "Redaction Criticism and the Two-Gospel Hypothesis" (1988 1995). From 1993 to 1995, after concluding his role as chair of the Acts group, Professor Tyson provided expert and helpful reviews of parts of three SBL seminar papers entitled "Narrative Outline of the Gospel of Luke according to the Two-Gospel Hypothesis." In light of the peer review given by Professor Tyson and others within the SBL, these seminar papers were eventually reshaped into major portions of the volume, *Beyond the Q Impasse: Luke's Use of Matthew.*[15]

It, therefore, seems appropriate that my contribution to this *Festschrift* should build upon this book which Joe Tyson so graciously helped us to improve. What I will say below concerns several topics of New Testament research to which Professor Tyson has made his own distinctive contributions: the synoptic problem, sequential parallelism in the synoptic gospels,[16] source criticism of the Gospel of Luke,[17] and literary

---

[13]In addition to Joe Tyson, others who reviewed *Mark as Composer* during that colloquy included Edward McMahon (Texas Christian University), "Narrative Structures and Deep Structures in Mark (On David Peabody's *Mark as Composer*)"; Allan J. McNicol (Institute for Christian Studies, Austin), "Linguistic Phraseology: A Tool for Solving the Synoptic Problem"; Philip L. Shuler (McMurry University, Abilene), "Mark and Gospel Genre"; William O. Walker (Trinity University, San Antonio), "Peabody's Methodology and Its Importance for Source Criticism"; and Frank Wheeler (Eastern New Mexico State University), "Mark as Composer and Textual Criticism." Martin Hengel (University of Tübingen) also evaluated the book during an oral presentation at the colloquy's close.

[14]Published forms of papers from these conferences appear in William S. Babcock, ed., *Paul and the Legacies of Paul* (Dallas: Southern Methodist University Press, 1990); and David L. Balch, ed., *Social History of the Matthean Community: Cross Disciplinary Approaches* (Minneapolis: Fortress, 1991).

[15]See *SBLSP* (1992): 98-120, on Luke 3:1–7:10; *SBLSP* (1993): 303-33, on Luke 7:11–9:50; *SBLSP* (1994): 516-73, on Luke 9:51–19:27; and *SBLSP* (1995): 636-87, on Luke 19:28–24:53. Professor Tyson responded to those sections of these coauthored papers dealing with Luke 9:1-50 in 1993, with Luke 14:1–16:31 in 1994, and with Luke 22:47–23:35 in 1995. The thoroughly reworked and developed form of these papers now appears as substantial parts of the following volume: Allan J. McNicol, David L. Dungan, and David B. Peabody, eds., *Beyond the Q Impasse: Luke's Use of Matthew: A Demonstration by the Research Team of the International Institute for Gospel Studies* (Philadelphia: Trinity Press International, 1996).

[16]See n. 1 above.

criticism and the gospels.[18] Although Professor Tyson does not advocate the two-gospel (neo-Griesbach) hypothesis, in 1985 he did conclude:

> It seems fair to say . . . that the Griesbach hypothesis, especially as represented in the work of W. R. Farmer, has now emerged as the leading alternative solution to the Synoptic problem. This fact suggests that future research on the source problem will be carried on largely by persons in the Griesbach and the two-source camps.[19]

So I now turn to some of this continuing research from the perspective of a person in the Griesbach camp.

II. Selected Historical Background on the Issue of Luke's Use of Matthew

One stumbling block preventing many scholars from accepting the view that the author of Luke was directly and literarily dependent upon Matthew has been the perceived differences in the sequential ordering of pericopes in Luke and Matthew. "If the author of Luke used Matthew," some may ask, "would he have rearranged the pericope order of Matthew so radically? And, if so, why did he do it?" Earlier advocates of the Griesbach hypothesis had difficulty providing plausible answers when such objections were raised against their hypothesis.

Johann Jacob Griesbach himself was heir to the so-called "Augustinian hypothesis" (that is, that Mark was literarily dependent upon Matthew and that Luke was literarily dependent upon both Matthew and Mark).[20] It, therefore, probably never occurred to Griesbach to provide a detailed demonstration that Luke had utilized Matthew[21] as a complement to his

---

[17]Joseph B. Tyson, "Source Criticism of the Gospel of Luke," *PerRS* 5 (1978): 144-50.

[18]See n. 5 above.

[19]Tyson, "The Two-Source Hypothesis: A Critical Appraisal," in *The Two-Source Hypothesis*, 452.

[20]I refer to this as the "so-called" Augustinian hypothesis primarily because of Augustine's own testimony in *De consensu evangelistarum* 4.10.11. For my analysis and conclusions about Augustine's statements about synoptic relationships here and elsewhere in the corpus of Augustine's writings, see my article, "Augustine and the Augustinian Hypothesis: A Reexamination of Augustine's Thought in *De consensu evangelistarum*," in *New Synoptic Studies: The Cambridge Gospel Conference and Beyond*, ed. William R. Farmer (Macon GA: Mercer University Press, 1983) 37-64.

[21]Griesbach did include some discussion of Luke's use of Matt in his Easter programme of 1783 at Jena entitled *Inquiritur in fontes, unde Evangelistae suas de resurrectione Domini narratione hauserint* (Jena: Strankmann-Fickelscherria, 1783). This Easter

demonstration that Mark had utilized both Matthew and Luke.[22] Scholars in the church before Griesbach (1745–1812) had affirmed Luke's direct literary dependence upon Matthew at least since the time of Augustine (354–430), if not since the time of Origen (ca. 185–ca. 254) or earlier.[23]

---

programme of 1783 was reprinted in 1794 and in 1825 (see below). Hans-Herbert Stoldt has included a discussion of this programme in *Geschichte und Kritik der Markushypothese*, 2nd ed. (Göttingen: Vandenhoeck & Ruprecht, 1986) 239-64. The first edition in 1977 did not include any equivalent to pp. 239-64 in the second edition, so these pages naturally have no equivalent in the English translation of the first edition, *History and Criticism of the Marcan Hypothesis* (Macon GA: Mercer University Press, 1980). However, pp. 239-64 of the second edition of Stoldt were reviewed by William Baird, "Luke's Use of Matthew: Griesbach Revisited," *PSTJ* 40 (July 1987): 35-38. Baird says that Griesbach had presented *Inquiritur* "during a celebration of Easter at Jena in 1783, eleven years before the publication of his monumental *Commentatio*." To clarify the history of Griesbach's work and its publication, one should note that Griesbach presented the essence of his "Demonstration that Mark was Written after Matthew and Luke" as the Whitsun programmes at Jena for 1789 and 1790. These Whitsun programmes were presented just six and seven years after Griesbach presented his *Inquiritur* as the Easter programme for 1783. But Baird is certainly correct to note that a combined and expanded form of these Whitsun programmes of 1789–1790 was published as Griesbach's *Commentatio* in 1794 which is, of course, as Baird affirmed, eleven years after Griesbach presented the *Inquiritur*. This expanded *Commentatio* was later reprinted by Gabler in 1825, as also noted by Baird (38n.5). Griesbach died in 1812, after the reprints of some of his work by Velthusen, Kuinoel, and Ruperti (1794–1799), but before the reprints by Gabler (1824–1825). See below.

[22]For a first expanded reprinting of the original Latin text of Griesbach's Whitsun programmes for 1789 and 1790 in Jena, see "Io. Iac. Griesbachii Theol. D. et Prof. Primar in academia Jenensi commentatio qua Marci Evangelium totum e Matthaei et Lucae commentariis decerptum esse monstratur, scripta nomine Academiae Jenensis (1789, 1790) jam recognita multisque augmentis locupletata" in *Commentationes theologicae*, ed. Johann Kaspar Velthusen (1740–1814), Christian Gottlieb (or "Theophilus") Kuhnol (or "Kuinoel") (1768–1841), and Georg Alexander Ruperti (1758–1839), 6 vols. (Leipzig: Johann Ambrose Barth, 1794–1799) 1:360-434. A second reprint of this work was provided in Johann Jakob Griesbach, *Opuscula academica*, ed. Johann Philip Gabler, 2 vols. (Jena: Frommanni, 1824–1825) 2:358-425. A third reprint of this Latin text, accompanied by a first English translation by Bernard Orchard, is now available in Bernard Orchard and Thomas R. W. Longstaff, eds., *J. J. Griesbach: Synoptic and Text-Critical Studies 1776–1976*, SNTSMS 34 (Cambridge: Cambridge University Press, 1978). In this volume, see esp. J. J. Griesbach, "Commentatio qua Marci Evangelium totum e Matthaei et Lucae commentariis decerptum esse monstratur" with introduction by Bo Reicke, 68-102; Bernard Orchard, "A Demonstration that Mark was Written After Matthew and Luke (A Translation of J. J. Griesbach's 'Commentatio qua Marci Evangelium totum e Matthaei et Lucae commentariis decerptum esse monstratur')" 103-35; cf. Bo Reicke, "Griesbach's Answer to the Synoptic Question," 50-67.

[23]William R. Farmer, "Patristic Evidence Reexamined: A Response to George Kennedy," in *New Synoptic Studies*, 3-15; Giuseppe Giov. Gamba, "A Further Reexamination of Evidence from the Early Tradition," in *New Synoptic Studies*, 17-35;

But some of Griesbach's early nineteenth-century followers such as Wilhelm Martin Leberecht de Wette (1780–1849)[24] and Friedrich Bleek (1793–1859)[25] came to the conclusion that Luke's direct literary dependence upon the text of Matthew was an insufficient explanation for common materials in Luke and Matthew. For instance, de Wette claimed:

> [T]he Gospel of Luke cannot be regarded throughout as only a free revision of Matthew, without the use of other sources. The proem i.1-4 shows the contrary. There is a degree of probability in favor of the theory that Luke arbitrarily undertook to assign the discourses of Jesus—which Matthew placed together—to certain incidents as occasions. . . . When he gives a corresponding equivalent for what he has not in common with Matthew . . . it proves that he had reference to Matthew. Cautious criticism, however, will not regard all these passages as manufactured by Luke, but will also suppose the use of tradition or of written sources. . . . In the same way Luke must have derived the larger passages, which he has in addition to Matthew, from a written source.[26]

In the note explaining the last statement above, de Wette continued:

> We may, with *Marsh* and others, regard a collection of discourses as this source. This collection, however, seems to have been enriched by scattered and unarranged excerpts from Matthew before it fell into Luke's hands; and, despite his acquaintance with Matthew, he preferred to follow it, and to give some of the discourses in less fitting connection.[27]

In short, de Wette believed that Luke's non-Matthean discourse tradition "overlapped" with discourse tradition that Luke also had available to him in Matthew. For some reason, though, Luke often preferred the non-Matthean discourse tradition in spite of the fact that it made Luke "give some of the discourses in less fitting connection" (than the parallel discourse[s] in Matthew).

While de Wette's speculations about Luke's use of sources in these cases seem inconsistent and doubtful, Bleek's views on Luke's use of Matthew are even farther removed from Griesbach's original position.

---

and Bernard Orchard, part 2, "The Historical Tradition," in *The Order of the Synoptics: Why Three Synoptic Gospels?* (Macon GA: Mercer University Press, 1987) 109-226.

[24]Wilhelm Martin Leberecht de Wette, "Explanation of the Relation between Matthew and Luke," in *A Historical-Critical Introduction to the Canonical Books of the New Testament* (Boston: Crosby, Nichols, 1858) 148-63.

[25]Friedrich Bleek, *An Introduction to the New Testament*, 2 vols. (Edinburgh: T.&T. Clark, 1869–1870). See "Relation Between Matthew and Luke," 1:275-81.

[26]De Wette, *A Historical-Critical Introduction*, 161-62.

[27]De Wette, *A Historical-Critical Introduction*, 163n.h.

Bleek affirmed Mark's direct literary dependence upon Matthew and Luke, but he hypothecated an Ur-Gospel that preceded these two synoptic gospels to explain the evidence of a relationship between them.[28] Thus, by the middle of the nineteenth century, two of Griesbach's most gifted disciples had come to deny in different ways a central feature of Griesbach's hypothesis, that is, Luke's direct literary dependence upon the text of Matthew wherever the degree of verbatim agreement would support such dependence. Thus, Bleek, if not both Bleek and de Wette, also helped to lay groundwork for the logia or "Q" hypothesis.

Outside the Griesbach school, the dominance of the two-source hypothesis among scholars since the second half of the nineteenth century has tended to hinder scholars from comparing Luke and Matthew directly (that is, unmediated by their alleged dependence upon Mark or "Q" or both). Until recently, even twentieth-century advocates of the two-gospel (or neo-Griesbach) hypothesis had yet to publish a comprehensive analysis of Luke's use of Matthew. The 1996 release of the book *Beyond the Q Impasse* fills that long-standing lacuna in the corpus of literature on the Owen-Griesbach (two-gospel) hypothesis.

In what follows, I intend to elaborate upon the demonstration in that book and to provide more detailed notes on Luke's orderly use of the sayings within the major speeches of Jesus in Matthew. But in order to understand these elaborations fully, one should consult *Beyond the Q Impasse* directly.[29]

As early as 1976, Bernard Orchard shared two important observations about Luke's use of Matthew:

> We here bring to light two facts hitherto unnoticed: firstly, there is a sequential parallel to the first part of each Matthean Discourse to be found in Luke's main structure in Luke's shortened form of it. . . . [S]econdly, Luke transfers to his Central Section the rest of the material that he takes out of these six Discourses, except for a few Sayings units which he joins on to his abbreviated versions of the Discourses in his main structure.[30]

---

[28]Bleek, *An Introduction to the New Testament*, 259, 275, 277, 279, 281.

[29]See McNicol, *Beyond the Q Impasse*, 151-244, for the discussion on Luke's travel narrative; and the related chart C, "The Travel Narrative (Luke 10:1–19:27)," which is found in a pocket inside the back cover.

[30]Bernard Orchard, *Matthew, Luke & Mark*, 2nd ed. (Manchester: Koinonia, 1977; [1]1976) 52. Tyson's review, "Bernard Orchard's *Matthew, Luke, and Mark*," was presented to the Southwest Seminar on Gospel Studies, 25 Sept. 1976.

What I have to say in this article is, at least in part, an attempt to establish further the evidential basis in support of Orchard's insights. Specifically, what I wish to demonstrate is that, when Luke moves material from the great discourses of Jesus in the Gospel of Matthew into his central section, he does so in an orderly manner. He rarely reuses what he has already utilized in "Luke's main structure in Luke's shortened form of [Matthew's discourse]." Luke, for the most part, adopts the sayings of Jesus that are contained in one of the great discourses in Matthew into the Lukan central section in the same order as those sayings appear in the parallel discourse in Matthew.

III. The Evidence of Luke's Sequential Use of the Sayings of Jesus from Matthew's Discourses

Below I take up Luke's use of the sayings within the several discourses in Matthew in an order which, I believe, begins with the more impressive evidence and concludes with the less impressive evidence. I will, therefore, provide notes on Luke's use of sayings material from the discourses in Matthew in the following order: (1) the parables discourse (Matt 13:1-53), (2) the "woes" discourse (23:1-39), (3) the mission discourse (9:35–11:1), (4) the last eschatological discourse (24:1–26:1), (5) the church discourse or community regulations (18:1–19:1), and (6) the sermon on the mount (4:23–7:29). To these six sections, I have added a seventh on Luke's use of material from Matthew 11–12 because Luke's travel narrative, according to the two-gospel (neo-Griesbach) hypothesis, is composed of the following elements:

(a) some remaining narrative units in Matthew (e.g., the balance of Matt 11–12) which Luke used in Matthew's general order;

(b) some remaining segments of Matthean units that Luke had otherwise previously utilized (e.g., Matt 8:11-12, 8:18-22, 17:19-20);

(c) sayings from all of Matthew's sayings collections, which Luke interspersed throughout Luke 10–19 mostly in the same order in which the sayings occur within Jesus' speeches in Matthew (but not necessarily in the same order as the speeches appear in Matt from which these sayings are drawn); and

(d) non-Matthean traditions worked into several teaching scenes where Luke thought them appropriate.[31]

---

[31]Cf. McNicol, *Beyond the Q Impasse*, 21, for a similar, brief sketch of Luke's literary

A. Luke's Use of Matthew's Parables Discourse (Matt 13:1-53)

Prior to the opening of the travel narrative, Luke made orderly use of the opening verses of Matthew's parables discourse—printed in plain type below (Matt 13:1-23 ‖ Luke 8:4-18). In subsequent parts of the travel narrative, Luke again made orderly use of other remaining material from Matthew 13—printed in bold type and indented below.

Matt 13:1-9	=	Luke 8:4-8. Parable of sower.
Matt 13:10-11, 13-15	=	Luke 8:9-10. Reason for parables.
Matt 13:16-17	=	**Luke 10:23-24. Blessed are your eyes.**
Matt 13:18-23	=	Luke 8:11-15. Interpretation of parable of sower.
(Matt 13:12)	=	Luke 8:18b. Haves and have nots.
Matt 13:24-30	=	Not in Luke. Parable of weeds.
Matt 13:31-33	=	**Luke 13:18-21. Parables of mustard and leaven.**
Matt 13:34-35	=	Not in Luke. Prophecy fulfillment.
Matt 13:36-43	=	Not in Luke. Interpretation of weeds.
Matt 13:44-46	=	Not in Luke. Parables of treasure and pearl.
Matt 13:47-50	=	Not in Luke. Parable of net and its interpretation.
Matt 13:51-52	=	Not in Luke. A scribe trained for the kingdom.
Matt 13:53	=	Not in Luke. When Jesus had finished . . .
		But cf. Matt 7:28-29 ‖ Luke 7:1a ‖ Luke 4:31-32.
Matt 12:46-50	=	Luke 8:19-21. Jesus' true family.[32]

---

procedures.

[32]Matt 12:46-50 are the verses that immediately precede Matthew's parables chapter (Matt 13:1-53). Luke simply reversed two contiguous units in Matt (Matt 13:1-23 ‖ Luke 8:4-15 and Matt 12:46-50 ‖ Luke 8:19-21) in composing Luke 8:4-21.

Sandwiched between these two contiguous units from Matt, the order of which Luke reversed, is a Lukan thematic summary (Luke 8:16-18). This Lukan thematic summary is made up of one verse from each of Matthew's first three discourses in the same order in which they appear in Matt. This arrangement may provide evidence of Luke's knowledge of the discourses of Jesus in Matt in the order in which they appear in Matt.

Matt 5:15	=	Luke 8:16. On uncovered light (cf. hidden city in Matt 5:14)
Matt 10:26	=	Luke 8:17. Nothing hidden/covered that will not be revealed.
Matt 13:12	=	Luke 8:18b. Those who have will get more and those who have not, will have even fewer of what they have taken away.

This Lukan thematic summary (Luke 8:16-18) is related to another at Luke 11:33-36 where Luke has again utilized Matt 5:15, but there, Luke conflated Matt 5:15 with Matt 6:22-23, on the eye as the lamp of the body which distinguishes light from darkness. The common motifs in Matt 5:14-16 and Matt 6:22-23 include: (1) lamp, (2) light/darkness, and (3) eye/seeing. But Luke rewrote Matt 5:15 at both Luke 8:16 and Luke 11:33, so that both Lukan thematic summaries include the same words: "in order that those who enter may see the light."

Within the travel narrative, Luke took up some remaining verses from
Matthew 13 in the same order in which they appear in Matthew (Matt
13:16-17 ‖ Luke 10:23-24 and Matt 13:31-33 ‖ Luke 13:18-21). Not
even a hint of the first two verses that Luke chose to utilize from
Matthew 13 (Matt 13:16-17 ‖ Luke 10:23-24) may be found in Luke's
previous use of Matthew 13:1-23 at Luke 8:4-18.

The parable of the weeds (Matt 13:24-30) immediately follows the
verses Luke had utilized earlier in composing the Lukan parable discourse (Matt 13:1-23 ‖ Luke 8:4-18). The interpretation of the parable
of the weeds appears later in Matthew 13:36-43. Between the parable of
the weeds (13:24-30) and its interpretation (13:36-43), neither of which
Luke chose to utilize in his gospel, fall the twin parables of the mustard
seed and the leaven (13:31-33). Luke next utilized both of these twin
parables (Matt 13:31-33 ‖ Luke 13:18-21) in the same order in which
they appear in Matthew. After Luke 13:21, Luke made no further use of
material from Matthew 13.

Luke 8:16-18 is also related to a Lukan interweaving transition at Luke 11:53–12:3
where Luke again utilized Matt 10:26(-27) and conflated it with Matt 16:1, 6; 23:1, and
perhaps some other fragments of Matt. Luke 8:16-18 is related to Luke 11:33-36 by the
common use of Matt 5:15, while Luke 8:16-18 is related to Luke 11:53–12:3 by the
common use of Matt 10:26.

We have seen that Luke 8:16-18 is sandwiched between Matt 13:1-23 ‖ Luke 8:4-15
and Matt 12:46-50 ‖ Luke 8:19-21. In this position, it functions as a "suture passage"
for the two contiguous literary units in Matt, the order of which Luke had reversed.

Luke 11:33-36 and 11:53–12:3 function in similar ways within the Gospel of Luke.
Luke 11:33-36 is sandwiched between a Lukan unit on spiritual power (Luke 11:14-32
‖ Matt 12:22-50) and a subsequent unit on woes against Pharisees and lawyers (Luke
11:37-52 ‖ Matt 23:1-36). Luke 11:53–12:2 also is sandwiched between the Lukan unit
on woes against the Pharisees and lawyers (Luke 11:37-52 ‖ Matt 23:1-16) and the
subsequent Lukan unit on fear and anxiety (Luke 12:4-34).

Given their literary functions in Luke, one may conclude that all three Lukan
passages (Luke 8:16-18, 11:33-36, 11:53–12:3) are most likely compositions of the author
of Luke. And, since the interconnections among these three Lukan passages are mediated
by Luke's use of Matt, we have here strong literary evidence of Luke's use of Matt. And
Luke 8:16-18, which is one of the products of the author of Luke, seems to have been
composed by someone who knew the structure of Matt at least from Matt 5:15–13:12,
including exactly three discourses of Jesus in the same order in which they appear in
Matt: (1) Matt 4:23–7:29 (cf. Matt 5:15 ‖ Luke 8:16), (2) Matt 9:35–11:1 (cf. Matt 10:26
‖ Luke 8:17) and (3) Matt 13:1-53 (cf. Matt 13:12 ‖ Luke 8:18).

B. Luke's Use of Matthew's "Woes" Discourse (Matt 23:1-39)

Luke's use of Matthew 23 within the travel narrative is also orderly.

Matt 23:1-36   = Luke 11:37-52. Woes against Pharisees and lawyers.
Matt 23:37-39   = Luke 13:34-35. Lament over Jerusalem.

Luke did radically recompose Matthew 23:1-36 in Luke 11:37-52, but a careful look at Luke 11:37-52 will reveal that Matthew 23:1-36 are precisely the verses that Luke used in composing Luke 11:37-52.

C. Luke's Use of Matthew's Mission Discourse (Matt 9:35–11:1)

The table below indicates that Luke made at least four uses of material from Matthew's mission discourse. During each usage, Luke adopted material from Matthew in Matthew's order. Material that Luke adopted during each of these four usages is indicated by a further indentation on the side of the equation reserved for Luke (1, 2, 3, or 4). What is most impressive in this table is Luke's orderly adoption of remaining sayings from Jesus' mission discourse in Matthew into the Lukan travel narrative (indented column 3, printed in bold type).

(1) Luke's first use of Matthew 9:35–11:1
    (2) Luke's second use
        (3) Luke's third use (within the travel narrative)
            (4) Luke's fourth use

Matt 9:35–10:16 =	Luke 6:12-15. Call of the twelve apostles.	
=	Luke 9:1-6. Commissioning of the twelve apostles.	
=		**Luke 10:1-12. Call and commissioning of 72 other disciples.**
Matt 10:17-22 =		Luke 21:12-19. Bearing witness.
Matt 10:24-25a =	Luke 6:40. A disciple is not above his teacher.	
Matt 10:26 =	Luke 8:17. Part of Lukan thematic summary (Lk 8:16-18).	
Matt 10:26-33 =		**Luke 11:53-12:9. On fear.**
(Matt 10:19-20) =		**Luke 12:11-12. On anxiety.**
Matt 10:34-37 =		**Luke 12:49-53. On divisions of family.**
Matt 10:37-38 =		**Luke 14:25-27. On conditions of discipleship.**
Matt 10:39 =		**Luke 17:33. On losing one's soul.**
Matt 10:40–11:1 =	Luke 9:46-48. Who is the greatest?	

Luke made first use of material from Matthew 9:35–11:1 at Luke 6:12-15 where he utilized the names of the twelve apostles in his narration of their call, just prior to the sermon on the plain (Luke 6:20–7:1). In this way, Luke depicted all twelve apostles as called and present for the sermon on the plain (6:20–7:1). Contrast Matthew's gospel where

Jesus is depicted as having called only four of his twelve closest disciples (Matt 4:18-22) prior to Jesus' preaching of the sermon on the mount (5:2–7:29). Luke then made use of Matthew 10:24-25 within the sermon on the plain and Matthew 10:26 as part of a Lukan thematic summary at Luke 8:16-18.

Luke returned to the opening verses of the mission discourse in Matthew 9:35–10:16 when he next narrated the commissioning of the twelve apostles (Luke 9:1-6). Then, just prior to the opening of his central travel narrative (9:51), Luke conflated the closing verses from Jesus' mission discourse in Matthew (Matt 10:40–11:1) with the opening verses of Jesus' community regulations in Matthew (Matt 18:1-2, 4-5 ‖ Luke 9:46-48).

Then, after composing a transitional section (Luke 9:37-62) that prepared for Luke 10:1-23 by questioning the adequacy of the twelve disciples and even some other would-be disciples of Jesus, Luke turned for a third time to Matthew 9:35–10:16 and used that material to compose his distinctive story of the call and commissioning of the seventy-two other disciples (Luke 10:1-12 ‖ Matt 9:35–10:16). Then, later in the travel narrative, although Luke made use of verses from Matthew 9:35–11:1 in five subsequent, but separated, Lukan literary contexts, Luke utilized every verse from Matthew 10:26-39 in the same order as these verses appear in Matthew.

Luke's shift of the order of Matthew 10:19-20 (on anxiety) in Luke 12:11-12 is explained by Luke's composition of a section within his travel narrative that focuses on the topic of rejecting fear and anxiety (Luke 12:4-34). Luke first utilized a Matthean segment of sayings on fear from Matthew 10:26-33 and then utilized a related segment on anxiety from Matthew 6:25-34, which even contains some doublets to Matthew 10:26-33. Moving Matthew 10:19-20 from its sequence in Matthew 10 into its new position in Luke 12:11-12 provided Luke with a smooth transition (Luke 12:11-12 ‖ Matt 10:19-20) from his discussion of fear (Luke 12:4-10 ‖ Matt 10:28-33 ‖ Matt 12:31-32) to his subsequent discussion of the related topic of anxiety (Luke 12:13-32 ‖ Matt 6:25-34, cf. "anxiety" in Matt 10:19 ‖ Luke 12:11).

Luke substituted most of the balance of this Matthean discourse (Matt 10:17-22) for its doublet at Matthew 24:9-15 in composing the contextual parallel to Matthew 24:9-15 at Luke 21:12-20.

D. Luke's Use of Matthew's Last Eschatological Discourse
   (Matt 24:1–26:1)

Luke's use of Matthew 24–25, the last eschatological discourse of Jesus, within the Lukan travel narrative is also orderly. But Luke seems to have utilized material from this discourse within this Lukan literary context in two successive sweeps that simply reverse the order of two blocks of contiguous material in Matthew. Luke's use of Matthew in Sweep B (Matt 24:23-41) ends exactly where Sweep A begins (24:42–25:13).

Sweep A
Matt 24:42-51   = Luke 12:35-48. Watchful, waiting, responsible servants.
Matt 25:1-13   = Luke 13:22-27. I do not know from where you come.
Sweep B
Matt 24:23-41   = Luke 17:20-33. Where is the kingdom of God?

E. Luke's Use of Matthew's Community Regulations
   (Matt 18:1–19:1)

Luke's use of Matthew's version of Jesus' community regulations also reflects an orderly progression in Luke's use of sayings material from this Matthean discourse.

Matt 18:1-2, 4-5   = Luke 9:46-48. Who is the greatest?
Matt 18:6-7   =   (On scandals. See Luke 17:1-2 below.)
Matt 18:8-9   =   Not in Luke. On moral surgery.
                           (Doublet at Matt 5:29-30
                           also omitted by Luke).
Matt 18:10, 12-14   = Luke 15:1-7. Parable of the lost sheep.
[Matt 18:11]   =   Is textually uncertain in Matt (cf. Luke 19:10)
(Matt 18:6-7)   =   Luke 17:1-2. On scandals.
Matt 18:15-17, 21-22 = Luke 17:3-4.
                           Forgiving a sinner within the community.
Matt 18:18-20   =   Not in Luke. Where two or three agree.
                           (Contrast divisions of two or three in Luke
                           12:49-53 ‖ Matt 10:34-37,
                           cf. Luke 14:25-27 ‖ Matt 10:37-38)
Matt 18:23-35   =   Not in Luke. But cf. "agreement with accuser"
                           in Luke 12:57-59 ‖ Matt 5:21-26.
(Matt 18:3)   =   Luke 18:17. Receiving the kingdom like a child.

The location of Jesus' discourse on community regulations in Matthew 18:1–19:1 determined the location of Luke's central travel narrative

(Luke 9:51–19:27; cf. Matt 18:1-2, 4-5 ‖ Luke 9:46-48). Luke's use of the remaining verses within this Matthean discourse was also orderly.

Luke utilized Matthew 18:1-5, but omitting Matthew 18:3, at Luke 9:46-48, just before Luke began to depart from following the sequential order of pericopes in Matthew within successive divisions of his narrative.[33] But that previously omitted verse from Matthew 18:1-2, 4-5 ‖ Luke 9:46-48 reappears in the parallel text of Luke precisely at the point where Luke generally began to follow the sequential order of pericopes in Matthew (Matt 19:13-15 ‖ Luke 18:15-16; Matt 18:3 ‖ Luke 18:17). This appearance is a striking example of the great care that Luke took in working with Matthew's text. That section of Luke's gospel that represents his major departure from following some kind of order of pericopes in Matthew (that is, Luke 10:1–19:12) seems to have been delimited by Luke himself by his usage of Matthew 18:1-5.

F.   Luke's Use of Matthew's Sermon on the Mount (Matt 4:23–7:29)

Luke's use of Matthew's sermon on the mount within the Lukan travel narrative appears to be the least orderly of all of Luke's uses of sayings material from Jesus' long speeches in Matthew, but that apparent disorder should be understandable because Luke had utilized more material from the sermon on the mount than he had from any other of Jesus' earlier discourses in Matthew, prior to the opening of the Lukan central travel narrative (Matt 4:23–7:29 cf. Luke 6:20–7:1; Matt 9:35–11:1, cf. Luke 6:12-16, 9:1-6; Matt 13:1-53, cf. Luke 8:4-18; and Matt 18:1–19:1, cf. Luke 9:46-48).

Luke utilized a great deal of material from Matthew's sermon on the mount in composing the Lukan sermon on the plain (Luke 6:20–7:1). Within his version of Jesus' great sermon, Luke utilized most of the sayings from the sermon on the mount in the same order as Matthew recorded them, including the same beginning, middle and ending.[34]

Luke's Use of Matthew within the Sermon on the Plain

Matt 5:2-12	= Luke 6:20-26. Beatitudes and woes.
Matt 5:43-45	= Luke 6:27-28. On love of enemies 1.
(Matt 5:38-42)	= Luke 6:29-30. On nonretaliation.
(Matt 7:12)	= Luke 6:31. The golden rule.
Matt 5:46-47	= Luke 6:32-34. On love of all.

---

[33]Compare chart A or B with chart C in McNicol, *Beyond the Q Impasse.*
[34]Cf. Orchard, *Matthew, Luke & Mark,* 65.

(Matt 5:43-45)   = Luke 6:35. On love of enemies 2.
Matt 5:48   = Luke 6:36. Be merciful as God is merciful.
Matt 7:1-2   = Luke 6:37-38. On judging/measure for measure.
(Matt 15:14)   = Luke 6:39. Blind leading the blind.
(Matt 10:24-25a)   = Luke 6:40. A disciple is not above the teacher.
Matt 7:3-5   = Luke 6:41-42. A speck versus a log in the eye.
Matt 7:15-20   = Luke 6:43-44. By their fruits.
‖ 12:33-35
(Matt 13:51-52?)   = Luke 6:45. Two kinds of treasure.
Matt 7:21   = Luke 6:46. Lord, Lord.
Matt 7:24-27   = Luke 6:47-49. Two houses.
Matt 7:28a   = Luke 7:1a. When Jesus had finished . . .
Matt 7:28b-29   = Luke 4:31-32. Crowds marveled.
                        He was teaching with authority. . . .

Luke's major reworking of Matthew's sequence of sayings within the sermon on the plain came in Luke's segment on love of enemies (Luke 6:27-36 ‖ Matt 5:38-48) where Luke twice utilized material from Matthew 5:43-45 in order to frame most of the Lukan account on this topic (Luke 6:27-28=Luke 6:35). Luke appropriately inserted the golden rule (Luke 6:31 ‖ Matt 7:12) and the sayings on nonretaliation from Matthew 5:38-42 (=Luke 6:29-30), verses that immediately precede Matthew 5:43-45, into his distinctively framed Lukan unit. Already within the sermon on the plain, we can also see Luke incorporating, on a small scale, materials from several Matthean discourses of Jesus, as Luke did on a large scale within the central travel narrative.[35]

We also see Luke conflating doublets in Matthew within the sermon on the plain (Matt 7:15-20 ‖ Matt 12:33-35 ‖ Luke 6:43-44) as he often does throughout the Lukan narrative.[36]

---

[35]See Matt 10:24-25a from the mission discourse in Matt 9:35–11:1 at Luke 6:40 and perhaps also Matt 13:51-52 from the parables discourse in Matt 13:1-53 at Luke 6:45. Compare also the insertion of the logion on "the blind leading the blind" from Matt 15:14 at Luke 6:39, if, in fact, this logion did not come into this location in Luke from non-Matthean tradition or simply from Luke's memory of the saying from some previous reading(s) of Matt.

[36]A list of Luke's conflations of Matthean "doublets" and other multiple contexts in Matt that contain verbal similarities would include, but would not necessarily be limited to, the following: (1) Luke 4:14-16 ‖ Matt 4:12-13 ‖ Matt 4:23-24 ‖ Matt 9:26, 31; (2) Luke 6:11-20 ‖ Matt 4:23–5:2 ‖ Matt 12:14-15 ‖ Matt 9:35–10:4; (3) Luke 6:43-44 ‖ Matt 7:15-20 ‖ Matt 12:33-35; (4) Luke 9:7-9 ‖ Matt 14:1-10 ‖ Matt 16:13-16; (5) Luke 9:48 ‖ Matt 10:40 ‖ Matt 18:5; (6) Luke 10:25-28 ‖ Matt 19:16-21 ‖ Matt 22:34-40; (7) Luke 11:14-15 ‖ Matt 9:32-34 ‖ Matt 12:22-24; (?) [Luke 11:29-32 ‖

Luke's Uses of Remaining Material from the Sermon on the Mount in the Travel Narrative

	Lukan unit on "prayer" (Luke 11:1-13)
Matt 6:5-15	= Luke 11:1-4. The Lord's prayer.
Matt 7:7-12	= Luke 11:9-13. On expectant prayer.

Matt 5:15, 6:22-23 = Luke 11:33-36. A Lukan thematic summary.

	Lukan unit on "rejecting fear/anxiety" (Luke 12:4-34)
Matt 6:25-34	= Luke 12:22-32. Do not be anxious.
Matt 6:19-21	= Luke 12:33-34. True treasure.

	Lukan unit on "who is truly judged?" (Luke 12:54–13:30)
Matt 5:21-26	= Luke 12:57-59. Agreement with accuser.
cf. Matt 18:23-35.	

	Lukan unit on "the Messiah's banquet instructions" (Luke 14:1-35)
Matt 5:13	= Luke 14:34-35. On salt.

	Lukan unit on "you cannot serve God and mammon" (Luke 16:1-31)
Matt 6:24	= Luke 16:13. On serving two masters.
Matt 5:17-18	= Luke 16:14-17. On the law and the prophets.
cf. Matt 11:11-12	
Matt 5:31-32	= Luke 16:18. On divorce.
cf. Matt 19:3-12.	

1. *Matthew 6:5-15 and 7:7-12.* Although Luke's remaining uses of sayings from Matthew's sermon on the mount may appear "disorderly" in the immediately preceding list, Luke's use of Matthew 6:5-15 ‖ Luke 11:1-4 followed by his use of Matthew 7:7-12 ‖ Luke 11:9-13 in composing the Lukan unit at Luke 11:1-13 still provides evidence of Luke's orderly use of Matthew. Luke sandwiched only the parable of the persistent neighbor (Luke 11:5-8) from non-Matthean tradition between these two uses of sayings from Matthew 6–7 in order. Luke made no use of

---

Matt 12:38-42 ‖ Matt 16:1, 4]; (8) Luke 12:37-39 ‖ Matt 24:42 ‖ Matt 25:13; (9) Luke 13:22-27 ‖ Matt 7:13-14, 21-23 ‖ Matt 25:1-13; (?) [Luke 13:30 ‖ Matt 19:30 ‖ Matt 20:16]; (10) Luke 16:18 ‖ Matt 5:31-32 ‖ Matt 19:9; (11) Luke 17:5-6 ‖ Matt 17:19-20 ‖ Matt 21:21-22; and (12) Luke 18:35-43 ‖ Matt 20:29-34 ‖ Matt 9:26-31.

sayings contained in Matthew 6 when he composed the sermon on the plain, so this is Luke's first use of material from Matthew 6.

2. *Matthew 5:15.* Luke made use of Matthew 5:15 not only in Luke 11:33-36, but also in Luke 8:16-18, two Lukan thematic summaries. One of these summaries, Luke 8:16-18, is also related to Luke 11:53–12:3, a Lukan interweaving transition, by the common use of Matthew 10:26. The interconnection of these Lukan compositions (Luke 11:33-36, 11:53–12:3) both related back to Luke 8:16-18 through common uses of different verses from Matthew (Matt 5:15, 10:26) also demonstrates Luke's orderly use of Matthew.[37]

3. *Matthew 6:22-34.* Luke's use of Matthew 6:22-23 ‖ Luke 11:33-36, followed immediately by his use of Matthew 6:25-34 ‖ Luke 12:22-32, is also orderly, especially when one notes that Luke came back in Luke 16:13, in an artful "clean-up" operation, to insert the one intervening verse previously omitted (Matt 6:24).

4. *Matthew 6:19-21.* Luke utilized Matthew 6:19-21 to conclude a Lukan unit that may be entitled "To Friends and Disciples: Reject Fear and Anxiety. Trust and Treasure God!" (Luke 12:4-34). Inappropriate fears and anxieties such as those about one's earthly goods and the storehouses for them (12:13-21) should be replaced by concerns for treasures in heaven and impregnable divine storage places for them (12:33-34).

5. *Matthew 5:21-26.* Luke's placement of his "verbal parallel" to Matthew 5:21-26 in Luke 12:57-59 was determined by his "contextual parallel" in Matthew 18:23-35. These two passages in Matthew include similar language which could be used to link them in the mind of a reader of Matthew (cf. Matt 5:25 and 18:34).

6. *Matthew 5:13.* In a manner similar to his use of Matthew 6:19-21 ‖ Luke 12:33-34, Luke also utilized Matthew 5:13 ‖ Luke 14:34-35 to conclude a Lukan unit. This latter unit may be entitled "To a Dinner Audience: The Messiah's Banquet Instructions" (Luke 14:1-35). A table condiment that has lost its savor is only worthy to be thrown out. This analogy is a fitting ending (Luke 14:34-35) to Jesus' teachings about table fellowship in Luke 14:1-33.

7. *Matthew 6:24, Matthew 5:17-18, Matthew 5:31-32.* Choosing not to exclude a few remaining teachings of Jesus in the sermon on the

---

[37]See n. 32 above for the fuller discussion.

mount from the Lukan gospel, Luke finally drew three more such teachings together into a limited literary context, Luke 16:13-18.

The first, Matthew 6:24 ‖ Luke 16:13, became in Luke the last of several aitiae (Luke 16:8b-13) to the parable of the unjust steward (Luke 16:1-8a) with which Luke had chosen to open yet another new section of the travel narrative. This section may be entitled "To the Disciples: You Cannot Serve God and Mammon" (Luke 16:1-31).

The second, which may be entitled "On the Permanence of the Law" (Matt 5:17-18 cf. Luke 16:17) is related to the third, which may be entitled "On the Intended Permanence of Marriage" (Matt 5:31-32 ‖ Matt 19:9 ‖ Luke 16:18). The reference to "the law and the prophets" in Matthew 5:17 probably helped encourage Luke also to draw into this context (Luke 16:13-18) the teaching from Matthew 11:12-13 about the relationship of John the Baptist to "the law and the prophets" and to insert here yet one more comparison of John the Baptist with Jesus, a favorite theme of Luke.

The entirety of this pastiche of verses from Matthew (Matt 5:17-18, 31-32, 6:24, 11:12-13 ‖ Luke 16:13-18) served Luke, in part, to introduce the closing parable in this section of Luke, the parable of the rich man and Lazarus (Luke 16:19-31). In that parable the rich man is taught that those who don't listen to "Moses [the law] and the prophets," (Matt 5:17 ‖ Matt 11:13 ‖ Matt 19:7 ‖ Luke 16:16, 29, 31) whose authority was evidenced through John (Matt 11:11-12 ‖ Luke 16:16-17), will still not listen even to one, like Jesus, who would rise from the dead (Luke 16:30-31).

Luke 16:13-18 is a typically Lukan interweaving transitional pericope that unites the parable of the unjust judge and its attendant aitiae on one side (Luke 16:1-13, cf. Matt 6:24) with the parable of the rich man and Lazarus on the other side (16:19-31). Like other similar pericopes composed by Luke (8:16-18, 11:33-36, 11:53-12:3),[38] this pericope is composed of a collection of verses drawn from several literary contexts in Matthew.

G. Luke's Use of Matthew 11–12

Within the travel narrative, Luke also makes orderly use of "narrative" material in Matthew 11–12 that still remained for him to utilize. Luke made earlier uses of some of this material:

---

[38]See n. 32 above.

Matt 11:2-19   = (Luke 7:18-35)
Matt 12:1-14   = Luke 6:1-11[39]
Matt 12:15-21   = Luke 6:17-19
Matt 12:46-50   = Luke 8:19-21

The combination of these earlier uses with the later ones in the Lukan travel narrative—indented and printed in bold type below—covers the whole of Matthew 11–12.[40]

Matt 11:2-19   = (Luke 7:18-35). John and Jesus.
Matt 11:20-24 =   **Luke 10:13-15. Woes against cities.**
Matt 11:25-30 =   **Luke 10:21-22. Jesus' prayer.**
Matt 12:1-14   = Luke 6:1-11. Eating and healing on the sabbath.
Matt 12:15-21   = Luke 6:17-19. Gathering of crowds and healings.
Matt 12:22-50 =   **Luke 11:14-32. On spiritual power.**
Matt 12:46-50   = Luke 8:19-21. Jesus' true family.[41]

IV. Summary Conclusion

True to his prologue (Luke 1:1-4), even within the travel narrative, Luke made orderly use of Matthew according to the two-gospel hypothesis. Although Luke repositioned many sayings of Jesus contained in the great discourses in Matthew into new Lukan literary units within the travel narrative, Luke made such orderly use of those sayings in Matthew that one can reconstruct the sequential parallelism of these sayings in Matthew and Luke.

The advocate of the two-source hypothesis need not give priority to the order of "Q" materials in Luke. Lukan redaction of Matthew may better explain the sequential parallelism of these sayings in Matthew and Luke than the "Q" hypothesis. What advocates of the two-source hypothesis may claim as evidence of composition and literary structure

---

[39]Luke made first use of Matt 11–12 at Luke 6:1-11 ‖ Matt 12:1-14 in the process of creating a Lukan unit of four controversy stories (Luke 5:17–6:11 ‖ Matt 9:1-17 and Matt 12:1-14). Luke continued to utilize Matt 12:15-21 in Luke 6:17-19 as part of his introduction (Luke 6:12-19, cf. Matt 4:23–5:1, Matt 12:15-21, Matt 9:35–10:4) to the sermon on the plain (Luke 6:20–7:1a ‖ Matt 5:2–7:29).

[40]There are, however, a few sentences that are parts of larger Matthean literary units that Luke has chosen to omit. And Luke has reasonably reordered Matt 12:22-50 internally.

[41]Luke utilized Matt 12:46-50 twice within his gospel, having come to it twice in following the order of Matt (cf. Luke 8:19-21 ‖ Matt 12:46-50 and Luke 11:27-28 ‖ Matt 12:46-50).

in "Q" is, on the two-gospel (neo-Griesbach) hypothesis, no more and no less than the fragmentary preservation of Lukan composition and literary structure within the reconstructed text of the hypothetical "Q" source.

The Gospel of Luke
in the Second Century CE

Arthur J. Bellinzoni

In an article published in 1992,[1] I traced the use of the Gospel of Matthew in second-century Christian literature from the Apostolic Fathers through Irenaeus. Such a study, I maintained, is central to an understanding of the development of the church's fourfold gospel canon. In this essay I hope to complement that earlier article by investigating the use of the Gospel of Luke in the second century CE.[2] This study is a prolegomenon that hopefully will lay the foundation for more detailed study of every passage that is relevant to the subject at hand.

I. Methodological Concerns

In the 1992 article, I indicated that several serious methodological problems complicate such a study. Thus, we must keep these critical issues before us. First, the difficulties involved in reconstructing the textual history of Luke during the first century of its transmission are enormous. Such difficulties make it virtually impossible to know to what extent the third-century archetypes of our best manuscript families conform either to the autograph of Luke or to the text(s) of Luke available to writers in the second century. Second, to the extent possible, we must attempt to fix the date and place of origin of the second-century Christian writings in which scholars have identified possible citations and allusions to the Gospel of Luke, if we hope to succeed in writing a credible history of the use of the Gospel of Luke in the second century. And third, scholars

---

[1] Arthur J. Bellinzoni, "The Gospel of Matthew in the Second Century," *SecCent* 9 (Winter 1992): 197-259. The present article draws freely from my 1992 study.

[2] Ever since I wrote the above-mentioned article on Matthew in 1992, I have thought about examining the use of Luke in the second century. The invitation from Tom Phillips to participate in this *Festschrift* in honor of Joseph Tyson afforded me the opportunity to undertake this study. The first draft, however, was more than three times the prescribed length, far too long for inclusion in the Tyson *Festschrift*. You therefore will notice that I have limited this paper to three pivotal figures from the middle of the second century (Marcion, Justin Martyr, and Tatian) and to Irenaeus, a critical figure toward the end of the second century. I hope to publish the longer and more complete version of this paper elsewhere.

must establish and agree upon criteria that determine what constitutes "use" of the Gospel of Luke by a second-century witness. That is, we must establish criteria that enable us to determine that it is *Luke* that has been used and not some other non-Lukan tradition that simply resembles Luke.

II. The Use of Luke in the First Half of the Second Century

Although I cannot present here a complete discussion on the use of Luke in the first half of the second century, my study has led to the conclusion that there was minimal use of the Gospel of Luke during this time. I focused my study on two general groups of texts: the Apostolic Fathers, and other early second-century writings (including early Christian apologists, apocryphal writings, extracanonical gospels, and gnostic writings). In examining the Apostolic Fathers, it was found that there was very little use of the Lukan gospel.[3] It is only as we approach the later Apostolic Fathers toward the middle of the second century, specifically *2 Clement* and the later writing included in Polycarp's *Letter to the Philippians*, that it appears likely that there were at least some knowledge and use of the Gospel of Luke.[4]

My conclusions were very similar after studying other writings of the first half of the second century. That is, there is generally little or no conclusive evidence to suggest that Luke was used in these writings.[5] Like-

---

[3] I examined the following texts or authors from the Apostolic Fathers in my study: *Did.* (95–100), Ignatius of Antioch (110–117), Polycarp's *Phil.* (#1, 110–117; #2, 138), *Barn.* (100–135), *Shepherd* of Hermes (ca. 150), and *2 Clem.* (120–160). I found that there was no evidence for the use of the Gospel of Luke in most of these texts, including the *Did.* (written in Syria or Palestine-Syria), Ignatius of Antioch (written in Syria, Ignatius's place of origin), the earlier writing included in Polycarp's *Phil.* (written in Asia Minor), *Barn.* (written possibly in Alexandria), and *Shepherd* (written in Rome).

[4] I did find some evidence for the use of Luke in the later writing included in Polycarp's *Phil.*, as well as evidence in *2 Clem.* (written in Rome or possibly Egypt) that Luke was used in harmony with Matt.

In the case of Polycarp of Smyrna, #1 and #2 (mentioned in n. 3 above) refer to two distinct documents incorporated into the current text of Polycarp's *Phil.* See Paul N. Harrison, *Polycarp's Two Letters to the Philippians* (Cambridge: Cambridge University Press, 1936).

[5] I examined the following texts or authors from the first half of the second century CE in addition to the Apostolic Fathers: Papias of Hierapolis (130), *Kerygma Petrou* (100–110), *Apology* of Quadratus (125), *Apology* of Aristides (138–147), *Gos. Naz.* (pre-170), *Gos. Eb.* (pre-150), *Gos. Heb.* (120–140), *Gos. Eg.* (pre-150), *Gos. Pet.* (pre-150), *Gos. Thom.* (pre-150), *Gos. Truth* (middle of second century), and *Ep. Apost.* (140–150). I found that there was also no evidence for the use of the Gospel of Luke in most of these

wise, there is not sufficient space to present the full discussion regarding the use of the Gospel of Luke in these early second century writings. Nonetheless, for the first half of the second century, the sources of Jesus' traditions seem to have been oral tradition or pregospel collections of traditions. There was apparently little or no significant use of the Gospel of Luke before 150.

III. The Use of Luke in the Middle of the Second Century

By the middle of the second century, the Gospel of Luke was known and used but had limited influence in certain Christian circles. Matthew, not Luke, was the more familiar and influential gospel. In no instance was Luke ever cited as Scripture, neither is there any hint whatsoever that Luke was so regarded in this period in any part of the Christian world. We turn now to an examination of the mid-second century and specifically to the critical figures who set a new direction with regard to the use of the Gospel of Luke: Marcion, Justin Martyr, and Tatian.

In all three of these writers, we see a careful and conscious use of one or more of the written gospels from the "ancient" past. In all instances, however, the older gospels were edited or reworked, continuing the general practice of the time of rewriting and redacting the ancient texts and thereby creating new editions of these traditional writings from the first century. What is particularly critical in the writings of these three figures is a conscious step toward the process of canonization—a step that was a clear departure from past practice. In one way or another each of these writers considered one or more of the gospels as authoritative; the gospels were on the road to being treated as Scripture.

A. Marcion

Clearly the single most important figure in the movement toward identifying specific Christian books as sacred Scripture was Marcion.

---

texts, including Papias's writings (written in Asia Minor); *Kerygma Petrou, Gos. Heb.,* and *Gos. Eg.* (written in Egypt); the apologies of Quadratus and Aristides (written in Athens); and *Gos. Naz.* (written in Syria).

The few Lukan allusions found in *Gos. Eb.* (written in Transjordan) but often used in harmony with Matt and possibly Mark, along with the disputed and/or dubious evidence in several extracanonical gospels (*Gos. Pet.* and *Gos. Thom.*, both written in Syria; and *Gos. Truth*, written in Egypt or Rome) are inadequate to afford us an understanding of whether the authors of these writings actually knew and used the Gospel of Luke. Only *Ep. Apost.* seems to have used Luke (as well as the other canonical gospels) extensively yet freely, but Luke is never cited as canonical Scripture.

Born about 100 in Sinope of Pontus in northeastern Asia Minor, Marcion sensed an incongruity between the God of the law revealed in the Jewish Scriptures (which until this time served as the only "Bible" of the Christian churches) and the merciful God of love, the Father of Jesus Christ. Marcion concluded that the two were, in fact, different Gods. Inasmuch as the Jewish Bible was concerned with the God of law, Marcion concluded that it should be dislodged from its position as Scripture in the Christian churches and replaced by Christian books, specifically the Gospel of Luke and ten letters of Paul.[6] Apparently, Marcion encountered the Pauline letters while in Asia Minor, and was so influenced by the teachings of Paul that, in his mind, Paul was the only legitimate apostle.[7] Sometime between 135 and 138, Marcion went to Rome, joined the church there, and apparently tried to prevail upon the Roman church to adopt his position. It is not clear whether he left voluntarily or was excommunicated from the Roman church, but following his departure from Rome around 144, he founded his own church, which spread rapidly.

Marcion's single book, *Antitheses* or *Contradictions* (no copies survive), was a catalog of contradictions between the teachings of the Old Testament and the teachings of Jesus. This work was designed to show how Christianity differed from what the Jewish prophets had foretold. Judaism and Christianity stood in "antithesis" to, or "contradicted" each other. The law and the gospel were irreconcilable. In undermining the authority of the Jewish Bible, Marcion needed to substitute another scriptural authority for use in the Christian churches, and so he created a new edition of the Gospel of Luke and the ten Pauline letters to purify them of what he regarded as later additions. Marcion's version of the Gospel of Luke followed the accepted procedures of the period by reworking and editing the ancient text. The distinctive feature of Marcion's redaction of the Gospel of Luke and the Pauline letters is that he never added to his sources but always abbreviated them.[8] From the Gospel of Luke, Marcion eliminated the birth narratives, the baptism and genealogy of Jesus (Luke 1:1–4:15), all quotations from the Old Testament, the

---

[6]These are, in order, Gal, 1–2 Cor, Rom, 1–2 Thess, Eph (or "Laodocians"), Col, Phil, and Phlm.

[7]John J. Clabeaux, "Marcion," in *ABD* (1992) 4:515.

[8]Hans von Campenhausen, *The Formation of the Christian Bible* (Philadelphia: Fortress, 1971) 161. It is von Campenhausen's view that Marcion's *Antitheses* served as an introduction to and justification for his canon.

parables of the fig tree (13:6-9) and the prodigal son (15:11-32), and Jesus' entry into Jerusalem and his cleansing of the temple (19:29-46).[9] What is significant about Marcion for our purposes is his elevation of the Gospel of Luke and Paul's letters to the status of Scripture and his simultaneous rejection of the Jewish Scriptures. Before Marcion, no canon of the New Testament existed, and probably no thought of one. He was the first person who can be demonstrated to have considered specific Christian writings as Scripture; his was the first Christian canon. Marcion's Bible in two parts—the Gospel of Luke and the letters of Paul—may well be responsible for providing the church with the broad outlines of what would eventually become the New Testament canon. It is important to note that, although the Gospel of Matthew was much better known and much more widely used than Luke, Marcion still rejected it, probably because of its supposed Judaizing tendencies.[10]

In his classical study of Marcion, Adolf von Harnack assumed that there was a fourfold gospel canon before Marcion; however, there is no evidence whatever for this position in the pre-Marcionite literature.[11] Nevertheless, von Campenhausen points out that "the majority of scholars . . . seem[s] still to prefer Harnack, in that they continue to maintain that Marcion's bible did not evoke the establishment of the catholic N.T. but merely accelerated a development in this direction which had already begun."[12] My own view on the matter is well stated by von Campenhausen:

> From every side we converge on the same result: the idea and the reality of a Christian Bible were the work of Marcion, and the Church which rejected his work, so far from being ahead of him in this field, from a formal point of view simply followed his example. . . . The first Christian canon remains his peculiar and unique creation, one in which neither churchman nor gnostic anticipated him.[13]

---

[9]Helmut Koester, *Introduction to the New Testament*, 2 vols. (Philadelphia: Fortress, 1982) 2:331.

[10]Koester, *Introduction to the New Testament*, 2:330; and von Campenhausen, *The Formation of the Christian Bible*, 159-60.

[11]Adolf von Harnack, *Marcion: Das Evangelium vom fremden Gott. Eine Monographie zur Geschichte der Grundlegung der katholischen Kirche*, 2nd ed. (Leipzig: Hinrichs, 1924; repr.: Darmstadt: Wissenschaftliche Buchgesellschaft, 1960); ET: *Marcion: The Gospel of the Alien God* (Durham NC: Labyrinth, 1990).

[12]von Campenhausen, *The Formation of the Christian Bible*, 149n.6.

[13]von Campenhausen, *The Formation of the Christian Bible*, 148.

Before Marcion, no one presented particular Christian books as the only authentic and normative documents of Christianity and then used those documents as the basis of Christian doctrine and preaching. Although perfection and inspiration of these books did not yet constitute in Marcion's time the essence of their canonical status, Marcion is, nevertheless, the creator of the concept of a canonical New Testament.[14]

Justin Martyr's *Dialogue with Trypho* may be a counterattack to Marcion's *Antitheses*, and Justin probably criticized Marcion in his lost book, *Against All Heresies*.[15] According to Eusebius (*Hist. Eccl.* 4.24.3), Theophilus of Antioch wrote a treatise *Against Marcion* around 180–190 (also lost), as did Rhodo (also lost) in the same period (*Hist. Eccl.* 5.13.1). Irenaeus in the same decade wrote about Marcion (*Against Heresies* 1.27.2; 3.3.4); and Tertullian (ca. 200) countered Marcionism with one of his major writings, *Against Marcion*. The Marcionite sect continued to flourish for about 200 years after Marcion's death.

Marcion's influence on orthodox Christianity cannot be overestimated. With Marcion came the principal impetus for the formation a New Testament canon—that is, for the identification of a limited number of traditional Christian books as authoritative writings. Apparently, in order to defend itself against Marcion and Marcionism, the church took the steps required to create its own canon of New Testament writings, an endeavor associated principally with Irenaeus and Tertullian.

B. Justin Martyr

Justin Martyr was the most important second-century Christian apologist. Born in Samaria, Justin lived in Ephesus, and finally moved to Rome where he died around 165. His writings include *Against All Heresies*, *Apology*, and *Dialogue with Trypho the Jew*.[16]

The relationship between the writings of Justin Martyr and the canonical gospels has been a subject of investigation for 150 years. Scholars have proposed various solutions to explain the literary relationship between Justin and the canonical gospels: the careless quotation from memory,[17] the use of at least one extra-canonical gospel,[18] the use of

---

[14]von Campenhausen, *The Formation of the Christian Bible*, 163.

[15]Actually the first attack against Marcion may have come from the Valentinian, Ptolemy, in his *Letter to Flora* (von Campenhausen, *The Formation of the Christian Bible*, 165).

[16]Robert M. Grant, "Justin Martyr," in *ABD* (1992) 3:1133-34.

[17]Karl Semisch, *Die apostolischen Denkwürdigkeiten des Märtyrers Justinus*

presynoptic material,[19] the use of only the canonical gospels,[20] and the systematic use of a postsynoptic harmony.[21] In my previous study of the sayings of Jesus in Justin's writings, I argued that Justin's quotations were based on a systematic harmonization of written gospels, including both Matthew and Luke and possibly also Mark.[22]

In my study, I concluded that Justin used written sources which harmonized parallel material from Matthew and Luke (and possibly also Mark) and which conflated related material from different parts of a single gospel (either Matthew or Luke). To explain Justin's use of harmonistic and conflated sources, I postulated the use of a written catechism as the source that he used for most of his sayings, and suggested that Justin and his pupils in the catechetical school in Rome during the mid-second century were probably responsible for the composition of this catechetical harmony.[23]

Helmut Koester has gone a step further than I did in my 1967 study by suggesting that Justin composed a *full* harmony of the Matthean and Lukan gospels and possibly Mark, "the one inclusive new Gospel which would make its predecessors, Matthew and Luke, obsolete."[24] Koester

---

(Hamburg: Perthes, 1848) 389ff.; and Theodor Zahn, *Geschichte des neutestamentlichen Kanons*, 2 vols. (Erlangen: Deichert, 1888) 2:463-585.

[18]Carl August Credner, *Beiträge zur Einleitung in die biblischen Schriften* (Halle: Buchhandlung des Waisenhauses, 1832) 266, and *Geschichte des neutestamentlichen Kanons* (Berlin: Reimer, 1860) 21-22; and Adolf Hilgenfeld, *Kritische Untersuchungen über die Evangelien Justins, der Clementinischen Homilien und Marcions* (Halle: Buchhandlung des Waisenhauses, 1850).

[19]Wilhelm Bousset, *Die Evangeliencitate Justins des Märtyrers in ihrem Wert für die Evangelienkritik* (Göttingen: Vandenhoeck & Ruprecht, 1891).

[20]Édouard Massaux, "Le Texte du Sermon sur la Montagne de Matthieu utilisé par Justin," *ETL* 28 (1952) 411-48; ET: "The Text of Matthew's Sermon on the Mount Used by Saint Justin," in *The Influence of the Gospel of Saint Matthew on Christian Literature before Saint Irenaeus*, 3 vols. (Macon GA: Mercer University Press, 1990–1993) 3:190-230.

[21]Moritz von Engelhardt, *Das Christenthum Justins des Märtyrers* (Erlangen: Deichert, 1878) 335ff.; William Sanday, *The Gospels in the Second Century* (London: Macmillan, 1876) 136n.1; and Ernst Lippelt, *Quae Fuerint Justini Martyris* AΠOMNHMONEY-MATA *Quaeque Ratione Cum Forma Syro-Latina Cohaeserint* (Halle: Buchhandlung des Waisenhauses, 1901) 35.

[22]Arthur J. Bellinzoni, *The Sayings of Jesus in the Writings of Justin Martyr* (Leiden: Brill, 1967).

[23]Bellinzoni, *The Sayings of Jesus*, 141-42.

[24]Helmut Koester, "The Text of the Synoptic Gospels in the Second Century," in *Gospel Traditions in the Second Century*, ed. William L. Petersen (Notre Dame IN: University of Notre Dame Press, 1989) 30.

cites my study of *I Apology* 16.9-13 as an excellent example of Justin's method of composing this harmony:[25]

I Apol. 16.9	=	Matt 7:21 = Luke 6:46.
I Apol. 16.10	=	Luke 10:16 which is a variant of Luke 6:47 with a phrase from Luke 6:46 not quoted in *I Apol.* 16.9.
I Apol. 16.11	=	harmonization of Matt 7:22-23 and Luke 13:26-27.
I Apol. 16.12	=	harmonization of Matt 13:42-43 and Luke 13:28.
I Apol. 16:13	=	combination of Matt 24:5 with Matt 7:15-16, 19.

Koester's summary of this passage is worth quoting in full:

> The writer of this new Gospel used Matthew 7 as the basis, moved from Matthew 7 to the proper Lukan parallel (6:46), replaced the following verse in Luke (6:47) with a variant found in Luke 10:16, returned to the Matthean context (7:22-23), harmonized it with the Lukan parallel (13:26-27), quoted the following Lukan verse (13:28), and harmonized it with the appropriate Matthean parallel (13:42-43), then returned to another saying from Matthew 7 (verses 15-16) and combined it with a variant from Matthew 24 (verse 5). This is a very complex procedure which the composition of catechetical materials would hardly require, but could well be the result of a systematic composition of a new Gospel on the basis of several older sources.[26]

I am not confident that Koester has proven that Justin's complex procedure of harmonizing and conflating Matthew and Luke (and possibly Mark) is better suited to the composition of an entire gospel than a mere catechism. Nonetheless, neither have I demonstrated conclusively the limited nature of Justin's composition. In fact, in retrospect I find Koester's thesis that Justin composed a full harmony of Matthew and Luke (and possibly Mark) very attractive.

Koester has also examined Justin's use of harmonized quotations of the synoptic narrative material and has shown that Justin "wants to bring the narrative texts into closer agreement with scriptural prophecy."[27] Justin's improvement of the narrative texts of Matthew and Luke was the result of his effort to establish a closer agreement with the texts of the

---

[25]Koester, "The Text of the Synoptic Gospels," 30. See also Bellinzoni, *The Sayings of Jesus*, 98-100, for a full discussion of the method of harmonization and conflation, the substance of which is illustrated in the accompanying diagram.

[26]Koester, "The Text of the Synoptic Gospels," 30.

[27]Koester, "The Text of the Synoptic Gospels," 18; see also Helmut Koester, *Septuaginta und synoptischer Erzählungsstoff im Schriftbeweis Justins des Märtyrers* (Heidelberg: Universität Heidelberg, 1956).

prophetic biblical passages.[28] Koester concludes that "Justin wants to create once again the *one* Gospel, now combining Matthew and Luke, strengthening at the same time the close bond between prophecy and fulfillment and thus expanding the text of this Gospel to achieve an even closer agreement than is evident in Matthew."[29] Koester's explanation for the creation of Justin's new gospel notes that Justin knew Marcion and opposed him; thus, he used this newly-created harmony of Matthew and Luke as an anti-Marcionite gospel. Whereas Marcion's work "severed ties" between gospel and Scripture and relied only on an expurgated version of Luke, Justin's harmony of Matthew and Luke joined the Lukan gospel with the more widely used and more Judaizing Matthean gospel and thereby sought to reestablish the close relationship between prophecy and fulfillment.[30] This thesis makes excellent sense when we recall that Justin's Christian faith was built on the Old Testament. His own testimony (*Dial.* 8.1) indicates that Justin converted to Christianity after reading the prophetic writings of the Jewish Scriptures.[31]

Justin called his source(s) for the words of the Lord τὰ ἀπομνημο-νεύματα τῶν ἀποστόλων, the "Memoirs of the Apostles" (*I Apol.* 67.3; *Dial.* 103.6) and sometimes also "gospels" (*I Apol.* 66.3), a designation for which he was the first written witness, but which he may have learned from Marcion. In any case, Justin indicates that the "Memoirs of the Apostles" were typically read in public worship along with the "writings of the Prophets" (*I Apol.* 67.3). This reference to the practice of reading these Christian writings as part of the church's public worship is very important, because it suggests that Christian congregations had begun to consider these writings as authoritative texts along with the ancient Scriptures of Judaism. This practice can certainly be considered as preparatory to, although not yet complete, canonization.[32] What is not clear is whether the gospels themselves or Justin's harmonized version of the gospels were read in public services in the church in Rome. It seems particularly tempting to conclude the latter.

---

[28]Koester, "The Text of the Synoptic Gospels," 32-33.
[29]Koester, "The Text of the Synoptic Gospels," 32.
[30]Koester, "The Text of the Synoptic Gospels," 32.
[31]See von Campenhausen, *The Formation of the Christian Bible*, 88-102.
[32]von Campenhausen, *The Formation of the Christian Bible*, 168.

C. Tatian

Like Marcion and Justin before him, Tatian was also a pivotal figure in the formation of the New Testament canon. Born in Assyria (Mesopotamia) of pagan parents, Tatian explored a number of religious and philosophical movements but found Christianity to be the one true "philosophy." Tatian was converted to Christianity probably in Rome about 150, and very possibly under the influence of Justin Martyr.

Unlike Justin, however, Tatian opposed everything Greek, perhaps because Justin had been martyred during the reign of the philosopher-emperor Marcus Aurelius. Following Justin's death (ca. 165), Tatian broke with the Roman church and returned to the East around 172, where he became the leader, if not the founder, of the sect of the Encratites (that is, the "Abstainers" or "the self-disciplined"), a religious group of Christians who rejected sexual intercourse, avoided the use of meat in any form, condemned the drinking of wine, and even went so far as to substitute water for wine in the celebration of the Eucharist. We know nothing about Tatian's death.

Only two of Tatian's works survive: the *Discourse to the Greeks* and the *Diatessaron*. The *Discourse* is a vehemently polemical treatise, which belittles and rejects the whole of Greek culture. In Tatian's mind, all things associated with Greek culture—mythology, philosophy, poetry, rhetoric, art, and science—are foolish, deceitful, immoral, and without value. Tatian's most famous work, however, is the *Diatessaron*, his harmony of the four gospels composed around 170.[33] Taking John as the

---

[33]Scholars disagree as to whether the *Diatessaron* was composed originally in Greek and then translated by Tatian into Syriac, or composed originally in Syriac, making use of an old lost Syriac translation of the gospels already in existence. The original manuscript of the *Diatessaron* is lost, but the text survives in a number of different forms: (1) two late manuscripts of an Arabic translation and one of a Persian translation; (2) the Latin Codex Fuldensis (541–546) arranges the gospels in a single consecutive narrative following the arrangement of Tatian's *Diatessaron*, although the text has been assimilated to that of the Vulgate; (3) Ephraem Syrus (ca. 306–373) wrote a commentary on the *Diatessaron* in Syriac (three-fifths of which was discovered in 1957 in the British Museum); a sixth-century Armenian version of Ephraem's commentary was published by the Mechitarist Fathers in Venice in 1836, and a Latin translation was published in 1876; (4) an Old German version of the Fuldensis Latin; (5) a medieval Dutch harmony probably modeled on the text of the *Diatessaron* was discovered at Liège in 1923 by D. Plooij; (6) a fragment containing fourteen imperfect lines of a Greek text of the *Diatessaron*, probably written before 256–257 (the date of the destruction of the site by the Persians), was discovered in 1933 at Dura Europos in Syria.

framework into which the synoptic gospels were then set, the *Diatessaron* arranged sections of all four gospels into one continuous gospel story. Like those who preceded him, Tatian revised his sources. He omitted the genealogies of Matthew and Luke and may even have drawn on apocryphal gospels for the form of some sayings. The words of Eusebius concerning Tatian are interesting in this regard: "Tatian composed in some way a combination and collection of the Gospels and gave this the name of the *Diatessaron*, and this is still extant in some places. And they say that he ventured to paraphrase some of the words of the apostles, as though correcting their style" (*Hist. Eccl.* 4.29.6). Although Tatian apparently held the four gospels in high regard, he obviously adopted a free attitude toward them. As a disciple of Justin, Tatian may have constructed his harmony in opposition to the Marcionite canon.

Written probably in Syria, the *Diatessaron* was used for a long time in the liturgy of the Syrian church, displaced only in the fifth century by the New Testament Peshitta of the four gospels, probably because Tatian was by then considered to be a heretic. Theodoret, bishop of Cyrrhus, west of the Euphrates, in his *Treatise on Heresies* 1.20 (*Haereticarum fabularum*, PG 83:372), written about 453, relates that he found more than 200 copies of the *Diatessaron* in the churches in his area. These he gathered up and replaced with the four gospels of the Syrian Peshitta.

If the original Greek or Syriac of the *Diatessaron* is ever discovered, or should it ever be possible to reconstruct the original Greek or Syriac version of Tatian's work from the several existing versions, we would have available to us an invaluable witness to the text of the gospels in the latter part of the second century. In any case, the publication of the *Diatessaron* in the second century is an important witness to the authority enjoyed by the four gospels, but Tatian's method of composition indicates that still one more mid-second century writer considered it appropriate to rework his gospel sources. Clearly, Tatian did not regard the four gospels themselves as sacred Scripture.

D. Conclusions

Our examination of Marcion, Justin Martyr, and Tatian reveals that these men were pivotal figures in the formation of the New Testament canon. While these men regarded one or more of the gospels as sacred Scripture, their importance is seen in the process they began that resulted in other individuals taking the steps toward canonization, probably in reaction to them.

Marcion is most responsible for developing the concept of a New Testament canon. His version of the Gospel of Luke was the core of his collection of authoritative Christian writings which were compiled by him to replace the Scriptures of Judaism. Marcion clearly knew the Gospel of Matthew, but he rejected it, apparently for its Judaizing tendencies, even though that particular gospel was in Marcion's time probably the most widely circulated and respected of all the gospel writings.

Whether Justin composed a full-fledged harmony of Matthew and Luke or simply used portions of Matthew and Luke (and perhaps Mark) in harmony, his text was almost certainly composed in reaction to Marcion's canon. Justin's reference to the reading of the "Memoirs of the Apostles" in public worship, along with the ancient Scriptures of Judaism, is an especially significant step toward canonization. It is not clear whether this reference is to the gospels themselves or Justin's harmonized and conflated readings, but probably the latter. If so, then it may not be our gospels, but rather Justin's harmony of Matthew and Luke (and possibly Mark), that was so honored in Justin's church.

Tatian seems to have taken the respective work of Marcion and Justin one step further. He used all four canonical gospels. Quite clearly, his *Diatessaron*, the "one [gospel] out of four" was the text that was read in Tatian's churches. As with Justin, Tatian's use of the Gospel of Matthew emphasized certain Judaizing elements that had been rejected by Marcion. But unlike Marcion and Justin, Tatian's inclusion of Mark and particularly the Gospel of John reached an even broader base of second-century Christianity.

Clearly, none of these three writers—Marcion, Justin Martyr, and Tatian—regarded the gospels in the form in which they were current as sacred Scripture, otherwise they would not have continued the practice of editing and reworking their sources, which included the Lukan gospel. Marcion produced a new edition of Luke; Justin Martyr harmonized and conflated parallel texts in Matthew and Luke (and possibly Mark); and Tatian used all four gospels but created a new "gospel" from them. Important steps had clearly been taken in the process of forming a Christian canon. However, the reaction to these men by the church fathers who followed them led eventually to the identification of the "ancient" gospels themselves as sacred Scripture. In the section that follows, I will try to identify some of the steps that resulted in the conviction that the four gospels themselves were perfect and inspired books.

IV. The Use of Luke in the Latter Half of the Second Century

We have already observed that the middle of the second century was the crucial period, or the turning point, for the formation of the New Testament canon. Marcion set the process in motion by identifying Luke and the letters of Paul as the core of the canon. Justin and Tatian each responded with respective harmonizations of gospels. All three of these men assumed that the gospel was *one*, that there apparently could be only *one* authoritative rendering of the gospel. It remained for those of the latter part of the second century to test the authority of one of the gospels or to create new gospel harmonies, but Irenaeus eventually provided the solution to the church's dilemma.[34]

A. Irenaeus

Irenaeus was born around 140 and died around 202. Inasmuch as Eusebius recorded that Irenaeus heard Polycarp as a boy (*Hist. Eccl.* 5.20.5-7), it is generally assumed that Irenaeus was a native of Polycarp's city of Smyrna in Asia Minor. Irenaeus studied at Rome, later became presbyter and, finally, around 178 became the bishop of Lyons in Gaul.

Irenaeus was undoubtedly the most important Christian theologian of the second century. He served as a major bridge between the Eastern and Western branches of Christianity. His principal work, *Refutation and Overthrow of knowledge falsely so-called*, generally called *Against Heresies* (*Adversus Haereses*), written about 180, is a detailed attack on gnosticism, particularly the valentinian system(s). The text of this work is preserved only in fragmentary form in Greek (by Hippolytus, Eusebius, and Epiphanius), but the entire text survives in a quite literal Latin translation, and sections of it are preserved in Syriac and Armenian. A second work, *Demonstration [or Proof] of the Apostolic Preaching* (mentioned by Eusebius, *Hist. Eccl.* 5.26), survives in an Armenian translation. Irenaeus's other writings are preserved only in fragmentary form.[35]

---

[34]In the original longer version of this section, I examined six representative writings or figures from the latter half of the second century (*Prot. Jas.*, Ptolemy's *Letter to Flora*, Apollinaris of Hierapolis, Athenagoras of Athens, Theophilus of Antioch, and Irenaeus) in an effort to show how the church gradually moved toward a solution of this problem of the "gospel" as the principal ingredient in the church's canon of sacred Scripture. My focus here, however, will be on Irenaeus of Lyons, the single most important figure in the formation of that canon.

[35]See Berthold Altaner, *Patrology* (New York: Herder and Herder, 1960) 152-53; and Johannes Quasten, *Patrology*, 3 vols. (Westminster MD: Newman, 1950) 1:293. See also

Irenaeus's attack against gnosticism emphasized the traditional elements of Christianity: the churches that were founded by an apostle, the episcopate as preserved from apostolic times in those churches, the canon of Scripture (especially the co-ordinate authority of the four gospels), and the religious and theological tradition of the church.

Irenaeus applied the term γραφή (Scripture) not only to the sacred writings of Judaism, but also to Christian writings of what would later become the New Testament. He regarded all these texts—the writings of Judaism *and* the Christian writings—as Scripture, which he used as proof texts. In determining the canonicity of the Christian writings, Irenaeus insisted that both apostolicity and ecclesiastical tradition should be demonstrated (*Adv. Haer.* 5.20.2). He referred to two such groups of Christian writings: the four gospels and the writings of the apostles.[36] In *Adversus Haereses* 3.11.11, Irenaeus wrote of a quadriform gospel (τετράμορφον τὸ εὐαγγέλιον), and he derived the number four (no more and no less) from a number of cosmological arguments, including the four cherubs and God's four covenants with humanity: Adam, Noah, Moses, and Christ. He explained:

> For it is impossible that the Gospel should be either more or fewer than these in number. For, since there are four regions of the world wherein they are, and four principal winds, and the church is a seed sown in the whole earth, and the Gospel is the church's pillar and ground, and the breath of life; it is natural that it should have four pillars, from all quarters breathing incorruption, and kindling men to life. Wherefore it is evident that the Maker of all things, the Word, who sits upon the Cherubim, and keeps all things together, when he was made manifest to men, gave us his Gospel in four forms, kept together by one Spirit. (*Adv. Haer.* 3.11.1-11)

Concerning the origin of these four gospels, Irenaeus wrote:

> Matthew issued a written Gospel among the Hebrews in their own dialect, while Peter and Paul were preaching at Rome and laying the foundations of the church. After their departure Mark, the disciple and interpreter of Peter, also handed down to us in writing what had been preached by Peter. Luke also, the companion of Paul, recorded in a book the Gospel that was preached by him. Afterwards, John, the disciple of the Lord, who also leaned upon his breast, himself published a Gospel during his residence at Ephesus in Asia. (*Adv. Haer.* 3.1.1-11)

Mary Ann Donovan, "Irenaeus," in *ABD* (1992) 3:457-61.

[36]In the writings of the apostles, Irenaeus included the epistles of Paul, Acts, 1 John, Rev, 1 Pet, and *Shepherd*.

To be sure, much of what Irenaeus wrote about the four gospels is fanciful and certainly more traditional in nature than historically reliable. Nonetheless, he did succeed in setting the church on the path that would eventually lead out of the confusion caused when Marcion settled on his canon comprised of the Gospel of Luke and the letters of Paul.[37] Irenaeus's New Testament canon was broader than Marcion's canon. Koester has summarized the issues very well:

> As for the gospels, Irenaeus did not try to create one exclusive authority; rather he accepted the four "separate" gospels (i.e., not in their harmonized form) of Matthew, Mark, Luke, and John. The idea that the gospels were four rather than one he tried to defend with a cosmological speculation that they corresponded to the four ends of the earth. It is clear that Irenaeus had to defend himself here against the widespread concept that, properly speaking, there could be only one gospel. . . . The inclusiveness of Irenaeus's conception of the Christian Scripture which is evident here has extraordinary significance. Everything that had been in use in the Christian communities from the beginning was included, if the tradition of the churches would confirm use.[38]

B. Conclusions

The second half of the second century was a particularly critical time in the history of the Christian church. This period witnessed the growth of gnosticism and the strong reaction against gnosticism in what was later called orthodox or catholic Christianity. Marcion, Valentinus, and their followers presented the most serious challenge that the church had witnessed since its inception, at least if we are to judge by the amount of polemic directed against their teachings.

Toward the end of the second century, Irenaeus argued the view that became the orthodox position of the church. In his attack on gnosticism, he emphasized the traditional elements of Christianity as found in a number of sources that were included in his canon, which for the first time clearly identified the authority of the four gospels as Scripture. In his arguments against the gnostics, Irenaeus called the four gospels γραφή and referred to them regularly in those arguments. Although Irenaeus quotes or alludes to the Old Testament 629 times in *Adversus Haereses*, there are 1,065 quotations or allusions to passages found in

---

[37]Koester, *Introduction to the New Testament*, 2:9-10.
[38]Koester, *Introduction to the New Testament*, 2:10-11.

what is now the New Testament.[39] Irenaeus rejected the notion that the gospel must be only *one* and established as canon the quadriform gospel—the four separate gospels that he believed had been in use in the Christian communities from the beginning and had apostolic origins. Irenaeus's position was the view that quickly prevailed, although the writings of Clement of Alexandria and Origen, the Pseudo-Clementine *Homilies*, and others, all later than Irenaeus, still reflect the use of gospel harmonies well into the third century.[40]

V. Final Observations

In the course of this paper I have investigated the use of the Gospel of Luke in the second century CE. In particular, I have focused my study on the writings of three pivotal figures from the middle of the second century and on the writings of one toward the close of that century—key individuals whose writings reflect the use of the Gospel of Luke.

Among the writings from the first half of the second century, including both the Apostolic Fathers and other writings of the period, there appears to have been little or no use of Luke per se, but rather use of presynoptic oral and/or written tradition. The sources of that tradition were the Christian communities which, based on their practical needs, handed down and made use of synoptic-like oral and written traditions.

In the middle of the second century, the situation changed dramatically. Marcion, originally from Asia Minor but living in Rome between 135 and 144, was apparently the first person to develop a canon of Christian Scriptures that was different from the sacred texts that the church accepted with Judaism. Marcion rejected the more popular Gospel of Matthew and created a new edition of Luke as his one gospel, to which he added ten letters of Paul to form his Christian canon of Scriptures. Marcion and his immediate successors apparently assumed that there could be only *one* gospel.

Both Justin Martyr and Tatian reflected similar assumptions about only *one* gospel. On the one hand, Justin Martyr, writing in Rome around 160 in reaction to Marcion, harmonized texts of Luke and Matthew (and possibly Mark) for reading, along with the "writings of the Prophets," in Christian worship services in Rome. In reaction to Marcion, Justin may have produced a full-blown harmony of Matthew and Luke as his one

---

[39]Johannes Werner, *Der Paulinismus des Irenäus* (Leipzig: Hinrichs, 1899) 7.
[40]Bellinzoni, *The Sayings of Jesus*, passim, esp. 141-42.

gospel. Justin apparently regarded this "gospel" on a par with the ancient Scriptures of Judaism. On the other hand, Tatian, born in Syria but converted to Christianity in Rome about 150, produced the *Diatessaron*, his harmony of the four gospels, about 170. This harmony also was produced probably in reaction to Marcion, and also may be a reaction to Justin's less inclusive two-gospel harmony.

What is significant to note here is that these developments occurred in the same general geographical area. Although it was probably in Transjordan or Rome that there was some initial, if tentative, use of Luke, it was clearly in Rome that the process of canonization began with Marcion (Luke), Justin (harmonized texts or perhaps even a full-blown harmony of Luke and Matthew), and Tatian (the *Diatessaron*, a harmony of Matthew, Mark, Luke, and John). In the latter part of the second century, however, there was somewhat greater use of the Gospel of Luke. It was with Theophilus of Antioch and especially with Irenaeus, originally from Smyrna but living later in Rome and then in Lyons at the end of the century, that the Gospel of Luke assumed the status of sacred Scripture. For Irenaeus, this assumption of sacred status for the Gospel of Luke was based on his understanding that Matthew, Mark, Luke, and John (the quadriform gospel) were apostolic. Both Irenaeus's view of apostolicity and Theophilus's view of inspiration provided the formula that the church later used to defend the authority of its New Testament: the four gospels were apostolic in origin and were written under the inspiration of the Holy Spirit.

The second-century Christian writings that reflect knowledge and use of Luke freely adapted the gospel and made significant alterations and modifications, sometimes harmonizing Luke with Matthew or otherwise radically modifying the text of the gospel. There is nothing in the literature before Irenaeus to suggest that church fathers in the second century felt obliged to preserve the Gospel of Luke in its original form.

What are the implications of this observation for textual criticism and for proposed solutions to the synoptic problems? Can we reasonably assume that there were scribes who faithfully copied the autographs of the gospels at a time when other writers were treating the texts quite freely? May not the so-called minor agreements of Matthew and Luke against Mark be most reasonably explained as second-century developments that reflect a tendency to rework the gospels in light of one another rather than as meaningful evidence for a particular solution to the synoptic problem?

We cannot hope to answer these questions here. As I mentioned at the outset, this study is but a first step, an overview, a prolegomenon. What is needed now is a rigorous examination of the use of synoptic tradition in the second century involving the skills of New Testament scholarship, patristics, and textual criticism. Scholars need to develop criteria to determine what constitutes a citation or allusion to the gospels. What we need now is a fresh reexamination of this question and of the evidence.

Acts and the Pauline Corpus Revisited: Peter's Speech at the Jerusalem Conference*

William O. Walker, Jr.

In a 1985 article entitled "Acts and the Pauline Corpus Reconsidered,"[1] I argued that the author of Acts "almost certainly knew, in some sense, at least some of the letters of Paul, [that] he made some use of these letters in the writing of his own work, and [that] there are plausible reasons why he, nevertheless, did not mention the letters or even indicate that Paul ever wrote letters."[2] As a part of the argument, I suggested "not only that the account of the so-called Jerusalem Conference in Acts 15 depends on Paul's reference to the same gathering in Galatians 2,[3] but also that, at least to some extent, the account in Acts is intended to correct impressions that might be conveyed by Paul's material."[4] The purpose of the present study is to treat more fully this suggestion regarding the relation between Acts 15 and Galatians 2, with particular reference to Peter's speech in Acts 15:7-11.

---

*This essay will also be presented at the 1998 international meeting of the Society of Biblical Literature in Cracow, Poland.

[1]William O. Walker, Jr., "Acts and the Pauline Corpus Reconsidered," *JSNT* 24 (1985): 3-23; repr.: *The Pauline Writings: A Sheffield Reader*, ed. Stanley E. Porter and Craig A. Evans (Sheffield: Sheffield Academic Press, 1995) 55-74. All references will be to the initial publication in *JSNT*.

[2]Walker, "Acts and the Pauline Corpus Reconsidered," 14.

[3]Scholars have long debated whether the Jerusalem gathering described in Acts 15:1-29 and that reported by Paul in Gal 2:1-10 are the same. On the positive side, the location, the central issue, and at least some of the principal characters are identical. On the negative side, the reported outcome is radically different: in Acts, it is the "apostolic decree" (Acts 15:22-29); according to Paul, it is "only they would have us remember the poor" (Gal 2:10). For a brief treatment of the issues involved, see, e.g., Charles B. Cousar, "Jerusalem, Council of," in *ABD* (1992) 3:766-68. For commentaries based upon the assumption that Acts and Galatians do in fact report the same gathering, see, e.g., Ernst Haenchen, *The Acts of the Apostles: A Commentary* (Philadelphia: Westminster, 1971) esp. 440-73; and Hans Conzelmann, *Acts of the Apostles: A Commentary on the Acts of the Apostles*, Hermeneia (Philadelphia: Fortress, 1987) esp. 114-22. For reasons not to be discussed here, I assumed when I wrote the 1985 article, and indeed still assume, that Acts 15:1-29 and Gal 2:1-10 do refer to the same gathering.

[4]Walker, "Acts and the Pauline Corpus Reconsidered," 11.

At the outset, one feature of Paul's material must be noted. According to most interpretations, Galatians 2:11-21[5] describes an occurrence that was later in time than the Jerusalem Conference reported in Galatians 2:1-10.[6] My own judgment, however, is that, in something of a "flashback" fashion, Galatians 2:11-21[7] represents simply Paul's further elaboration of the controversy in Antioch that led to the Conference in Jerusalem.[8] Indeed, I would suggest that the "false brethren secretly brought in, who slipped in to spy out our freedom which we have in Christ Jesus" (Gal 2:4) and the "certain men [who] came from James" (Gal 2:11) are the same people.[9] They came from Jerusalem to Antioch and instigated a controversy there that involved both Peter (Gal 2:11-12) and (at least temporarily) Barnabas (Gal 2:13) in opposition to Paul. As a result, Paul, Barnabas, and Titus went to Jerusalem (Gal 2:1), and the conference followed.[10] Thus, in my view, it is the entire chapter in Galatians that represents Paul's account of the Jerusalem Conference, not just verses 1-10.[11] Even if this is not correct, however, the author of Acts, if he knew (and used?) Galatians in constructing his own account of the Conference, almost certainly knew (and used?) all of chapter 2, not just verses 1-10. Thus, in what follows, I shall treat the entire chapter as a unit.

With this point clarified, I now return to the question of the relation between Peter's speech in Acts 15:7-11 and Paul's material in Galatians 2. Scholars have occasionally noted that "the argument of [Peter's] speech is remarkably Pauline,"[12] with particular attention to Acts 15:11:

---

[5]Or perhaps only vv. 11-14.

[6]See, e.g., F. F. Bruce, *The Epistle of Paul to the Galatians: A Commentary on the Greek Text*, NIGTC (Exeter: Paternoster, 1982) 128: "it is most natural to take this as an incident that followed the conference of vv 1-10." For a defense of this view, see, e.g., George Ogg, *The Chronology of the Life of Paul* (London: Epworth, 1968) 89-98.

[7]Or at least vv. 11-14.

[8]For a cogent defense of this view, see, e.g., Johannes Munck, *Paul and the Salvation of Mankind* (Richmond VA: John Knox, 1959) 100-103.

[9]Biblical quotations in this essay are from the Revised Standard Version (copyright ©1952 by the Division of Christian Education of the National Council of the Churches of Christ in the United States of America) unless otherwise noted.

[10]For the argument that the *twofold* reason for the trip to Jerusalem was divine revelation and the appearance of the "false brethren," see William O. Walker, Jr., "Why Paul Went to Jerusalem: The Interpretation of Galatians 2:1-5," *CBQ* 54 (1992): 503-10.

[11]It may be, to be sure, that some or all of vv. 15-21 represents Paul's later reflection on the issues and not what he actually said to Peter in Antioch. Nevertheless, it is my own judgment that the entire chapter has in mind the controversy in Antioch and the conference in Jerusalem.

[12]F. J. Foakes-Jackson, *The Acts of the Apostles*, MNTC (London: Hodder and

"But we believe that we shall be saved through the grace of the Lord Jesus, just as they will."[13] What has not been noted, however, at least to my knowledge, is the remarkable similarity, both ideational and verbal, between *Peter's speech as a whole* (Acts 15:7-11) and *Paul's report regarding the Jerusalem Conference* (Gal 2). Also unnoticed or at least not emphasized, so far as I can ascertain, has been what might be termed the surprising "transfer of roles" from Paul to Peter that appears when one moves from Galatians 2 to Acts 15:7-11.

First, regarding the transfer of roles. In Galatians, *Paul* claims not only that it is he, Paul, who has "been entrusted with the gospel to the uncircumcised" and Peter with that "to the circumcised" but also that this division of responsibility was recognized and approved by the reputed "pillars" of the Jerusalem church: James, Cephas,[14] and John (Gal 2:7-9). Here, *Paul* is the apostle *par excellence* to the Gentiles and Peter is the apostle to the Jews.[15] In Acts 15:7, however, *Peter* alludes to the conversion of the Gentile centurion Cornelius (Acts 10:1–11:18) as evidence of God's decision "in the early days" that it was to be by his, Peter's, mouth that "the Gentiles should hear the word of the gospel and believe." Here, *Peter* is the apostle *par excellence* to the Gentiles, and, at least by implication, others are responsible for the mission to the Jews.[16] To be sure, it might be argued that the division of responsibility mentioned by Paul represents a *later* development[17] and that Peter was indeed the original pioneer in the mission to the Gentiles. Taken simply at face value, however, the two passages appear to be in direct conflict. The role claimed by *Paul* in Galatians is claimed by *Peter* in Acts.

Perhaps even more surprising, however, is the fact that, in articulating his claim to this role in Acts 15:7-11, Peter employs ideas and even words that are remarkably reminiscent of Paul's ideas and words in Galatians 2, where the latter claims the same role for himself. Thus, not

---

Stoughton; New York: Harper and Brothers, 1931) 137.

[13]See, e.g., Haenchen, *The Acts of the Apostles*, 446: "Peter speaks in terms familiar to us from Paul."

[14]Regarded by most scholars, correctly in my judgment, as simply the Aramaic equivalent of the Greek Πέτρος.

[15]In Gal 2:9, to be sure, James and John are also included in the mission to the Jews. Nevertheless, the emphasis clearly is on Peter.

[16]This latter point, I believe, is implied in Acts 15:7: "Brethren, you know that in the early days *God made a choice among you* . . . " (emphasis added).

[17]Perhaps even an agreement made at the Jerusalem Conference.

only is there a transfer of *roles* from Paul to Peter when one moves from Galatians 2 to Acts 15:7-11; there is also a transfer from Paul to Peter of essentially the same *ideas and words*. Indeed, as the following examples indicate, virtually everything in Peter's speech at the Jerusalem Conference (Acts 15:7-11) has parallels either in Paul's report regarding the same Conference (Gal 2) or in other passages in Galatians.

1. In Galatians 2:7, *Paul* refers to his message to the Gentiles as "gospel."[18] Similarly, in Acts 15:7, *Peter* speaks of his message to the Gentiles as "gospel."[19]

2. In Galatians 2:7, as already noted, *Paul* speaks of a division of responsibility whereby he is to be the missionary to the Gentiles and Peter to the Jews. In Acts 15:7, *Peter* at least suggests a similar division of responsibility,[20] but here he is to go to the Gentiles and others to the Jews.

3. In Galatians 2:7-8, *Paul*, somewhat obliquely to be sure, attributes to divine decree his own selection as missionary to the Gentiles and that of Peter as missionary to the Jews.[21] In Acts 15:7, *Peter* appeals to God's "choice" as the basis for his selection as missionary to the Gentiles.[22]

4. In Galatians 2:6, *Paul* insists that "God shows no partiality." In Acts 15:9, *Peter* asserts that God "made no distinction." To be sure, Peter has in mind a distinction between Jews and Gentiles, while Paul refers to himself and the leaders of the church in Jerusalem. Nevertheless, the basic point appears to be essentially the same: God does not play favorites as far as the life and mission of the church are concerned.

5. In Acts 15:8, *Peter* cites the Gentiles' reception of the Holy Spirit as proof that his mission to the Gentiles was approved by God.[23] This has no parallel, to be sure, in Paul's report regarding the Jerusalem Conference; in the passage immediately following this report, however, *Paul* cites reception of the Spirit by the Galatian Christians (presumably

---

[18]"The gospel to the uncircumcised."

[19]"The word of the gospel."

[20]As already suggested, this appears to be implied in the words, "God made a choice among you."

[21]Paul's use of the passive voice, "I had been entrusted . . . Peter had been entrusted" (Gal 2:7), surely implies that it was God who had done the entrusting, and this is made more explicit by his statement that "he who worked through Peter for the mission to the uncircumcised worked through me also for the Gentiles" (Gal 2:8).

[22]"Brethren, you know that in the early days God made a choice among you, that by my mouth the Gentiles should hear the word of the gospel and believe."

[23]"God . . . bore witness to [the Gentiles], giving them the Holy Spirit just as he did to us."

Gentiles) as evidence of the validity of his "gospel" and thus of his mission to the Gentiles (Gal 3:2-5).

6. In Acts 15:10, Peter refers to the law as a "yoke" (ζυγός). Again, there is no parallel to this in Paul's report regarding the Jerusalem Conference; in Galatians 5:1, however, Paul refers specifically to the law as "a yoke [ζυγός] of slavery."[24]

7. More fully, in Acts 15:10, *Peter* speaks of the law as a "yoke upon the neck of the disciples which neither our fathers nor we have been able to bear" and accuses certain others of attempting to impose this "yoke" upon Gentile believers. In Galatians 2:14, *Paul* is critical of none other than Peter, who, though himself a Jew, "live[s] like a Gentile and not like a Jew" but would "compel the Gentiles to live like Jews." The idea is at least similar to that in Acts: even Jews do not keep the law, and yet some would compel the Gentiles to do so.

8. In Acts 15:10-11, *Peter* rejects the law as a means of salvation and declares that both Jews and Gentiles are "saved through the grace of the Lord Jesus." In Galatians 2:16,[25] *Paul* asserts (to Peter of all people!) "that a person is not justified by works of the law but through faith in Jesus Christ . . . because by works of the law shall no one be justified" (Gal 2:16).[26] Thus, Acts has *Peter* express precisely the same view about law and gospel as *Paul*, according to Galatians, expressed *to Peter*.[27]

9. In Acts 15:9, Peter asserts that God "cleansed [the] hearts" of both Gentiles and Jews "by faith."[28] As already noted, *Paul* insists in Galatians 2:16[29] that "justification" is based not upon "works of the law" but rather upon "faith in Christ."[30]

10. In Acts 15:11, *Peter* declares that salvation comes "through the grace [χάρις] of the Lord Jesus." In Paul's report of the Jerusalem

---

[24]According to Conzelmann, *Acts of the Apostles*, 117, however, "The concept of the Law as an unbearable burden is neither the common Jewish view . . . nor is it Pauline."

[25]And elsewhere!

[26]Adaptation of RSV. Many would translate διὰ πίστεως Ἰησοῦ Χριστοῦ as "through the faith/faithfulness of Jesus Christ;" see, e.g., Richard B. Hays, *The Faith of Jesus Christ: An Investigation of the Narrative Substructure of Galatians 3:1–4:11*, SBLDS 56 (Chico CA: Scholars Press, 1983) passim; and George Howard, *Paul: Crisis in Galatia*, 2nd ed., SNTSMS 35 (Cambridge: Cambridge University Press, 1990) passim.

[27]Karl Heinrich von Weizsäcker, *The Apostolic Age of the Christian Church*, 2 vols. (New York: Putnam, 1894, 1895) 1:211.

[28]Cf. also Acts 15:11: "we believe that we shall be saved. . . . "

[29]And elsewhere!

[30]Or "Christ's faith/faithfulness."

Conference, to be sure, "grace" (χάρις) appears only in a rather general sense, "the grace that was given to me" (Gal 2:9). Earlier in the letter, however, *Paul* refers specifically to the "grace of Christ" (χάρις Χριστοῦ) and to "his [i.e., God's] grace" (ἡ χάρις αὐτοῦ; Gal 1:6, 15).[31] Moreover, as F. J. Foakes-Jackson noted, "Salvation by the grace of the Lord Jesus is . . . a characteristically Pauline doctrine."[32]

In short, virtually every idea and much of the actual wording of Peter's speech in Acts 15:7-11 have parallels either in Paul's report regarding the Jerusalem Conference (Gal 2) or elsewhere in the Galatian letter. Indeed, the Acts passage is so remarkably similar to the material in Galatians as to suggest that the author of Acts almost certainly knew this letter and, indeed, used it as a source in constructing Peter's speech at the Jerusalem Conference. It is also surely worthy of note that Acts 15:7-11 is one of only two passages in Acts that articulate what might be called a "Pauline" soteriology[33] and that this soteriology is here attributed not to Paul but rather to Peter.

It appears, therefore, that, for some reason, the author of Acts here wishes to have *Peter*, not Paul, express the views more typically associated with *Paul* and, at the same time, to have Peter replace Paul as the pioneer missionary to the Gentiles. Why would this be? Two theoretical possibilities can almost immediately be rejected: (1) given Paul's dominating role in the following chapters of the Book of Acts, it appears most unlikely that the author's goal is a denigration of Paul; and (2) in light of the fact that Peter disappears completely from the narrative immediately following the Jerusalem Conference, it is also unlikely that the goal is to elevate Peter's status and role.

Perhaps a clue to the author's intention is to be found, however, in a comparison of Acts 15:1-2, which introduces the account of the Jerusalem Conference in Acts, and Galatians 2:11-14, which, according to my

---

[31] In Gal 1:6, there are textual variants: some MSS read "grace of Jesus Christ," some "grace of God," and some only "grace." By far the best attested reading, however, is "grace of Christ."

[32] Foakes-Jackson, *The Acts of the Apostles*, 137.

[33] The other is in Paul's speech in Antioch of Pisidia (Acts 13:16-41), where he is represented as saying (vv. 38-39): "Let it be known to you therefore, brethren, that through this man forgiveness of sins is proclaimed to you, and by him every one that believes is freed from everything from which you could not be freed by the law of Moses." For significant differences between this statement and Paul's actual views, however, see, e.g., Philipp Vielhauer, "On the 'Paulinism' of Acts," in *Studies* (1966) 41-43.

interpretation, also refers to events immediately preceding the Conference. Both of these passages speak of the following: (1) a controversy, (2) in Antioch, (3) sparked by "certain men" (τινας),[34] and (4) who came to Antioch "from" (ἀπό) elsewhere. The similarities both in general content and in specific wording suggest the likelihood of some literary relation between the two passages—almost certainly meaning, as already suggested, that the author of Acts knew and used the Galatians passage in constructing his own narrative. Despite the similarities, however, there are three important points at which the passages differ significantly.[35]

1. According to Paul, the men who created the controversy in Antioch came specifically from *James*, the leader of the church in Jerusalem; according to Acts, however, they came simply from *Judea*.[36] In other words, Paul suggests that James was involved, even if only indirectly, in instigating the controversy in Antioch, while Acts here suggests and later insists that the controversy was sparked only by certain persons from Judea who acted on their own initiative, without authorization from the leaders in Jerusalem.[37]

---

[34]Personal translation. See also Acts 15:24: "certain men (τινες) from us" (my translation). In Gal 2:12, the reading τινα ("a certain man") appears in P[46]. See, e.g., Frank J. Matera, *Galatians*, Sacra Pagina 9 (Collegeville MN: Liturgical, 1992) 85: "This is an interesting reading in light of 5:10 which could be interpreted as referring to an individual disturbing the Galatian community. The reading of P[46], however, is not supported by any of the other important manuscripts, and it probably arose because of the well attested variant ἦλθεν (3rd sing.) in the same verse."

[35]Indeed, there might appear to be a fourth. According to Acts, the subject of controversy was, at least initially, whether Gentile believers must be circumcised in order to be saved (Acts 15:1); according to Paul, however, the specific point at issue in Antioch was whether Jewish Christians should eat with Gentile Christians (Gal 2:12). This, however, is probably not a real contradiction. Acts refers to circumcision as "the custom of Moses" (Acts 15:1), thus pointing to the law as the basic issue. Moreover, Paul identifies the opposition as "the circumcision party" (Gal 2:12) and, in his ensuing discussion, refers repeatedly to the law as the real point at issue (Gal 2:16, 19, 21).

If, as most interpreters hold, Gal 2:11-21 refers to events subsequent to the Jerusalem Conference, another important difference emerges: Paul reports that controversy in Antioch continued and perhaps even intensified after the Conference, while Acts suggests that all outstanding difficulties were, in fact, resolved at the Conference. As already indicated, however, I do not accept this interpretation of the sequence of events.

[36]Indeed, the reference in Acts 15:1 is so vague as to allow the possible interpretation that the men were not even Christians; they might have been non-Christian Jews. Later in the chapter, however, it is made clear that they were, in fact, Christians (v. 24).

[37]See Acts 15:24: "Since we have heard that certain men from us have troubled you with words, unsettling your minds, although we gave them no instructions . . . " (adaptation of RSV).

2. According to Paul, *Peter* (another of the leaders of the church) became directly involved (on the wrong side!) in the controversy in Antioch; in Acts, however, there is no mention of Peter ever being in Antioch or of his involvement in the opposition to Paul.

3. According to Paul, "even *Barnabas* was carried away" by the insincerity of "the circumcision party"; in Acts, however, there is no reference to Barnabas's involvement in the controversy except as an ally of Paul.[38]

These three differences between Acts 15:1-2 and Paul's report in Galatians 2:11-14 can actually be reduced to one: whether Barnabas and particularly Peter and James were involved in the controversy in Antioch in opposition to Paul. According to Paul, they were. According to Acts, they were not so involved, and, indeed, at the Jerusalem Conference, all three were in basic agreement with Paul.[39] In light of both the similarities and the differences between the two passages, it is my own judgment that the author of Acts almost certainly was familiar with and made use of Paul's material in Galatians, but that he deliberately altered this material in such a way as to remove James, Peter, and Barnabas from any type of involvement in the opposition to Paul. This alteration of the material includes the following.

1. The author of Acts omits any reference to *James* (and, indeed, any reference specifically to Jerusalem) in his depiction of the people who instigated the controversy in Antioch (Acts 15:1; cf. Gal 2:12). Ernst Haenchen suggests that he here "wishes to avoid creating the impression that the τινες are a Jerusalem delegation."[40] Even more to the point, I believe, he wishes to avoid any involvement of the *leadership* of the Jerusalem church (e.g., James) in the controversy in Antioch.

2. As already noted, the author omits any reference to *Peter* even being in Antioch (cf. Gal 2:11), thus removing him from any involvement in the controversy there.

---

[38]Later, to be sure, Acts does report "a sharp contention" between Paul and Barnabas, but the subject of debate is simply whether to take John Mark along on "the second missionary journey" (Acts 15:36-40). See the essay by C. Clifton Black in this volume for a differing view.

[39]The position of James, according to Acts, might be regarded as something of a "mediating" one, but James is by no means portrayed as an "opponent" of the Pauline position.

[40]Haenchen, *The Acts of the Apostles*, 442-43. Note that the more general "Judea" appears, not the more specific "Jerusalem."

3. The author also omits any reference to *Barnabas* except as an ally of Paul.[41]

4. At the Jerusalem Conference, the author attributes to none other than *James* the resolution of the controversy—a resolution that, as he portrays it, was accepted and endorsed by all parties involved, including Paul (Acts 15:13-21, cf. 22-31).

5. Also at the Jerusalem Conference, the author attributes precisely to *James* the declaration that the people who instigated the controversy in Antioch had acted without authorization from the Jerusalem leadership (Acts 15:24).

6. In his most brilliant move of all, the author attributes to none other than *Peter*, at the Jerusalem Conference, essentially the same ideas and indeed much of the actual language used by Paul in his own report regarding the gathering. Thus, he succeeds in portraying Peter as not only the chief spokesperson for the "Pauline" position but also as the one who, by divine decree, anticipated Paul as missionary *par excellence* to the Gentiles. There is, of course, real irony in this: in Galatians, it is precisely Peter who is the object of Paul's scathing criticism for being led astray by "the circumcision party"; in Acts, however, it is Peter who, more than anyone else, articulates Paul's vision of the Gentile mission.

Again, the question must be raised: What is the purpose of the author of Acts in thus altering Paul's account of the controversy in Antioch and the Conference in Jerusalem? Although this cannot here be worked out in any detail, my own view is that the author's purpose is neither to exalt Peter nor to denigrate Paul but rather to "rehabilitate" Paul in the minds of those Christians who, for whatever reason, look upon him with suspicion.[42] He does this by indicating that Paul's activities as missionary to the Gentiles and his views regarding soteriology are neither idiosyncratic nor dangerous; rather, they were anticipated and articulated by none other than Peter, supported by James, and endorsed by the assembled "apostles" and "elders" who led the early church in Jerusalem. In other words, Paul was not a "maverick" as some might suspect; both

---

[41]As already noted (n. 38 above), the author of Acts does later describe a controversy between Paul and Barnabas, but the issue is totally unrelated to that of the Jerusalem Conference.

[42]For further detail, see Walker, "Acts and the Pauline Corpus Reconsidered," esp. 14-17.

his activities and his ideology were squarely within the mainstream of "apostolic" Christianity.[43]

A final word: If this interpretation of the relation between the two accounts of the Jerusalem Conference is correct, two of the three points in the thesis of my 1985 article are thereby substantiated: the author of Acts "almost certainly knew, in some sense, at least some of the letters of Paul, [and] he made some use of these letters in the writing of his own work."[44]

---

[43]To be sure, except at 14:14, the author of Acts never refers to Paul as an "apostle," the title Paul so insistently claims for himself in his letters (and particularly in Galatians!).

[44]Walker, "Acts and the Pauline Corpus Reconsidered," 14.

Acts 9:1-29 and Early Church Tradition*

John T. Townsend

Recent studies on Acts have tended to deal with the questions which concern the book as a whole, such as genre and theology. More traditional questions concerning historical accuracy and sources have tended to assume less importance, perhaps because much of what we can know has already been argued at length. A comparison of Acts 9:1-29 with Galatians 1:11-20 plus 1 Corinthians 11:22-23, however, can yield two significant pieces of information. The first is that the tradition behind the passage in Acts 9 seems to derive ultimately from those whom Paul is opposing in Galatians 1:1-11. The second is that any such opponents could easily have arrived at their views without any feelings of enmity towards Paul.

Acts 9 and Galatians 1:11-20 plus 1 Corinthians 11:22-23 both begin with Paul's calling[1] and include his first visit to Jerusalem as a believer.[2] While both accounts exhibit several points of agreement, there are also several points of disagreement.[3] These disagreements, however, are valuable clues to the knowledge and accuracy of the author of Acts. Paul was obviously aware of his own movements. Moreover, he was unlikely to lie greatly to readers who might be in a position to investigate his truthful-

---

*This chapter is an updating and abridgment of a paper presented at the 1988 meeting of the Society of Biblical Literature in Chicago, and printed in *SBLSP* (1988): 119-31.

[1]Substituting the word "calling" for "conversion" follows the suggestion of Krister Stendahl, *Paul Among the Jews and Gentiles* (Philadelphia: Fortress, 1976) 7-23. Similarly Hans Dieter Betz, *Galatians*, Hermeneia (Philadelphia: Fortress, 1979) 64, 69-70. See R. F. Collins, "Paul's Damascus Experience: Reflections on the Lukan Account," *LS* 11 (1986): 99-103; Herbert G. Wood, "The Conversion of St Paul: Its Nature, Antecedents and Consequences," *NTS* 1 (1954/1955): 279: "Paul was converted to Christ rather than to Christianity"; James D. G. Dunn, *A Commentary on the Epistle to the Galatians*, BNTC (London: Black, 1993) 62-67, and "Paul's Conversion—A Light to Twentieth Century Disputes," in *Evangelium Schriftauslegung Kirche: Festschrift für Peter Stuhlmacher zum 65. Geburtstag*, ed. Jostein Adna et al. (Göttingen: Vandenhoeck & Ruprecht, 1997) 77-93.

[2]This identification has been challenged by Pierson Parker, "Once More, Acts and Galatians," *JBL* 86 (1967): 175-82; Heinrich Schlier, *Der Brief an die Galater*, KEKNT 7 (Göttingen: Vandenhoeck & Ruprecht, 1951) 66-78; and by D. F. Robinson, "A Note on Acts 11:27-30," *JBL* 63 (1944): 169-72, but their views have found few followers.

[3]See, e.g., Justin Taylor, *Les Actes des deux apôtres*, vol. 5, *Commentaire historique (Act. 9, 1-18, 22)*, Ebib (Paris: Gabalda, 1994) 5.

ness.[4] Therefore, where Acts and Galatians disagree, there must be an initial presumption that the inaccuracy lies in Acts.

In both accounts, the main outline of the story and certain details remain the same. Both agree that Paul had once been a zealous persecutor of what became the Christian sect and that divine intervention persuaded him to join this sect in or near Damascus. Both also agree that he had been forced to escape Damascus in a basket and that he had later visited certain Jerusalem church leaders. In addition, the accounts agree in representing Paul as a missionary preacher, although Acts hesitates to represent him also as an apostle.

Among these points of agreement, though, are significant points of disagreement. According to Galatians, Paul was called to preach to Gentiles to the apparent exclusion of Jews (Gal 1:16; 2:2, 8), but Acts 9 also includes Israel. According to Acts, Paul (Saul before Acts 13:9) sought the company of other Christians soon after his Damascus experience, while Galatians denies that he did so.[5] According to Acts, Paul's first evangelistic activity was in the Damascus synagogues; Galatians implies that his first preaching was in Arabia.[6] According to Acts, Paul fled Damascus to escape Jews; 2 Corinthians 11:32-33 maintains that he was fleeing the ethnarch of King Aretas.[7] According to Acts, the interval between Paul's encounter with Jesus and his subsequent visit to Jerusalem which followed it was a matter of days,[8] while Galatians affirms

---

[4]On this point, see below.

[5]According to Hans Conzelmann, *Acts of the Apostles: A Commentary on the Acts of the Apostles*, Hermeneia (Philadelphia: Fortress, 1987) 71, Acts 9:6 asserts that "in contrast to Gal. 1:12-13 Paul does not learn of the gospel in the vision itself. He is directed to the Church, which is the mediator of this teaching." This distinction seems overdrawn. The vision in Acts 9 certainly included the revelation that Jesus had overcome death and should be confessed as Lord. Such a revelation is indeed the gospel. The rest is commentary.

[6]See, e.g., Dunn, *A Commentary on the Epistle to the Galatians*, 69-70; Jerome Murphy-O'Connor, "What Was Paul Doing in Arabia?" *BibRev* 10/5 (1994): 46-47, and "Paul in Arabia," *CBQ* 55 (1993): 315-17. Most exegetes identify Arabia with North Arabia just south of Damascus, but cf. N. T. Wright, "Paul, Arabia, and Elijah (Galatians 1:17)," *JBL* 115 (1996): 683-92, who places Paul on Mt. Sinai.

[7]Cf. Rudolf Pesch, *Die Apostelgeschichte*, 2 vols., EKKNT 5 (Zürich: Benziger, 1988) 1:311, who suggests that "die Nachstellung durch den Nabatäer-Ethnarchen durch die Juden veranlaßt gewesen sein kann"; similarly Ernst Haenchen, "The Book of Acts as Source Material for the History of Early Christianity," in *Studies* (1966) 268-69.

[8]It seems unlikely that the "many days" of Acts 9:23 indicates a period of more than a year, as maintained by Adolf von Harnack, *The Acts of the Apostles* (New York: Putnam, 1909) 23, 28n.1, and Eugene Jacquier, *Les Actes des Apôtres*, Ebib (Paris:

it was a matter of years. Acts and the epistles also differ considerably in their descriptions of this visit. In Galatians, Paul swears before God that the visit lasted only two weeks and that, aside from Peter, he saw no other apostle but James the Lord's brother.[9] In fact, Paul claims that the Judean Christians did not even know what he looked like.[10] According to Acts, however, Paul met "the apostles" and engaged in public preaching and disputing. There also seems to be disagreement over whether Paul was to be regarded as an apostle. Throughout Acts 9, indeed throughout all of Acts, the author of Luke-Acts seems to be downplaying Paul's apostleship. Apart from passing allusions in Acts 14:4, 14 to Barnabas and Paul as apostles, Acts never refers to Paul as an apostle but reserves the title for Jerusalem church leaders, presumably the twelve. In fact, Acts 1:21 laid down one requirement for apostleship that Paul could never have fulfilled: the requirement that an apostle must have been with Jesus throughout his earthly ministry.[11] Thus, it is not surprising to find Acts 13:3 describing what appears to be a kind of ordination for Paul before he sets forth on his main missionary work (cf. also Acts 9:15; 22:14-15).[12] In addition to these contradictions, Acts 9 has two major

---

Gabalda, 1926) 296-97.

[9]Whether the text of Gal 1:19 implies that James was an apostle or not depends upon the interpretation of εἰ μή. See Marie-Joseph Lagrange, *Saint Paul: Épître aux Galates*, 2nd ed., Ebib (Paris: Gabalda, 1950) 18-19; Schlier, *Der Brief an die Galater*, 31; and Johannes Munck, "Paul, the Apostles and the Twelve," *ST* 3 (1949): 106.

[10]The assertion that Judea in Gal 1:22 excludes Jerusalem (e.g., Louis Finkelstein, *The Pharisees: The Sociological Background of Their Faith*, 2nd ed., 2 vols. [Philadelphia: Jewish Publication Society of America, 1940] 1:24; cf. Charles S. C. Williams, *A Commentary on the Acts of the Apostles*, HNTC [New York: Harper, 1957] 126-27) is supported by little evidence. See B. W. Bacon, "Acts Versus Galatians: The Crux of Apostolic History," *AJT* 11 (1907): 156; Schlier, *Der Brief an die Galater*, 32; cf. Ernest DeWitt Burton, *A Critical and Exegetical Commentary on the Epistle to the Galatians*, ICC (New York: Scribner's, 1920) 62ff., 435-36.

[11]Gerhard Lohfink, *The Conversion of St Paul: Narrative and History in Acts* (Chicago: Franciscan Herald Press, 1976) 29-30; Ernst Haenchen, *The Acts of the Apostles* (Philadelphia: Westminster, 1971) 113ff.; Hans Conzelmann, *The Theology of St. Luke* (New York: Harper & Row, 1960) 215ff.; but cf. Jacob Jervell, "Paulus in der Apostelgeschichte und die Geschichte des Urchristentums," *NTS* 32 (1986): 378-92, who argues that Acts takes the apostolic title away from Paul because he is more than an apostle, i.e., a super-apostle. See also J. C. Beker, "Luke's Paul as the Legacy of Paul," in *SBLSP* (1993): 511-19, esp. 518.

[12]See Joseph Coppens, "L'imposition des mains dans les Actes des Apôtres," in *Les Actes des Apôtres: Traditions, rédaction, théologie*, ed. Jacob Kremer, BETL 48 (Leuven: Leuven University Press, 1979) 417-20, who argues that Paul and Barnabas could be called apostles in Acts 14 because they had been ordained as apostles in Acts 13:1-3; but

additions. The first is the imaginative elaboration of Paul's miraculous encounter with Jesus. The second is the story about the restoration of his sight and his baptism by a certain Ananias.

The details of Acts 9:1-29 clearly disagree at many points with the corresponding accounts found in the Pauline epistles, and the two cannot be harmonized.[13] Faced with such disagreements, it is easy, perhaps too easy, to begin with the assumption that the account in Galatians must be completely historically accurate. Certainly Paul knew the facts about what he had done; but given the canons of ancient rhetoric, just how much would Paul slant the truth in a *narratio* such as that in Galatians 1–2? Still, one should not overemphasize Paul's likely use of such rhetorical freedom. A *narratio* had to be plausible, and a statement is most easily plausible when true.[14]

For this study, however, the question of Paul's historical accuracy need not be decisive. What we can learn from Galatians with absolute certainty is what Paul wanted the Galatians to believe about his activity, and from this knowledge it is possible to infer some of the views of those whom Paul opposed. Even though there are difficulties both in fully describing such opponents and in interpreting Paul predominantly through a "mirror" reading, still it is not too difficult to isolate specific points that the apostle is denying.[15] Surprisingly, these specific points of denial bear a striking resemblance to the account in Acts 9:1-29, as shown by Olaf Linton.[16] In other words, Paul seems to be denying much of what Acts 9 says about him.[17] Acts 9:1-29, therefore, reflects a tradition at least as old as the epistle to the Galatians,[18] and those studying the differences

---

cf. Jervell, "Paulus in der Apostelgeschichte," 379.

[13]Betz, *Galatians*, 63; and Taylor, *Les Actes des deux apôtres*, 5:27-29.

[14]Betz, *Galatians*, 60. For a questioning of Paul's accuracy apart from rhetorical considerations, see Jack T. Sanders, "Paul's Autobiographical Statements in Galatians 1–2," *JBL* 85 (1966): 335-43.

[15]Johan S. Vos, "Paul's Argumentation in Galatians 1–2," *HTR* 87 (1994): 1-2; and Betz, *Galatians*, 5-6.

[16]Olaf Linton, "The Third Aspect: A Neglected Point of View: A Study in Gal. 1–2 and Acts 9 and 15," *ST* 3 (1949): 79-95. Cf. Taylor, *Les Actes des deux apôtres*, 5:27-29.

[17]See Helmut Koester, "Gnomai Diaphoroi: The Origin and Nature of Diversification in the History of Early Christianity," *HTR* 58 (1965): 314-15: "No doubt, Luke was a student of Paul's opponents rather than of Paul himself." So also Robert Jewett, *A Chronology of Paul's Life* (Philadelphia: Fortress, 1979) 17.

[18]Cf. Linton, "The Third Aspect," 95, who concludes: "It is therefore very probable that the account of Acts derives from older sources, surely not identical with those current in Galatia, but akin to them." Cf. also Georg Strecker, "Die sogenannte zweite Jerusalem-

between this section of Acts and the Pauline epistles should begin, not with some supposed purpose on the part of the author of Luke-Acts,[19] but with the origin of the tradition which the author has used.

How might such a tradition about Paul have arisen? Was it necessarily a deliberate perversion of Paul's activity on the part of his enemies? Perhaps not.[20] First of all, we can assume that the ultimate source for any story or detail in Acts which finds confirmation in the Pauline epistles is the event itself, or at least what both Paul and his opponents agreed was the event itself. Thus, the tradition in Acts 9:1-29 must contain the following original nucleus about Paul's activities upon which both he and his opponents agreed:

> Paul, a Jewish persecutor of Christians, had experienced a miraculous change of heart in or near Damascus. Sometime later he had to escape from Damascus in a basket and then visited Jerusalem. He also became a great Christian evangelist.

Since the tradition contains no mention of Paul's Arabian visit, we may assume as a working hypothesis that those who formed the tradition did not know of that visit.[21]

As for the other disagreements in the Acts tradition, we need to ask whether they arose from real enemies of Paul or whether such disagreements were natural assumptions by those who only knew the short story outlined above. How might even someone who was pro-Paul have filled

---

reise des Paulus (Act 11:27-30)," *ZNW* 53 (1962): 71. Concerning a possible verbal relation between Acts 9 and Gal 1, see Linton, "The Third Aspect," 81-82. For an argument that Acts depends on the epistles, see Thomas L. Brodie, "Luke's Redesigning of Paul," *IBS* 17 (1965): 98-128.

[19]See Jules Cambier, "Le voyage de S. Paul à Jérusalem en Act. 9:26ss. et le schéma missionaire théologique de S. Luc," *NTS* 9 (1961/1962): 249-57.

[20]Paul's opponents in Galatia need not have regarded themselves as his enemies. While disagreeing with some of his claims, they may actually have held him in high esteem. Even if they never regarded him as the equal of the Jerusalem apostles, they like the author of Acts may well have respected Paul as an evangelist. See Linton, "The Third Aspect," 85-86, 95; and Conzelmann, *Acts of the Apostles*, 73. See also John Coolidge Hurd, Jr., *The Origin of I Corinthians* (London: S.P.C.K.; New York: Seabury, 1965; new ed.: Macon GA: Mercer University Press, 1983), who presents Paul's opponents in 1 Cor as people led astray by the apostle's earlier preaching. For a truly hostile approach to Paul, see Pseudo-Clement, *Homilies* 17.13-19.41.

[21]But cf. Stanislas Giet, "Les trots premiers voyages de saint Paul à Jérusalem," *RSR* 41 (1953): 338ff., according to whom Acts 9 contains a hiatus where one would expect a mention of the Arabian visit. Similarly, Jacquier, *Les Actes des Apôtres*, 296, who thinks that perhaps the author of Luke-Acts did know of this visit.

out such a fragmentary account? What would one expect Paul to have done in his circumstances? He certainly had changed from persecutor to church leader. But would he have done so wholly through a divine revelation and without any church instruction? Would he not, as the Acts tradition claims, be expected to spend some time with nearby Christians and then without too much delay to visit the Jerusalem church leaders? Moreover, since Paul was known as a great evangelist, one would easily make the correct assumption that he would soon begin preaching. After all, even though he may not have been an apostle of Christ, at least to those like Luke who would limit the title to the twelve, he was a truly great evangelist! Now where would one expect a learned Pharisee to preach his new revelation? In the local synagogues, of course—in the synagogues of Damascus. Then, since the tradition builders apparently knew nothing of an Arabian visit, they might easily assume, as they did, that Paul remained in Damascus until his escape in a basket. Nor would they have had any reason to suppose that he was fleeing an Arabian king. Therefore, Acts 9 makes the quite plausible assumption that Paul was fleeing Jews, at least partly because it was already assumed that Paul's first preaching had been in the Damascus synagogues. As for Paul's apostleship, was it not enough for him to be the great missionary without giving him a title which many would reserve for the twelve?

The Acts tradition was aware that Paul went to Jerusalem after his escape from Damascus. It was certainly easy to assume further that Paul would have visited the Jerusalem apostles soon after his encounter with the risen Jesus.[22] After all, those responsible for the tradition in Acts 9 appear to have known of no activity which would have delayed the visit some years. According to Acts, therefore, Paul remained in Damascus only long enough for him to linger there with the disciples "several days" (ἡμέρας τινάς) and to build up enough animosity to force his flight from the city after "many days" (ἡμέραι ἱκαναί).

The tradition apparently contained little accurate information concerning Paul's first Jerusalem visit after his Damascus experience, apart from the fact that he did visit there.[23] The tradition builders seem to have used their version of Paul's stay in Damascus as a model for his activity in

---

[22]Bernard Orchard, "The Problem of Acts and Galatians," *CBQ* 7 (1945): 378.
[23]Cf. Williams, *A Commentary on the Acts of the Apostles*, 23; and Cambier, "Le voyage de S. Paul," 257.

Jerusalem.[24] Of course, in Jerusalem Paul had no need to gain his sight or to receive baptism; however, as in Damascus, Paul spends his time in meeting church leaders—in this case the Jerusalem apostles—and in preaching. Also as in Damascus, his preaching resulted in a plot that forced his flight from the city.[25] Moreover, the assumption that this visit took place soon after his miraculous encounter with Jesus leads to the further assumption that the Jerusalem Christians were unaware Paul was no longer persecuting them. Acts 9, therefore, quite understandably depicts them as fearing Paul before Barnabas gave him a suitable introduction.

Of course, the fact that the author of Acts 9:1-29 has relied on an earlier tradition need not imply that he left this tradition untouched.[26] Just as the author of Luke-Acts edited the material which he used from the Gospel of Mark,[27] it is likely that he also edited the tradition he used here.[28] One detail which may be a Lukan addition is the naming of Barnabas as the one who introduced Paul to the Jerusalem apostles. Another is the use of the word "Hellenists" to describe those in Jerusalem with whom Paul disputed. A third is the double vision to Paul and to Ananias, a device also used in the Cornelius story of Acts 10:1–11:18.[29] Regarding Barnabas, Luke's motive for bringing Paul and Barnabas

---

[24]See David Gill, "The Structure of Acts 9," *Bib* 55 (1974): 546-48.

[25]See Charles H. Talbert, *Acts*, Knox Preaching Guides (Atlanta: John Knox, 1984) 40-41, who also finds a chiastic arrangement in the stories of Paul at Damascus and at Jerusalem.

[26]See Collins, "Paul's Damascus Experience," 107-18, who argues for a three-stage history in the development of the account: the traditional story from Damascus, the pre-Lukan story, and Acts 9. But cf. Jacob Jervell, "Paul in the Acts of the Apostles: Tradition, History, Theology," in *Les Actes des Apôtres*, ed. Kremer, 297-98, who notes that the difficulty in distinguishing between the author and his traditions is reflected in the contradictory results of recent monographs on the subject. See also Taylor, *Les Actes des deux apôtres*, 5:10-29, esp. 13, who follows the source theory of M.-É. Boismard and Arnaud Lamouille, *Les Actes des deux apôtres*, 3 vols., Ebib (Paris: Gabalda, 1990) 1:1-51, esp. 3-5, and who argues that, while Luke's source did not know Galatians, Luke himself did.

[27]See Frank C. Burkitt, "The Use of Mark in the Gospel according to Luke," in *Beginnings*, 2:106-20.

[28]For a study of this editing, see Gerd Lüdemann, *Das frühe Christentum nach den Traditionen der Apostelgeschichte* (Göttingen: Vandenhoeck & Ruprecht, 1987) 121-25. On the special concerns of Luke in relation to Marcionites and Jewish Christianity, see my "The Date of Luke-Acts," in *Luke-Acts: New Perspectives from the Society of Biblical Literature Seminar,* ed. Charles H. Talbert (New York: Crossroad, 1984) 47-62. On the Jewishness of Paul in Acts, cf. Jervell, "Paulus in der Apostelgeschichte," 384-86.

[29]Lüdemann, *Das frühe Christentum*, 116.

together would be to serve as a prelude to their association in the subsequent chapters. The designation of the Hellenists[30] as a group with whom Paul disputed in Jerusalem may simply indicate that some tradition builder thought that someone like Paul, so closely associated with the Diaspora, would likely seek out those of Greek culture.[31] This detail, however, may also be the product of the author of Luke-Acts who, having already recorded that Stephen had found violence while preaching in the Greek synagogues of Jerusalem, thought that a violent reaction to Paul's Jerusalem preaching might well have sprung from the same source and designated this source by what may well have sprung from the same source and designated this source by what may well be a word of Lukan coinage, namely "Hellenists."[32]

There are two sections in the narrative of Acts 9:1-29 which the Pauline epistles neither confirm nor deny. The first is the story of how Paul, who had been blind since his encounter with Jesus, received his sight through the laying on of hands[33] and was then baptized. There is, of course, little reason to doubt that Paul was indeed baptized.[34] More-

---

[30]The meaning of Ἑλληνιστής (Acts 9:29; also Acts 6:1 and, according to rather strong textual evidence, Acts 11:20) is uncertain. The word is usually thought to designate a Greek-speaking Jew or Jewish Christian. So, for example, Hans Windisch, "Ἕλλην," in *TDNT* 2:509-10; Haenchen, *The Acts of the Apostles*, 260n.3, 266-67; Conzelmann, *Acts of the Apostles*, 61; similarly C. F. D. Moule, "Once More, Who Were the Hellenists?" *ExpTim* 70 (1959): 100-102; Edwin C. Blackmann, "The Hellenists of Acts 6:1," *ExpTim* 48 (1937): 542-43; and Alfons Weiser, *Die Apostelgeschichte*, 2 vols., OTNT 5 (Gütersloh: Mohn, 1981) 168-69. Some critics, however, disagree, including Henry J. Cadbury, "The Hellenists," in *Beginnings*, 5:59-74, who concludes that Ἑλληνιστής has essentially the same meaning as Ἕλλην. Against Cadbury's interpretation, see Haenchen, *The Acts of the Apostles*, 260n.1, 266-67; and Windisch, "Ἕλλην," *TDNT* 2:509.

[31]There is reason to doubt the unconfirmed assertions of Acts 9:11, 21:39, 22:3 (cf. 9:30, 11:2) that Paul was originally from Tarsus. Robert Kraft of the University of Pennsylvania has maintained for many years that Luke may have invented Paul's birth in Tarsus because he misunderstood the expression "Saul the Tarsian," which in Aramaic reads, *Sha'ul Tarsaya* (Hebrew: *Sha'ul haTarsi*), and means "Saul the Weaver." Thus, it would not have been too difficult to misinterpret "Paul" or "Saul the Tarsian" to mean "Saul, the man from Tarsus." See my paper, "The Contributions of John Knox to the Study of Acts: Some Further Notations," in *Cadbury, Knox, and Talbert: American Contributions to the Study of Acts*, ed. Mikeal C. Parsons and Joseph B. Tyson (Atlanta: Scholars Press, 1992) 86-87.

[32]See Windisch, "Ἕλλην," *TDNT* 2:508-509.

[33]According to Acts 22:12-16, Paul actually received ordination at the hands of Ananias. See Kirsopp Lake, "The Conversion of Paul and the Events Immediately Following It," in *Beginnings*, 5:189-90. However, one must note that this account appears in a speech and represents the interpretation of the author of Luke-Acts. See my article, "The Speeches in Acts," *ATR* 43 (1960): 150-59.

[34]But cf. Reginald H. Fuller, "Was Paul Baptized?" in *Les Actes des Apôtres*, ed.

over, the story contains concrete details which are difficult to explain as someone's deduction or bias.[35] The one who baptized Paul was a certain Ananias, who is otherwise unknown. The account even names the street and house where the baptism occurred. If such details involved well-known people and places, one might see them as creative elaboration, but these details do not fit such a category. Thus, Acts may well preserve a reliable tradition that Paul received his baptism in the house of Judas on the street called Straight in Damascus by a certain Ananias.[36] That Paul regained his sight at this time, however, is questionable. According to the tradition, Paul's miraculous experience had left him blind, and he was obviously not blind during his ministry. Perhaps the tradition builders simply felt that a likely time for Paul to have regained his sight was at his baptism. Moreover, that Paul regained his sight presupposes that he had lost it in the first place; and as shown below, the latter presupposition is also questionable.[37] The only other detail for which the story does not account is the vision (ὄραμα) which guided Ananias to Paul. Tradition required that the two meet to fulfill the divine plan, and Acts commonly makes use of visions in such situations (Acts 10:3, 10-17; 11:5; 16:9-10; 18:9), in particular the double vision as found here. After all, Luke was certainly aware that the prophet Joel promised that such would occur during the messianic age (3:1=2:18 in the NRSV; cf. Acts 2:17).[38]

Kremer, 505-508, who argues that for Paul, Peter, the twelve, and others the apostolic calling was the equivalent of baptism.

[35]See Strecker, "Die sogenannte zweite Jerusalemreise des Paulus," 71-72; but cf. Taylor, *Les Actes des deux apôtres*, 5:16-17.

[36]Against this deduction, see Kirsopp Lake and Henry J. Cadbury, "English Translation and Commentary [Acts]," in *Beginnings*, 4:102-103, who argue that such details may be found elsewhere in Acts (in particular in 10:6); but apart from 10:6, the details in these other passages tend to be well-known geographical or political facts (e.g., 9:38, 18:12). See also Pesch, *Die Apostelgeschichte*, 1:301-302, 305; but cf. Lake, "The Conversion of Paul," 191: "It is quite unnecessary to suppose that the story of Ananias is fiction." Similarly Haenchen, *The Acts of the Apostles*, 328.

[37]But cf. Weiser, *Die Apostelgeschichte*, 1:228, who regards this healing as very likely.

[38]Although it is unlikely that the story of Paul's baptism is without foundation, its position immediately following the call may well be open to question. Luke has a tendency to relate all the Pauline stories that take place in a given city to Paul's first visit there. Since both Paul's initial encounter with Jesus and his later baptism are connected with Damascus, Luke would have put them together whether they belonged together chronologically or not. See Chris U. Manus, "Conversion Narratives in the Acts," *ITS* 22 (1985): 185.

The second section of Acts 9:1-29 without a parallel account in the Pauline epistles is the detailed elaboration of Paul's Damascus experience. In Galatians, the apostle simply affirms that God revealed his son in (ἐν) him.[39] Acts 9, however, adds that Paul saw a heavenly light, before which he fell to the ground blind, while he heard the voice of Jesus, who made himself known to Paul. Since Luke composed the speeches in Acts,[40] there is little reason to doubt that he would have composed suitable words for Jesus to speak to Paul (in vv. 4-6), especially since the parallel accounts in Acts 22:8 and Acts 26:14-15 give somewhat different versions.[41] That Acts 9 reports a light from heaven is hardly surprising since, in the ancient world of the early church, brilliant lighting was expected with heavenly appearances.[42] Moreover, Paul's blindness may have been added merely as a testimony to the intensity of the light.[43] In addition, the setting of the account in Acts 9 may be partly due to an expanded tradition. The tradition builders were aware that the event took place in the environs of Damascus and that Paul had formerly persecuted the church. Taken together, these facts easily suggest that Paul's business in Damascus was the persecution of Christians.[44] Following Paul's initial

---

[39]The exact meaning of these words in Gal 1:16 is uncertain. Cf. Burton, *Galatians*, 49ff.; Lagrange, *Saint Paul*, 14; Schlier, *Der Brief an die Galater*, 26-27; and Dunn, *A Commentary on the Epistle to the Galatians*, 64. Note also that, in addition to Gal 1:11-17, most exegetes add 1 Cor 9:1 and 15:8; but Betz, *Galatians*, 71 affirms the need for caution on this point. Some critics also maintain that 2 Cor 12:2-4 describes the apostle's miraculous Damascus experience. See my arguments in "The Contributions of John Knox," 84-86. Cf. James D. Tabor, *Things Unutterable: Paul's Ascent to Paradise in its Greco-Roman, Judaic, and Early Christian Contexts*, Studies in Judaism (Lanham MD: University Press of America, 1986). Although Tabor does not consider the possibility of this epiphany being the Damascus experience, his interpretation of the epiphany could fit such a consideration. See also Betz, *Galatians*, 69, who explains that Paul's brevity in Gal is due to the fact that a rhetorical *narratio* called for brevity.

[40]Townsend, "The Speeches in Acts," 150-59.

[41]See Conzelmann, *Acts of the Apostles*, 71-73, 187, 210-11.

[42]Cf. Num 9:15-16; 2 Kgs 2:11f., 6:17; Ezek 1:4-28; Luke 2:9; Acts 7:55; Rev 1:16, 21:23, 22:5; etc. Cf. also Conzelmann, *Acts of the Apostles*, 72. See Harald Riesenfeld, *Jésus transfiguré, l'arrière-plan récit évangélique de la transfiguration de Notre-Seigneur*, ASNU 16 (Copenhagen: Munksgaard, 1947) 97-114; and Conzelmann, *Acts*, 71.

[43]See Acts 22:11, which is more specific. Cf. 2 Kgs 6:17-18, Ezek 1:28, and 2 Cor 3:7ff. See also Haenchen, *The Acts of the Apostles*, 323, 626.

[44]Various exegetes have pointed out parallels between Paul's experience in Acts 9 and various other ancient stories. Hans Windisch, "Die Christusepiphanie vor Damaskus und ihrer religionsgeschichtlichen Parallelen," *ZNW* 31 (1932): 1-23, sees parallels with the experience of Heliodorus in 2 Macc 3:1. So also Talbert, *Acts*, 39-40; and Christoph Burchard, *Die dreizehnte Zeuge* (Göttingen: Vandenhoeck & Ruprecht, 1970) 54-105, who

experience of the risen Jesus, Acts 9 has him spend three days in blindness during which time he abstained from food and drink. Again, such expansions are not surprising. The three days need only have been used as a conveniently short period,[45] perhaps suggested by the fact that Jesus spent three days in the darkness of the grave. The fasting served as a suitable indication of Paul's repentance[46] and would also have been the normal preparation for his impending baptism.[47] Of course, it is possible that some of the above details represent what actually happened, but they can just as easily be seen as a rather commonplace expansion of the simple fact that God revealed his son to Paul, the persecutor, in or near Damascus.

In summary, Acts 9:1-29 can be understood as reflecting a tradition which arose from a simple elaboration of certain bits of accurate information. While some of this elaboration may well stem from the author of Luke-Acts, the similarity of this tradition with what Paul was denying in Galatians 1 suggests that it goes back to those against whom the apostle

---

in addition cites parallels of the Lukan account with *Joseph and Aseneth*. Charles W. Hedrick, "Paul's Conversion/Call: A Comparative Analysis of the Three Reports in Acts," *JBL* 100 (1981): 415-32, finds a parallel in the healing and conversion of Ptolemy in the Coptic Acts of Peter. Norman A. Beck, "The Lukan Writer's Stories about the Call of Paul," *SBLSP* (1983): 215, makes use of 1 Macc 15:15-21 and Dan 10:2-21. Gerhard Lohfink, "Ein alttestamentliche Darstellung für Gotteserscheinungen in der Damaskus-berichten (Apg. 9; 22; 26)," *BZ* 9 (1965): 247-53, and Manus, "Conversion Narratives in the Acts," 173-81, find parallels in the Hebrew scriptures, while Marvin W. Meyer, "The Light and Voice on the Damascus Road," *Forum* 2 (1986): 27-35, compares scriptural parallels plus the texts from Nag Hammadi and Ras Shamra. Cf. also Conzelmann, *Acts of the Apostles*, 73. For a form-critical analysis of the account in Acts 9 as a "commissioning account," see Collins, "Paul's Damascus Experience," 107-18; Walter Vogels, "Les récit de vocation des prophètes," *NRT* 95 (1973): 1-24; Walther Zimmerli, *Ezekiel: A Commentary on the Book of the Prophet Ezekiel*, 2 vols., Hermeneia (Philadelphia: Fortress, 1979) 1:100; also Benjamin J. Hubbard, "The Role of Commissioning Accounts in Acts," in *Perspectives on Luke-Acts*, ed. Charles H. Talbert (Danville VA: Association of Baptist Professors of Religion; Edinburgh: T.&T. Clark, 1978) 187-98. Against Zimmerli, see Odil H. Steck, "Formgeschichtliche Bemerkungen zur Darstellung des Damaskusgeschehens in der Apostelgeschichte," *ZNW* 67 (1976): 20-28. Cf. also Manus, "Conversion Narratives in the Acts," 179-81.

[45]See Friedrich Nötscher, "Zur Auferstehung nach drei Tagen," *Bib* 35 (1954): 313: "Daß die Dreizahl in Mythus, Religion und Kult eine große Rolle spielt, ist längst beobachtet worden." Following this assertion, Nötscher adds a survey of various studies on the number three in Greek and Semitic antiquity.

[46]Haenchen, *The Acts of the Apostles*, 323.

[47]See *Did.* 7:4; Justin Martyr, *I Apol.* 61; Tertullian, *De Baptismo* 20; and Lake and Cadbury, "English Translation and Commentary [Acts]," 102.

was writing. Of course, it is possible that those who formed the tradition did not see themselves as enemies of Paul. This possibility is certainly true for the author of Luke-Acts.[48] As for Paul, his reaction to this tradition is reflected in Galatians and suggests that he did not look so benignly upon those who misrepresented him. Even if Paul ever stopped to consider the possibility that such people were not really his enemies, he would probably have thought, "With friends like these, who needs enemies?"

---

[48]So Jervell, "Paulus in der Apostelgeschichte," 378-92.

Part II

Lukan Themes, Characters, and Rhetoric

John Mark in the Acts of the Apostles*

C. Clifton Black

Among the colorful *dramatis personae* on the teeming stage of Acts, John Mark is a pallid bit player, one whose performance receives short shrift among commentators. The present essay attempts an exercise of exegetical redress. We shall test the hypothesis that some of Luke's religious concerns acquire greater depth and resonance if we attend more closely to the subtle shadings of John Mark's portrayal in the second volume of the Evangelist's narrative. Latent in this proposal is an assumption congenial with the redaction-critical perspective, as well as with some currents in narrative criticism: namely, that the depiction of John Mark, like that of other figures in Acts, assists Luke in formulating or bolstering particular theological convictions whose historical interest is not coterminous with strictly historical preoccupations.[1] By scrutinizing John Mark, we shall find that Luke's characterization of that elusive figure constitutes an interesting piece in the kaleidoscopic pattern of images of Judaism in Lukan thought, to which much of Joseph Tyson's scholarship has directed our attention.[2]

I. The Portrayal of John Mark in Acts

A. Acts 12:12

We begin at Acts 12:12,[3] where, in passing, Luke mentions "John, whose other name was Mark," as the son of a certain Mary, in whose

---

*This essay is a revised version of material that first appeared in *PerRS* 20 (1993): 235-54; and subsequently in C. Clifton Black, *Mark: Images of an Apostolic Interpreter*, Studies on Personalities of the New Testament (Columbia: University of South Carolina Press, ©1994) 25-49. Use of this material here is with the permission of the publisher.

[1]With the pioneering *redaktionsgeschichtlich* treatment of Ernst Haenchen, *The Acts of the Apostles: A Commentary* (Philadelphia: Westminster, 1971) 90-116, one might compare the approaches of Robert C. Tannehill, *The Narrative Unity of Luke-Acts: A Literary Interpretation*, 2 vols. (Philadelphia and Minneapolis: Fortress, 1986, 1990) 2:1-8; and John A. Darr, *On Character Building: The Reader and the Rhetoric of Characterization in Luke-Acts*, LCBI (Louisville KY: Westminster/John Knox, 1992).

[2]See esp. Joseph B. Tyson, *Images of Judaism in Luke-Acts* (Columbia: University of South Carolina Press, 1992).

[3]Peter's colleague in Acts 3–4 is most likely John the son of Zebedee, not John Mark. See Black, *Mark: Images of an Apostolic Interpreter*, 26-27.

house in Jerusalem Peter took refuge after his miraculous release from prison (Acts 12:6-12). Beyond the familial connection, in 12:12 we learn nothing directly about John Mark.[4] Indirectly, we learn that his mother is a Jerusalemite woman of substance: Mary is served by a maid (παιδίσκη, 12:13) and owns a house, access to which was gained by a gateway or porch (ὁ πυλών, 12:13), and large enough to accommodate a congregation of believers who had gathered to pray, presumably for Peter's welfare (12:5, 12). Interestingly, in Luke's narrative John Mark is introduced in order to identify his mother, Mary; it is not the other way around, as we might have expected. Equally intriguing and perhaps contrary to expectation is the fact that neither here nor anywhere in Acts is John Mark explicitly associated with Peter. When, after his comical detention at the door (12:13-16), Peter finally gains entry to Mary's house, he stays only long enough to describe his miraculous jailbreak and to ask that the report be relayed to James and the other believers in Jerusalem (12:17). Luke neither states nor intimates what has sometimes been assumed: "Presumably Mark was at home in those days, and so found himself in association with early representatives of the new religious movement,"[5] Peter in particular. In fact, the narrator of Acts whisks Peter off the premises almost as quickly as he arrives: "Then [Peter] left and went to another place" (12:17). In Acts 12:12-17 the name of John Mark is tangentially used to identify Peter's influential patron, Mary, not to establish any connection between her son and that apostle. On a first reading of Acts, oblivious to other early Christian traditions or literature, a reader would have no reason to expect that John Mark would ever reappear.

B. Acts 12:25

Therefore, at Acts 12:25, it is surprising to learn that John Mark has been inducted into an apostolic entourage: "Then Barnabas and Saul returned [to Antioch: see 13:1], after completing their mission at Jerusalem, taking along with them John, whose other name was Mark."[6] The

---

[4]In particular, no connection is wrought between Mary's house in Acts 12 and the site of the Last Supper in Luke 22 (contra F. F. Bruce, *The Acts of the Apostles: The Greek Text with Introduction and Commentary* [Grand Rapids MI: Eerdmans, ²1952, ¹1951] 246-47, and elsewhere).

[5]Shirley Jackson Case, "John Mark," *ExpTim* 26 (1914–1915): 372-76 (quotation, 372).

[6]For discussion of the text-critical problems that complicate satisfactory translation of this verse, consult Bruce M. Metzger, *A Textual Commentary on the Greek New Testa-*

reader's expectations are given a new twist: perhaps, one might suppose, this John Mark will emerge as a major protagonist in the drama of Acts. After all, he is traveling in the company of Barnabas and Saul, who by now have emerged as key missionary delegates, operating at the behest of the significant Christian centers at Jerusalem and Antioch (9:26-30; 11:19-30). Moreover, both of those leading characters were themselves introduced as minor figures who first appeared, then immediately disappeared (cf. 4:36-37; 8:1a) in a manner that contributes to the narrative unification of Acts and seems characteristic of its implied author.[7] On the other hand, one cannot be certain of John Mark's potential influence, since he does not appear to be the fully equal partner of those whom he accompanies: rather than uniformly collocating all three missionaries, Luke completes his update on Barnabas and Saul with a subordinate clause to the effect that John Mark "was taken along [συμπαραλαβόν-τες] with [them]." In this team John Mark is the junior partner, whose character awaits further disclosure.

From among all the Christian faithful in Jerusalem, why was John Mark selected to accompany Barnabas and Saul? Intriguingly, Luke never explains. Henry Barclay Swete gave voice to perhaps the most common suggestion: "It was for Barnabas to seek fresh associates in his work, and John was a near relative of Barnabas"[8]—a theory that rests, in turn, upon the coordination of John Mark in Acts 12–13 with the reference to Mark in Colossians 4:10. Yet, while Luke identifies Mary as John Mark's mother—as though Mark would have been more widely known than Mary—he never identifies Barnabas and John Mark as cousins. If Luke's intention, in Acts 12:12, was to relate Mary to someone with whom his readers might be better acquainted, and if Luke had known of the cousinship of Mark and Barnabas, why would he not have identified Mary as kinswoman to Barnabas? Equally lacking in narrative foundation is the proposal that Barnabas and Paul lodged with Mark's mother during their stay in Jerusalem,[9] or that "Mark was taken on Paul's first missionary

---

ment (London/New York: United Bible Societies, 1971) 398-400.

[7]Tannehill, *The Narrative Unity of Luke-Acts*, 2:78, 99. Note also Philip's introduction and delayed development in Acts 6:5, 8:26-40.

[8]Henry Barclay Swete, *The Gospel According to St Mark*, 3rd ed. (London: Macmillan, 1927) xvi.

[9]F. F. Bruce, *Commentary on the Book of Acts*, NICNT (Grand Rapids MI: Eerdmans, 1954) 258.

journey because his eyewitness reminiscences supplied an element in the Gospel preaching that neither Paul nor Barnabas could supply."[10]

So the question stands: Why is John Mark suddenly aligned with Barnabas and Saul in Acts 12:25? In the absence of clear narrative clues, any response is necessarily conjectural. One possibility, tradition-critical in orientation, is that Luke learned of this association from one of his sources and simply reported it, without knowing its rationale or without interest in explaining it. Another alternative pays closer attention to the narrative logic of Acts: one may inquire into the allusive reverberations between John Mark and the characters and events with which, in 12:25, he is related. For example, through his mother Mark is indirectly associated with both wealth and piety, as typified by the Christians gathered at Mary's house in fervent prayer (12:12). In similar terms Luke has already introduced and sketched Joseph Barnabas: the "son of encouragement"[11] who laid the proceeds from the sale of certain real estate at the apostles' feet (4:36-37) and, as a leading delegate of both the Jerusalem and Antiochene churches (11:22, 30),[12] manifested goodness, fidelity, and fullness of the Holy Spirit (11:24a). Moreover, John Mark is identified by Luke as a Jerusalemite (12:12; 13:13): his presence at the start of Paul's first major missionary journey into Gentile territory (13:4–14:28) effectively, albeit tacitly, represents the reach of Jerusalemite Christianity, whose general influence is maintained in Acts yet harmonized with other potent spheres of Christianity beyond Judean boundaries. (Earlier, at 4:35-36, Barnabas, a Cypriot, has subjugated himself to the Jerusalem apostles, who bestow on him a new name; somewhat later, at 9:26-30, Saul, a Cilician [see 21:39; 22:3; 23:34], is accredited by Barnabas before the Jerusalem apostolate.) Furthermore, in the light of events to come, it may not be sheer happenstance that the beginning of John Mark's travels with Barnabas and Saul coincides with

---

[10]G. J. Paul, *St. John's Gospel: A Commentary* (Madras, India: Christian Literature Society, 1965) 16n.1. For alerting me to this suggestion and for making the quotation available to me I am indebted to Beverly R. Gaventa.

[11]Contrary to Luke (Acts 4:36), the name "Barnabas" means "son of Nebo," not "son of encouragement." Nevertheless, in Acts the characterization holds, even if its etymological association does not.

[12]One might even say that Barnabas is the "senior member" of those delegations. Consider Paul's nominal subordination to Barnabas in Acts 9:27; 11:25-26, 30; 12:25; 13:1-2, 7; 14:14. On the pivotal role played by Barnabas in Acts, see Luke Timothy Johnson, *The Literary Function of Possessions in Luke-Acts*, SBLDS 37 (Missoula MT: Scholars Press, 1977) 53, 203-204.

different narratives of divine intervention and rectification amid human thickheadedness or outright hubris (12:14-16 [Rhoda and the Jerusalemite congregation]; 12:18-23 [Herod Agrippa]). While these narrative allusions are not farfetched, their attenuation must nevertheless be conceded. Luke simply asserts that, on the threshold of a significant missionary expedition, Barnabas and Saul took John Mark with them. It is left for the reader to ponder why.

C. Acts 13:5b

When next we meet John Mark in Acts, it is during the mission of Barnabas and Saul (now referred to as Paul, 13:9) in Cyprus, Barnabas's homeland (4:36). "When they arrived at Salamis, they proclaimed the word of God in the synagogues of the Jews; and they had John as a ὑπηρέτης" (13:5). With respect to the characterization of Mark in this verse, at least two problems arise. Of the two the minor question involves Luke's mention of "John" and the ambiguity of that reference. As there has been no mention of anyone else named "John" in the few verses intervening 13:5 and 12:25, which contained Luke's last mention of "John, whose other name was Mark," surely we are meant to construe John Mark as the referent in 13:5b.

More difficult to discern is Luke's intention in describing John (Mark) as a ὑπηρέτης and, therefore, how that appositive should best be translated. In classical Greek the root meaning of ὑπηρέτης is that of a galley slave, one who pulled the oars in the lower tier of a trireme (a ship with three rows or banks of oars on each side).[13] Already in Herodotus (*History* 3.635.111) and Plato (*Politicus* 289c), the term is used to refer more generally to an underling, a servant or attendant. Rather quickly the word comes to be employed for all sorts of subordinate relations in domestic, political, or religious spheres, and this general and varied usage persists in the writings of Hellenistic Judaism (thus, LXX Prov 14:35; Wis 6:4; Isa 32:5; similarly in *Ep. Arist.* 111, Philo, and Josephus). More technically, in the works of the later Attic historians, Thucydides (*Peloponnesian War* 3.17) and Pseudo-Xenophon (*Cynegeticus* 2.4.4; 6.2.13), ὑπηρέτης is used in military contexts to designate

---

[13]See James Hope Moulton and Wilbert Francis Howard, *A Grammar of New Testament Greek*, 3rd ed., 4 vols. (Edinburgh: T.&T. Clark, 1929) 2:328. This connotation of the noun may linger in Paul's metaphor at 1 Cor 4:1.

an armed foot soldier's attendant (who carried the warrior's baggage, rations, and shield) or any adjutant, staff officer, or aide-de-camp.

Occurring six times in Luke-Acts, ὑπηρέτης is employed in no single and consistent way. Rather, Luke's usage captures various nuances within the term's semantic field.

1. The more general sense of subordinate service, albeit within a religious framework, is suggested in the preface to the third gospel (Luke 1:2: "those who from the beginning were eyewitnesses and servants of the word") and in Paul's description, before Agrippa, of his appointment by the Lord as Jesus' "servant and witness" (Acts 26:16). The same connotation appears to be present in Luke's use of the verbal cognate, ὑπηρετέω (Acts 13:36; 20:34; 24:23).

2. The more specific nuance of a cultic functionary is present in Luke 4:20, with reference to the liturgical assistant to a synagogue's president.

3. The more specific use of the term, denoting military "officers" who answered to the high priest and Sanhedrin, appears in Acts 5:22 and 26.

Which, if any, of these connotations is predominant with reference to John Mark in Acts 13:5? In the recent history of scholarship, variations and elaborations of possibilities 1 and 2 above have been propounded.

(a) Among others, Hans Conzelmann and Ernst Haenchen opine that only the most general sense of "assistance" is appropriate to Acts 13:5.[14] In overall agreement are other scholars, like Swete, who nevertheless attempt to define that assistance in more precise terms, "such as arrangements for travel, the provision of food and lodging, conveying messages, negotiating interviews, and the like."[15]

(b) Wide currency has been given to a more technical interpretation of Mark as ὑπηρέτης in Acts 13:5. B. T. Holmes has argued that the term probably entailed the function of looking after documents: "Mark handled a written memorandum about Jesus in the course of the first Gentile mission in Cyprus."[16] Similarly, though attempting even finer etymological precision, R. O. P. Taylor proposed that ὑπηρέτης in Acts

---

[14]Hans Conzelmann, *Acts of the Apostles: A Commentary on the Acts of the Apostles,* Hermeneia (Philadelphia: Fortress, 1987) 99; and Haenchen, *The Acts of the Apostles,* 397.

[15]Swete, *The Gospel according to St Mark,* xvi.

[16]B. T. Holmes, "Luke's Description of John Mark," *JBL* 54 (1935): 63-72 (quotation, 64).

13:5 was functionally equivalent to the חזן, the priestly assistant in the cultus of Palestinian and later Rabbinic Judaism ("ministers of the Temple" in *m. Tamid* 5.3 and *t. Sukk.* 4.11-12). Thus, for Taylor, John Mark was "the schoolmaster—the person whose duty was to impart elementary education[, which] consisted in teaching the actual wording of the sacred records, the exact and precise statements of the facts and dicta on which their religion was based."[17] It is this kind of image that various scholars presuppose of Acts 13:5 when they speak of Mark as the teacher or catechist authorized by Paul and Barnabas.[18]

Clearly we must allow the context of Acts 13:5b to lead us to the most reasonable exegesis. First to be noted is the commissioning scene in Acts 13:1-3. Gathered at Antioch, worshiping and fasting, are various prophets and teachers: Barnabas, Symeon Niger, Lucius of Cyrene, Manaean, and Saul. John Mark is not mentioned as one such προφήτης or διδάσκαλος, even though we have just been informed that he had been accompanying Barnabas and Saul (12:25). Similarly, John Mark is not expressly singled out, as are Barnabas and Saul, as one set apart for the particular work to which they have been called by the Holy Spirit (13:2). Nor is it even clear, in 13:3, that Mark is among those who, after fasting and prayer, either laid hands upon the Spirit's delegates or had others' hands laid upon him. If the reader of Acts is intended to regard John Mark as an emissary with prerogatives for teaching or catechesis, then Luke has left unexploited a fitting juncture in the narrative at which that point might have been clearly communicated.

Dispatched by the Holy Spirit, the delegates proceed to Seleucia, the ancient port city of Antioch, and from there sail to Salamis, Cyprus, where they proclaim the word of God in Jewish synagogues (13:4-5a). In a dependent clause (13:5b) Luke adds that they had John Mark as a ὑπηρέτης. While proclamation could be included in this ὑπηρέτη-

---

[17]R. O. P. Taylor, "The Ministry of Mark," *ExpTim* 54 (1942–1943): 136-38 (quotation, 136); and F. H. Chase, "Mark (John)," in *Dictionary of the Bible*, ed. James Hastings, 5 vols. (Edinburgh: T.&T. Clark, 1909) 3:245-46. In more recent study cf. Mary Ann Beavis, *Mark's Audience: The Literary and Social Setting of Mark 4.11-12*, JSNTSup 33 (Sheffield: Sheffield Academic Press, 1989) 63-67.

[18]Thus, E. P. Blair, "Mark, John," in *IDB* (1962) 3:277-78; and William Barclay, "A Comparison of Paul's Missionary Preaching and Preaching to the Church," in *Apostolic History and the Gospel: Biblical and Historical Essays Presented to F. F. Bruce on His Sixtieth Birthday*, ed. W. Ward Gasque and Ralph P. Martin (Grand Rapids MI: Eerdmans, 1970) 165-75, esp. 169-70.

σις, the wording and syntax of Acts 13:4-5 mitigate against construing Mark's role in exalted terms. First, since John is distinguished from those whom he assists, the implied subject of εἶχον in 13:5b must refer to Barnabas and Saul, which in turn suggests that Luke has had those apostles most prominently in mind in the statement of itinerary at 13:4-5a. Second, almost as an afterthought, Luke informs the reader that Barnabas and Saul are still accompanied by John Mark (13:5b), a datum that, on a first reading of Acts, we would have had no reason whatever to presume. As in 12:25 John still appears in a subordinate position: to judge by Luke's phraseology, neither here nor soon afterward (in 13:7) does John appear to stand on equal footing with his patrons, who are very much the focal missionaries in the narrative. (This remains so throughout the next scene, which portrays the confrontation between the missionaries and Elymas the magician [13:6-12]: again John Mark drops from sight, and Saul, in particular, steps into the spotlight.) Third, and perhaps most telling, Acts 13:5b explicitly says that John was present as an assistant, neither to the Holy Spirit (cf. 13:2, 4) nor to the Lord (cf. 26:16) nor to the word (cf. Luke 1:2), but to Barnabas and Saul. While not overtly denigrated, John Mark's status is significantly qualified: though indeed a *servus*, he is a *servus servorum Dei*.

The thrust of the narrative, therefore, favors a neutral interpretation of ὑπηρέτης: John Mark was simply at the disposal of Barnabas and Saul. Accordingly, all speculation about the kinds of service that he rendered, whether sanctified (preaching or teaching) or mundane (handling baggage or booking passage), probably veers away from Luke's intentions. Of all references to a ὑπηρέτης in Luke-Acts, John Mark's attribution as such in Acts 13:5b is arguably the most colorless.

D. Acts 13:13b

At Acts 13:13 we encounter Luke's most tantalizing reference to John (Mark). Having worked their way from Salamis, on the east coast of Cyprus, through the whole of the island to the western port at Paphos, Paul and his companions (οἱ περὶ Παῦλον) set sail northwest for Perga, the principal seaport of Pamphylia, in southern Asia Minor. "John, however, withdrew from them and returned to Jerusalem" (13:13b).

In both classical and Hellenistic Greek, the verb ἀποχωρεῖν means, generally, "to go away from" or "to depart," though it can carry the connotation of retirement or withdrawal after a defeat (such as an army might do in battle: Thucydides, *Peloponnesian War* 2.89). Beyond Acts

13:13 this verb appears only twice in the New Testament. At Luke 9:39, with reference to a demonic spirit, it may, though need not, carry this nuance of capitulation (and probably does not do so in Matthew 7:23). The other verb in Acts 13:13b, ὑποστρέφειν, may simply be translated as "to return," its most common connotation in Luke-Acts (see, e.g., Luke 1:56; Acts 1:12), or it can convey the more negative nuance of retreat under fire (Homer, *Iliad* 5.581, 12.71; Herodotus, *History* 7.211, 9.14; Thucydides, *Peloponnesian War* 3.24; cf. Luke 11:24 and 23:48). The precise timing of John Mark's separation from Paul and company is vague. Later, at Acts 15:38, we shall learn that John accompanied Paul and Barnabas as far as Pamphylia; without that clarification the wording of 13:13b could have suggested that John withdrew from the others at Paphos, the point of their Asian embarkation. Somewhat clearer, at 13:13b, is the probably adversative import of the connective particle, δέ: at the outset of their mission to Asia, the apostles headed in one direction; John, however, went in the other. Similarly, if δέ is again taken as an adversative at the beginning of 13:14, we are helped in geographically positioning all of the principals: at Perga (not Paphos) John Mark withdrew, but Paul and Barnabas traveled on to Antioch of Pisidia.

Why did John Mark turn away from Paul's coterie and return to Jerusalem? Suggested explanations have ranged all over the exegetical map: from his missionary commitment, limited from the start, up to but not beyond Syrian Antioch or Cyprus;[19] to his general unwillingness to participate in Paul's mission to the Gentiles;[20] to his resentment at his cousin Barnabas's falling into second place behind Paul;[21] to his consternation at the prospect of crossing the formidable Taurus Mountains of northern Pamphilia;[22] to his sense of responsibility to his mother back in Jerusalem;[23] and even to his preference for Mary's home-cooking![24] Not sur-

---

[19]Kirsopp Lake and Henry J. Cadbury, "English Translation and Commentary [Acts]," in *Beginnings*, 4:147.

[20]R. Alan Culpepper, "Paul's Mission to the Gentile World: Acts 13-19," *RevExp* 71 (1974): 487-97, esp. 488.

[21]Bruce, *The Acts of the Apostles* (1951) 259. Again notice the assumption of Luke's acquaintance with Col 4:10.

[22]Gerhard A. Krodel, *Acts*, Augsburg Commentary on the New Testament (Minneapolis: Augsburg, 1986) 231.

[23]Swete, *The Gospel according to St Mark*, xvii.

[24]Krodel, *Acts*, 231, probably proposed with tongue in cheek.

prisingly, other interpreters have judged it futile to speculate on reasons left undisclosed by the narrator.[25]

One may sympathize with those who refuse to engage in uncontrollable speculation about John Mark's intentions at Acts 13:13. Neither, however, should we succumb to another temptation: that of peremptorily dropping the matter without pondering Luke's intentions in presenting the story as he has. John Mark's unexplained return to Jerusalem is not unlike the Philippian magistrates' unexplained about-face regarding the arrest of Paul and Silas (16:35), the ambiguity surrounding the condition of Eutychus and the degree of symbolism, if any, that pervades the story of his resuscitation (20:7-12), and the contradiction between Governor Felix's promise to render a verdict on Paul's case and his subsequent failure to do so (24:22-27). In all of these cases, the narrator of Acts withholds information from the reader and thereby permits multiple interpretations. In his study of Hebrew narrative, Meir Sternberg distinguishes between "gaps," either temporary or permanent omissions of material that are relevant to interpretation, and "blanks," omissions judged by the narrator to be unimportant or irrelevant.[26] What kind of omission do we find in Acts 13:13b?

The safest answer is that at this stage we cannot tell. Not only does Luke withhold from the reader any explanation for John's activity; on a first or naïve reading of Acts it is not even clear that John's return to Jerusalem is inherently problematic. After all, John is a Jerusalemite (12:12), and throughout the narrative the Jerusalem church functions as the principal base and collective arbiter of early Christianity's operations (Acts 1:4, 12; 9:26-30; 11:1-18, 27-30; 15:1-35; 16:4; 21:15-26). That John should withdraw to Jerusalem at this juncture is mysterious, but not intrinsically sinister.

On the other hand, Luke has left some clues in the narrative that, while not decisive, do produce wisps of suspicion around John Mark's conduct. First, there is the fact that John's standing does not appear equal to that of Barnabas and Saul. To this point he has been a passive figure,

---

[25]Haenchen, *The Acts of the Apostles*, 407; and Conzelmann, *Acts of the Apostles*, 105.

[26]Meir Sternberg, *The Poetics of Biblical Narrative: Ideological Literature and the Drama of Reading*, Indiana Studies in Biblical Literature (Bloomington: Indiana University Press, 1985) 230-40. Sternberg's concepts have been insightfully appropriated by Tannehill, *The Narrative Unity of Luke-Acts*, 2:199-200, 248-50, 306-307, who does not explore the possibility of intentional obscurity with reference to John Mark in Acts 13:13.

taken along by the other two missionaries; because we as readers have not witnessed his assertion of positive Christian values or conduct, we cannot be sure of his character. (Although relations among believers tend to be portrayed in Acts as remarkably harmonious [notably, 2:43-47; 4:32-37], Luke by no means suppresses all Christian malfeasance [see 5:1-11; 8:9-24].) Second, we may recall, and now wonder, that John Mark was neither explicitly set apart and dispatched by the Holy Spirit nor confirmed by the Antiochene church for missionary enterprise (13:1-4). Third, immediately preceding the notice of John's separation from his patrons, the reader is told of a Roman proconsul's conversion and Paul's ensuing confrontation with Elymas the magician (13:6-12). From this story emerge some suggestive points for interpreting the character of Mark.

First, the story of Elymas details an instance of human obstinacy and corruption, which must be overcome by divine intervention. Luke's first references to John Mark (12:12, 25) bracketed different stories (Peter's reception [12:12-17]; Herod's atrocities [12:18-23]) that also convey those themes.

Second, the two references to John in Acts 13 (his assistance of Barnabas and Saul, v. 5b; his departure from them, v. 13b) frame a story whose outcome is the conversion to Christianity of a prominent Gentile. While John's response to this event is indiscernible, we know that the Jerusalemite has been directly associated with missionary activity within Jewish synagogues (v. 5a), and soon we shall learn (in Acts 15) that all qualms attaching to Jewish and Gentile relations were not allayed at the Jerusalem conference described in Acts 11:1-18.

A third point may be noted, even though we cannot know how or if it be related to John Mark. It is with the story of Elymas and Sergius Paulus that the erstwhile relationship between Barnabas and Saul is reversed (cf. 9:26-30; 11:19-30; 12:25; 13:1-2, 7), and Paul becomes the "senior member" of the missionary team: from here onward Paul's name is usually mentioned first or representatively (13:13, 43, 45, 46, 50; 14:9, 11; 15:2, 35; though cf. 14:14; 15:12, 25), and Paul's authority, preaching, and fortunes markedly assume center stage (13:9-12, 16-41; 14:9-11, 19-20; 15:36). Indeed, although Paul and Barnabas are described as jointly acting or preaching (13:43, 46-47, 50-52; 14:1-7, 14-18, 21-28; 15:2-4, 12, 22, 30-35), no specific activity of Barnabas alone is portrayed throughout the first missionary journey, the Jerusalem conference, or its immediate aftermath (Acts 13:1–15:35). While its significance is uncertain, it remains the case that John Mark exits the narrative of Acts at precisely the point where Paul moves into ascendance and the role of Barnabas recedes.

At any rate, these associations, tensions, and reversals attending John Mark's entry into and exit from the narrative of Acts are exceedingly subtle. At 13:13b we simply cannot determine whether John's disappearance is an inconsequential "blank" or a significant "gap," or, if the latter, whether that omission is temporary or permanent. In the face of apostolic triumph amid adversity (13:42-52; 14:1-28; 15:30-35), the cryptic statement of John Mark's withdrawal might plant in the reader's mind a seed of suspense. It could just as easily pass unnoticed. Having read no farther than 13:13b, the reader could easily suppose that John Mark has made his last bow in Acts.

E. Acts 15:36-40

The narrative continues with Acts 13–14 offering a representative portrait Paul's missionary endeavors in a Gentile world: bold preaching and miraculous deeds, favorably though not universally received (13:14-50); encounters with Gentile polytheism and mostly Jewish persecution in Iconium, Lystra, and Derbe (13:51–14:20); the pastoral fidelity of Paul and Barnabas to their newly organized churches (14:21-25). In a progress report made to the congregation in Syrian Antioch, where they had received their commission by the Spirit, Paul and Barnabas credit God for opening a door of faith among Gentiles (14:26-28). A potentially catastrophic rupture between the congregations of Antioch and Jerusalem is averted in Acts 15:1-35, with the consensus decision of the apostles and elders that Gentile converts to Christianity need not be circumcised but, rather, adhere only to the basic Mosaic requirements in Leviticus 17:1–18:30 (Acts 15:19-21, 28-29). At stake in this "apostolic decree" are several Lukan desiderata: the intrinsic legitimacy of the Gentile mission, the absolution of Gentiles from conversion to Judaism, and a *modus vivendi* between Jewish and Gentile believers in Christ.

On the verge of a new voyage, at Acts 15:36, Paul proposes to Barnabas a return visit with believers in every city that they have previously missionized.

[37]Now Barnabas was also eager to take with them John, the one called Mark. [38]Paul, however, believed it best not to take with them this one, who had deserted them at Pamphylia and had not gone with them to the work. [39]And so sharp a disagreement arose that they separated from each other: taking Mark with him, Barnabas sailed away to Cyprus. [40]And choosing Silas, Paul

set out, having been commended to the grace of the Lord by the [Antiochene] brothers. [41]And he went through Syria and Cilicia, bolstering the churches. (Acts 15:37-41)

After a lengthy absence John Mark unexpectedly returns to the narrative. Now we know that this character's omission since Acts 13:13b has constituted a temporary gap, not an irrelevant blank. Straightaway, we also learn how John Mark's withdrawal was regarded by Paul: the latter was not favorably disposed to the former's return to Jerusalem (see Acts 13:13), thus confirming our worst fears concerning John Mark's behavior. This assessment is supported by the strikingly harsh tone of this small tableau, which is apparent from Luke's selection and placement of words.

1. We might note the two main predicates in verses 37 and 38: Barnabas "was desiring" (ἐβούλετο) to bring Mark, while Paul "was insisting" (ἠξίου) that they not do so. Both verbs are conjugated in the imperfect tense, indicating continuous action in the past: in this case, persistent and deliberate attitudes in mutual opposition.[27]

2. The vocabulary used to portray the characters' actions in this passage is tart. John Mark is described as the one who in Pamphylia had withdrawn from them: the participle τὸν ἀποστάντα stems from ἀφίστημι, a verb that typically connotes desertion, defection, or apostasy (see Luke 8:13; Acts 5:37-38; LXX Jer 3:14; 1 Macc 11:43; and often throughout the LXX with reference to falling away from God).[28] The term used to portray Paul and Barnabas's "sharp disagreement" (v. 39), παροξυσμός, suggests, not only the English derivative, "paroxysm" (a

---

[27]Some grammarians consider significant the different tenses of the cognate infinitives in verses 37 and 38: the former, συμπαραλαβεῖν ("to take with," in the aorist), referring to a snap decision by Barnabas "with [the] easy forgetfulness of risk" (Moulton and Howard, *A Grammar of New Testament Greek*, 1:130); the latter, συμπαραλαμβάνειν ("to take with," in the present tense), suggesting Paul's refusal to have Mark along day after day. Other scholars, however, reject such a distinction, insisting that the aorist, properly understood, is a nondescriptive tense that may be employed for any kind of action, not merely that which is pointed or instantaneous (Frank Stagg, "The Abused Aorist," *JBL* 91 [1972]: 222-31). The strongest grammatical clues in Acts 15:37-38 are to be found in the main verbs, not in their supplementary infinitives. For correction of this aspect of my analysis in an earlier version of this essay, I am gratefully indebted to private correspondence with Professor Stagg.

[28]The transitive form of the verb is used by Herodotus (*History* 1.76, 154), Thucydides (*Peloponnesian War* 1.81), Josephus (*Ant.* 8.198; 20.102), LXX Deut 7:4, and Luke (Acts 5:37) to describe one who misleads others or incites a revolt. In the patristic literature ἀφίστημι may be used to refer to one's withdrawal from church communion (Irenaeus, *Adv. Haer.* 3.4.2) or apostasy (*Herm. Sim.* 8.8.2; Irenaeus, *Adv. Haer.* 1.13.7).

sudden, violent outburst), but also the more vivid Greek verbal cognate, παροξίζω ("to have a sharp odor"). An English colloquialism captures the sense of it: at Antioch, Barnabas and Paul "raised a stink" with each other over John Mark's inclusion.

3. By the placement of a demonstrative pronoun at the end of verse 38, John Mark is emphatically identified as the defector: Παῦλος δὲ ἠξίου τὸν ἀποστάντα . . . καὶ μὴ συνελθόντα αὐτοῖς . . . μὴ συμπαραλαμβάνειν τοῦτον (woodenly translated, "Him who had deserted and had not accompanied them, . . . Paul thought it better not to take along *this one*"). Observe also the balanced contrast between the missionaries after their parting of the ways: Barnabas took Mark and sailed away to Cyprus; Paul chose Silas and departed for Syria and Cilicia (vv. 39-41). Not only do the erstwhile partners separate; they head out, with new associates, in opposite directions.

The history of this text's exegesis has tended to highlight things neither stated nor reasonably implied by Luke. For example, family feeling, expressed by an elder to a younger cousin, has often been proposed as the motivation for Barnabas's intervention on Mark's behalf.[29] Perhaps even more prominent has been the suggestion that the author of Acts 15:36-40 knows more than he is willing to admit of the apostolic controversy narrated in Galatians 2:11-14, and that Luke consequently shifts the cause of Barnabas's and Paul's separation away from missionary substance to the seemingly less volatile matter of colliding personalities (Paul's steadfastness contrasted with John Mark's unreliability).[30]

Doubtless Acts 15:36-40 bears an underdeveloped quality, which might suggest Luke's discomfiture at airing this portion of early Christianity's "dirty linen" (particularly as it involves two heroic apostles). Yet Luke's concern for personalities can be misconstrued. He never mentions, and may not have known, the tradition underlying Colossians 4:10, to the effect that Barnabas and Mark were cousins. Certainly this item is never offered in explanation of Barnabas's judgment in Acts 15:37-39. Nor does it seem accurate to speak of Luke's account as "neutral"[31] or to reduce it to less consequential matters of personality: in fact, παροξυσμός

---

[29]Krodel, *Acts*, 294; and Luke Timothy Johnson, *The Acts of the Apostles*, Sacra Pagina 5 (Collegeville MN: Liturgical, 1992) 282-83.

[30]Conzelmann, *Acts of the Apostles*, 123; and Paul J. Achtemeier, *The Quest for Unity in the New Testament Church: A Study in Paul and Acts* (Philadelphia: Fortress, 1987) 41-42.

[31]Haenchen, *The Acts of the Apostles*, 474.

is anything but a neutral term for depicting the disagreement between Paul and Barnabas, which is left quite unresolved and arguably entails more than Paul's pique with a blemish in Mark's character.

However delicate its rendering, Acts 15:36-40 amounts to a disturbing, if not traumatic, rift within Luke's narrative, and John Mark stands at its epicenter. The falling-out between Paul and Barnabas ruptures the common mind and concerted action within the Christian community: traits that Luke has taken great pains to establish in the narrative of Acts (e.g., 2:41-47; 4:32-37).[32] Even more pointedly, as Richard Cassidy notes,[33] the reader of Acts has been encouraged to regard Barnabas with great favor: as magnanimous (4:36-37), insightfully supportive of the newly converted Saul (9:26-27; 11:25-26), and, in Luke's own words, "a noble man, full of the Holy Spirit and of faith" (11:24a). To the reader of Acts, Barnabas's estrangement from Paul is both startling and distressing, especially since their breach is never repaired. Even though Paul functions as an agent of reconciliation elsewhere in the narrative (15:1-31; 16:3-4; 21:18-26), after Acts 15:36-40 no further contact between him and his closest colleague is ever reported.

Within the narrative, we are permitted access neither to Mark's motive for returning to Jerusalem (13:13b) nor to Barnabas's reason for reintegrating him into the missionary team (15:37). We are told what Paul thinks: that it was best not to take with them one who had resigned and had not participated with them "in the work" (εἰς τὸ ἔργον, 15:37). What is "the work" that (the Lukan) Paul has in mind? The absolute use of τὸ ἔργον occurs six times in Acts. The first, employed by Gamaliel in his cautionary speech to the Sanhedrin (5:38), is so vague in its reference that it is variously translated as "undertaking" (NRSV), "movement" (NJB), or "[an idea's] execution" (NEB). Often translated as "deed," the singular term also appears twice in 13:41, in a quotation from the LXX (Hab 1:5). The remaining occurrences in Acts of τὸ ἔργον are all relatively proximate to one another: 13:2, referring to that work for which Barnabas and Saul were specially set apart by the Holy Spirit; 14:26, regarding that work which those two missionaries fulfilled in Cyprus, Pamphylia, Pisidia, and Galatia; and 15:38, the work from which

---

[32]Consult Howard Clark Kee, *Good News to the Ends of the Earth: The Theology of Acts* (London: SCM; Philadelphia: Trinity Press International, 1990) 86-89.

[33]Richard J. Cassidy, *Society and Politics in the Acts of the Apostles* (Maryknoll NY: Orbis, 1987) 26, 66-67, 190n.38.

John Mark recoiled. Evidently, the particular "work" that Luke has in mind is the propagation of faith even among Gentiles, the door to which God had opened (thus the climax of Paul's first missionary journey at 14:27; see also 10:1–11:18). If that is the case, then it is this same work that, in Paul's (read Luke's) estimation, John Mark rebuffed. And if that is how Acts 15:38 is to be understood, then its conventional interpretation misses the bull's-eye by a considerable margin: in Luke's judgment, the problem with John Mark would be not that he simply "threw in the towel." Rather, Mark recalcitrantly had given up on a Christian mission extended to Gentiles as well as to Jews.[34]

Several scraps of circumstantial evidence seem to buttress this conclusion. First, even though Acts tells us precious little about Mark, clearly he is a Jerusalemite with undeniable sympathy for that city (12:13, 25; 13:13b). Through his civic affiliation, Mark (better known by his Jewish name, John; 13:5b), is thus associated with the locus for the Judaizing party: those who held the position, "Unless you are circumcised according to Moses' custom, you cannot be saved" (Acts 15:1; cf. Gal 2:12). Indeed, throughout the second half of the narrative in Acts, no little tension is generated by observant Jews or Jewish Christians who repeatedly oppose Paul's liberal mission among Gentiles.[35] Second, we have learned of Mark's assistance of his apostolic mentors in the context of proclamation in Jewish synagogues (Acts 13:5); precisely at the point where a Gentile proconsul is converted, John Mark withdraws from their mission, back to Jerusalem (13:6-13). Third, immediately preceding Mark's reentry into the narrative is the articulation of a plan of communion between Christian Jews and Gentiles, endorsed by the apostles in Jerusalem and joyously confirmed at Antioch (15:1-35). Fourth, immediately following the apostolic estrangement over John Mark in 15:36-39, Paul forms a new missionary team (15:40–16:5). In place of Barnabas, he enlists Silas, a believer from among the leading Jerusalemites (15:22b, 27, 32). Into the position of assistance formerly occupied by John Mark

---

[34]While the extension of God's salvation to Gentiles appears to have been the particular impetus for John Mark's resignation, Robert L. Brawley correctly emphasizes that Paul's mission in Acts is not restricted to Gentiles, since many Jews accept the preaching of Paul and Barnabas (13:42-43; 14:1, 27). See Brawley, *Text to Text Pours Forth Speech: Voices of Scripture in Luke-Acts*, Indiana Studies in Biblical Literature (Bloomington and Indianapolis: Indiana University Press, 1995) 169n.37.

[35]See Lawrence M. Will's perceptive discussion, "The Depiction of the Jews in Acts," *JBL* 110 (1991): 631-54, esp. 640-43.

steps Timothy (16:1-5), whose mixed parentage symbolizes the ethnic alliance of Jews and Gentiles that, in Luke's judgment, should be the wave of Christianity's future.

To be sure, Luke could have been more direct, and much of the preceding is speculative. But if my conjecture be accepted, then the trouble with John Mark in Acts 15:35-40 entails something more profound than a character flaw or lapse of judgment. In effect, Mark may represent in Acts an aborted future for Christianity: a religious outgrowth of Judaism that stubbornly remained within the confines of old Israel. If so, then the narrative of Acts would suggest a mitigated tragedy, not only for an Israel that largely rejected a message of the fulfillment of its most cherished hopes,[36] but also for early Christianity—one of whose forms may have been stunted, being too closely wedded to an ethnically exclusivist conceptualization of that hope.

But would Luke have us infer that Barnabas, Mark's advocate (15:37-39), supported a position so parochial and ultimately unavailing? Does not Luke persistently present Barnabas as a mediating figure between Jews and Gentiles, between Jerusalem and Antioch (Acts 11:19-30; 13:1-28; 15:1-35)?

This, indeed, is the case and perhaps helps us to appreciate the poignancy of the episode in Acts 15:35-40. From his initial appearances at 4:32-36 and 9:26-27, Barnabas has been sympathetically portrayed by Luke as a "son of encouragement," the defender of underdogs, the standard-bearer of Christian unity and generosity. If, however, we have rightly construed John Mark's role in Acts, then the character of Barnabas is situated, in Acts 15:35-40, on the horns of a dilemma from which he cannot escape being impaled. If Barnabas cast his lot with Paul (another Jew with missionary proclivities toward Gentiles) and split with John Mark, whose sympathies were narrower, then the Christian enterprise would be internally fractured. If he broke with Paul and sided with Mark (as, for probably different reasons, he had once stood beside Paul [9:26-30]), the result would be precisely the same. Luke may not have known Paul's account, similar though not identical, of the apostolic row at Antioch over the question of Jewish relations with Gentiles (Gal 2:11-

---

[36]Robert C. Tannehill, "Israel in Luke-Acts: A Tragic Story," *JBL* 104 (1985): 69-85. On the exegetical debate attending Luke's perception of the Jews, consult Joseph B. Tyson, ed., *Luke-Acts and the Jewish People: Eight Critical Perspectives* (Minneapolis: Augsburg, 1988).

14). Acts 15:35-40, however, whispers something of the same painful and perhaps unresolved controversy, dramatized in terms of Barnabas's effective ensnarement in a tactically divisive, and unavoidable, Catch-22. Perhaps it is just for this reason that Luke handles the split between Paul and Barnabas over John Mark with such a light touch: in 15:35-40, as in 15:1-5, we encounter one of the few instances in Acts where opposition to Christianity's future is expressed "in-house" by other, more traditionally observant, Jewish Christians. Unlike the Jerusalem controversy, which ended in a compromise satisfactory to all (the apostolic decree in Acts 15:22-35), here we find a fracture within the Christian movement that proved immediately if not indefinitely irreparable.[37]

For reasons left inexplicit, yet in a manner consistent with his character in Acts, Barnabas separates from Paul and takes Mark back to Cyprus. With the benefit of hindsight, we may now understand why, since chapter 13, the pronounced leadership of Barnabas has been subtly receding: that character is preparing to vanish entirely, his place in the narrative to be assumed by his colleague, Paul. As commentators regularly observe,[38] a positive outcome may be intimated by this sad state of affairs: with the division between Barnabas and Paul and their respective entourages, from Luke's point of view the Gentile mission may have been effectively doubled. Though such an ironically providential twist would cohere with his theology, evidenced elsewhere,[39] in fact Luke is not utterly clear about this prospect: while considered Gentile territory, Cyprus has been previously missionized (13:4-12), and no itinerary beyond that island is suggested for Barnabas and John Mark. On the contrary, these two characters completely fade out of the narrative, never to be smoothly reconciled with the evangelical mission thereafter associated with Paul. The same could be said, both historically and theologically, for the narrower vision with which John Mark appears to have been associated.

---

[37]In private correspondence (6 March 1991) Beverly R. Gaventa has commented on a cognate contrast between the antagonists in Acts 15 and those in Acts 5:1-11 and 8:9-24: "Perhaps Luke treats Mark (and Barnabas) with such care because they are not villains in the blatant sense [that Ananias, Sapphira, and Simon Magus are]. [Mark and Barnabas] are reputable members of the community, whose position (on the Gentile mission) Luke will not endorse."

[38]Among others, see Bruce, *Commentary on the Book of the Acts* (1954) 319; Haenchen, *The Acts of the Apostles*, 474; and Achtemeier, *The Quest for Unity in the New Testament Church*, 42.

[39]See Acts 8:1 and 26:32, where persecution and imprisonment become vehicles for the gospel's dissemination.

II. Concluding Observations

In the Book of Acts John Mark plays a minor but highly suggestive role.

1. He is patently associated with the early Christian community at Jerusalem (12:12; 13:13), perhaps latently aligned with the piety and wealth of those among its number (12:12).

2. He is directly associated with Barnabas and Paul, at whose invitation he renders general service at the start of their first mission to Cyprus (12:25; 13:5). He is not expressly kin to Barnabas (cf. Col 4:10), nor is he directly or indirectly linked with Peter (though the latter repairs to the home of Mark's mother, Mary: 12:12; cf. 1 Pet 5:13).

3. He is implicitly connected with the Christian mission exercised within Jewish synagogues (13:5) and implicitly detached from the broader sweep of that mission among Gentiles (13:13; 15:38).

4. In general, John Mark is cast in an obscure (13:5, 13) or outrightly derogatory light (15:38-39), arguably owing (in Luke's view) to his reticence or refusal to engage in Paul's missionary labors among Gentiles. Evidently for this reason, in Luke's account, he is the cause of the breakup between Barnabas and Paul (15:39b-40).

5. With his patron, Barnabas, John Mark disappears from the Lukan narrative after chapter 15, never to return.

These results prompt some general reflections. First, although it has proved tempting to blend elements from Acts and the New Testament letters, consolidating them into a unitary image of John Mark—the Jewish-Christian backslider who, with his cousin's help, returned to the Pauline and Petrine fold[40]—that temptation probably should be resisted. From this analysis there has emerged no evidence whatever that Luke was knowledgeable of, much less dependent on, Pauline (Phlm 24), Deutero-Pauline (Col 4:10; 2 Tim 4:11), or Petrine (1 Pet 5:13) sources for his portrayal of Mark as an apostolic associate.[41]

Second, although the Lukan Mark lacks sharp definition, and the reader of Acts must work hard to discern this character's significance, it

---

[40]In recent scholarship observe the tendencies of Pierson Parker, "The Authorship of the Second Gospel," *PerRS* 5 (1978): 4-9, and Clayton N. Jefford, "Mark, John," in *ABD* (1992) 4:557-58.

[41]For all of their sketchiness, the various depictions of Mark in the New Testament manifest the superficial similarity and distinctive differences that would be expected of documents that appear to have been literarily independent of one another, yet traditionally interrelated at some level. See Black, *Mark: Images of an Apostolic Interpreter*, 50-73.

can scarcely be doubted that John Mark's primary role in Acts is that of counterpoint for its principal characters. Through Mark's presence and behavior, Luke subtly discloses or confirms the values and purposes of Barnabas, Paul, and even God, who through the Holy Spirit initiates and sustains their missionary program.

Finally, if the outcomes of this essay hold, then the ambivalence toward Judaism within Luke-Acts, noted by this volume's honoree,[42] is not the only intra-religious tension that pulses within this literature. John Mark and Paul, with Barnabas caught somewhere betwixt, appear in Acts to represent conflicting visions of early Christianity: one so firmly committed to the significance of Jesus Christ for the Jewish people that it prescinded from outreach beyond Israel; the other acknowledging an open door of faith for both Jews and Gentiles, in fulfillment of God's restoration of Israel. Although Luke's heart lies with the second, his account remembers John Mark and thus laments, without denying, the existence of the first.

---

[42]Tyson, *Images of Judaism in Luke-Acts*, esp. 187-89.

Irenic or Ironic?
Another Look at Gamaliel
before the Sanhedrin (Acts 5:33-42)

John A. Darr

I. Introduction

The Gamaliel of Acts has fared remarkably well in the hands of most ancient and modern Christian interpreters. The Pharisee who was esteemed by all the people (Acts 5:34), who dissuaded the Sanhedrin from executing the apostles (5:35-40), and who educated Saul in Jewish law (22:3), has long been treated as a treasured character in the Christian imagination. As construed by the vast majority of exegetes, Gamaliel straddles that indistinct but strategic boundary between nascent Christianity and formative Judaism, a station fairly brimming with apologetic and ecumenical potential in Christianity's ongoing attempts to define itself in relation to the other descendants of second temple Judaism.

In Origen's *Contra Celsus*, for example, Gamaliel is a paragon of open-mindedness and wisdom, a model of the sage Jewish teacher and leader who (unlike Origen's opponent) does not simply presume that Christian doctrine is heretical, but rather gives "extremely wise" counsel to fellow Jews to remain open to the possibility of Christianity's correctness (57). The *Recognitions of Clement* goes further, portraying Gamaliel as a closet believer to whom the apostles grant a special dispensation to remain on the council as a Christian spy and advocate (1.65-71).[1] Luke's picture of Gamaliel has so fired the Christian imagination that some

---

[1] Such developments are clear examples of narrative breeding narrative, a significant phenomenon in the development of the gospel tradition, and of Christian traditions in general. Characters in particular seem to elicit new stories among curious, creative readers/(re)writers. Such rewriting and fleshing out of intriguing characters are not that different from what interpreters have always done (Frank Kermode, *The Genesis of Secrecy: On the Interpretation of Narrative* [Cambridge MA: Harvard University Press, 1979] 99).

authors have even written gospels under the Pharisaic leader's name.[2] For what better witness to Jesus' passion and resurrection could one wish?

This virtual canonization of Luke's Gamaliel is continued by many recent interpreters. He is "the genuine Jew on the verge of affirming Christianity."[3] Like the Pharisees at Paul's later ordeal before the council (Acts 23:1-10), he is a heroic defender of Christians and, in fact, is favorably inclined toward them.[4] Although Gamaliel is not a Christian, he is still "a person of insight and reason" who "serves as spokesman for the implied author."[5] Indeed, he speaks "with an authority that is heard by the members of the Sanhedrin and by the reader as well," for "his words approximate the ideological point of view of the narrator."[6] Gamaliel and a few of his fellow Pharisees in Luke's second volume provide a valuable counterweight to Luke's otherwise bleak and incriminating portrayal of official Judaism. They are bright spots in Luke's portrayal of Judaism because, unlike other Jewish leaders, they "could hardly behave better toward Christians if they were the Church's fairy godmother."[7] They stand for the courageous but bygone "bridge" generation of Jews who link Gentile Christianity to its ancestral Jewish roots, or for the "ideal" Jews of Luke's own day, that is, those who relate openly, irenically, and sympathetically to both Jewish and Gentile Christians.[8]

---

[2]On the (so-called) "Gospel of Gamaliel," parts of which are embedded in a larger Coptic writing, see Marcus Antonius van den Oudenrijn, "The Gospel of Gamaliel," *New Testament Apocrypha*, ed. Edgar Hennecke and Wilhelm Schneemelcher, 2 vols. (Philadelphia: Westminster, 1963) 1:508-10. The urge to view Gamaliel as a sympathetic witness and evangelist appeals to moderns as well. Gerald Heard's novel, written from the point of view of the Pharisaic leader, is a good case in point (*The Gospel according to Gamaliel* [New York: Harper and Brothers, 1945]).

[3]Robert L. Brawley, *Luke-Acts and the Jews: Conflict, Apology, and Conciliation*, SBLMS 23 (Atlanta: Scholars Press, 1987) 98.

[4]David A. Neale, *None But the Sinners: Religious Categories in the Gospel of Luke*, JSNTSup 58 (Sheffield: JSOT Press, 1991) 104, refers to the representation of Pharisees in Acts as "almost heroic." J. A. Ziesler, "Luke and the Pharisees," *NTS* 25 (1978–1979): 147, argues that Gamaliel's speech is "plainly friendly to the Christians."

[5]Robert C. Tannehill, *The Narrative Unity of Luke-Acts: A Literary Interpretation*, 2 vols. (Philadelphia and Minneapolis: Fortress, 1986, 1990) 2:66-67.

[6]David B. Gowler, *Host, Guest, Enemy, and Friend: Portraits of the Pharisees in Luke and Acts* (New York: Peter Lang, 1991) 279.

[7]Jack T. Sanders, *The Jews in Luke-Acts* (Philadelphia: Fortress, 1987) 111.

[8]The former argument is made by Sanders, *The Jews in Luke-Acts*, 112-30. The latter view belongs to Robert L. Brawley, "The Pharisees in Luke-Acts: Luke's Address to Jews and His Irenic Purpose" (Ph.D. diss., Princeton University, 1978) 13; and *Luke-Acts and the Jews*, 84-106. Such readings are simplistically allegorical and are based on highly questionable apriori assumptions about Luke's actual social and religious environment.

It can hardly be denied that Gamaliel's actions and speech at the trial of the apostles have some positive implications. He courageously resists the momentum of mob violence that grips his fellow council members. His discourse encouraging a patient, wait-and-see attitude is a model of practical wisdom for all religious and political leaders who must deal with upstart sects. Whatever we might speculate about Gamaliel's motivations, his actions within the drama do result in a reduced sentence and (ultimately) emancipation for the protagonists. But do these patent observations warrant the overwhelmingly positive evaluations of Luke's Gamaliel so common among Christian critics? Would one of Luke's intended readers, who, like the implied author, "followed everything carefully from the beginning" (Luke 1:3) be likely to applaud Gamaliel after reading about him in Acts 5:33-41 (and again in 22:3)? Bucking conventional wisdom, several scholars have recently begun to argue against the notion that the Gamaliel episode (Acts 5:33-42) casts the Pharisaic leader in a good light.[9] None of these critics has devoted a full study to Gamaliel in Acts (their comments have all been made in the course of treating larger issues or passages), but their observations point in a common direction. When viewed in its broader narrative context and subjected to a close reading, the account of Gamaliel before the Sanhedrin proves to be fraught with irony that strongly calls into question laudatory evaluations of the Pharisaic leader. The purpose of this study is to buttress and confirm these discrete, preliminary suggestions of an ironic depiction of Gamaliel in Acts by providing a fuller and more focused analysis of the evidence.

II. The Reader and the Rhetoric of Irony

Like humor, irony is difficult to define. Perhaps a good place to begin is a basic dictionary definition: irony is "the dramatic effect achieved by

---

They betray modern ecumenical and apologetic concerns that cannot be demonstrated to have existed in Luke's context.

[9]Luke T. Johnson, *The Literary Function of Possessions in Luke-Acts* (Missoula MT: Scholars Press, 1977) 116-17n.3, 197-98; and *The Acts of the Apostles*, Sacra Pagina 5 (Collegeville MN: Liturgical, 1992) 102-103; Brian E. Beck, *Christian Character in the Gospel of Luke* (London: Epworth, 1989) 130-44; Jack Dean Kingsbury, "The Pharisees in Luke-Acts," in *The Four Gospels 1992: Festschrift Frans Neirynck*, ed. Frans van Segbroeck et al., 3 vols., BETL 100 (Leuven: Leuven University Press, 1992) 2:1503-1507; and John A. Darr, *On Character Building: The Reader and the Rhetoric of Characterization in Luke-Acts*, LCBI (Louisville: Westminster/John Knox, 1992) 116-20.

leading an audience to understand an incongruity between a situation and the accompanying speeches, while the characters in the play remain un-aware of the incongruity."[10] While this definition is geared to the theater, it is entirely apropos to narratives like the one before us. Whether pointed or subtle, irony always involves different levels of knowledge between the reader and the characters in the story. The reader, who is prompted by the narrator and who is privy to "insider" information, knows much more than do most characters. Thus the reader is often able to detect disparities (frequently tinged with humor or paradox) between what a character says, does, or thinks, and what a true understanding of the circumstances or significance of their situation merits.

The power of irony lies in its ability to strengthen the reader's identification with the narrator and, concomitantly, to distance the reader from certain characters ("We know more than they do"). Successful irony always reaffirms the superiority of the narrative's dominant point of view, and it does so at the expense of unwitting characters. What Mary Ann Tolbert says about the rhetoric of irony in Mark applies equally well to Luke-Acts:

> If irony serves to bind more closely together the audience and the narrator . . . by underscoring their joint knowledge and point of view, it also serves to distance the audience from the witless victims of irony, whether they be high priests or disciples. The rhetorical effect of irony, then, is twofold: it builds and strengthens community among those with superior knowledge, and it excludes and denigrates those with inferior knowledge. It thus appears to be a very appropriate literary strategy for a Gospel so seemingly concerned with "insiders" and "outsiders."[11]

Like the other New Testament narratives, Luke-Acts is suffused with irony. The irony of these early Christian stories is fueled by the notion that, although the ultimate revelation of God has occurred in the recent past (in Jesus), those who should have most readily recognized it did not, while those who should not have recognized it did. In other words, the criterion for distinguishing between insiders and outsiders is perception: those who truly see and hear are insiders, while those who merely look and listen are outsiders, regardless of gender, ethnicity, religious affilia-

---

[10]*American Heritage Dictionary of the English Language* (Boston: Houghton Mifflin, 1969) 692a.

[11]Mary Ann Tolbert, *Sowing the Gospel: Mark's World in Literary-Historical Perspective* (Minneapolis: Fortress, 1989) 103.

tion, or age. This failure of the supposed insiders to perceive the revelation provides prime territory for irony—particularly when read in light of Isaiah 6:9; and the evangelists take full advantage of it. Each gospel plays off the basic ironic structure in discrete ways, with different characters or groups playing the roles of insiders and outsiders. In Mark, for example, the disciples, whom one would expect to be the ultimate insiders, end up playing the role of imperceptive outsiders. By the end of the story, Peter and his comrades have misunderstood, betrayed, denied, and abandoned Jesus, despite being privy to more information than any other characters. Matthew and Luke take pains to rehabilitate the disciples in their accounts and make them (still somewhat ironic) learners rather than complete failures. Perhaps the only consistent feature among the evangelists with regard to perceptional irony involves the depiction of the Jewish leadership groups as obtuse, although even here one must be attentive to important nuances among the gospels. The Pharisees in Luke are not identical to the Pharisees in Matthew, John, or Mark; each group character requires analysis within its own literary context.

In order to recognize irony in a particular episode of Luke-Acts, therefore, we must be aware of the insider knowledge sequentially accumulated by the reader to that point in the narrative.[12] We must also be alert to those signals in the passage which prompt readers to access and apply this cache of privileged information. Four cues in Acts 5:33-42 trigger the reader into retrospection that encourages a construal of Gamaliel as problematic rather than heroic, oblivious rather than insightful, ironic rather than irenic. In order of appearance, these cues are: (1) a note that Gamaliel was a member of the Sanhedrin; (2) a description of him as Pharisee and teacher of the law (νομοδιδάσκαλος; 5:34); (3) an observation that he was "held in honor by all the people" (5:34); and (4) Gamaliel's speech, especially his references to other messianic movements and the plan (βουλή; 5:38-39) of God. These indicators bring to mind prior narrative phenomena steeped in irony, and so predispose the reader to view Acts 5:33-42 ironically as well. In what follows, we shall

---

[12]My argument depends heavily on the assumption that Luke and Acts form a narrative unity when read in sequence. The unity of Luke and Acts remains the dominant scholarly view, despite recent questioning (Mikeal C. Parsons and Richard I. Pervo, *Rethinking the Unity of Luke and Acts* [Minneapolis: Fortress, 1993]). A full articulation of the pragmatic (audience-oriented) methodology utilized here appears in Darr, *On Character Building*, 16-59.

examine each of these cues in turn, and ask about their implications for an ironic perception of Gamaliel.

III. Unwitting Witness: Gamaliel as Council Member

By the time the reader encounters the Gamaliel episode of Acts 5:33-42 within the narrative continuum of Luke-Acts, the Sanhedrin is firmly established as a highly ironic character group. Irony surrounds the council because of its prior interactions with both Jesus and the apostles. This atmosphere of irony strongly conditions how the reader evaluates Gamaliel and his speech. Thus, a brief retrospection on the Sanhedrin is appropriate for the reader (and for us).

A. Jesus' Hearing before the Sanhedrin (Luke 22:66-71)

Two aspects of Luke's unique version of this incident are significant for our purposes. First, Luke depicts the whole assembly of the Sanhedrin as participating in the hostile questioning of Jesus. This depiction is a radical departure from Mark's report that the high priest alone posed the accusatory questions (Mark 14:60-64).[13] From the perspective of character theory, Luke's depiction encourages the reader to view the council as a collective character. Readers already have a proclivity to build group characters synecdochically; by presenting the Sanhedrin as querying Jesus in concert, Luke reinforces the reader's tendency to construe the council consistently, homogeneously, and collectively.[14] Unless directly countermanded by the narrator, another authoritative voice (Jesus), or other contradictory information, the reader will continue to build consistency by imputing group traits to individual members and, reciprocally, individual members' traits to the group.[15]

A close reading of the narrative reveals that neither the narrator nor any other authoritative textual evidence serves to dissociate Gamaliel from the Sanhedrin and its decisions concerning Jesus and his followers. This lack of dissociation is particularly conspicuous when Gamaliel is juxtaposed with another council member, Joseph of Arimathea. The

---

[13]Frank J. Matera, "Luke 22,66-71: Jesus before the ΠΡΕΣΒΥΤΕΡΙΟΝ," *ETL* 65 (1989): 47.

[14]Rudolf Bultmann, *The History of the Synoptic Tradition*, trans. John Marsh, rev. ed. (New York: Harper and Row, 1968; [1]1963) 188, in his discussion of the synoptic similitudes, pointed out the common practice of construing groups of people as a single person in these compact narratives.

[15]Darr, *On Character Building*, 93-94.

reader is prompted to compare and contrast Gamaliel and Joseph because they are the only two council members who are individuated in the narrative. In other words, the individualization of just two constituents of this group triggers σύγκρισις (comparison and contrast of somewhat similar characters), an ubiquitous and firmly entrenched Greco-Roman literary convention.[16] The fact that Luke assumes his readers are familiar with σύγκρισις (and so expects them to draw upon it at appropriate junctures) is incontrovertible given his strong reliance on this convention in the paralleling of John the Baptist and Jesus, especially in the infancy narratives of Luke 1–2.[17] Joseph is described by the narrator as "a member of the council, who was a good and righteous man (he had not agreed to their plan or deed) . . . and who waited for the kingdom of God" (23:50-51). The adjectival phrase "good and righteous" (ἀγαθὸς καὶ δίκαιος) clearly refers to primary narrative values in Luke-Acts. Furthermore, the note that Joseph anticipated the kingdom of God identifies him as one of Luke's "insiders." The parenthesis (or narrative aside) draws attention to and emphasizes the importance of Joseph's disagreement with both the planning and the execution of the Sanhedrin's actions against Jesus. By contrast, Gamaliel receives no commendation from the narrator except the ambiguous note that the people honored him (see below); nor is he exculpated of the council's "plans and deeds" regarding Jesus and the apostles. In lieu of any indication to the contrary, therefore, the reader is very likely to associate Gamaliel with the council, to implicate him in the Sanhedrin's prior decisions and its overall anti-Christian agenda, and to anticipate that his actions and speech will be consistent with his group's characterization to this point in the narrative.[18] The latter point is especially significant because anticipation strongly conditions the reader's actualization of any newly encountered narrative unit.[19]

---

[16]Contra Steve Mason, "Chief Priests, Sadducees, Pharisees, and Sanhedrin in Acts," in *The Book of Acts in Its Palestinian Setting*, ed. Richard Bauckham, The Book of Acts in Its First Century Setting 4 (Grand Rapids MI: Eerdmans, 1995) 151, who dismisses the comparison of Gamaliel and Joseph out of hand.

[17]Darr, *On Character Building*, 66-68. This phenomenon has been observed by many interpreters.

[18]Darr, *On Character Building*, 118.

[19]Redaction critics and most narratologists, who often hold a static notion of the literary work, still have not awakened to the necessity of interpreting episodes in terms of sequential reading activity, or what we might call narrative flow.

Second, as John P. Heil has amply demonstrated, ironies permeate the interaction of the Sanhedrin with Jesus in Luke.[20] Three of these ironies have special importance for our inquiry:

(1) The council's actions are patently ironic. The gathering of "elders, chief priests, and scribes" to interrogate and condemn Jesus is intended to thwart the charismatic Jesus and his movement. This gathering is no open and equitable inquiry; it has been plotted for some time (Luke 20:19-20; 22:4-5). What the Sanhedrin does not know—but the reader does know—is that Jesus has predicted that precisely these types would gather against him, and further, that their antagonistic action is necessary for him to achieve his ultimate agenda: "The Son of man must suffer many things, and be rejected by the elders and chief priests and scribes, and be killed, and be raised up on the third day" (9:22). By collaborating in his execution they are, paradoxically, abetting him by setting the stage for his resurrection and exaltation to the right hand of God (22:69), from which position he will then judge them! The audience thus realizes that the plan of God is to be fulfilled both in spite of and because of the malevolent opposition of the Sanhedrin.[21]

(2) The council's speech is ironic. What they say concerning Jesus' identity can be construed as affirming the opposite of what they intend. Lest the reader miss this rather subtle irony, the Lukan Jesus points it out. Following Jesus' implicit claim to be the Son of man who will sit at the right hand of the power of God (Luke 22:69), the entire (πάντες) Sanhedrin says, Σὺ οὖν εἶ ὁ υἱὸς τοῦ θεοῦ (22:70a). This clause can be understood as either interrogative ("Are you, then, the Son of God?") or declarative ("Then you are the Son of God"). Rather than depending upon conjectures about the council members' voice inflection or textual punctuation, the reader is urged to consider the literary context of this remark to determine its grammatical mood and narrative function. Jesus' immediate response, "You [emphatic] say that I am," certainly assumes that their utterance is in some sense declarative rather than strictly interrogative; at the very least, his sharp rejoinder plays off the syntactical ambiguity by pointing up that their words could well be taken as confirming his divine provenance.[22] The reader, therefore, would con-

---

[20]John P. Heil, "Reader-Response and the Irony of Jesus before the Sanhedrin in Luke 22:66-71," *CBQ* 51 (1979): 271-84. Much of this section is dependent on Heil's insightful study.

[21]Heil, "Jesus before the Sanhedrin," 277-80.

[22]Joseph A. Fitzmyer, *The Gospel according to Luke: A New Translation with Intro-*

strue this aspect of the episode as follows: in an attempt to trap Jesus into explicitly affirming his divine sonship, the Sanhedrin itself formulates the logical conclusion to Jesus' preceding remarks concerning the Son of man. From Jesus' perspective, their utterance is not to be taken as a question, but as a peremptory declaration (albeit with accusatory overtones) meant to elicit assent on Jesus' part. Instead of responding directly to this (supposedly) incriminating statement, however, Jesus chooses to point out that, ironically, they have just professed what they do not believe (but what the reader knows to be true). In the verbal jousting of the Sanhedrin hearing, therefore, the one who was supposed to be trapped by his own words (20:20) ensnares his interlocutors in the net of their words.

(3) The Sanhedrin's exultant rhetorical question caps its attempts to get Jesus to say something that can incriminate him: "What more witness (μαρτυρίας) do we need, for we ourselves have heard (it) from his own lips?" Unlike Mark, Luke has no false witnesses appear before the council. Jesus alone bears witness, but this witness bears the seeds of irony.[23] What the council believes to be evidence for condemnation—Jesus' implicit claim to be Christ and Son of God—the reader knows to be evidence for belief. The clueless members of the council, "in seeking to condemn Jesus as a false Christ, are actually condemning themselves of failure to believe in Jesus as the true Christ."[24] Although they observe the one who is the ultimate revelation, they fail to recognize him. Unwitting witnesses, they look and look, but do not see, they listen and listen, but do not hear (see Isa 6:9).[25]

---

duction and Commentary, 2 vols., AB 28, 28A (Garden City NY: Doubleday, 1981, 1985) 2:1468, understands Jesus' response as an ironic "half-yes" that "implies an affirmation, yet stresses that it is their [the Sanhedrin's] way of putting it."

[23]Matera, "Jesus before the ΠΡΕΣΒΥΤΕΡΙΟΝ," 56-57.

[24]Heil, "Jesus before the Sanhedrin," 278.

[25]The rhetorical structure of Luke-Acts is built entirely around the concept of witnessing. The ideal character (and the ideal reader) is a true witness, one who recognizes and responds correctly to the divine revelation and then faithfully and boldly reports it to others (John A. Darr, "Narrator as Character: Mapping a Reader-Oriented Approach to Narration in Luke-Acts," *Semeia* 63 [1993]: 56-57). That the Sanhedrin is oblivious is confirmed by Jesus' criticism of them, "If I tell you, you will not believe; and if I ask you, you will not answer" (Luke 22:67b-68).

B. The Apostles and the Sanhedrin (Acts 4:5-22; 5:17-42)

The council's tragic imperceptibility (with its attendant ironies) is reiterated and reinforced in the early part of Acts. Although convinced that they "need no more witness" (Luke 22:71) concerning Jesus, its members get exactly that. The risen Lord specifically characterizes his apostles as his witnesses (Luke 24:48; Acts 1:8b), and they identify themselves in the same manner before the Sanhedrin (5:32). The apostles, represented by Peter and John, are arrested and bear witness before the council on two separate occasions. In both cases Peter boldly implicates the leaders in Jesus' death and delivers unambiguous testimony concerning God's choice of Jesus as savior (4:8-12; 5:29-32). Unlike Jesus' elliptical testimony, the apostles' witness is direct and unequivocal. There can be no excuse for misunderstanding it, and yet the reader is given no indication that the council recognizes and responds to their message of salvation. At the end of the first hearing, the Sanhedrin threatens the apostles, orders them not to speak or teach in Jesus' name, and then releases them. The narrator makes clear that the release of the apostles is due to neither mercy nor respect, but is motivated out of fear of the people, who have become enamored with the apostles' miracles (4:17-21). At the second hearing, the high priest charges the apostles with intending "to bring this man's blood upon us" (5:28), clearly an ironic statement since the reader knows that the leaders bear responsibility in the matter. Peter promptly obliges the council by accusing them of hanging Jesus on a tree.[26] The upshot of this second hearing is that the council is ready to execute the apostles and so reprise a regrettable action they have just sought to repudiate (5:33)! Once again, absolutely no indication is given that the Sanhedrin has recognized the divine message despite being confronted directly with it. To the contrary, as seen in the leaders' ironic speech and behavior, they seem bent on perpetuating their unwitting antagonism. This antagonism sets the stage for Gamaliel's dramatic speech.

In summary, the Sanhedrin has been depicted consistently as a group character. To the reader, the council members appear to have acted in unison to harass and ensnare both Jesus and his followers. Apart from Joseph of Arimathea, none of the individual council members (including Gamaliel) has sought to counter their strong opposition to the new move-

---

[26]Johnson, *The Acts of the Apostles*, 102.

ment. Unbeknownst to the council, its opposition actually furthers the agenda of its messianic opponents. Ironically, the leaders' speeches sometimes contradict and implicate themselves. Thus, the reader brings these significant facets of the reading lens (or "context of expectations") to Acts 5:33-42. Unless Gamaliel is depicted in an extremely idiosyncratic manner (which he is not), the reader will look for ways in which he perpetuates the Sanhedrin's ironic roles of antagonist and facilitator, accuser and "unwitting witness."

IV. Obtuse Observer:
Gamaliel as Pharisee and Teacher of the Law

Scholarly interest in Luke's Pharisees has burgeoned in recent years, with lively debates developing especially among biblical literary critics.[27] All agree that Luke has a particular interest in the Pharisees and that their role is significant, but the nature and function of their narrative portrayal are disputed. This is not the place for a complete study of the Pharisees in Luke-Acts; their ubiquity precludes such an effort in this essay.[28] Instead, I wish simply to bring forward aspects of the Lukan Pharisees' characterization that bear directly on our subject: (1) their consistent portrayal as a group character; (2) their obtuseness as a primary trait; and (3) their didactic function as a paradigm of many of the story's anti-values.

Luke takes pains to reinforce the reader's perception of the Pharisees as a collective character, just as he did with the Sanhedrin (see above). The Pharisees and teachers of the law make a sweeping entry into the story; Pharisaic representatives from every village in the regions of Jesus' ministry (Galilee, Judea, and Jerusalem) are on hand when Jesus heals the paralytic (Luke 5:17-26). Furthermore, the narrator presents this geographically diverse group as united in their response to Jesus, much as the Sanhedrin will be united in their later questioning of him. These cues

---

[27]A major catalyst for recent study of the Pharisees (including my own efforts) has been the pioneering work of Professor Joseph B. Tyson. See esp. "The Opposition to Jesus in the Gospel of Luke," *PerRS* 5 (1978): 144-50; "Conflict as a Literary Theme in the Gospel of Luke," in *New Synoptic Studies: The Cambridge Gospel Conference and Beyond*, ed. William R. Farmer (Macon GA: Mercer University Press, 1983) 303-27; and (ed.) *Luke Acts and the Jewish People: Eight Critical Perspectives* (Minneapolis: Augsburg, 1988).

[28]See Darr, *On Character Building*, 85-126, where I provide a much fuller discussion of the portrayal, role, and function of the Pharisees in Luke-Acts.

at the beginning of the Pharisees' storyline encourage the reader consistently to construe the Pharisees as a group character throughout the remainder of the narrative. Furthermore, at critical junctures, the narrator and Jesus (the most authoritative voices in the text) promote this collective characterization of the Pharisees by criticizing them in general (11:39-44; 12:1-3; 16:14-15). When individual (or small parties of) Pharisees encounter Jesus, therefore, their behavior and speech will be understood as representative of the group; and, conversely, traits attributed to the larger group will accrue to individual members.[29]

The primary character trait of the Pharisees in Luke-Acts is spiritual obtuseness. Apart from the disciples, this leadership group is afforded more opportunity to see and hear Jesus than any other character or group. Yet they consistently fail to recognize and respond to him. Despite an intricate knowledge of the tradition and an almost obsessive curiosity with Jesus, they never quite "get" it. They are the great observers who never truly perceive, the scrutinizers who never recognize.[30] Their obliviousness is heightened by contrast with sinners and tax collectors who quickly comprehend and correctly respond to Jesus.[31] Luke does not hesitate to tap the inherent irony of this strange state of affairs. For example, even as Simon the Pharisee determines in his heart that Jesus cannot be a prophet (since he interacts with a sinful woman), Jesus proves himself to be a prophet by reading Simon's thoughts. Jesus then insinuates that it may well be Simon rather than the woman who is the outsider (Luke 7:39-47).[32]

---

[29]Darr, *On Character Building*, 93-94. In light of these textual cues and reading dynamics, efforts to identify discrete types of Pharisees in Luke-Acts appear misguided.

[30]Luke's idiosyncratic use of παρατηρέω and παρατήρησις regarding the Pharisees (Luke 6:7; 14:1; 17:20) is particularly telling (Darr, *On Character Building*, 98, 106, 112-13).

[31]Such reversals are ubiquitous in Luke (see Neale, *None But the Sinners*).

[32]Robert C. Tannehill, "Should We Love Simon the Pharisee? Hermeneutical Reflections on the Pharisees in Luke," *CurTM* 21 (1994): 432, notes that the Simon episode is open-ended, and makes a plea for us to view Simon more sympathetically, i.e., as one who is on a threshold of deciding for or against Jesus. This view is all but impossible to take, however, unless we agree to counter-read (or under-read) the text, or to diminish the authority of the narrator (see 430) and Jesus, both of whom severely condemn the Pharisees in general. It is not sufficient to point out a gap; one must also be prepared to take into consideration all textual cues and data for filling that gap, even if they do not result in readings conducive to modern preaching and the interpretive ideal of loving our neighbor (432-33). Tannehill tips his hand by appealing to contemporary homiletical and ecumenical concerns which are values in their own right, but may well be intrusive and dis-

The censure of the Pharisees is harsh and consistent, and culminates with Jesus' stinging condemnation of the group, a consequent rise in the level of their hostility toward Jesus and their plot to entrap Jesus (Luke 11:42-54). Later incidents which, if isolated from the narrative flow, would seem to reflect well on the Pharisees, actually assume a dark and ironic aspect. At 13:31-35, for example, when Pharisees advise Jesus to "go away and depart from here for Herod wants to kill you," the reader is likely to believe their report (based on prior textual data about the tetrarch) but distrusts their motives in delivering it. Given their hostility toward Jesus, they may well want him out of their territory.[33] From the perspective of one who has read the narrative sequentially, therefore, no positive value accrues to the Pharisees because of their warning of Jesus. Indeed, as Robert C. Tannehill insightfully observes, their advice is tinged with irony when read in the context of Jesus' response: surely he must "go," but he goes toward death (in Jerusalem) rather than away from it.[34] Once again, this irony plays off the reader's cognizance of God's plan over against the Pharisees' ignorance of it.

Luke's caricature of the Pharisees performs a valuable function: their hostility and obtuseness (and the ironies engendered thereby) discourage readers from themselves being resistant to and unperceiving of "the things fulfilled among us" (Luke 1:1). Put positively, the Pharisees are another of Luke's rhetorical devices for developing perceptive and receptive readers. In distancing itself from oblivious and recalcitrant Pharisees, the audience increasingly identifies with the narrative's dominant point of view and is encouraged to reject the anti-values exhibited by the

---

tortive to a literary-historical interpretation of Luke's late first-century writing.

[33]Darr, *On Character Building*, 105-106; concurring: Gowler, *Host, Guest, Enemy, and Friend*, 236-41; and Raymond E. Brown, *The Death of the Messiah: From Gethsemane to the Grave. A Commentary on the Passion Narratives in the Four Gospels*, 2 vols. (New York: Doubleday, 1994) 1:770. Joel B. Green, *The Theology of the Gospel of Luke* (Cambridge: Cambridge University Press, 1995) 73-74; and *The Gospel of Luke*, NICNT (Grand Rapids MI: Eerdmans, 1997) 537-38, argues against this reading by pointing out the need to take into account not only readerly anticipation, but also retrospection and the modifications it might entail. But Green appears to misconstrue the reading process by disregarding the "primacy effect," which holds that what comes first in a narrative conditions the reader's understanding of what comes later, and therefore, that the critic is to weigh earlier data more heavily than later information. That is, properly understood, a reader's retrospection is not neutral (as Green seems to assume), but rather is always strongly preconditioned by anticipation (Meir Sternberg, *Expositional Modes and Temporal Ordering in Fiction* (Baltimore: Johns Hopkins University Press, 1978) 93-96.

[34]Tannehill, *The Narrative Unity of Luke-Acts*, 1:196.

Pharisees: self-righteousness, greed, fraud, love of money, pride, lack of compassion, and so forth. In terms of the present study, the most significant shortcoming of the Pharisees is that they "rejected the plan [βουλή] of God for themselves" by refusing to undergo John's baptism (7:30). Without the baptism of repentance for the forgiveness of sins, it is impossible (in this story world) for a person to recognize the revelation of God in Jesus.

Before moving ahead, we must draw attention to the final dramatized incident involving Jesus and Pharisees. When, during the triumphal entry, the disciples acclaim Jesus as messiah, Pharisees ask Jesus to rebuke them (Luke 19:39). This request epitomizes Pharisaic hostility to the new movement. Although not necessarily violent in their opposition, they not only stubbornly refuse to see and hear for themselves, but also wish to suppress the witness to others. Their antagonism is not bloody like that of the high priests, scribes, and Sadducees, but their stance remains wholly inimical to the outworking of God's purpose on earth. The reader next encounters a Pharisee in Acts 5:34 with the introduction of Gamaliel. Will he break the strongly cast mold, or will he reprise the ironic obtuseness of the Pharisees exhibited in the first volume of Luke's narrative?

V. Gamaliel and the Vagaries of Honor by the People

Many critics view the narrator's remark that Gamaliel was "honored by all the people" (Acts 5:34) as establishing the Pharisaic leader's reliability in the mind of the reader. Even a cursory survey of how "the people" (λαός) have been characterized to this point, however, reveals the flaws in such a view. A holistic and sequential review of the narrative evidence confirms that the only consistent characteristic of the people in Luke-Acts is their inconsistency. They are a fickle lot, alternating quickly between supporting Jesus and his disciples and rejecting them. As the new movement begins to take hold in Jerusalem, the people respect it (2:47). At the same time, however, Peter soundly rebukes the people for their full participation in the condemnation and execution of Jesus (2:23, 36; 3:13; 4:27). In an ironic twist, Gamaliel himself underscores the capriciousness of the people by referring to their willingness to follow false prophets like Judas (5:37). Early on, Jesus warned his followers, "Woe to you when all men speak well of you, for so their fathers did to the false prophets" (Luke 6:26). Even more damning is Jesus' castigation of the Pharisees for seeking honor among people rather than with God

(Luke 16:15). Against this backdrop, one could even see attribution of honor by the people as a backhanded compliment, though we need not go that far. In short, Gamaliel may well be respected by the λαός, but the λαός are not respected by the reader. As virtual paradigms of unreliability, the people can by no means establish any other character's reliability. In conclusion, the narrator's note that Gamaliel was honored by the people does not establish Gamaliel as a reliable character, but rather explains why he carries weight in the Sanhedrin, which was sensitive to pressures from the populace (Acts 4:2, 21).[35]

VI. Gamaliel's Ironic Speech

Given the facts that Gamaliel is a Pharisee, teacher of the law, and member of the Sanhedrin, and that he has not been exculpated of the council's recent decisions and actions regarding Jesus and his followers, Luke's intended reader assumes that Gamaliel opposes the apostles and hopes for the demise of their movement. Furthermore, the one who reads the narrative sequentially has every reason to anticipate that Gamaliel will be spiritually oblivious to the divine revelation unfolding before him. The dynamic of consistency building encourages the reader to look first for ways in which these expectations of antagonism and obtuseness are fulfilled in Gamaliel's speech. Only if such indicators are absent, and specifically insightful and irenic signifiers also appear, will the reader consider construing Gamaliel's intent as conciliatory.

But, of course, the reader finds plenty of evidence confirming Gamaliel's spiritual blindness and belligerence toward Peter and his cohorts. First, Gamaliel ignores Peter's definitive testimony about Jesus being raised from the dead (Acts 5:29-32; see also 4:9-12); instead, the Pharisaic leader focuses on the issue of political strategy—how best to deal with the messy problem at hand. As we have seen, Lukan characters are evaluated largely in terms of how well they recognize and respond to divine revelation. Gamaliel receives poor marks on this score. Second, Gamaliel's speech posits distance rather than identification between himself and the apostles. He refers to the apostles three times as "these men" (5:34, 35, 38), but refers to his colleagues as "Men, Israelites" (5:35).[36] Third, the logic of his argument from historical antecedents

---

[35]Darr, *On Character Building*, 118.

[36]Kingsbury, "The Pharisees in Luke-Acts," 1505; also Rudolf Pesch, *Die Apostelgeschichte*, 2 vols., EKKNT 5 (Zürich: Neukirchener, 1986) 1:219.

draws an (implicit) analogy between the Christian messianic movement and two failed messianic movements.[37] Theudas and Judas arose, claimed to be something special, drew people unto themselves, and were destroyed. Then their movements dispersed and disappeared. The thrust of Gamaliel's argument, therefore, is that the Jesus movement, which went through similar developmental stages, will probably also disperse and disappear. If history tells us anything, says Gamaliel, the Christians have failure written all over them. The reader will note especially that Gamaliel puts forward no examples of successful movements (e.g., the Maccabees) as possible parallels to Jesus and his followers. Fourth, Gamaliel is not censured or ostracized in any way by members of the Sanhedrin. Instead, they take his advice, have the apostles lashed, and tell them once again not to witness. The council's response to that advice implies that, at least from their perspective, Gamaliel was not witnessing along with the apostles. He was simply advising the council to return to their prior strategy of threatening the apostles not to witness and then waiting for the movement to die out. This tactic is reminiscent of the Pharisees' attempt to throttle Jesus' disciples during the triumphal entry, and thereby reinforces the reader's sense of continuity between those Pharisees and this Pharisee (Gamaliel). In short, much evidence confirms the reader's expectations that Gamaliel would be obtuse and hostile.

Gamaliel's speech also fulfills other expectations of the reader about him. As a constituent of two character groups (the Pharisees and the Sanhedrin) that have been characterized as acting and speaking in highly ironic ways within the narrative thus far, Gamaliel can rightly be expected to voice ironies too. And indeed he does. Before indicating these ironies, however, we must debunk the widespread but misleading notion that the syntax of Gamaliel's conditional statements in Acts 5:38-39 proves that he is favorably inclined toward the apostles' claims concerning the divine origin of their movement. Relying on a questionable entry in Blass's and Debrunner's grammar,[38] many interpreters argue that the shift from ἐάν with the subjunctive in 5:38 ("if this plan or undertaking be from men") to εἰ with the indicative in 5:39 ("but if it be from God") denotes a movement in the speaker's mind from mere possibility ("it might be from men") to high probability or actual fact

---

[37]Darr, *On Character Building*, 120; Kingsbury, "The Pharisees in Luke-Acts," 1505; and Johnson, *The Acts of the Apostles*, 103.
[38]BDF 372.1.

("but it is of God").[39] Often cited to buttress this reasoning is the fact that εἰ plus the indicative can convey a causal force ("but because it is from God"). On the basis of that argument, for example, John T. Squires feels free to disregard the conditional mood altogether and assert that "Gamaliel . . . declares that what the apostles are doing is not a human undertaking (5:38), but is truly of God."[40]

A careful reappraisal of the evidence, however, reveals that Squires and his interpretive predecessors placed far too much weight on one of several possible readings of Gamaliel's statements. Conditional clauses are a notoriously complex and mutable aspect of Greek syntax; we should tread lightly here, especially when speculating about the reader's apprehension of a speaker's convictions about the reality of a set of conditions. In fact, Gamaliel's position concerning the validity of the apostles' claim to be of God cannot be determined with reference to syntax alone. As Max Zerwick observed about so-called "real" conditions in Greek sentences, "the 'reality' of the condition does not mean that the speaker regards the condition as fulfilled, indeed the opposite may be the case, but only that the condition in question is treated not as a generality but as a case which for one reason or another is a concrete one."[41] For example, speakers may raise cases that are untrue, but assume them to be true for the sake of the argument at hand. When Jesus says, "If I cast out demons by Beelzebul" (Luke 11:19 [εἰ plus present indicative]), he does not thereby admit to being the devil's pawn; rather, he refers to a concrete case raised by his adversaries, and thus the condition is considered "real."[42]

But the issue remains that Gamaliel uses two different kinds of conditional constructions in his speech. What, if anything, does his shift from ἐάν with the subjunctive to εἰ with the indicative imply? Often

---

[39]Ernst Haenchen, *The Acts of the Apostles: A Commentary* (Philadelphia: Westminster, 1971) 253n.2; Hans Conzelmann, *Acts of the Apostles: A Commentary on the Acts of the Apostles*, Hermeneia (Philadelphia: Fortress, 1987) 43; Brawley, *Luke-Acts and the Jews*, 89; Tannehill, *The Narrative Unity of Luke-Acts*, 2:67; Gowler, *Host, Guest, Enemy, and Friend*, 278; and John T. Squires, *The Plan of God in Luke-Acts*, SNTSMS 76 (Cambridge: Cambridge University Press, 1993) 58.

[40]Squires, *The Plan of God in Luke-Acts*, 58.

[41]Max Zerwick, *Biblical Greek Illustrated by Examples* (Rome: Pontifical Biblical Institute, 1963) 103.

[42]Zerwick, *Biblical Greek Illustrated by Examples*, 103.

overlooked, but worthy of quotation here, is Zerwick's interpretation of these controversial protases in Gamaliel's speech.

> The latter condition [5:39a], the "real" one, may well be rendered "but if in fact . . . , " but this does not necessarily imply that Gamaliel thought that this was the fact. He might indeed have been led to use the "real" form of condition because in his opinion it was "real" in the sense that the condition was fulfilled; but he may equally have expressed the condition as a "real" one for the same reason as in the case discussed in the last paragraph [see above, Jesus and Beelzebul], namely, because this was the contention of the apostles, and so the concrete supposition to be discussed; but even apart from this there is yet another psychological explanation of the use of a "real" condition for the second member despite the generality of the other member . . . : in a sense, the condition "if it be from God" is a more actual and pressing one (and hence calls for expression as a "real" condition); if the work happens to be of men, it does not matter very much what is done about it; but if in fact it is of God it matters very much.
>
> It is an astonishing fact that even scholars sometimes overlook what has just been said and seem to forget that, εἰ even in a "real" condition still means "if" or the like.[43]

Zerwick rightly concludes that a categorical argument to the effect that the speaker of these conditional clauses must believe that the apostles are truly of God is "unfounded, since such an explanation is only one among several which would account for the text."[44] In the final analysis, then, syntax alone cannot help us determine whether Gamaliel actually believes the condition to be true. But knowledge of the broader narrative context (which we have tried to lay out at length) allows us to draw some conclusions about how the reader would process this text. The reader knows the condition in Acts 5:39 to be real but, based on the overwhelming narrative evidence thus far, is strongly disinclined to view Gamaliel as believing it. Rather, the reader views Gamaliel as choosing to voice a real condition in these circumstances simply because this grammatical form highlights the more pressing case raised by his adversaries, not because he holds it to be true. If we are correct, the reader is once again in the pleasurable position of savoring an irony much like that at Jesus' trial. There, the Sanhedrin, in badgering Jesus, unwittingly voiced what it did not believe ("Then you are the Son of God" [Luke 22:70]); and

---

[43]Zerwick, *Biblical Greek Illustrated by Examples*, 104.
[44]Zerwick, *Biblical Greek Illustrated by Examples*, 105.

here, for the sake of argument, Gamaliel posits (if somewhat conditionally) what he does not believe ("They are of God").

When read from the perspective we have developed here, other aspects of Gamaliel's speech appear ironic as well. As Luke T. Johnson points out, Gamaliel unwittingly uses the loaded language of "rising up" to describe the advent of the failed prophets Theudas and Judas. But, as witnessed by the apostles, Jesus "has been 'raised up' in a new and powerful way."[45] And, even as Gamaliel speaks of the dispersion and dissipation of these supposedly analogous movements, the reader knows that the numbers of believers in Jesus are actually growing by the thousands (Acts 2:41; 4:4). Finally, it can only strike the reader as tragically ironic that a leader of the very group that has "rejected the plan of God for themselves," and therefore has been completely unable to perceive God's activity all around them (including in the recent hearing), takes it upon himself to lecture his cohorts in the Sanhedrin about discerning the plan of God.[46]

The long Christian fascination with Luke's Gamaliel is understandable. Here might be a prototype for Jewish appreciation of Christianity, a figure to help bridge the hurtful gap between sibling faiths. Too often, however, the apologetic or ecumenical wish has become the interpretive conclusion. Even today the temptation to see Gamaliel as a positive locus for interfaith dialogue is strong. He is frequently (and wrongly) viewed as rehabilitating the image of the Pharisees (bad in the gospel but good in Acts). The Pharisees, in turn, are then unfairly burdened with the responsibility of representing "real" Jews of both Luke's day and our own day. Thus Gamaliel represents those Jews who are more tolerant of Christianity and its claims. But such an idealistic appropriation of the Pharisaic leader and council member is possible only if one isolates Acts 5:33-42 from its larger narrative context. When perceived in light of a sequential reading of the story, Gamaliel's action in the Sanhedrin appears not so much irenic as ironic.

---

[45]Johnson, *The Acts of the Apostles*, 103.

[46]Darr, *On Character Building*, 119 (thanks to A. Smith for first pointing this out to me); and Johnson, *The Acts of the Apostles*, 103.

Conversion in the Acts of the Apostles: Ancient Auditors' Perceptions

Charles H. Talbert

Conversion is a central focus of Acts, maybe *the* central focus.[1] There are at least ten conversion narratives in Acts[2] plus numerous statements by the narrator about such phenomena. In 1979, Paulist Press published *The Salvation of the Gentiles* by Jacques Dupont, which contained an essay on "Conversion in the Acts of the Apostles."[3] Dupont contended the following concerning conversion in Acts: (1) that it belonged to the moral category of conversion which was concerned with sin and forgiveness, (2) that it involved a "turning from" as well as a "turning to," (3) that its catalysts were miracles and preaching, (4) that its roots were in divine grace, and (5) that it resulted in a continuing change of life. Looking back on Dupont's study, one may conclude that the only point that needs modification is the first one. In Acts, instances are identifiable of both the moral and the cognitive types of conversion (e.g., the account that includes Simon in Acts 8 is an example of cognitive conversion because his worldview, even after his baptism, includes magic; 13:4-12; 14:8-18; 17:22-31).[4] With this one adjustment, I want to employ Dupont's descrip-

---

[1]Thomas M. Finn, *From Death to Rebirth: Ritual and Conversion in Antiquity* (New York: Paulist, 1997) 27, says conversion is the major theme of Acts.

[2]Finn, *From Death to Rebirth*, 27, says there are twenty one. In the summer of 1995, my student, Craig Joseph, and I attempted to build a database of ancient conversion accounts and, on the basis of an examination of that collection to determine whether or not there was a set form for a conversion story. We concluded that it is possible to isolate five stable components in these ancient conversion narratives: (1) the context, (2) the catalysts leading to conversion, (3) the counter-forces which pose an obstacle or opposition, (4) the conversion itself, and (5) the confirmation of the genuineness of the conversion by postconversion evidence. These results essentially confirmed an earlier attempt by Robert Allen Black, "The Conversion Stories in the Acts of the Apostles" (Ph.D. diss., Emory University, 1985). A reading of Acts then showed ten narratives which contained these five components: (1) 2:1-47, (2) 3:1–4:37, (3) 8:4-25, (4) 8:26-40, (5) 9:1-22, (6) 10:1-48, (7) 13:6-12, (8) 13:13-52, (9) 16:11-15, and (10) 16:25-34.

[3]Jacques Dupont, *The Salvation of the Gentiles* (New York: Paulist, 1979) 61-84. Cf. further R. Michiels, "La conception lucanienne de la conversion," *ETL* 41 (1965): 42-78; and Augustin George, *Études sur l'oeuvre de Luc*, Sources bibliques (Paris: Editions Gabalda, 1978) 351-68.

[4]Nancy Shumate, *Crisis and Conversion in Apuleius' Metamorphoses* (Ann Arbor:

tion of conversion in *this* study of Acts and ask a further question: How would ancient auditors have heard Acts' description of Christian conversion?[5] An answer to this question will be attempted, mostly but not exclusively, on the basis of a comparison of Acts with selected conversion narratives from antiquity.[6] We will take up in order the five parts of our modified version of Dupont's description of conversion in Acts.

I. Moral and Cognitive Conversions

First, if we grant the modification of Dupont's proposals as stated above, Acts describes some conversions as primarily moral, which involve issues of sin and forgiveness (e.g., 2:38; 3:19; 5:30-31; 10:43; 13:38; 26:17-18), and others as essentially cognitive, which involve a shift of basic paradigms about the world, that is, a movement from idolatry to the worship of the living God (e.g., 13:4-12; 14:8-18; 17:22-31). How would people outside of messianic Judaism have heard this depiction?

On the one hand, a moral type of conversion was known to both Jewish and pagan[7] persons alike. (1) *Jewish.* One example will suffice. Although the material is not in the form of a conversion narrative, the synoptic traditions about John the Baptist (Matt 3:1-12; Mark 1:2-8; Luke

---

University of Michigan Press, 1996) works out the contrast between a moral type of conversion in which the stress is ethical, a movement from vice to virtue in which the convert recognizes his/her shortcomings in light of a heightened awareness of morality, and a cognitive type of conversion in which there is a collapse of an entire system of premises and assumptions about how the world works and its replacement by one radically different, a change of worldviews. In Acts, Jews and God-fearers are offered forgiveness for sins through Jesus (a moral type of conversion) while pagans are called upon to experience a shift from polytheism to monotheism (a cognitive type of conversion).

[5]The audience-oriented approach taken here is like that of Peter J. Rabinowitz, "Whirl Without End: Audience-Oriented Criticism," in *Contemporary Literary Theory*, ed. G. Douglas Atkins and Laura Morrow (Amherst: University of Massachusetts Press, 1989) 81-100; "Truth in Fiction: A Reexamination of Audiences," *CrIn* 4 (1977): 121-42; and *Before Reading: Narrative Conventions and the Politics of Interpretation* (Ithaca NY: Cornell University Press, 1987) 15-46. Rabinowitz defines the "authorial audience" as the readers that the author has in mind in creating the text. These readers possess the sociocultural knowledge and interpretive skills necessary to actualize the text's meaning. Unlike some contemporary uses of the expression "implied reader," the term "authorial audience" locates the interaction of text and reader in a particular sociohistorical context.

[6]The database of conversion narratives from antiquity may be found in my *Reading Acts* (New York: Crossroad, 1997) in the section on Acts 9:1-31. Some scholars would also include Dio Chrysostom's *Thirteenth Discourse* and Aelius Aristides' *Sacred Tales*. I have reservations about both and so have omitted them.

[7]See Finn, *From Death to Rebirth*, 45-46, for a discussion of the term.

3:1-14) relate John's call for a repentance/conversion that involved the forgiveness of sins and a change of behavior in an ethical direction. Such a view of conversion was far from unique in ancient Judaism.

(2) *Pagan.* Conversion to philosophy belongs to the moral type, although the categories employed are those of vice and virtue rather than sin and forgiveness. Two examples will suffice.[8] The first example is the case of Polemo. In *Double Indictment* (ca. 165 CE), Lucian presents the judicial case, Drink versus the Academy, in which Drink accuses the Academy of luring away her faithful servant, Polemo. In section 17, the Academy responds.

> One day he reached my door. He found it open: I was discoursing to a company of my disciples, as is my want, upon virtue and temperance. He stood there, with a flute-girl at his side and the garlands on his head, and sought at first to drown our conversation with his noisy outcry. But we paid no heed to him, and little by little our words produced a sobering effect, for Drink had not the entire possession of him: he bade the flute-girl cease, tore off his garlands, and looked with shame at his luxurious dress. Like one waking from sleep, he saw himself as he was, and repented his past life; the flush of drunkenness faded and vanished from his cheek, and was succeeded by a blush of shame; at last, not (as plaintiff would have you believe) in response to any invitation of mine, nor under any compulsion, but of his own free will, and in the conviction of my superiority, he renounced his former mistress there and then, and entered my service.[9]

This is a conversion from vice to virtue.

A second example of philosophical conversion of the moral variety is Lucian's *Wisdom of Nigrinus* (mid-second century CE). Lucian presents a dialogue between two friends, one (Lucian?) who has been converted by exposure to Nigrinus and the other who is befuddled by his friend's new behavior (1-5). The friend sets the tone with his comment about the other's behavior since he came back. "You don't deign to notice us anymore, you don't associate with us, and you don't join in our conversations; you have changed all of a sudden. . . . [W]hat is the cause of all this?" The other answers: "I have come back to you transformed . . . into a happy and blissful man—in the language of the stage, 'thrice blessed.' " The friend replies: "In so short a time?" The other responds:

---

[8]One could also refer to the conversion of the brother of Apollonius of Tyana in Philostratus, *Life of Apollonius of Tyana* 1.13.

[9]Translation from F. G. Fowler and H. G. Fowler, *The Works of Lucian of Samosata*, vol. 3 (Oxford: Clarendon, 1949) 155-56.

"Yes. Don't you think it wonderful, in the name of Zeus, that once a slave, I am now free; once poor, now rich indeed; once witless and befogged, now saner?" The friend replies: "I don't clearly understand what you mean." The other then tells of his experience. He was going to Rome to see an oculist about eye trouble. While there he went early one morning to pay his respects to Nigrinus the Platonic philosopher, something he had not done for some time. Nigrinus began to speak to him. He praised philosophy and the freedom it gives; he ridiculed the things that are commonly counted blessings like wealth and reputation, dominion and honor, purple and gold. As a result, the other says: "I couldn't imagine what had come over me." The other now regarded all these things as paltry and ridiculous and was, in his words, "glad to be looking up, as it were, out of the murky atmosphere of my past life to a clear sky and a great light." He forgot his eye ailment as he became sharper-sighted in his soul. "There you have it! I am going about enraptured and drunk with the wine of his discourse."[10] This dialogue, then, is also indicative of a conversion from vice to virtue.

In both examples of conversion to philosophy given above, the conversion is moral. There is a renunciation of a lifestyle (drunkenness, luxury) that is now replaced with a higher virtue (sobriety, simplicity). At the same time, the philosophic convert remains within the pagan, polytheistic worldview. His conversion is moral not cognitive.[11]

On the other hand, a cognitive type of conversion was also known to both Jewish and pagan persons in antiquity. (1) *Jewish.* The five major conversion narratives from ancient Judaism about which I know[12] have

---

[10]The quotations are LCL translations.

[11]Wayne A. Meeks, *The Origins of Christian Morality: The First Two Centuries* (New Haven: Yale University Press, 1993) 28, agrees with A. D. Nock that "being or becoming religious in the Greco-Roman world did not entail . . . moral transformation." His position is critiqued by Thomas M. Finn, review of *The Origins of Christian Morality: The First Two Centuries*, by Wayne A. Meeks, *CBQ* 57 (1995): 602. There are texts that cast doubt on the long held stereotype about Greek religion: (1) Euripides, *Bacchae* lines 72-77 ("O blessed he who in happiness knowing the rituals of the gods makes holy his way of life and mingles his spirit with the sacred band."); (2) Theophrastus, *On Piety*, extant in fragments attested by Porphyry (*De abstinentia*), discusses the relationship between ethics and sacrifice (e.g., "One must go to the sacrifices having a soul pure from evils."); (3) Porphyry, *De abstinentia*, quotes an inscription at the entrance to the sanctuary at Epidauros: "Pure must one be when entering the temple. . . . But purity is thinking holy things." Among pagans, it was not just in philosophy that conversion meant a changed lifestyle. This is not to deny that in some pagan religion ethics were irrelevant; it is to say that not all pagan cultic religion was devoid of ethical concern.

[12]I am not counting the conversion of Naaman in 2 Kgs 5. This seems closer to

one thing in common: they all understand conversion as the movement from a worship of idols to the worship of the living God. This commonality is found in the following accounts: the conversion of Achior, an officer in the Ammonite army (Jdt 14; second century BCE); the conversion of Aseneth (*Joseph and Aseneth*; 100 BCE–100 CE);[13] the case for Izates as recounted by Josephus (*Ant.* 20.2.3-4, 34-48); Job (*T. Job* 2–5; 100 BCE–100 CE); and Abraham (*Apoc. Ab.* 1–7; 100–200 CE). The conversion of these Gentiles to Judaism was understood as a cognitive shift from a polytheistic frame of reference to a monotheistic worldview.

(2) *Pagan.* Nancy Shumate's *Crisis and Conversion in Apuleius' Metamorphoses* offers a reading of the novel as a narrative of religious experience and specifically as a narrative of conversion. Throughout this work, Shumate contends that Lucius's conversion is not moral but cognitive. She asserts: "The axis upon which the conversion of Lucius turns is one of epistemological rupture rather than moral reform."[14] Conversion of this type involves a comprehensive and radical shift from one paradigm of interpreting and constructing reality to another. In spite of having a secondary moral component, this model is primarily a cognitive one.[15] It is a mistake to see Lucius's transformation as punishment for his moral sins (lust and striving after forbidden knowledge) and to see Isis as an agent of moral purification.[16] Rather, Lucius's conversion is a move from one plausibility structure to another, from one worldview to another. It is a process of changing a sense of root reality, the ground of being that orients and orders experience.[17] Shumate concludes: "Lucius begins with his worldview bounded by conventional structures of meaning and is thrown off-balance when these structures collapse. For this reason it is in the end the structuring function of Isis . . . to which he is especially attracted."[18] Both Jewish and pagan persons, therefore, knew of cognitive type conversions.

---

adhesion than conversion.

[13]Randall D. Chesnutt, *From Death to Life: Conversion in Joseph and Aseneth,* JSPSup 16 (Sheffield: Sheffield Academic Press, 1995) 150: "Conversion in Joseph and Aseneth is . . . conceived as a transition from death and destruction which characterize the predicament of the godless to the life and immortality enjoyed by those who worship the true God, and creation imagery is the descriptive language used most often."

[14]Shumate, *Crisis and Conversion,* 34.

[15]Shumate, *Crisis and Conversion,* 139.

[16]Shumate, *Crisis and Conversion,* 147.

[17]Shumate, *Crisis and Conversion,* 173-74, 184.

[18]Shumate, *Crisis and Conversion,* 50.

When Mediterranean auditors heard Acts read and encountered both its moral and cognitive types of conversion, they would have been sensitized already to both types of life transformation in their ancient milieu. In respect to the possibility of moral and cognitive conversions, Acts would have posed little formal discontinuity between Christian conversion and that of nonmessianic Jews and Greco-Roman pagans.

II. "Turning From" and "Turning To"

Second, Dupont argues further that conversion in Acts involves both a "turning from" and a "turning to" (e.g., 14:15-16, turning from idols to the living God; 26:18, turning from darkness to light, from Satan to God).[19] This, of course, fits A. D. Nock's definition of conversion: an experience that involves belief that the old was wrong and the new is right. According to Nock, this is different from "adhesion" in which one turns toward a deity and an accompanying lifestyle without ever breaking off from another prior deity or lifestyle. In Nock's view, Judaism, Christianity, and pagan philosophy demanded conversion while cultic paganism expected only adhesion.[20] What the ancient textual evidence shows, however, is that there is a "turning away" and a "turning towards" not only in Judaism and in philosophy but also surprisingly in some forms of cultic paganism.

(1) *Jewish.* The Hellenistic-Jewish romance, *Joseph and Aseneth*, tells the story of a pagan girl, Aseneth, who converts to Judaism as a condition for marrying Joseph. In 9:2, we hear that she "repented of her (infatuation with the) gods whom she used to worship, and spurned all the idols." In 13:11-12, she cries out to the God of Joseph:

> Behold now, all the gods whom I once used to worship in ignorance:
> I have now recognized that they were dumb and dead idols,
> and I have caused them to be trampled underfoot by men, . . .
> And with you I have taken refuge, O Lord my God.[21]

Aseneth turns from idols to the living God of Joseph. This conversion from idolatry to the living God is characteristic of all five of the postbib-

---

[19]The language of turning (ἐπιστρέφειν and cognates) is shared by pagans, Jews, and Christians.

[20]A. D. Nock, *Conversion* (London: Oxford University Press, 1933) 7, 14, 134, 179.

[21]The translation is from *The Old Testament Pseudepigrapha*, 2 vols., ed. James H. Charlesworth (Garden City NY: Doubleday, 1983, 1985) 2:223.

lical narratives of Gentile conversion to Judaism that I have mentioned above.

(2) *Pagan.* On the one hand, in philosophical conversions there is the same double turning that we have seen in conversions of Gentiles to Judaism.[22] For instance, in *Wisdom of Nigrinus*, Lucian (or another) turns from luxury to the simplicity of the philosophic way. The case is similar with Polemo. Lucian says that, once exposed to the Academy's discourse, Polemo "repented of his past life," he "renounced his former mistress," and he "entered my service" (*Double Indictment* 17).[23] In Philostratus's *Life of Apollonius of Tyana*, a youth is converted from scepticism to belief in the immortality of the soul by an appearance of Apollonius to him after the philosopher's departure from this life (8.31). On the other hand, in the type of cultic paganism reflected in Apuleius's *Metamorphoses*, Lucius turns from hostile fate and magic as a way to manipulate that fate, to the goddess Isis for her protection.[24] Isis, not magic, saves, so Lucius comes to believe.

What is seldom recognized is that cultic paganism often involved the dual turning.[25] Two examples will suffice to show this to be the case. One example is found in Plutarch's *Obsolescence of Oracles* (434.45d-f), which captures the conversation of Greeks about the decreased consultation and utilization of the country's oracles.

> "I do not know," said Demetrius, "the state of affairs there at present; for as you all know, I have been out of the country for a long time now. But when I was there, both the oracle of Mopsus and that of Amphilocus were still flourishing. I have a most amazing thing to tell as the result of my visit to the oracle of Mopsus. The ruler of Cilicia was himself still of two minds toward religious matters. This, I think, was because his skepticism lacked conviction, for in all else he was an arrogant and contemptible man. Since he kept about himself certain Epicureans, who, because of their admirable nature studies, forsooth, have an arrogant contempt, as they themselves aver, for all things such as oracles, he sent in a freedman, like a spy into the ene-

---

[22]The origins of this dualism would be Plato, *Republic* 518c-d, where he speaks of the conversion of the soul as the movement from darkness to light.

[23]Not all stories of conversion to philosophy explicitly involve the double turning: e.g., Porphyry's *Life of Plotinus* 3 speaks only of his following Ammonius continuously for eleven years.

[24]This was regarded as an exception by Nock, *Conversion*, 138-55.

[25]This is not to deny that some conversion narratives tell only of adhesion, e.g., Ovid, *Metamorphoses* 3.574-698, tells of the adhesion of one Acoetes to the worship of Dionysius.

my's territory, arranging that he should have a sealed tablet, on the inside of which was written the inquiry without anyone's knowing what it was. The man accordingly, as is the custom, passed the night in the sacred precinct and went to sleep, and in the morning reported a dream in this fashion: it seemed to him that a handsome man stood beside him who uttered just one word 'Black' and nothing more, and was gone immediately. The thing seemed passing strange to us, and raised much inquiry, but the ruler was astounded and fell down and worshipped; then opening the tablet he showed written there the question: 'Shall I sacrifice to you a white bull or a black?' The result was that the Epicureans were put to confusion, and the ruler himself not only duly performed the sacrifice, but ever after revered Mopsus."[26]

Here a pagan person turns from skeptical philosophy to traditional religion.

A second example of the dual turning in the conversion to cultic paganism is found in the first book of Horace's *Odes* (ca. 23 BCE). Ode 34 describes the poet's renunciation of skeptical philosophy and his return to the traditional state religion:

> My religious devotions were mean and infrequent.
> I strayed, a foolish man of wisdom,
> But now I set my sails
> in reverse, compelled to trace
>
> abandoned routes; for Jove who normally
> parts the clouds by fire crossed
> the *empty* sky with his thundering
> horses and aerial chariot
>
> by which the solid earth and wandering
> rivers, the dreaded Taenaran cave,
> the Atlantic shore, and the Styx
> are shaken. God can raise
>
> the depths, diminish distinction, reveal
> the obscure. Rapacious Fortune on whirring
> wings delights in moving
> crowns from head to head.[27]

Here Horace claims he moved from religious skepticism back to traditional religion because of his experience of the inexplicable phenomenon

---

[26]LCL translation.

[27]Translation from David Mulroy, *Horace's Odes and Epodes* (Ann Arbor: University of Michigan Press, 1994) 93-94.

of thunder on a clear day. He remains within a pagan frame of reference, but he has been converted from one form of paganism to another.[28]

Since both Jewish and pagan persons had knowledge of conversion as a "turning from" and as a "turning to," they would have felt little formal discontinuity if and when they heard the narrative of Acts with its depiction of conversion in these terms.

III. Miracles and Preaching as Catalysts

Third, Dupont contends that in Acts the catalysts of conversion are preaching (e.g., 2:37-38; 4:3; 10:44; 11:19-21) and miracles (e.g., 4:33; 9:32-34; 9:36-43; 14:3). This fits nicely into the ancient Greco-Roman context of both Jewish and pagan persons.[29]

(1) *Jewish.* On the one hand, Josephus (*Ant.* 20.2.3-4, 34-48) tells of the conversion of the royal house of Adiabene. It happened because a certain Jewish merchant, whose name was Ananias, taught the women who belonged to the king to "worship God according to the Jewish religion." Ananias also persuaded Izates, the king's son, to embrace Judaism as well. Here conversion is prompted by teaching. On the other hand, in Judith, the conversion of Achior, an officer in the Ammonite army, is effected when he hears that Judith has slain the Assyrian general, Holofernes. "And when Achior saw all that the God of Israel had done, he believed in God with all his heart, and accepted circumcision and was adopted into the household of Israel" (Jdt 14:10). Both teaching and marvels functioned as catalysts for conversion in ancient Judaism.

(2) *Pagan.* On the one hand, conversion to philosophy was usually due to hearing the teaching of the philosopher. So Polemo is brought from drunkenness to sobriety by exposure to the words of Xenocrates. Diogenes Laertius says that, in spite of the young man's intrusion, Xenocrates "without being at all disturbed went on with his discourse as

---

[28]This evidence demands a rather severe revision of Nock's categories. This is important because Nock's distinction between Jewish and Christian conversion and cultic pagan adhesion underlies most New Testament scholarship today. See, e.g., Meeks, *The Origins of Christian Morality*, 28; John E. Stambaugh and David L. Balch, *The New Testament in Its Social Environment*, LEC (Philadelphia: Westminster, 1986) 45-46; and Martin Goodman, *Mission and Conversion: Proselytizing in the Religious History of the Roman Empire* (Oxford: Clarendon, 1994) 27.

[29]Ramsay MacMullen, "Two Types of Conversion to Early Christianity," *VC* 37 (1983): 174-92 and elsewhere, contends that early Christianity grew mainly through demonstrations of divine power/miracles. There would have been a cultural predisposition in this direction apart from Christianity.

before, the subject being temperance. The lad, as he listened, by degrees was taken in the toils" (*Lives of Eminent Philosophers* 4.3.16-18). Also, Lucian (or another) becomes enraptured and transformed as a result of hearing the words of Nigrinus in Rome. Lucian, speaking of Nigrinus, says: "Beginning to talk on these topics and to explain his position, . . . he poured enough ambrosial speech over me to put out of date the famous sirens . . . and the nightingales and the lotus of Homer. A divine utterance!" (*Wisdom of Nigrinus* 17). On the other hand, conversion within cultic paganism was usually linked to a miracle. Lucius becomes a devotee of Isis when she effects his transformation from a donkey to human form. The ruler of Cilicia becomes a worshipper of Mopsus as a result of a miracle of knowledge. Horace changes orientation from skeptical philosophy to traditional religion because of an unprecedented event that was, to him, best explained in terms of traditional mythology.[30]

Whether one was Jewish or pagan, preaching/teaching and miracle were the normal catalysts of conversion in antiquity. If and when such people of antiquity heard the narrative of Acts, they would have felt at home in its religious world, at least in respect to the forces which it depicts as the catalysts of conversion.

IV. Divine Grace

Fourth, Dupont argues that in Acts the roots of conversion are in divine grace. God grants salvation (5:31; 11:18; 13:48; 15:9, 14; 16:14). The same assumptions are found in nonmessianic Jewish and pagan traditions.

(1) *Jewish*. In the *Testament of Job* 2–5 we hear of the conversion of Job from idolatry to faith in the living God, the creator. The process involves two steps. First there is a time of reasoning in which Job's critical faculties undermine the status of idols. Then there is a divine disclosure which grants Job the true knowledge he seeks. This act of divine grace enables Job to make the transition from idolatry to true faith. In the *Apocalypse of Abraham* 1–7, the patriarch's conversion follows the same two steps noted in the case of Job. Abraham is initially involved in a rational critique of idols (1–6); he then is the recipient of a divine disclosure which enables the transition to faith in the living God (6–7). In

---

[30]The Christian Apocryphal Acts express the conviction that more than anything else miracles initiate the process of conversion. Cf. Eugene V. Gallagher, "Conversion and Salvation in the Apocryphal Acts of the Apostles," *SecCent* 8 (1991): 13-30.

both of these Jewish documents, the process of conversion is possible only because divine grace grants an individual what is needed.

(2) *Pagan.* The same emphasis may be found in pagan sources as well. Shumate's study of Apuleius's *Metamorphoses* shows how the preparation for Lucius's conversion operates on an almost entirely passive subject. In theological terms, this conversion occurs because of grace.[31] Furthermore, just as in the cases of Job and Abraham, Lucius's transition to devotion to Isis is made possible only by her self-disclosure to him. This comes on the beach, in her actions on his behalf to restore him to human form, and by her later invitation to him to be initiated. Lucius's conversion is by grace from first to last. In the accounts of conversion to philosophy one does not normally hear such an explicit emphasis on divine grace. Nevertheless, Dio Chrysostom says that "whatever wise and true words about the gods and the universe there are to be found among men, none have ever lodged in human souls except by the divine will" (*Discourse* 1.57). The assumptions of pagan philosophy allowed for the possibility of belief in the graced nature of conversion.

Once again, the ancient Mediterranean auditors who heard the Acts of the Apostles would sense continuity between the larger cultural expectations about conversion and those depicted in Acts. Nonmessianic Judaism and Greco-Roman paganism allowed for a common belief in deity as the ultimate author of change.[32]

V. A Continuing Change of Life

Fifth, the final aspect of Dupont's portrayal of conversion in Acts is that Christian conversion involves a continuing change of life. This belief was not alien to Mediterranean antiquity generally.

(1) *Jewish.* The account of the conversion of Achior, which we introduced earlier, emphasized the ongoing significance of his newfound faith and circumcision by closing with the note that he remained committed to Judaism "unto this day" (Jdt 14:10). There was permanence to the conversion. In the *Testament of Job*, the hero makes his commitment to renounce idols and worship the creator. He says to God: "'Till death I will endure: I will not step back at all" (5:1).[33] Subsequent events depict Job as showing endurance, as not growing weary, and as finally triumph-

---

[31]Shumate, *Crisis and Conversion*, 121-22.
[32]Finn, *From Death to Rebirth*, 240.
[33]Translation is from Charlesworth, *The Old Testament Pseudepigrapha*, 1:841.

ing over Satan (27:4-5). Thus, his conversion also apparently involved a continuing commitment to the convert's change of life-orientation.

(2) *Pagan.* On the one hand, a continuing change of life-orientation was characteristic of a true conversion to philosophy. Diogenes Laertius says of Polemo who was converted by listening to Xenocrates' words about temperance: "He became so industrious as to surpass all the other scholars, and rose to be himself head of the school in the 116th Olympiad" (*Lives of Eminent Philosophers* 4.3.16-18). Seneca claimed that what is stated in the conversion narrative itself is typical of the life of philosophy:

> I understand, Lucilius, that I am not only being improved but that I am being transformed. I do not already promise or hope that nothing is left in me that needs change. . . . The very fact that the soul sees failings in itself which it previously ignored is a proof of its change to a better state. (*Epistle* 6.1)[34]

Plutarch speaks to the same issue:

> What possible form of argument, my dear Sosius Senecio, will keep alive in a man the consciousness that he is growing better in regard to virtue, if it is a fact that the successive stages of his progress produce no abatement of his unwisdom. . . . [I]n the study of philosophy, neither progress nor any sense of progress is to be assumed, if the soul does not put aside any of its gross stupidity and purge itself thereof, and if . . . it is wedded to the evil. (*How a Man May Become Aware of His Progress in Virtue* 75.1b-d)[35]

The argument moves on the assumption that conversion to philosophy involves a change of life by degrees and in stages during one's entire lifetime.

On the other hand, the persistent effects of a change can be found in cultic paganism as well. Plutarch's account of the conversion of a ruler of Cilicia to belief in the oracle of Mopsus ends with the statement that "the Epicureans were put to confusion, and the ruler himself not only duly performed the sacrifice, but ever after revered Mopsus" (*Obsolescence of Oracles* 434.45d-f).

Whether it be a Jewish or pagan person in Mediterranean antiquity, conversion was believed to involve a change of orientation that continued throughout one's lifetime.[36] Once again, the ancient auditors who heard

---

[34] LCL translation.
[35] LCL translation.
[36] Both Jews and pagans were aware of and concerned about conversions away from

the Acts narrative and reflected on its depiction of Christian conversion would have sensed little formal discontinuity in the way conversion was described.

This essay began with a slightly modified form of Jacques Dupont's description of Christian conversion as depicted in the Acts of the Apostles. It then sought to determine whether or not auditors from non-messianic Judaism, on the one hand, and pagan philosophy and cultic paganism, on the other, would have heard continuities or discontinuities in the depiction of conversion in the narrative of Acts. This brief comparison has enabled us to see that, insofar as the formal components of conversion are concerned, non-Christian auditors in antiquity would have sensed enough continuities with the depiction of Christian conversion in Acts to be able to understand it.[37] Their difficulty, if they felt one, would have been with the object/content of the Christian conversion experience (that is, Christ), not with its formal components.

---

their positions to others. 1 Macc (1:10-15, 41-50; 2:15-22) tells of Jewish conversion in Palestine to pagan ways under Antiochus Epiphanes. Cf. Harry A. Wolfson, *Philo: Foundations of Religious Philosophy in Judaism, Christianity, and Islam*, 2 vols. (Cambridge MA: Harvard University Press, 1948) 1:73-85, who identifies at least three reasons for Jewish conversion to paganism in Alexandria. Aulus Gellius, *Attic Nights* 3.13.1-5 tells of Demosthenes' leaving Plato for Callistratus; 5.3 tells how Protagoras forsook philosophy for rhetoric.

[37] An obvious question to be raised at this point has to do with whether or not pagans and nonmessianic Jews engaged in aggressive proselytizing as did the messianists and Christians. The issue is focused especially on nonmessianic Judaism. Since the work of Schürer and Juster at the beginning of this century, most scholars have subscribed to the view that Jewish proselytizing reached a peak of intensity in the first century CE. In recent years there has been some dissent (e.g., J. Munck, D. Rokeah, E. Will, and C. Orrieux, and most recently, Martin Goodman and Scott McKnight). James Carleton Paget, "Jewish Proselytism at the Time of Christian Origins: Chimera or Reality?" *JSNT* 62 (1996): 65-103, surveys the evidence and arguments and concludes that some Jews proselytized, contra Goodman and McKnight. Shaye J. D. Cohen, *From the Maccabees to the Mishnah*, LEC (Philadelphia: Westminster, 1987) 57, draws a similar conclusion: "There is no evidence of an organized Jewish mission to the Gentiles, but individuals seem to have engaged in this activity on their own."

The Place of Jerusalem on the Lukan Landscape: An Exercise in Symbolic Cartography*

Mikeal C. Parsons

I. Introduction

The cover of the *New Yorker* magazine on 29 March 1976 bears a well-known image by Saul Steinberg. The most striking feature, of course, is that it locates visually and spatially the city of New York at the very center of the world. The map is, as such, an example of cosmological cartography, that is, making a map of one's symbolic universe. The *New Yorker* cover was immensely popular and spawned the production of hundreds, perhaps thousands, of copycats where various towns, cities, states, and countries produced their own versions of the map, propagandistically locating their own political unit at the center of the world.

Galileo's struggle to establish a heliocentric cosmology by disabusing his fellow humans of the notion that the earth was at the center of the universe is evidence of the stubborn tenacity with which people cling to various forms of geocentricity and ethnocentricity. Images like the *New Yorker* cover remind us that these notions are remarkably resilient. We may all carry maps of the world in our heads shaped by our geography lessons in elementary school, the globe in our studies, and the breathtaking satellite photos of the earth on the television or the computer screen. At some level, we have these other symbolic maps which locate various places and persons in spatial relationship to each other in terms of their relative importance to our daily orbits. We are all, then, cartographers of the symbolic maps which order our worlds.

Such cosmological cartography is not a recent phenomenon.[1] As early

---

*Professor Tyson has been a valued colleague in the Southwest region of the Society of Biblical Literature for many years. My personal association with him goes back to 1986 when he, as chair of the national SBL Acts group, invited me to deliver a paper at the 1987 SBL meeting on the contributions of Charles Talbert to Lukan studies. Subsequently, he and I coedited a volume, *Cadbury, Knox, and Talbert: American Contributions to the Study of Acts* (Atlanta: Scholars Press, 1992), in which those original essays (and some subsequent responses) were collected. Professor Tyson has always been generas 600 BCE, the Babylonians had produced a cosmological map on a clay tablet. Notable among its features are the placement of Babylon at the center of the map and the placement of various topographical features (Euphrates River, mountains, oceans) in relationship to Babylon.[2] The text accompanying the map describes various beasts and regions which lie beyond the ocean encircling the Babylonian world, what will be called in later maps the *terrae incognito*.[3] Similarly, evidence suggests that many other early cultures—Egyptians, Chinese, Mayans—also located their holy places at the center of the world.

The *Madaba map* is a sixth-century CE mosaic of Palestine and lower Egypt with legends in Greek.[4] This map is the earliest extant Christian map. Here Jerusalem is given a prominent position and an exaggerated size. The "Holy City" is "portrayed in great detail as an oval walled city with its principal gateway in the north."[5] We see here with the Madaba map a tradition of Christian scholars visualizing the *Terra Sancta*, the Holy Land with its accompanying Holy City, at the center of the inhabited world.

But surely no group produced more such cosmological maps than Christian geographers of the medieval period.[6] In the section labeled "The Geography of the Imagination," of his encyclopedic work *The Discoverers*, Daniel Boorstin laments:

---

ous in his support, gracious in his critique, and uncompromising in his expectations for intellectual honesty and excellence from himself, his colleagues, and his students. I am delighted to contribute this essay to a *Festschrift* honoring his contributions to the literary study of Luke/Acts.

[1]On the history of cartography in antiquity, see J. B. Harley and David Woodward, eds., *History of Cartography*, vol. 1, *Cartography in Prehistoric, Ancient, and Medieval Europe and the Mediterranean* (Chicago: University of Chicago Press, 1987).

[2]Catherine Delano Smith, "Cartography in the Prehistoric Period in the Old World: Europe, the Middle East, and North Africa," in *History of Cartography*, 1:85.

[3]A. R. Millard, "Cartography in the Ancient Near East," in *History of Cartography*, 1:111. The largest dimensions of the original clay tablet are 12.5×8 cm. It is currently housed in the British Museum.

[4]The extant map is 5×10.5 m, but originally the mosaic may have been as large as 24×6 m and composed of more than 2 million pieces of colored cubes, preserved in a church in Madaba, Jordan.

[5]O. A. W. Dilke, "Cartography in the Byzantine Empire," in *History of Cartography*, 1:265.

[6]However, see the medieval texts, *Midras Konen* and *Seder Rabba diBeresit*, which belonged to the rabbinic cosmographical tradition; see N. Sed, *La mystique cosmologique juive* (Paris: Ecole des Hautes Études en Science Sociales, 1981); cited by Philip S. Alexander, "Geography and the Bible (Early Jewish)," in *ABD* (1992) 2: 977-88.

Christian geographers in the Middle Ages spent their energies embroidering a neat, theologically appealing picture of what was already known, or was supposed to be known.
Geography had no place in the medieval catalogue of the "seven liberal arts." . . . Lacking the dignity of a proper discipline, geography was an orphan in the world of learning. The subject became a ragbag filled with odds and ends of knowledge and pseudo-knowledge, of biblical dogma, travelers' tales, philosophers' speculations, and mythical imaginings.[7]

More than 600 of these so-called *Mappaemundi* have survived from the medieval period. Their makers were responsible for what Boorstin calls "the Great Interruption" in the advance of scientific knowledge of the world's surface. The most famous medieval maps are the *T-O maps* credited to Isidore of Seville (560–636), a renowned encyclopedist and historian who succeeded his brother as bishop of Seville in ca. 600 CE.[8] The Isidorian T-O map is thus named because the whole inhabited earth was depicted as a circular dish (an "O"), divided by a T-shaped flow of water. East was placed at the top, the means then used for "orienting" a map.[9] Above the "T" was the continent of Asia, which was associated with Noah's son Shem; Africa in the South was linked with Ham; Europe was associated with Japheth. Jerusalem was either presumed or shown to be at the center of the world, the *umbilicus terrae*, as the Latin Vulgate put it.[10]

I propose in this essay to trace the reader's understanding of one particular place, Jerusalem, within the plot of Luke/Acts[11] by comparing it with other depictions of Jerusalem in other ancient Jewish writings. At the end of the article, I shall compare my findings with Joseph Tyson's analysis of the image of Jerusalem.

---

[7]Daniel J. Boorstin, *The Discoverers* (New York: Random House, 1983) 100.

[8]On the various types of medieval *Mappaemundi*, see David Woodward, "Medieval *Mappaemundi*," in *History of Cartography*, 1:286-370. Of special interest is the chart on 298 which shows that of the maps from the eighth through fifteenth centuries, the tripartite maps account for more than fifty percent of those extant, reaching a high of more than ninety percent in the ninth century.

[9]Boorstin, *The Discoverers*, 101.

[10]Boorstin, *The Discoverers*, 101.

[11]"Luke/Acts" (with a forward slash) rather than the more common "Luke-Acts" (with a hyphen, representing the view that Luke and Acts are one continuous narrative) is used throughout this essay (except in direct quotations) and is a typographical representation of my views of the literary relationship between Luke and Acts (interrelated yet independent). This argument is detailed in Mikeal C. Parsons and Richard I. Pervo, *Rethinking the Unity of Luke and Acts* (Minneapolis: Fortress, 1993).

Obviously, with Luke/Acts, I am dealing with literary texts, verbal maps as such, not drawn or visual maps. Although the ancients did occasionally draw out mental maps and models, few drawn maps from antiquity are extant today, not even from the Greeks who made such rich contributions to scientific cartography. The fact that so few of these maps have survived is not an irreparable loss. If we have sufficiently detailed verbal descriptions which convey clear visual images, we can translate these descriptions onto paper.[12]

The question is whether or not the Lukan writings are open to such cartographic interpretation. I am not arguing that Luke stands in the scientific geographical tradition of Eratosthenes, Strabo, and Ptolemy. It is interesting in this regard, however, that Strabo (*Geography* 1.1.2) and others credit Homer with being the founder of the study of geography, even though Homer was a poet not a philosopher (using Strabo's terminology) and evidently never intended to draw a map. Strabo is forced to admit, in the course of defending Homer against his critics, that Homer at times "was wont to add a mythical element to actual occurrences, thus giving flavor and adornment to his style" (*Geography* 1.2.9).[13]

Luke, too, "added flavor and adornment to his style" through his abiding interest in and use of geographical references in his theological agenda. Luke's interest in spatial features and spatial metaphors can be quantified to an extent. With the help of semantic domain lexicons, a close examination of the New Testament writings shows that only the book of Revelation comes anywhere close to the consistent quantity and variety of geographical terms found in Luke and Acts.[14] Thus, while Luke was not a geographer per se, he was interested in geography, and it will

---

[12]On the problems associated with "verbal maps," see Alexander, "Geography and the Bible," 977-88.

[13]LCL translation.

[14]Johannes P. Louw and Eugene A. Nida, *Greek-English Lexicon of the New Testament Based on Semantic Domains*, 2nd ed., 2 vols. (New York: United Bible Societies, 1989), in their first volume list "Geographical Objects and Features" as the first semantic domain. A frequency analysis (using version 2.0 of the *AcCordance* software program) of its various subdomains demonstrates that, even after adjusting the results to take into account the fact that Luke and Acts are much longer than any other NT document, the Lukan writings demonstrate a higher rate of frequency for spatially related terms than any other NT document. In many cases, the subdomains of domain 1 were represented by terms which are found only in Luke/Acts among the NT documents. Similar results were found in analyses of domains 80 ("Space"), 81 ("Spatial Dimensions"), 82 ("Spatial Orientations"), and 83 ("Spatial Positions"). I wish to thank my graduate assistants, Stanley Harstine and Mark Proctor, for their help in conducting these analyses.

be instructive to create a map of Luke's symbolic world based on his literary texts.[15] We now turn our attention to the place of Jerusalem on the Lukan landscape.

II. Mapping the Lukan Landscape:
The Place of Jerusalem in Luke/Acts

In his watershed redactional study, *The Theology of St. Luke*, Hans Conzelmann argues that with the Gospel of Luke "the process by which the scene [of Jerusalem and its surrounding setting] becomes stylized into the 'Holy Land' has begun."[16] The legacy of Conzelmann in modern scholarship is not hard to find. Luke Johnson claims: "The geographical structure of Luke-Acts makes Jerusalem the center of Luke's narrative."[17] And Joseph Fitzmyer concludes: "Though Luke never uses the expression, Jerusalem functions for him as 'the navel of the earth.' "[18] In this view, Luke's understanding of Jerusalem as the "Holy Land" or the *umbilicus terrae* may logically be viewed to have culminated in the *Mappaemundi* of medieval Christian scribes which visually and symbolically located Jerusalem at the center of the world.

On the other hand, W. D. Davies claims that Luke recognized that "what we might call a demotion of Jerusalem" was "a necessity for the church of his day."[19] He continued:

> In Jewish expectation Jerusalem was the city of the End: an eschatological mystique surrounded it. Early Christians could easily succumb to this mystique, and some, as we shall see in Acts, were tempted to do so. Luke was aware of that mystique and of its accompanying seduction. He saw that it was necessary, quite deliberately, to transcend it.[20]

In this essay I would like to argue that Luke neither intentionally marginalized or "demoted" Jerusalem (as Davies suggests) nor stylized it as the "Holy Land" (as Conzelmann argued), but rather presented it in

---

[15]The "map" metaphor forms the basis for the introduction ("Orienting the Reader") to my forthcoming commentary on Acts in the Narrative New Testament series.

[16]Hans Conzelmann, *The Theology of St. Luke* (New York: Harper, 1961) 70.

[17]Luke Timothy Johnson, *The Gospel of Luke*, Sacra Pagina 3 (Collegeville MN: Liturgical, 1991) 11.

[18]Joseph A. Fitzmyer, *The Gospel according to Luke*, 2 vols., AB 28, 28A (Garden City NY: Doubleday, 1981, 1985) 1:168.

[19]W. D. Davies, *The Gospel and the Land: Early Christianity and Jewish Territorial Doctrine* (Berkeley: University of California Press, 1974) 255.

[20]Davies, *The Gospel and the Land*, 255-56.

ambivalent terms (*pace* Tyson, as we shall see). I will contribute to this discussion by placing Luke's view of Jerusalem within the context of first-century Jewish views of Jerusalem which presumably would have been familiar to Luke's "implied reader." In order to accomplish this task, I am interested, then, in a literary analysis which lays bare the spatial relations of Luke's narrative world, what I am calling an exercise in symbolic cartography. By engaging in this task, I wish to gain theological insight into the symbolic world of Luke and Acts and Jerusalem's place within it.

I begin by noting two cartographic categories necessary for our analysis. From the Lukan writings, we may construct either a topographical map or a geopolitical map.[21] A topographical map depicts spatial relationships that would be observed from an aerial photograph or a relief map. Geopolitical space refers to spatial areas which are defined by human-made boundaries of civic or governmental units. The implied reader of Luke/Acts will know that God is creator of both topographical and the geopolitical space. In Acts 4:24, the Christian community at prayer draws on an OT topos: "Lord God, who made the heaven and earth and sea and everything in them."[22] In his speech to the Lycaonians of Lystra, Paul also refers to the "living God who made the heaven and the earth and the sea and all that is in them" (14:15). According to Paul's Areopagus speech, the God who is Lord of topographical space is also the same God who "made from one person every nation to live on all the face of the earth, having determined allotted periods and the boundaries of their habitation" (17:26). The word "boundaries" (ὁροθεσία) occurs only here in the NT, though elsewhere in Greco-Roman literature it carries (as here) the geopolitical sense of borders or boundaries between nations.

On a topographical map one would see rivers, lakes, seas, wilderness areas, mountains, cities and villages (although not their names), and roads, that is, the physical features of the earth, both natural (e.g., mountains) and human made (e.g., roads). We must include on this topographical map Luke's view of a three-tiered universe, one we have come to expect in the writings of biblical and postbiblical Judaism. There is the

---

[21]I have modified the terminology from Elizabeth Struthers Malbon, *Narrative Space and Mythic Meaning in Mark* (San Francisco: Harper & Row, 1986), who also speaks of architectural space.

[22]This phrase occurs verbatim in the Greek version of Exod 20:11; Neh 9:6; Isa 37:16; Ps 145:6 [MT 146:6]. Biblical quotations in this essay are taken from the NRSV unless otherwise noted.

earth, with heaven above and hell or Hades below. Luke shows relatively little interest in providing detailed descriptions of either the tier above, heaven, or the tier below, Hades.

The attention of Luke's audience is fixed on the middle tier, the surface of the earth. As the readers adjust their vision from the more global picture of the three-tiered universe to the specific features of the Lukan landscape, they encounter a variety of topographical features: natural places like the countryside, the desert, fields, rivers, valleys, mountains, hills, lakes, grainfields, seacoasts, rocks, holes, nests, and human-made space like cities and villages, roads, streets, wells, courtyards, temples, houses, and synagogues. A number of these, such as the desert, mountains, and countryside, have special significance along the Lukan landscape.

One topographical feature is worthy of comment, in light of our quest to locate Jerusalem in Luke's symbolic world. The "road" or "way" (ὁδός) in Luke and Acts plays an important role for the understanding of the authorial audience. The term, however, functions less as a static setting in which a certain action takes place (though this element is not entirely missing; cf. 9:57, 18:35, 19:36, 24:32). Rather the word is used to depict Jesus' career as a course or way. It is well-known that the central section of Luke's gospel is set within the framework of a journey narrative, but the way of Jesus is not only expressive of his physical arrival in Jerusalem or of his progress toward his passion. At the outset, the journey is described as Jesus' ἀναλήμψις, literally his "taking up." This "taking up" refers to the entire complex of events that forms Jesus' transit to the Father: his passion, death, burial, resurrection, and ascension/exaltation. Jesus' journeying along the way is also depicted in Luke as an "exodus." In the transfiguration scene in Luke 9:28-36, only Luke of the synoptic gospels reports that Jesus, Moses and Elijah were speaking of Jesus' "departure" or exodus, "which he was to accomplish at Jerusalem" (9:31). The way of Jesus becomes paradigmatic for Jesus' followers; the journey motif fits "Luke's conception of the life of faith as a pilgrimage, always on the move."[23] It is not surprising, then, that the favorite term for the Christian movement in Acts is simply the "Way" (cf. 9:2; 19:9, 23; 22:4; 24:14, 22).

---

[23]Charles Talbert, *Reading Luke: A Literary and Theological Commentary on the Third Gospel* (New York: Crossroad, 1982) 113.

The goal of Jesus' journey is Jerusalem, our city of inquiry, which brings us to a discussion of geopolitical space in Luke's narratives. While some interesting comments may be made on a number of geopolitical sites in Acts (especially cities like Caesarea, Antioch, Ephesus, Athens, and Rome and provinces like Judea and Samaria), our focus remains on Jerusalem. The evidence demonstrating the importance which Luke attaches to Jerusalem is easy for the reader to find and is well documented in the commentaries. On the one hand, Luke Johnson's comments are typical:

> The infancy account leads to the presentation of Jesus in the Temple (2:22) and his discovery there as a young boy (2:41-51). In the Lukan temptation account, the order of the last two temptations in Matthew is reversed, so that the climax is reached in Jerusalem (4:9). At the end of the Galilean ministry, the transfiguration account explicitly prepares for the journey to Jerusalem and Jesus' death there (9:31). The journey itself begins with a solemn announcement (9:51), and continues with multiple references to Jesus' destination (13:22, 33-44; 17:11; 18:31; 19:11, 28). Luke has all of Jesus' resurrection appearances take place in the environs of the city, and in the last of them, Jesus instructs the disciples, "stay in the city" (24:49).
>
> In Acts the geographical movement is *away* from Jerusalem. The ministry in Jerusalem (Acts 1–7) is followed by the evangelization of Judea and Samaria (8–12), then Asia Minor and Europe, ending in Rome. Each outward movement, however, also circles back to Jerusalem (see Acts 12:25; 15:2; 18:22; 19:21; 20:16; 21:13; 25:1). Luke is concerned to show that the expansion of Christianity into the wider world and among the Gentiles took place in continuity and communication with the original community in Jerusalem.[24]

On the other hand, ominous and negative images are associated with Jerusalem. Along the way to Jerusalem, Jesus laments: "Yet today, tomorrow, and the next day I must be on my way, because it is impossible for a prophet to be killed outside of Jerusalem. Jerusalem, Jerusalem, the city that kills the prophets and stones those who are sent to it! How often have I desired to gather your children together as a hen gathers her brood under her wings, and you were not willing!" (Luke 13:33-34). Later, Jesus foretells the destruction of Jerusalem with details unparalleled in the other gospels:

> "When you see Jerusalem surrounded by armies, then know that its desolation has come near. Then those in Judea must flee to the mountains, and

---

[24]Johnson, *The Gospel of Luke*, 14-15.

those inside the city must leave it, and those out in the country must not enter it; for these are days of vengeance, as a fulfillment of all that is written. . . . and Jerusalem will be trampled on by the Gentiles until the times of the Gentiles are fulfilled." (Luke 21:20-22, 24b; cf. 19:11)

If one includes the image of the temple depicted in Luke and Acts, the picture is even more ambivalent. On a positive note, the gospel does begin and end in the temple, but by the time we reach Stephen's speech in Acts 7, the temple (or at least the prevailing attitudes toward it) is the object of Stephen's harsh critique: "Yet the Most High does not dwell in houses made with human hands" (7:48).

Even after the acknowledgment of the theological centrality of Jerusalem for Luke, it still remains to be seen if Jerusalem occupies the central *place* in Luke's world. We find some clues in the Pentecost narrative (a passage briefly treated by Tyson in his latest book[25]). In Acts 2:5, we read that "there were devout Jews from every nation under heaven living in Jerusalem." The reference to "devout Jews from every nation under heaven living in Jerusalem" implies that Jerusalem is the "mother city" of the world, because Jews are living in every nation. And in verses 9-11, representative nations are listed. The list of nations in Acts 2:9-11 may be an "update" of the table-of-nations tradition found in Genesis 10, a point rarely examined by interpreters.[26]

The implied reader has already been introduced to the table-of-nations tradition in Luke 10:1ff. in the so-called mission of the seventy. The mission of the seventy foreshadows the Gentile mission. The textual problem of whether the number is seventy or seventy-two only serves to strengthen the connection with the table-of-nations tradition of Genesis, since the variant may go back to the differences between the Hebrew text of Genesis which lists seventy nations and the Greek, which lists seventy-two. From a very early point, then, readers (the scribes) connected the mission of the seventy(-two) with the table of nations in Genesis 10 to symbolize the universality of their mission.

---

[25]Joseph B. Tyson, *Images of Judaism in Luke-Acts* (Columbia: University of South Carolina Press, 1992) 100-11.

[26]On the importance of the table-of-nations tradition for Luke, see James M. Scott, "Luke's Geographical Horizon," in *The Book of Acts in Its Graeco-Roman Setting*, ed. David W. J. Gill and Conrad Gempf, The Book of Acts in Its First Century Setting 2 (Grand Rapids MI: Eerdmans, 1994) 483-544. I do not, however, follow Scott (530-41) in his argument that the entire book of Acts is organized around the missions to Shem (Acts 2:1–8:25), Ham (8:26-40), and Japheth (9:1–28:31).

The context in Acts 2 is eschatological, and it foreshadows the Gentile mission. In his Pentecost sermon, Peter interprets the gift of the Holy Spirit by reference to Joel 3 (LXX). But he adds a significant phrase missing in the Greek text of Joel: "And it shall be, *in the last days, says God*, I will pour out my spirit on all flesh" (2:16; emphasis added). At the end of his speech, he will allude to inclusion of the Gentiles as recipients of the promise of salvation and spirit: "For the promise is for you, for your children, and *for all who are far away, everyone whom the Lord our God calls to him*" (2:39; emphasis added).

III. Mapping the Larger Context:
Jerusalem in Postbiblical Jewish Thought

How would Luke's implied reader have understood these references to Jerusalem? Here we need to turn to extratextual information, by noting the various views of the cosmological place of Jerusalem held by Jewish interpreters, who were roughly contemporary with the Lukan writings. The implied reader of Luke/Acts may have been aware of at least four attempts to locate Jerusalem in relationship to the rest of the world.[27]

1. *The table of nations in Genesis 10 established Jerusalem at the center of the world and that position continues to be a present reality.* Some texts draw on the table-of-nations tradition in Genesis 10 to argue that the establishment of Jerusalem as the center of the world, an act of God in conjunction with the division of lands among the sons of Noah, is inviolable and static. Jerusalem's status as the center of the world reflects present reality despite any outward appearances (including the subjugation of the Jews by a foreign power). Most prominent among these texts is *Jubilees* 8–10. *Jubilees* evidently draws on the old Ionian world map which was accommodated to the Bible.[28]

Though the Ionian maps of Anaximander and others are no longer extant, it is traditionally accepted that these ancient maps were circular, with Greece in the middle and Delphi at the center. At the oracle in Delphi, there was purportedly an *omphalos* (navel), a stone that symbol-

---

[27]I am not suggesting that the implied reader necessarily had knowledge of these *specific* texts, but rather was generally familiar with the positions they articulated.

[28]See Alexander, "Geography and the Bible," 980-82. All translations of second temple Jewish texts, unless otherwise noted, are taken from the translations in *The Old Testament Pseudepigrapha*, 2 vols., ed. James Charlesworth (Garden City NY: Doubleday, 1985).

ized the center not only of east and west, but the connection between higher and lower tiers of the three-tiered universe. It is not clear how seriously later Greeks took these maps. Herodotus offered a scathing critique of those maps (*History* 4.36), and there was also the satirical tradition which said that Zeus, in an attempt to find the center of the world, released two birds flying east and west in opposite directions; the birds collided with one another and fell to the earth at Delphi. The *omphalos* was thus erected on the spot where the fowl fell!

The author of *Jubilees* evidently took the tradition very seriously and envisaged the inhabited world as a roughly circular land mass surrounded by ocean. The center of the world—its "navel" (*omphalos*)—is Zion, not Delphi, as on the Ionian map. *Jubilees* 8:12 reads: "And the lot of Shem was assigned in the document as the middle of the earth." Later *Jubilees* reports that "Mount Zion (was) in the midst of the navel of the earth." For the writer of *Jubilees*, the table of nations, and Israel's position in it, is seen to have timeless value and eternal validity, even for the second century BCE, when *Jubilees* was most likely written.[29]

2. *Jerusalem is the center of the world as indicated by the diaspora.* A more modest claim regarding the central place of Jerusalem in the present world argues that Jerusalem is rightly called the "mother city" because Jews live in every part of the inhabited world. Philo of Alexandria promotes this view in his *Embassy to Gaius*.[30] Philo includes a letter allegedly by King Agrippa I to the Emperor Gaius in which he explains:

> While she (the Holy City), as I have said, is my native city, she is also the mother city not of one country, Judea, but of most of the others in virtue of the colonies sent out at different times to the neighboring lands. . . . So that if my own home-city is granted a share of your goodwill the benefit extends not to one city but to myriads of the others situated in every region of the inhabited world whether in Europe or in Asia or in Libya, whether in the mainlands or in the islands, whether it be seaboard or inland. (281-83)[31]

3. *Jerusalem is the center of the land of Israel, not of the world.* On the other end of the spectrum are those writers who, in light of historical

---

[29]On the *omphalos* tradition in OT studies, see Brevard S. Childs, *Myth and Reality in the Old Testament*, SBT 27 (Naperville IL: Allenson, 1960); and Samuel Terrien, "The Omphalos Myth and Hebrew Religion," *VT* 20 (1970): 313-38.

[30]For another comparison of Philo and Luke on geographical perspectives, see Peder Borgen, "Philo, Luke and Geography," in *Philo, John, and Paul: New Perspectives on Judaism and Early Christianity*, BJS 131 (Atlanta: Scholars Press, 1987) 273-85.

[31]LCL translation.

realities, modified the view of Jerusalem as the center. The most important of these writers is Josephus. Josephus presents his own updating of the table-of-nations tradition (*Ant.* 1.122-47). His depiction is very different from that of *Jubilees*. He does not follow *Jubilees'* schema of correlating the three sons of Noah with the three Ionian continents. More importantly, in light of the destruction of the temple and fall of Jerusalem, he relinquishes the notion that Jerusalem is the center of the earth. When he does refer to Jerusalem as the "navel" (*War* 3.52) he restricts the concept to mean the "navel of the country [i.e. Judaea]" not the world.

4. *At the end times, Jerusalem will be (re)established or once again recognized as the center of the world.* Other texts declare that Jerusalem will be (re)constituted or at least recognized again to be at the center of the world in an eschatological act of God. This view goes back at least to the time of Ezekiel where we read that, in the eschatological battle between God and his enemy, the prince Gog will say, "I will go up against the land of unwalled villages . . . to seize spoil and carry off plunder; to assail the waste place that are now inhabited, and the people . . . who live at the navel of the world" (Ezek 38:10-12; cf. also Isa 66:17-20). This view was also seen in several second temple Jewish texts, roughly contemporary with Luke and Acts. In the *Psalms of Solomon* (a document likely from the first century CE), we read this eschatological vision:

> Sound in Zion the signal trumpet of the sanctuary;
>> announce in Jerusalem the voice of one bringing good news,
>> for God has been merciful to Israel in watching over them.
> Stand on a high place, Jerusalem, and look at your children,
>> from the east and the west assembled together by the Lord.
> From the north they come in the joy of their God;
>> from far distant islands God has assembled them. . . .
> Jerusalem, put on (the) clothes of your glory,
>> prepare the robe of your holiness,
> for God has spoken well of Israel forevermore. (11:1-3, 7)[32]

First Enoch's eschatological vision of Jerusalem "at the center of the earth" (26:1) and the reference in the *Sibylline Oracles* to the "heavenly race of the blessed Jews, who live around the city of God in the middle

---

[32]R. B. Wright, "Psalms of Solomon," in *The Old Testament Pseudepigrapha*, vol. 2, ed. James H. Charlesworth (Garden City NY: Doubleday, 1985) 661-62.

of the earth, are raised up even to the dark clouds" (5:249-50) also bear witness to Jerusalem's place in the center of the world at the end times.

For the implied reader, the text of Luke/Acts does not explicitly refer to Jerusalem as the "center" of the world, as *Jubilees* does, neither does it limit its role to the land of Israel only, as Josephus does. Already in Isaiah 66:18-20, the table-of-nations tradition was updated by a partial list of "the nations," and a *pars pro toto* list also found in the *Sibylline Oracles* (3:512-19). Remember that both *Jubilees* and Josephus update the table of nations, though in ways very different from Luke.

It is difficult to escape the conclusion that the implied reader would have understood Luke, like *Jubilees* and Josephus, to be drawing on the table of nations to locate Jerusalem on his symbolic map. But the implied reader would presumably also have concluded that Luke is willing neither to state baldly that Jerusalem is indeed at the center of the world (as *Jubilees* does) nor to demote Jerusalem to the center only of the land of Israel (as Josephus does); after all Jews from every nation under heaven have come there. Rather, like Philo, Luke uses the fact of the diaspora to imply that Jerusalem is still important, though he avoids Philo's language that Jerusalem is the "mother city." Luke asserts the importance of Jerusalem in an eschatological context foreshadowing the Gentile mission.

So to sum up: for the implied reader conversant with these various options for "locating" Jerusalem, Luke locates Jerusalem by drawing on a familiar "thesaurus"; the implied reader recognizes the following: (1) Luke's use of table-of-nations tradition (with *Jub.*, Isa, and Josephus); (2) the appeal (with Philo) to the diaspora to establish Jerusalem's place; and (3) the eschatological setting of many references to Jerusalem (with Ezek, *Pss. Sol.*, *1 Enoch*, and the *Sib. Or.*). But Luke's view presents the implied reader with a fifth alternative, which at this point may be stated negatively: Jerusalem does not stand in the center of Luke's symbolic world.

This last statement contradicts Conzelmann's conclusion and flies into the face of much contemporary Lukan scholarship. If not at the center, then where? Luke conveniently answers that question for us twice. Jerusalem stands at the *end* of the story of Jesus as the goal of his journey and at the *beginning* of the story of the church as the starting point for Christian witness in the world. I will deal with this second point in more detail. At the end of Luke's gospel, Jesus commands his disciples: "Thus it is written, that the Messiah is to suffer and to rise from the dead on the third day, and that repentance of sins is to be proclaimed in his name to all nations, *beginning from Jerusalem*. And you are witnesses of these things" (24:47-48; emphasis added). And Jesus says in Acts 1:8: "you will be my witnesses in Jerusalem, in all Judea and Samaria, and to the end of the earth."

For Luke, Jerusalem is not the city of the end time. His symbolic world does not picture the nations swarming to Jerusalem to receive the gospel. Jerusalem is associated with the end only in the sense that it stands at the beginning of the end, the beachhead for the Gentile mission. There is, of course, a spatial dimension to Luke's eschatology. When the disciples ask Jesus "is this the time when you will restore the kingdom to Israel?" Jesus brushes aside their temporal question and replaces it with a spatial response: "It is not for you to know the times or periods . . . but you will be my witnesses in Jerusalem . . . to the end of the earth" (Acts 1:7-8). For Luke, there is a real sense in which the parousia cannot occur until the Christian witness reaches the end of the earth. That is to say, the temporal dimension of eschatology is interrelated to its spatial dimension.[33] But Jerusalem is not the center of Luke's symbolic world, and he is no Christian Zionist as Conzelmann implies, but neither is Jerusalem simply demoted as Davies insists. Luke's view, then, may be stated positively: Jerusalem was, on the one hand, an ending to the story of Jesus and, on the other hand, the beginning of the church's end-time witness, which included but was not restricted to the Gentile mission.

IV. Comparison with Joseph Tyson's *Images of Judaism in Luke-Acts*

This conclusion regarding Luke's ambiguous presentation of Jerusalem is similar to that drawn regarding Judaism in general by Joseph Tyson in his book *Images of Judaism in Luke-Acts*. Tyson finds an "ambivalence in Luke-Acts in regard to the images of Judaism," an ambivalence he ex-

---

[33]This spatial dimension of Luke's eschatology has attracted scathing critique. Many have identified the commission of Acts 1:8 exclusively with the Gentile mission and then argued that Luke has a "theology of glory," a triumphalist attitude that depicts the gospel steamrolling through the Mediterranean basin, converting anything that moves. But while to be a "witness" in the Lukan world includes the Gentile mission, more generally it means to bear testimony to the redemptive work achieved by God through Christ, and often involves a dimension of suffering. On the theme of suffering in Luke/Acts, see the various writings of David Moessner, esp. " 'The Christ Must Suffer,' The Church Must Suffer: Rethinking the Theology of the Cross in Luke-Acts," in *SBLSP* (1990): 165-95.

plains as the attempt "to wean the implied reader away from Judaism and convince him to accept the Christian message."[34] Tyson makes similar observations regarding the city of Jerusalem and the temple.[35]

Tyson reaches this conclusion by utilizing the work of Wolfgang Iser and R. Alan Culpepper to draw a profile of the implied reader of Luke/Acts based on the implied reader's knowledge of locations, persons, languages, events, measurements and money, religious practices, and literature. Following Culpepper's lead, Tyson argues that unexplained references to characters, places, and events mean that "an implied author makes some assumptions about the intellectual capacity of an implied reader."[36] He maintains further that the modern critic

> may identify some of the assumptions about the implied reader by being attentive to allusions that appear in the text, characters that are not fully identified, references that require geographical knowledge, events that are not fully explained, as well as indications of language, customs, and literary competence.[37]

For Tyson, the emergent implied reader of Luke/Acts is similar in perspective to "those characters in Acts that are called 'Godfearers.'"[38] This implied reader becomes "the benchmark against which other readings may be judged."[39]

Tyson brings much clarity to the bewildering maze of positive and negative images of Judaism in the Lukan writings. His decision to analyze those images by attending to their occurrences within the narrative

---

[34]Tyson, *Images of Judaism in Luke-Acts*, 183. See also Tyson's work on Jerusalem and the temple in his *The Death of Jesus in Luke-Acts* (Columbia: University of South Carolina Press, 1986) 84-113.

[35]Tyson, *Images of Judaism in Luke-Acts*, 24, 53, 74-76, passim. Tyson, for example, refers to the powerfully negative image of the temple doors being shut for the last time in Acts 21:30, observing that from "this point on, no Christian enters the Temple, nor does it function in any way in the following narratives" (184).

[36]Tyson, *Images of Judaism in Luke-Acts*, 23.

[37]Tyson, *Images of Judaism in Luke-Acts*, 23.

[38]Tyson, *Images of Judaism in Luke-Acts*, 36.

[39]Tyson, *Images of Judaism in Luke-Acts*, 22. Though I myself prefer Peter Rabinowitz's terminology and definition of the *authorial audience* as the theoretical model for understanding the role of the reader, for the sake of consistency and because I see basic continuity between Tyson's "implied reader" (with certain extratextual knowledge) and my "authorial audience," I will refer here to the "implied reader" of Luke/Acts. On the notion of the authorial audience, see Peter J. Rabinowitz, "Truth in Fiction: A Reexamination of Audience," *CrIn* 4 (1977) 126; and Mary Ann Tolbert, *Sowing the Gospel: Mark's World in Literary-Historical Perspective* (Minneapolis: Fortress, 1989) 52-55.

plot of Luke and Acts is a significant advance over those studies which sought either to excavate the various "sources" of Judaism in Luke/Acts or to catalogue the references to Jewish persons, places, festivals or rituals with no regard to their placement in the overall narrative(s).

I would like to argue that the next step in such an analysis is to contextualize these images of Judaism within the context of other postbiblical representations of Judaism.[40] Tyson's work appeared at a time when biblical literary criticism was heavily influenced by and indebted to formalist approaches which tended to view the text as an autonomous entity. To his credit, Tyson attempted to resist this impulse by noting that literary analysis of the gospels required acknowledging "extratextual knowledge on the part of the implied reader."[41] I am not persuaded, however, that the textually encoded implied reader (even with extratextual knowledge) furnishes an adequate theoretical model for dealing with the text in its ancient literary context. And while Tyson's very attractive thesis (that the "implied reader" of Luke-Acts bears striking resemblance to the Lukan "Godfearer") fits well with my comparison of the Lukan view of Jerusalem with other postbiblical representations, I do not think this overall thesis can be properly evaluated until compared more comprehensively with the "images of Judaism" in other second temple texts, reconstructed with the same literary sensitivity employed by Tyson on Luke/Acts. This essay is one small step in that direction.

The rule of thumb for me is simple to state, but difficult to execute. Interpretation requires that we place a word in the context of a sentence, a sentence in the context of a paragraph, a paragraph in the context of a section, a section in the context of a literary text, and a text in context of its larger social and literary environment.[42]

---

[40]Of course, one can apply a variety of reader-response approaches to a biblical text which do not attempt to reconstruct an encoded or ancient audience. Tyson, however, clearly wants to avoid an "idiosyncratic" reading (see Tyson, *Images of Judaism in Luke-Acts*, 20).

[41]Tyson, *Images of Judaism in Luke-Acts*, 23. See John A. Darr, *On Character Building: The Reader and the Rhetoric of Characterization in Luke-Acts*, LCBI (Louisville KY: Westminster/John Knox, 1992), who has been especially sensitive to the necessity for constructing the extratext of the reader.

[42]See Charles Talbert, "Once Again: Gospel Genre," *Semeia* 43 (1988): 53, for a similar formula, though his construal is in the context of the importance of genre criticism for biblical studies.

V. Conclusion

At the conclusion of a well-known essay, Jonathan Z. Smith remarked, " 'Map is not territory'—but maps are all we possess."[43] All too often in the history of Lukan scholarship, debate has turned to the relationship between the territory, that is, the historical events of early Christianity, and the map, the ways in which Luke represented, construed, and/or invented those events. As important as those issues often are, preoccupation with them can distract us from interpreting the texts in their final form. Joseph Tyson belongs in that category of scholars who helpfully remind us that since "maps are all we possess" we should take care to read them as carefully as we can.[44] I, for one, am grateful for the sure-footed way Professor Tyson has led so many of us through the thicket we know as Luke/Acts!

---

[43]Jonathan Z. Smith, *Map Is Not Territory: Studies in the History of Religions* (Leiden: Brill, 1978) 309.

[44]And, of course, Professor Tyson has not only been a "reader of maps"; his work on the Lukan view of Judaism is itself an act of symbolic cartography, fueled by his interest in redrawing the map of contemporary Jewish-Christian relations in ways that foster "more benign convictions about Jewish-Christian relations in our own time" (Tyson, *Images of Judaism in Luke-Acts*, 189).

The Rhetorical Character of Luke 1–2

Philip L. Shuler

I. Introduction

The relationship between chapters 1–2 and the rest of Luke's gospel has long been a subject of scholarly discussion. On the one hand, Hans Conzelmann completed his classic study on the Gospel of Luke with little notice of the first two chapters. For him, these two chapters simply played no essential role in his examination of Luke's literary and theological purposes.[1] On the other hand, some more recent discussions, including that of Professor Joe Tyson, have argued that Luke 1–2 are integral to the Lukan narrative and play a vital role in one's understanding of the Lukan literary corpus (both Luke's gospel and Acts).[2]

The present paper argues for the latter view: namely, that Luke 1–2 are vital to the Lukan narrative agenda, and further that Luke's literary rhetorical style in these two chapters places him squarely in the category of accomplished Hellenistic authors. Our purpose is to demonstrate how Luke has structured the first two chapters in order to prepare his readers for the portrait of the adult Jesus he is constructing. Chapters 1–2, therefore, are central to the Lukan narratives, both the gospel and Acts.

We acknowledge from the outset that the present research presupposes the two-gospel hypothesis source paradigm.[3] Working from this hypothesis may seem irrelevant to the reader, given the difficulties involved in placing the birth narratives of Matthew alongside those of

---

[1]Conzelmann regarded the first two chapters of Luke as late additions to the book and not an integral part of Luke's gospel. See *The Theology of Luke* (San Francisco: Harper, 1961) 118, 172.

[2]Joseph B. Tyson, "The Birth Narratives and the Beginning of Luke's Gospel," *Semeia* 52 (1990): 101-18.

[3]One of the reasons I am especially honored to make this contribution rests not only with the distinguished career of Prof. Joe Tyson, but also with the way Prof. Tyson constantly fosters critical thought even when he may disagree with the paradigm fundamental to that research. While he does not hold to the two-gospel source paradigm, he has nevertheless been consistently strong in his belief that such research was important and necessary. He has not hesitated to offer helpful reviews and critiques of work in progress. His comments and suggestions have consistently been most helpful; his stature as a scholar with a commitment to unqualified academic excellent is unassailable.

Luke. To say, however, that Luke cannot easily be placed in direct parallel with Matthew's gospel does not mean that Luke did not know Matthew's work, nor that he failed to rely upon it in any way. Indeed, a glance at the common parallels suggest Luke's awareness of the Matthean text. Consider the following parallel information:

	Matthew	Luke
1. Mary and Joseph will serve as parents for Jesus	(1:16, 18, 19, 20, 24; 2:11, 13, 19)	(1:27-56; 2:1, 5, 16, 19, 34)
2. Joseph is betrothed to Mary	(1:18)	(1:27; 2:5; cf. 1:35)
3. Virginity of Mary	(1:18, 23)	(1:27, 34)
4. Conception by Holy Spirit	(1:18, 20)	(1:35)
5. Jesus' family is from the line of David	(1:1, 6, 17, 20)	(1:27, 32, 69; 2:4, 11)
6. Angelic annunciation	(1:20)	(1:30)
7. Child's name given	(1:21)	(1:13, 31; 2:21)
8. Jesus as savior	(1:21)	(2:11)
9. Child visited	(2:11)	(2:16)
10. Visitors worhsip	(2:2, 11)	(cf. 2:20)
11. Jesus is born in Bethlehem	(2:1, 5, 6)	(2:4, 15)
12. Herod is king	(2:1)	(1:5)
13. There is "great joy"	(2:10)	(1:14; 2:10)
14. Use of "righteous"	(1:19)	(1:6; 2:25)
15. "Fear"	(1:20; 2:22)	(1:12, 13, 29-30, 65; 2:9)
16. Abraham	(1:1-2, 17)	(1:55, 73)
17. Family's hometown is Nazareth	(2:23)	(1:26; 2:4, 39, 51)
18. Genealogy	(1:1-17)	(cf. 3:23-38)

Of course, such comparative lists do not conclusively prove the validity of the two-gospel hypothesis paradigm. However, the above list increases in significance if one is working from this paradigm. Clearly, both Matthew and Luke share many of the same details about Jesus' birth. However, they have formulated their own respective narrative accounts, and the literary results are vastly different.

II. Luke 1:1-4.
The Prologue

Luke is the only synoptic evangelist to introduce his gospel with a prologue. In form and function, Luke 1:1-4 is typical of the introductions found in various Hellenistic genres (e.g., histories, apologies, and lives). Luke's prologue reflects close affinities with epistolary and oratorical works,[4] and is comparable to prologues found in βίος narratives (e.g., in Plutarch, Suetonius, and Diogenes Laertius).

Matthew has opened his account of Jesus with the word, βίβλος (Matt 1:1). This reference is sufficient to remind Luke of the accepted procedure in Hellenistic "books," namely, one begins a "book" with a statement of authorial intent. Accordingly, Luke formulates his own prologue in which he reveals his methodological procedures ("having followed all things closely," Luke 1:3a) and the literary purpose for his narrative (he is not the first to "compile a narrative," 1:1). Luke proposes to present an "orderly account" of all that has taken place (1:3b).

Luke's prologue is not specific about the genre of Luke (or Acts, for that matter). One notes the absence of genre designators in the title—designators such as "life," "history," "gospel"—or even references to Jesus, his followers, or the church. This absence causes the reader no little perplexity. Ambiguity about the genre of Luke-Acts encourages questions about whether the documents are a single work in two volumes, a work with an attached sequel, or simply two distinct works (each with its own purpose). Is Luke's gospel some kind of "life" or "history?" Is Acts "history" or some kind of "life?" Perhaps an additional question is: does Luke really know what he intends to write? A negative answer to the last question seems inconceivable, given the rhetorical skill evident in Luke 1–2. These chapters are rhetorically and meticulously crafted. For this reason, I conclude that the ambiguity is intentional.

With such ambiguity Luke is able to link the two volumes, the Gospel of Luke and Acts, that separately present two different subjects: Luke's gospel contains the "life" of Jesus and Acts is a "history" (or perhaps a "life") of the development of the early Christian community for which the βίος of Jesus is hermeneutically crucial. In order to grasp fully the implications and impact of Luke's gospel, one needs only to continue reading the second volume, Acts. Conversely, to understand fully the story of the church as recorded in Acts, Luke's gospel is imperative. Luke himself makes this point in Acts by referring directly to the previous volume (Τὸν μὲν πρῶτον, Acts 1:1), which clearly is Luke's gospel. The address to "Theophilus" also links the two volumes (Luke 1:3; Acts 1:1). In this way, Luke's work parallels that of Philo in *Moses* (written in two distinct parts). The major difference between the

---

[4]Vernon Robbins, "Prefaces in Greco-Roman Biography and Luke-Acts," *PerRS* 6 (1979): 95-103.

two authors is that both of Philo's volumes are concerned with Moses (prophet and priest in book 1, and king in book 2) whereas Luke's first volume is concerned with the person of Jesus and his second volume is concerned with the church that emerged immediately following and in response to Jesus' resurrection and ascension.[5]

A closer look at the Lukan prologue reveals much about Luke's style as an Hellenistic author. He is making use of the best sources available to him. Based on Luke's words, there is little difficulty seeing Matthew as one of the πολλοί. Luke has consulted others in the process of writing his own διήγησις ("narrative," Luke 1:1). This term for a narrative is commonly found in ancient documents including the βίοι of Plutarch (cf. *Lycurgus* 1.3; *Cimon* 2.3; *Agis and Cleomenes* 2.6). Luke supports the validity of his διήγησις by insisting both that his sources were "eyewitnesses and ministers of the word" (1:2) and that he has carefully examined his sources. Having both carefully (ἀκριβῶς) followed these testimonies of the events (1:3) and also supplemented these with his own direct information, Luke writes his διήγησις. Luke also describes his narrative as καθεξῆς (1:3), by which he seems to mean "sequential" or "chronological."[6] Luke's statement of literary purpose may be summarized in the following manner: "After I examined all things closely, including the testimonies of eyewitnesses and ministers of the word, it seemed good for me also to write a narrative in sequence."

Luke's use of the descriptive term καθεξῆς need not be understood as applying to his gospel only. Since Luke is writing to his own community whose self-identity revolves around the person and work of Jesus, the term καθεξῆς may refer to the sequential order of events recorded in both Luke's gospel and Acts (that is, Jesus' life, the activities of his followers, of the church, and of the Gentile mission). In this way, Luke preserves the essential historical sequence of events that are related in Luke's gospel and Acts without quibbling over the chronological details within the respective works.

In the prologue, Luke addresses his narrative to Theophilus (which may be either an historical individual or a symbolic designation) in the

---

[5]In addition to Philo's work on Moses, one would benefit by comparing Luke's prologue with the prologues of Josephus's *Against Apion* (1.2) and of Xenophon's *Agesilaus* (1.1).

[6]Michael D. Goulder, *Luke: A New Paradigm*, 2 vols., JSNTSup 20 (Sheffield: JSOT Press, 1989) 1:199-200.

form of direct address as was common to biographical writers like Plutarch (*Theseus* 1.1; *Dion* 1.1; *Demosthenes* 1.1) and Josephus (*Against Apion* 1.1.1; 2.1.1).[7] Finally, because he has "followed all things closely," received the testimonies of "eyewitnesses and ministers of the word," and drawn from his own experiences, Luke punctuates his prologue with a claim of the narrative's reliability (ἀσφάλειαν, Luke 1:4). This authorial concern for narrative reliability is common to ancient prologues (cf. Plutarch, *Lycurgus* 1.3; *Numa* 1.4; *Nicias* 1.5; Josephus, *Against Apion* 1.1.47-52; and Philo, *Moses* 1.4).

III. Luke 1:5–2:40.
The Narratives Involving John and Jesus: An Overview

In this long passage, Luke expands upon Matthew's account by recording not only the birth of Jesus but also the birth of John the Baptist, and he does so in parallel fashion. The germinal idea for the presentations of these two births may derive from the two significant personages in Jesus' background which Luke finds in Matthew 1:1, namely, the traditions of David (Jesus) and Abraham (John). Admittedly, one cannot push these comparisons too far. Davidic references do appear elsewhere in sections associated with John (e.g., Luke 1:69) and Abraham is mentioned in passages referring to Jesus (e.g., 1:55). Still, the associations of John with Abraham and of Jesus with David is striking.

The parallel pattern by which Luke presents these stories of annunciation and birth is a beautifully crafted one. It may be diagrammed as follows.

John's annunciation (1:5-25) ‖ Jesus' annunciation (1:26-38)
Mary visits Elizabeth (1:39-56)
John's birth account (1:57-79) ‖ Jesus' birth account (2:1-39)
Nurture statement (1:80) ‖ Nurture statement (2:40)
Jesus visits the temple (2:41-51)
Nurture conclusion (2:52)

The diagram conveys both the progression of Luke's narrative and the parallel structure Luke employs to prepare for his portrait of Jesus. The parallelism involves John the Baptist and Jesus, beginning with the announcement to Elizabeth and Zechariah that she, though advanced in age, will give birth to John, and its parallel in the announcement to Mary

---

[7]Robbins, "Prefaces in Greco-Roman Biography and Luke-Acts," 107.

that she, though a virgin, will give birth to Jesus. The second set of parallels is the respective accounts of the birth of John and the corresponding birth of Jesus. Each birth account concludes with a parallel nurture statement. After the annunciation stories, there is a single episode involving Mary's visit to Elizabeth during which time the narrative clearly emphasizes the superiority of Jesus. Following the birth accounts, another single episode focuses entirely on Jesus who, at the age of twelve years, visits the temple with his parents. The third climactic nurture statement referring once more to Jesus (Luke 2:52)—in parallel with the earlier one concerning John (1:80) and the later one again concerning Jesus (2:40)—concludes both parallel series of accounts with the reader fully prepared for and now focused on Jesus' adult ministry. Clearly, Jesus has emerged as the major figure around whom God's plan of salvation will unfold.

The contents of this section correspond to the encomium rhetorical rules, namely, that an author will recount things that happen before, during, and after a birth, if deemed appropriate (cf. Aristotle, *Rhet. Alex.* 3-4; Cicero, *De Part. Orat.* 11; and Quintilian, *Inst. Orat.* 3.7.10-18). Two additional concerns account for the rhetorical parallel structure of Luke 1–2: (1) the clear delineation of the relationship between John and Jesus, and (2) the identification of John and Jesus and their subsequent ministries with God's plan of salvation. Underlying the Lukan parallelism in this section is the rhetorical technique of comparison (cf. Aristotle, *Rhetoric* 1.9.20-25 and *Rhet. Alex.* 142a25-30).

Plutarch's *Lives* provides numerous examples of the rhetorical use of comparison in Hellenistic biographical introductions. Explicit comparisons based upon the similarity of persons' character, deeds, and vocational accomplishments are frequently evident in *Theseus* (2.1-2), *Solon and Publicola* (21), *Demosthenes* (3.2-3), *Pericles* (2.4), *Dion* (1.1-2), and *Tiberius and Caius Gracchus* (2). One notes especially Plutarch's discussion (*Dion* 1.1-2) where the similarities between the teachings of Brutus and Dion (a "disciple" of Plato) are related to the teachings of Plato. In another comparison, Plutarch even notes that the lives of Demosthenes and Cicero are so similar that "it would seem that the Deity originally fashioned them on the same plan" (*Demosthenes* 3.2-3). Comparisons by means of contrast are found in the introductions of *Lycurgus and Numa* (1.1-2), *Aristides* (2.1-2), and *Tiberius and Caius Gracchus* (3). In the case of *Theseus* and *Tiberius and Caius Gracchus*, these two share familial relationship.

With Luke's gospel, while the literary technique of comparison is typical of its literary environment, the execution is distinctive. In the works cited above, the comparisons are made without employing the type of "back and forth" or antiphonal parallel structure found in Luke. In Luke's case, the superiority of one character over another becomes increasingly clear to the reader as each unit unfolds. Jesus' superiority to John is evident in the manner by which Luke places these units in antiphonal parallel with the more significant character occupying the second position in the parallel. The inserted single units, Mary visits Elizabeth and Jesus visits the temple, coupled with the three nurture statements accentuate the pivotal role of Jesus. The reader focuses more narrowly upon Jesus as each comparison is presented. Luke is at home in the Greco-Roman literary milieu of comparison.

IV. Luke 1:5-25.
The Annunciation of John

Following the prologue, Luke turns his attention to "the things that have been accomplished." The first things to be accomplished concern John; therefore, his ministry becomes the precise point at which each canonical evangelist begins to address the life of the adult Jesus. Luke demonstrates the continuity between Jesus and John by relating John's divine origin prior to, yet in concert with, Jesus. The angel Gabriel visits Zechariah and Mary (Luke 1:19, 26) in order to explain that the circumstances of the two births derive from divine activity.

John comes "in the spirit and power of Elijah . . . to make ready for the Lord a people prepared" (Luke 1:17). The announcement of John's birth is likewise the announcement of the one who is to come, the Lord. As is generally true with encomiastic compositions, the focus is upon the narrative's subject, Jesus, the one expected even though his name has not yet appeared in the text!

Luke identifies John's parents as worthy of praise (Luke 1:6). The attention placed upon the age of Zechariah and Elizabeth (1:7, 18) calls forth the typology of Abraham and Sarah. More specifically, one notices the parallel themes in the circumstances surrounding both Isaac's birth and John's birth as described by Luke. Isaac's father Abraham kept the commandments and ordinances (Gen 26:5) as did John's parents (Luke 1:6). Sarah, Isaac's mother, was barren (Gen 11:7), as was Elizabeth, John's mother (Luke 1:7). Isaac's parents were "advanced" in years (Gen 18:11), as were John's parents (Luke 1:7). In both instances, the promised birth produces the response of doubt in the form of a question (Gen 15:8; Luke 1:18). In both, assurance comes in the statement that no "word" is impossible "with" God (Gen 18:14; Luke 1:37). A statement of neighbors rejoicing appears in both accounts (Gen 21:6; Luke 1:58). In this rhetorical manner, John gains authority in the eyes of the reader, and Jesus gains even more authority through the unfolding comparisons that Luke orchestrates. Additionally, Luke may have received this idea of an Abraham/Isaac typology related to John from his reading of the reference to Abraham in the first verse of Matthew's gospel (Matt 1:1).

Important themes that one will encounter while reading the Lukan corpus appear in this unit. The activity of the Holy Spirit (e.g., Luke 1:15), miraculous deeds that indicate divine intervention (1:20-23), and the temple are three such themes.[8]

V. Luke 1:26-38.
The Annunciation of Jesus

Luke's account of the annunciation of Jesus closely parallels that of John the Baptist. The points of parallel may be listed as follows.

John	Jesus
1. Date of announcement (1:5)	1. Date of announcement (1:26)
2. Names of parents (1:5)	2. Names of parents (1:27)
3. Parents praised (1:6)	3. Mary favored (1:28-30)
4. Age of parents (1:7, 18)	4. Virginity of mother (1:27)
5. Angel appears to Zechariah (1:11)	5. Angel appears to Mary (1:26)
6. Angel, named Gabriel (1:19)	6. Angel, named Gabriel (1:26)
7. Told not to fear (1:13)	7. Told not to fear (1:30)
8. Conception (1:13)	8. Conception (1:31)
9. Child named (1:13)	9. Child named (1:31)
10. Filled with Holy Spirit in womb (1:35)	10. Holy Spirit comes upon Mary (1:35)
11. Great before the Lord (1:15)	11. Son of Most High (1:32)

Luke has used the device of comparison to demonstrate the excellence of Jesus: if the annunciation of John is impressive, the annunciation of Jesus is even more impressive. For example, the angel speaks directly to Mary in the annunciation of Jesus (perhaps because Luke sees her to be the climactic point of Matthew's genealogy; Matt 1:16) while Zechariah is the recipient in the account of John's annunciation. The

---

[8]Tyson has convincingly identified the role of the temple in Luke-Acts. See Tyson, "The Birth Narratives and the Beginning of Luke's Gospel," 112-15.

angel is identified before the annunciation to Mary (Luke 1:26), but Zechariah learned the name of the angel only after the message was delivered (1:19). Elizabeth conceives John in her old age (1:24, cf. 1:7), but Mary conceives Jesus while still a virgin (1:26-27, 34). Zechariah and Elizabeth are praised (1:6), but Mary is twice addressed as "the one who has found favor with God" (1:28, 30). John is said to be "filled with the Holy Spirit from his mother's womb" (1:15), whereas "the Holy Spirit will come upon" Mary, an image that affirms that Jesus is "Son of God" (1:35).[9]

Future greatness is affirmed in both instances: John will be great "before the Lord" (Luke 1:15) while Jesus will be called "the Son of the Most High" and he will be given "the throne of David" (1:32). In the eyes of the reader, Jesus' stature begins to move gradually to center stage through the comparison.

The Lukan theme of the role of the Holy Spirit is again accentuated, as is the angelic visitation. Also, the miraculous deed is present for Mary's benefit in the reference to the conception of Elizabeth, "who was called barren" (Luke 1:36).

VI. Luke 1:39-56.
Mary Visits Elizabeth

In dramatic fashion, Luke brings together the accounts of two separate annunciations, those of John and Jesus, in his account of Mary's visit with Elizabeth. Here, the reader discovers that the two characters are related. Luke notes the familial relationship between Mary and Elizabeth at Luke 1:36, a relationship that explains the reasons for Mary's visit.

Luke continues his rhetoric of comparison in the following ways. When Mary and Elizabeth meet, Elizabeth's baby (John) leaps within her womb and she is "filled with the Holy Spirit" (1:41). The theme of "being filled with the Holy Spirit" is common in Luke-Acts (1:15, 41, 67; Acts 2:4; 4:8, 31; 9:17; 13:9). Elizabeth's words acknowledge divine presence and recognize excellence, thereby exalting Mary's baby (Jesus).

---

[9]See David Cartlidge and David L. Dungan, *Documents for the Study of the Gospels* (Philadelphia: Fortress, 1994) 129-36. Other Hellenistic works containing stories that attribute birth to divine initiation include Plutarch's *Alexander* (2.1–3.2), *Fabius Maximus* (1.1-2), *Romulus* (5); Suetonius's *(De Vita Caesarum)* Vergil (3-5) and *Augustus* (2.94.1-7), Diogenes Laertius's *Plato* (3.1-2), and Philostratus's *Apollonius of Tyana* (1.4-6). Works that claim divine descent include Xenophon's *Agesilaus* (1.2), and Plutarch's *Numa* (3.4) and *Theseus* (2.1-2). This list is by no means exhaustive.

Elizabeth describes Mary as "the mother of my Lord" (1:43) and says that Mary is to be blessed because of the baby she carries in her womb (1:42). Even Elizabeth's baby acknowledges this presence by moving within her womb (1:44). As elsewhere, "belief" (1:45; cf. 1:20) and fulfillment of prophecies internal to his narrative are integral to Luke's account. To be sure, blessed is the one who carries the Lord in her womb; and equally blessed is the one who believes that the word of the Lord will be fulfilled.

The rhetorical impact of this section is clear. Luke affirms that far greater events are taking place than the circumstances of two women giving birth. The comparison between Jesus and John is carried to the level of their mothers. The stage is, thereby, set for Mary's Magnificat in which essential aspects of Jesus' adult ministry are set forth. The focus is upon God (1:46-47, 49) who has done (and will do) great things for his people. He has shown his strength by scattering the proud, putting down the mighty, and exalting the lowly (1:51-52). He has fed the hungry and helped his servant Israel (1:53-54). God is said by Mary to be "my savior" (1:47), and Mary affirms that he will do all of this through the child now being carried in her womb.[10] Mary's Magnificat represents the high point within Luke's narrative thus far. God's redemptive plan is unfolding before Luke's readers with synchronous harmony.

VII. Luke 1:57-80.
The Birth of John

Luke has set the stage. The time for the expected events has now arrived. The antiphonally structured narrative turns once more to John. The story of John's birth and circumcision provides the occasion for Luke to see the completion of the miraculous deed initiated in John's annunciation, that is, the restoration of speech to Zechariah (Luke 1:63-64, cf. 1:20).

This restoration occurs when Zechariah concurs with Elizabeth on the naming of the child, John, a name that does not accord with established tradition. "His name is John" (Luke 1:63) but he will be called "the prophet of the Most High" (1:76). Note that Jesus, by contrast, is called "the son of the Most High" (1:32).

There are no known parallels to the account of John's birth in the canonical gospel traditions (except for the comparison Luke makes with

---

[10]Cf. Jesus' inaugural sermon in Luke 4:16b-30 and his sermon on the plain (6:20–7:1).

Jesus' birth). Goulder argues for a further development of the Abraham typology.[11] Elizabeth, like Sarah before her, gave birth to a "son" when the time was fulfilled for her to "bear" (Gen 21:1f.; cf. Luke 1:57). Genesis states that "whoever hears will rejoice" with Sarah (Gen 21:6), even as Luke states that Elizabeth's neighbors and relatives "heard" and "rejoiced" with her (1:58). Genesis notes that "Isaac was circumcised on the eighth day" (Gen 21:4), and Luke notes that Elizabeth's child also "was circumcised on the eighth day" (1:59). Like Isaac, John also received a name that was given or implied by divine beings (cf. Gen 21:3 with Gen 18:9-15; Luke 1:60, 63 with Luke 1:13).

The Benedictus emphasizes the prophetic spirit of John's ministry by making reference to God's visitation (Luke 1:68), by the validating reference to words spoken by holy prophets of old (1:70; cf. the speeches in Acts, e.g., 3:21), by the prophetic references to being saved from "enemies" and from those who "hate" (Luke 1:71, 73; note the reference to the promise to Abraham, cf. Acts 3:25), and by the goal of prophetic ministry (Luke 1:74-75: "that we . . . might serve him without fear, in holiness and righteousness before him all of the days of our life").

As a prophet, John is to "go before the Lord to prepare his ways, to give knowledge of salvation to his people in the forgiveness of their sins" (Luke 1:76b-77). John will participate in the dispensing of light to those sitting in darkness (1:79; cf. Matt 4:12-16), a signal that, by his ministry of preparation, John simultaneously participates in God's act of salvation through Jesus Christ.

Lukan themes that appear in Luke-Acts are evident in the mercy shown to Elizabeth (Luke 1:58) and in the mercy shown to the poor (a theme that is present both in 1:72 and is prominent in Luke's sermon on the plain, esp. 6:36). Other reoccurring Lukan themes also appear. Once more, the theme of "being filled with the Holy Spirit" (1:67) recurs as does the theme of Israel's salvation in Zechariah's pronouncement that "God . . . has visited and redeemed his people" (1:68).

Luke provides closure to the scenes of the birth announcements in the form of an encomiastic nurture statement (as described in the rules of encomium writing by Hermogenes):[12] "And the child grew and became strong in spirit, and he was in the wilderness till the day of his manifesta-

---

[11]Goulder, *Luke: A New Paradigm*, 1:237-38.
[12]D. L. Clark, *Rhetoric in Greco-Roman Education* (New York: Columbia University Press, 1957) 196-97.

tion to Israel" (Luke 1:80). In addition to this nurture statement regarding John, Luke provides two other such statements regarding Jesus (1:80; 2:40, 52).

VIII. Luke 2:1-40.
The Birth of Jesus

Based on our analysis of Luke's use of the rhetorical technique of comparison, the moment toward which the whole antiphonally structured introduction has been moving now arrives. The focus is on the birth of Jesus. The points of parallel between Luke's accounts of the birth of John and the birth of Jesus may be listed as follows.

John	Jesus
1. Time arrived (1:57)	1. Time arrived (2:6)
2. Birth of a son (1:57)	2. Birth of a first-born son (2:7)
3. Zechariah speaks, blessing God (1:64)	3. Angel speaks/multitude of heavenly hosts speak (2:10-13)
4. Neighbors afraid (1:65)	4. Shepherds afraid (2:9)
5. Neighbors lay up in heart (1:66)	5. Mary ponders in heart (2:19)
6. Circumcised on eighth day (1:59)	6. Circumcised on eighth day; origin of name from the angel repeated (2:21)
7. Zechariah filled with Holy Spirit (1:67)	7. Holy Spirit comes upon Simeon, inspires him with revelation (2:25-27)
8. Praise by canticle of Zechariah (1:68-79)	8. Praise by persons and oracles (1:68-79) of Simeon and Anna (2:25-38)
9. Salvation for Israel (1:68-69)	9. Salvation given all peoples (2:31-32)
10. Prepares and goes before the Lord (1:76)	10. Set for rise and fall of many in Israel and suffering (2:34-35)
11. Child grows and becomes strong (1:80)	11. Child grows, becomes strong, wise, and favored by God (2:40; cf. 2:52)

In contrast with John's birth, Jesus' birth reveals careful documentation of circumstance and time (an enrollment under Quirinius; Luke 2:1-3) as well as of place (Jesus' parents are said to live in Nazareth and must travel to Bethlehem; 2:4). Bethlehem is identified as the "city of David" (2:4). The God who acts for and in behalf of the lowly (1:46-55, esp. 1:48) now acts in a lowly stable (2:6-7). The fact that there was "no place for them in the inn" (2:7) may, for Luke, foreshadow the rejection of Jesus in Nazareth on the occasion of his inaugural sermon (4:16-30) and perhaps even on the occasion of his passion.

As with Elizabeth, the "time came" for Mary "to be delivered" (Luke 2:6, cf. 1:57). Both gave birth to a son, a "firstborn" son in Mary's case (2:7, cf. 1:57). Luke's account of John's birth (1:5-25, 57-80) records the events that occur after his birth (2:8f.). Luke's account of Jesus' birth also records the events that occur after his birth (2:1-7). Luke expands on these events. Angels and heavenly hosts greet the shepherds, giving praise to God at Jesus' birth (2:8-14). The response to both births is similar (cf. 1:65, 2:18). Luke says that "all who heard" about the things that happened to Zechariah "laid them up in their hearts" (1:66) while he says that Mary "kept all these things, pondering them in her heart" (2:19, cf. 2:51).

Both John and Jesus are said by Luke to have been circumcised and named on the eighth day, but the account of Jesus' circumcision explicitly refers back to the time when his name had been given by the angel, Gabriel (Luke 2:21, cf. 1:31; for the announcement of John's name and its assignment, see 1:57-63, 1:13).

Canticles serve here to accentuate the future role of Jesus (Luke 2:29-32, 34-35; cf. 1:46-55) as they did for John (1:14-17, 68-79). Luke describes the Jerusalemite, Simeon, as δίκαιος (2:25) even as Zechariah and Elizabeth, John's parents, had been so described earlier (1:6; cf. Matt 1:19 where Joseph, the would-be parent of Jesus, is also described as δίκαιος).

Simeon finds fulfillment after seeing the child and declares salvation to be "a light for revelation to the Gentiles and for glory to thy people, Israel" (Luke 2:30-32). For the parents of Jesus, however, there is not only blessing, but also the ominous allusion to Jesus' future suffering (2:33-35). Further significance is added to the event by the story involving the prophetess Anna (2:36-38).

Luke brings his comparison to glorious climax. And this child, Jesus, "grew and became strong" (2:40a), as John had previously done (1:80). In addition to describing the growth and development which both Jesus and John experienced (1:80), Luke supplements his description of Jesus by explaining that Jesus was also "filled with wisdom; and the favor of God was upon him" (2:40b).

This passage is replete with themes common to Luke's gospel and Acts: the activity of the Holy Spirit (amplified considerably in Luke 2:25-27), the death of Jesus (2:34-45, significant both in the gospel and in Acts), the mission to the Gentiles (2:32), and the temple (2:27, 37). Indeed, all that which has been discussed above regarding Luke's account of the significance of Jesus' birth will be developed later in the remaining portions of Luke's gospel and in Acts. It would be difficult for one to find in ancient literature a birth account that more effectively prepared the reader for an adult career, death, and subsequent developments stemming from this person than Luke has done in the first two chapters of his gospel (in preparation for the whole of Luke-Acts).

It is significant to note that Luke frames this portion of his introduction in several ways. First, the section begins with Zechariah in the temple (1:5-23) and ends with Jesus and his parents in the temple (2:22-38). Secondly, John's parents are described as "walking in all the commandments and ordinances of the Lord, blameless" (1:6), while Jesus' birth account concludes with his parents having "performed everything according to the law of the Lord" (2:39a) before returning to Nazareth from the temple (2:39b). In this way, Luke has skillfully crafted a tightly structured section, one that effectively sets forth both Jesus' superiority over John and also the major themes to be further explored in his narrative(s).

IX. Luke 2:41-52.
Jesus' Temple Journey as a Youth

Luke has stated that John will not reappear until the time of his "manifestation" (1:80). The comparison of the birth of Jesus with the birth of John prepares for the shift of focus from Jesus and John to Jesus alone. In this story Luke completes that shift.

When Jesus is twelve years old, he goes with his parents, as is their custom, to the temple in Jerusalem at the Passover feast (Luke 2:41). The parents become separated from Jesus and begin their homeward journey with the mistaken assumption that he is with other relatives. After a day's travel, they look for him unsuccessfully among their relatives and friends, and find it necessary to return to Jerusalem to continue the search. "They found him in the temple" with the teachers, listening to them and asking them questions (2:46). This scene depicts a typical student-teacher relationship that would be appropriate in either a Jewish or a non-Jewish, Hellenistic setting. In this setting, Jesus excels. He is the model pupil, and his actions impress all who witness his excellent performance. "All who heard him were amazed at his understanding and his answers" (2:47). When his parents do find him, they express their anxiety. In response, Jesus offers little consolation that his parents are able to understand ("Did you not know that I must be in my Father's house?" 2:49, cf. 2:50). The family then returns home together and Mary, once more, "ponders in her heart" (2:51; cf. 2:19).

The story is a beautiful account, at home in the Hellenistic literary environment. In it, Luke demonstrates Jesus' excellence at a young age and prepares the reader for a career in which Jesus will have numerous occasions to engage religious leaders, both friendly and hostile. Each time, Jesus will emerge unscathed.

While there are many parallels in Hellenistic βίος literature, one appropriate example appears in Plutarch's *Cicero* (2.2):

> [W]hen he was of an age for taking lessons, his natural talent shone out clear and he won name and fame among the boys, so that their fathers used to visit the schools in order to see Cicero with their own eyes and observe the quickness and intelligence in his studies for which he was extolled, though the ruder ones among them were angry at their sons when they saw them walking with Cicero placed in their midst as a mark of honor. (Cf. Philostratus, *Apollonius of Tyana* 1.7; Philo, *Moses* 1.5.21-23.)

Cicero's youthful prowess in his academic studies serves Plutarch's portrait of Cicero's career as an orator; so also Jesus' spiritual insight, exemplified in this temple scene at the age of twelve, serves Luke's portrait of Jesus as messiah. Jesus' excellence is demonstrated here and throughout Luke's gospel; it will continue in the lives of those who follow after him in Luke's account of the disciples and apostles in Acts.

As the annunciation and birth accounts of John and of Jesus were framed by scenes and activity in the temple, so now Luke similarly frames his entire introduction (1:5–2:52). Luke's introduction began with Zechariah in the temple (1:9). It now ends with a demonstration of Jesus' excellence in that same temple (2:46), thereby marking the conclusion of the preliminary section of Luke's βίος of Jesus (1:1–2:52). It remains only to point to the continued direction of Jesus' development in a final, climactic nurture statement: "And Jesus increased in wisdom and in stature, and in favor with God and man" (2:52). The truth of this statement has just been demonstrated in the account of this temple visit (2:46-47).

From a literary standpoint, this episode provides an impressive double inclusio around the preliminary account of Jesus' βίος. The first inclusio opens before the births of John and Jesus, with Zechariah in the temple (Luke 1:8-11), continues through Jesus' birth (2:1-8) and closes with Jesus' family in the temple (2:22-40). Another closing of an inclusio that opened with a reference to the temple (either 1:9 or 2:37, or both) appears in the one canonical account of Jesus' youth which is also set exclusively in the temple (2:41-51).

X. Conclusion

The trip this paper has taken through Luke 1–2 has produced results that are worth emphasizing. To begin with, Luke has composed his gospel and Acts in a fashion that incorporates both Jewish and non-Jewish, Hellenistic literary traditions. He relies significantly upon Old Testament traditions and has done so in a manner consistent with Hellenistic encomium literature. To be more specific, Luke has composed a prologue that serves both parts of his Luke-Acts διήγησις. Next, he has followed the style of Hellenistic βίος narratives by incorporating the events that precede birth, the events of birth, and the events following birth, including a story of Jesus as a boy.

In point of fact, Luke has recorded the births (including events before, during, and after these births) of two persons, John the Baptist and Jesus. Luke's distinctive contribution is his employment of the Hellenistic rhetorical device known as comparison in an antiphonally designed sequence for the purpose of clarifying the relationship between John and Jesus for his readers. He arranges the annunciation stories of John and Jesus in parallel literary units and brings the stories together with an account of Mary's visit to Elizabeth so that the reader can grasp the preparatory nature of John's role and the more significant role to be played by Jesus. John is an Elijah-type prophet, preparing people for the salvation God will initiate in the person of Jesus.

Then Luke places the accounts of the births of John and Jesus in parallel with one another. Each account serves as the fulfillment of the respective annunciation pronouncements. In addition, the parallel structure of these birth units, a reflection of Luke's use and development of the rhetorical technique of comparison, leads the reader to recognize that this baby born to the virgin, will bring salvation to both Jew and Gentile alike, yet he will suffer in the process. At this point, the focus shifts from the relationship between John and Jesus to the mission of Jesus alone.

The trip Jesus makes to the temple at the age of twelve, the final story in this introductory section of Luke's gospel, stresses the excellence of the youthful Jesus which signals the excellence that will be apparent throughout his career and evident in his followers at a later time.

While fulfilling his literary purposes, Luke has introduced significant themes that will be further developed later in both parts of his narrative, Luke-Acts. Most prominent are the identity of Jesus as the Messiah, the Gentile mission, God's great reversal that favors the poor and the lowly, the temple, and the vital activity of the Holy Spirit. There is little doubt that Luke 1–2 serve Luke's larger two-volume work effectively.

Luke clearly marks off chapters 1–2 as a literary unit by skillfully framing it twice. First, the theme of the temple frames the series of stories between the annunciations of the birth of John and of the birth of Jesus (1:5–2:40). Second, this entire preliminary section is once again framed by the addition of Luke's account of Jesus' visit to the temple (2:41-52). By framing Luke 1:5 2:52 in this manner, Luke uses this preliminary section to prepare his readers for his portrait of the adult Jesus in true Hellenistic narrative fashion. Luke 1–2 serve as a beautiful example of a creative rhetorical structure designed to introduce persuasively a narrative βίος of Jesus.

From Enthymeme to Theology in Luke 11:1-13*

Vernon K. Robbins

Luke 11:1-13 presents an abbreviated version of the Lord's prayer followed by nine verses that elaborate parts of the prayer.[1] Among the notable rhetorical features in this text is a series of rationales (beginning with "for," "because," or "since"), including one in the Lord's prayer itself. These rationales invite a special way to analyze this passage.[2] Rationales in discourse create enthymemes. An enthymeme is an assertion that is expressible as a syllogism.[3] A special characteristic of an enthymeme is to leave a premise or conclusion unexpressed, with a pre-

---

*I am grateful to H. J. Bernard Combrink, David Armstrong-Reiner, Lynn R. Lutes, and Thomas D. Stegman for their probing rhetorical exegeses of this sequence in Luke for my Ph.D. seminar on rhetorical criticism in the New Testament at Emory University during the spring of 1997. In addition, I am highly indebted to Gordon D. Newby, Laurie L. Patton, R. Alan Culpepper, and Margaret E. Dean for their supportive, critical reviews of this ongoing work.

[1]Matt 6:9-13 contains an expanded version of the Lord's prayer. See Vernon K. Robbins, "Divine Dialogue and the Lord's Prayer: Sociorhetorical Interpretation of Sacred Texts," *Dialogue* 28 (1995): 117-46, for a sociorhetorical analysis of the abbreviated and expanded versions of the Lord's prayer in Matt, Luke, *Did.*, and the *Book of Mormon*.

[2]Cf. Burton L. Mack and Vernon K. Robbins, *Patterns of Persuasion in the Gospels* (Sonoma CA: Polebridge, 1989); Richard B. Vinson, "A Comparative Study of the Use of Enthymemes in the Synoptic Gospels," in *Persuasive Artistry: Studies in New Testament in Honor of George A. Kennedy*, ed. Duane F. Watson, JSNTSup 50 (Sheffield: JSOT Press, 1991) 119-41; Wesley H. Wachob, "The Rich in Faith and the Poor in Spirit: The Socio-Rhetorical Function of a Saying of Jesus in the Epistle of James" (Ph.D. diss., Emory University, 1993); Vernon K. Robbins, *The Tapestry of Early Christian Discourse: Rhetoric, Society, and Ideology* (London: Routledge, 1996), *Exploring the Texture of Texts: A Guide to Socio-Rhetorical Interpretation* (Philadelphia: Trinity Press International, 1996), "The Dialectical Nature of Early Christian Discourse," *Scriptura* 59 (1996) 353-62, and "The Present and Future of Rhetorical Analysis," in *The Rhetorical Analysis of Scripture: Essays from the 1995 London Conference*, ed. Stanley E. Porter and Thomas H. Olbricht, JSNTSup 146 (Sheffield: Sheffield Academic Press, 1997) 32-41; Anders Eriksson, *Traditions as Rhetorical Proof: Pauline Argumentation in 1 Corinthians*, ConBNT 29 (Stockholm: Almquist & Wiksell International, 1998); and L. Gregory Bloomquist, "The Place of Enthymemes in Argumentative Texture," forthcoming.

[3]George A. Kennedy, *Aristotle, On Rhetoric: A Theory of Civic Discourse* (New York: Oxford University Press, 1991) 297-98; and Patrick J. Hurley, *A Concise Introduction to Logic*, 2nd ed. (Belmont CA: Wadsworth, 1985) 230-35.

sumption that the premise or conclusion is obvious from the overall context. Enthymemic discourse, then, is discourse that presumes a context to fill out its meanings. The question then becomes the context a particular enthymeme evokes. Every text somehow enacts the social, cultural, and ideological context in which it was written. A reader who stands outside that context uses that enacted context as a medium for another context. Readers, from their own contexts, may be preoccupied with looking back on the context in which the work was written, may intentionally intertwine looking back with looking forward to another context, or may simply use the context embedded in the discourse as a medium for a new context.

Literary works vary in the manner in which they present enthymemes in their discourse. A literary work may articulate premises somewhere in the work that are exactly or approximately equivalent to the unexpressed premises evoked by enthymemes in another location. This kind of work creates an enthymemic network in the text that may invite readers to turn most of their attention toward negotiating the reasoning in the work's inner content rather than negotiating the reasoning in relation to social, cultural, and ideological contexts outside the work. In contrast, a literary work may not articulate unexpressed premises or conclusions for its enthymemes. This kind of text invites the reader into a process of evoking contexts of various kinds outside the work to understand these enthymemes.

A major thesis in this essay is that the Gospel of Luke interweaves enthymemic networks in the text with social, cultural, ideological, and theological enthymemes that evoke contexts outside the work. In some instances, unexpressed premises or conclusions for enthymemes are expressed elsewhere in the work and create an explicit enthymemic network in the text. In the same portion of text, however, the premises or conclusions missing from the enthymemes may reside in social, cultural, ideological, and theological environments outside the text. These enthymemes create a conventional context that provides a matrix for depicting conventional, ideological, and/or idiosyncratic thought and behavior. Conventional behavior enacts the inductive and deductive logic of generally accepted social, cultural, ideological, and theological reasoning. Ideological behavior participates in presuppositions, dispositions, and values that reflect "the needs and interests of a group or class at a particular time in history."[4] Idiosyncratic behavior counters conventional actions and thought, creating an especially dynamic context for new meanings and meaning effects.

In the context of social, cultural, ideological, and theological enthymemes, abductive reasoning may redirect and reconfigure inductive and deductive reasoning. Abductive reasoning is a procedure of discovery that works off of suggestion rather than formal logic.[5] Early Christians used generally presupposed premises as a fertile environment for flashes of insight—"suggestions" or "hypotheses" for life—that introduce new social, cultural, ideological, and theological reasoning. Commitment to this reasoning provided a distinctive identity for early Christians. Sometimes they intertwined conventional premises and conclusions in an unconventional manner to explain their way of life; they placed special value on this reasoning which they shared in common with one another. At other times they intertwined new insights with conventional premises or conclusions. Both procedures were a matter of bottling and aging new wine while still enjoying the old, as well as creating a new wardrobe without destroying all of the old garments. The Gospel of Luke exhibits both kinds of interweaving in the "kingdom wisdom" presented in 11:1-13. Unusual interweaving of conventional premises and conclusions as well as new insights in the presence of conventional insights create new social, cultural, ideological, and theological patterns. This essay describes both processes at work in the discursive progression in Luke 11:1-13.

I. Chreia and Enthymeme in Luke 11:1-4

Luke 11:1 presents a span of time in which Jesus prays, then a disciple, speaking for all the disciples, asks Jesus to teach them how to pray. When Jesus responds by speaking to all the disciples (11:2-4), the beginning of this unit exhibits conventional features of a "responsive" (ἀπο-

---

[4]David B. Davis, *The Problem of Slavery in the Age of Revolution 1770–1823* (Ithaca NY: Cornell University Press, 1975) 14; John H. Elliott, *A Home for the Homeless: A Social-Scientific Criticism of 1 Peter, Its Situation and Strategy* (Philadelphia: Fortress, 1981; repr. Philadelphia: Fortress, 1990) 268; Robbins, *The Tapestry of Early Christian Discourse*, 193; and Robbins, *Exploring the Texture of Texts*, 96.

[5]See Bruce J. Malina, "Interpretation: Reading, Abduction, Metaphor," in *The Bible and the Politics of Exegesis: Essays in Honor of Norman K. Gottwald on His Sixty-fifth Birthday*, ed. David Jobling et al. (Cleveland: Pilgrim, 1991) 253-66; and John H. Elliott, *What Is Social-Scientific Criticism?* (Minneapolis: Fortress, 1993) 48-49; cf. Rebecca S. Chopp, *The Power to Speak: Feminism, Language, God* (New York: Crossroad, 1989).

κριτικόν) chreia.[6] An intriguing part of the disciple's statement is his comparison of Jesus with John the Baptist who, according to this disciple, taught his disciples to pray (11:1; cf. 5:33). However, no extant text reveals any prayer attributed to John the Baptist.[7] Comparison is a standard rhetorical feature of biographical literature in antiquity,[8] and one feature of Lukan discourse is to highlight the character of Jesus through comparison with John the Baptist.[9] An additional feature in the opening sentence is the unnamed disciple's address of Jesus as κύριε (lord or master). This mode of address is an implicit act of praising Jesus, which also occurs in the preceding episode, both in the narration (10:39, 41) and in the speech of Martha (10:40) as she provides hospitality for him in her home. Thus, Luke 11:1 communicates such a high esteem for Jesus that it exhibits an intriguing relation to the first step in the elaboration of a chreia. Hermogenes asserts that an elaboration should begin with "encomium in a few words for the one who spoke or acted."[10] Luke 11:1-13 begins with honorific address to Jesus and comparison that evokes a tone of authority for Jesus' speech.

Jesus responds to the disciple by reciting the Lord's prayer in abbreviated form. An ability to expand and abbreviate traditional stories and sayings with respectable grammatical and syntactical skill is fundamental to progymnastic rhetorical composition, which is the mode of writing the Gospel of Luke exhibits.[11] Luke may have found this abbreviated version in "Q,"[12] but, if he did not, he has abbreviated the prayer for this con-

---

[6]Ronald F. Hock and Edward N. O'Neil, *The Chreia in Ancient Rhetoric*, vol. 1, *The Progymnasmata* (Atlanta: Scholars Press, 1986) 87.

[7]See Joseph A. Fitzmyer, *The Gospel according to Luke*, 2 vols., AB 28, 28A (New York: Doubleday, 1981, 1985) 2:902, for references to Essene forms of prayer some scholars have thought might be relevant to a discussion of prayer-forms that John the Baptist might have used.

[8]Comparison (σύγκρισις) is a primary dynamic underlying Plutarch's *Parallel Lives*. Most of the fifty lives highlight the characteristics of either a Greek or Roman leader through comparison with one or more other leaders with whom they are compared.

[9]Cf. Luke 3:18-20; 5:33; 7:18-35; 9:7-9, 18-19; 16:16; 20:1-8; see Ron Cameron, " 'What Have You Come Out To See?' Characterizations of John and Jesus in the Gospels," *Semeia* 49 (1990): 35-69. See also the essay by Philip L. Shuler in this volume.

[10]Hock and O'Neil, *The Progymnasmata*, 177.

[11]For the meaning of "progymnastic" rather that fully developed "oratorical" rhetorical skills, see Vernon K. Robbins, "Progymnastic Rhetorical Composition and Pre-Gospel Traditions: A New Approach," in *The Synoptic Gospels: Source Criticism and the New Literary Criticism*, ed. Camille Focant, BETL 110 (Leuven: Leuven University Press, 1993) 111-47.

[12]John S. Kloppenborg, *Q Parallels: Synopsis, Critical Notes and Concordance*

text.[13] In its abbreviated form, the Lord's prayer contains an address ("Father"), two petitions of praise, and three petitions for communal benefaction.[14]

Address: Father

Petitions of praise:
(1) Hallowed be thy name.
(2) Thy Kingdom come.

Petitions for communal benefaction:
(3) Give us each day our daily bread.[15]
(4) Forgive us our sins, for we ourselves
forgive every one indebted to us.
(5) Lead us not into temptation.

The opening address introduces the image of God as Father, the two petitions of praise request that God manifest his holiness and enact his power with his rule, and the three petitions for communal benefaction ask God to provide daily bread and forgiveness, and not to lead people into testing.

The second petition for communal benefaction in the Lord's prayer differs from the other two petitions by containing a rationale. In its current discursive context in Luke, this petition is a cultural enthymeme, that is, the enthymeme expresses a point of view held by people who were born or educated into this particular tradition, rather than by people who accepted the belief and practice that shaped society generally. The enthymeme is a petition by a specific community of people for a benefit from God. Only in this instance does a petition in the prayer give a

---

(Sonoma CA: Polebridge, 1988) 82-85; and Shawn Carruth and Albrecht Garsky, *Documenta Q 11:1b-4* (Leuven: Peeters, 1996).

[13]An expanded chreia features amplification within the chreia itself, while a chreia elaboration regularly features recitation of the chreia in an abbreviated form; see Vernon K. Robbins, "Introduction: Using Rhetorical Discussions of the Chreia to Interpret Pronouncement Stories," in *The Rhetoric of Pronouncement*, ed. Vernon K. Robbins, *Semeia* 64 (Atlanta: Scholars Press, 1994): xii-xvi.

[14]Cf. Fitzmyer, *The Gospel according to Luke*, 2:898; Fred B. Craddock, *Luke* (Louisville KY: Westminster/John Knox, 1990) 153-54; Luke T. Johnson, *The Gospel of Luke*, Sacra Pagina 3 (Collegeville MN: Liturgical, 1991) 179; and Sharon H. Ringe, *Luke* (Louisville KY: Westminster/John Knox, 1995) 162-65.

[15]For variations in the translation, and the reasons for the variations, see Fitzmyer, *The Gospel according to Luke*, 2:904-906.

reason why God should grant the request,[16] and the reason is because the people who pray the prayer also forgive everyone indebted to them. This petition participates in an enthymemic network of reasoning related to "Forgive, and you will be forgiven" (6:37-38):

Luke 6:37-38	Luke 11:4
Rule. The measure you give will be the measure you get back. [*Case.* Judging, condemning, forgiving, and giving are measures given.]	
Result. Judge not, and you will not be judged; condemn not, and you will not be condemned; **forgive, and you will be forgiven**; give, and it will be given to you; good measure, pressed down, shaken together, running over, will be put into your lap.	[*Rule.* **Forgive, and you will be forgiven.**]
	Case. We forgive every one indebted to us. *Result.* Forgive us our sins.

One result in the enthymemic reasoning in 6:37-38 is that forgiving is an action related to judging, condemning, and giving. In the context of early Christian discourse, the passive voice in the second part presupposes that God is the one who forgives the person who has forgiven someone else.[17] The manner in which a person judges, condemns, forgives, and gives relates directly to the manner in which God judges, condemns, forgives, and gives to this person. In other words, these actions are part of the text's "sacred texture,"[18] in which human actions are intricately interconnected with divine actions. There is not space here to pursue all the topics in this network. Let us notice, however, that the statement about giving bridges back to the statement in the Lord's prayer where petitioners pray, "Give us this day our daily bread." As the statement bridges back, it would be natural for an implication to be evoked con-

---

[16]The version of the Lord's prayer commonly recited by Protestant Christians concludes with the supporting premise: "For thine is the Kingdom and the power and the glory forever." In other words, the reason it is presupposed that God the Father can grant the petitions in the prayer is the Father's possession of kingdom, power, and glory.

[17]God is the presupposed agent of the forgiveness in the second part, not the person who has been forgiven; see Ernst Käsemann, *New Testament Questions of Today* (London: SCM, 1969) 66-107.

[18]Robbins, *Exploring the Texture of Texts*, 120-31.

cerning giving that would replicate the reasoning concerning forgiving.[19] In other words, it would be natural to reason: "Give us this day our daily bread, because we give bread to others who need it." We will see some of the implications of this in the section below.

When Luke 11:4 is placed in the enthymemic network that includes Luke 6:37-38, there is a problem in the syllogistic logic. If the reasoning in relation to the rule "Forgive, and you will be forgiven" were strictly inductive deductive, it would be as follows.[20]

Deductive	**Inductive**
	Case. We forgive every one indebted to us.
	[*Result.* God will forgive us.]
Rule. Forgive, and God will forgive you (Luke 6:37).	*Rule.* Forgive, and God will forgive you (Luke 6:37).
Case. We forgive every one indebted to us (Luke 11:4).	
[*Result.* God will forgive us.]	

The statement in the Lord's prayer is "Forgive us our sins," not "God will forgive us." Therefore, something has changed. According to modern analysis, this change is a result of abduction. Despite the rule, "Forgive, and you will be forgiven," the formulator of the enthymeme in Luke 11:4 experienced God as a being who does not grant forgiveness simply on the basis of forgiving the indebtedness of another person. The experience of the speaker overrides the inductive-deductive reasoning and produces an alternative result. Richard L. Lanigan describes reasoning like this as rhetorical rather than descriptive or dialectic.[21] Its logic concerns particular individuals and groups of people and is characteristic of the "cultural psychology of a rhetor."[22] Rather than staying within an inductive-deduc-

---

[19]For replication, see Bruce J. Malina, *The New Testament World: Insights from Cultural Anthropology*, rev. ed. (Louisville KY: Westminster/John Knox, 1993) 39-40, passim.

[20]For display of an inductive-deductive cycle of reasoning, see Richard L. Lanigan, "From Enthymeme to Abduction: The Classical Law of Logic and the Postmodern Rule of Rhetoric," in *Recovering Pragmatism's Voice: The Classical Tradition, Rorty, and the Philosophy of Communication*, ed. Lenore Langsdorf and Andrew R. Smith (Albany NY: SUNY Press, 1995) 58.

[21]Lanigan, "From Enthymeme to Abduction," 52-53.

[22]Lanigan, "From Enthymeme to Abduction," 62; cf. Vernon K. Robbins, "Pragmatic Relations as a Criterion for Authentic Sayings," *Forum* 1/3 (1985): 35-63; and Shawn Carruth, "Strategies of Authority: A Rhetorical Study of the Character of the Speaker in

tive cycle, "particular" reasoning uses abductive reasoning as an assistant to imagine transcendent realities that can never be seen or deduced. The reasoning in the petition in 11:4 reaches beyond the inductive-deductive reasoning to grasp the transcendent reality of God and God's forgiveness. When this happens, the reasoning adds the necessity to "ask" God, and it inverts the "case" and the "result" in the deductive reasoning:[23]

Abductive	Deductive	Inductive
		Case. We forgive every one indebted to us.
[*Rule.* Forgive, and God will forgive you (**if you ask God to forgive your sins**) (6:37).]		*Result.* **Forgive us our sins!**
Result. **Forgive us our sins** (11:4a)!	[*Rule.* Forgive, and God will forgive you (**if you ask God to forgive your sins**).]	[*Rule.* Forgive, and God will forgive you (**if you ask God to forgive your sins**).]
Case. We forgive every one indebted to us (11:4b).	*Case.* We forgive every one indebted to us.	
	Result. **Forgive us our sins!**	

The statement "Forgive, and you will be forgiven" could function as a statement about human relationships, where one person forgives another, if there were no language about God in the context. The presence of language about God, however, creates a consciousness of the nature of God and God's forgiveness. In turn, this creates an awareness that our ability to forgive is in fact defective in relation to God's ability. This "discovery" produces an inversion of the deductive reasoning so that our asking of God to forgive us creates the "case" whereby we "forgive others." In technical terms, in abductive reasoning the result of the deductive reasoning (a petition to God to forgive us our sins) becomes the because-motive (abductive "result") that produces the case (we forgive every one indebted to us).[24]

An underlying reason why people must ask God for forgiveness probably is that Father God (11:2) is a patron whom one must approach in "lowliness" if one is to receive from him. Thus, the abductive

---

Q 6:20-49," in *Conflict and Invention: Literary, Rhetorical, and Social Studies on the Sayings Gospel Q*, ed. John S. Kloppenborg (Philadelphia: Trinity Press International, 1995) 107-10.

[23]For a display of the enthymeme argument cycle, see Lanigan, "From Enthymeme to Abduction," 62.

[24]Lanigan, "From Enthymeme to Abduction," 63.

reasoning is related to well-known cultural reasoning. Bruce J. Malina, John H. Elliott, and others propose that the meanings of God the Father emerge primarily from the social system of patronage and clientage in Mediterranean society.[25] It is God's natural role to enter into patron-client contracts whereby he provides benefactions for various kinds of services his clients render to him. But a client must approach this patron in "lowliness" in order to receive the benefactions. A major stimulus for reconfiguring "God will forgive us our sins" into the petition "Forgive us our sins," then, appears to be the presence of the principle, "those who lower themselves will be exalted." This reasoning occurs inductively in Luke 18:13-14.

> *Case.* A tax collector lowers himself by standing afar, not lifting up his eyes to heaven, beating his breast and saying, "God, be merciful to me a sinner" (18:13).
> *Result.* The tax collector is justified (exalted) (18:14).
> *Rule.* All who exalt themselves will be lowered, and those who lower themselves will be exalted (18:14).

Inductive reasoning that the tax collector's action brings forgiveness (justification) evokes the principle that God exalts those who lower themselves. The principle that "those who lower themselves are exalted" has widespread currency in Mediterranean culture.[26] Thus, deductive application of this principle is readily available for use by any group within its environs. In Lukan reasoning, the principle by which the tax collector received the benefit of forgiveness can be expressed in these terms: Do not expect forgiveness on the basis of anything good you might have done, but "lower yourself," asking God for forgiveness simply on the basis of his mercy.

Once we have seen the enthymemic network concerning forgiveness that interconnects Luke 11:4, 6:37-38, and 18:13-14, we are in a position to go to another location in the Lukan text. Luke 23:34 depicts Jesus as saying, "Father, forgive them, for they know not what they are doing."[27]

---

[25]Bruce J. Malina, "Patron and Client," *Forum* 4/1 (1988): 2-32; and John H. Elliott, "Patronage and Clientage," in *The Social Sciences and New Testament Interpretation*, ed. Richard L. Rohrbaugh (Peabody MA: Hendrickson, 1996) 144-56.

[26]See Vernon K. Robbins, *Ancient Quotes and Anecdotes: From Crib to Crypt* (Sonoma CA: Polebridge, 1989) 37-38.

[27]Possibly 23:34 was added by a later scribe. Luke 23:34 is absent from P⁷⁵, א¹, B, D*, W, Θ, etc. but present in א*·², (A), C, D², L, Ψ, etc. Whether originally in the text of Luke, or added later, it is fully consonant with the principle that is taught by Luke 11:4;

This statement itself is enthymemic, evoking a premise about God forgiving people who do not know what they are doing.

> [*Rule.* The Father forgives people who do not know what they are doing.]
> *Case.* They do not know what they are doing.
> *Result.* Father, forgive them.

For our purposes here, it is instructive to observe that Jesus' statement has a relation to the "case" in the cycle of enthymemic reasoning established by 11:4 ("We forgive every one indebted to us. . . . "). Since Jesus' action in 23:34 exhibits an enactment (an example or paradigm) of a generalized form of the principle, it can be helpful to display the reasoning in an inductive (case + result = rule) rather than deductive syllogism.[28]

Deductive	**Inductive Enthymemic Enactment**	**Deductive**	
		[*Rule.* People should imitate the actions of God.] *Case.* The Most High is kind to the grateful and the selfish (6:35). [*Result/Rule.* People should be kind to the grateful and selfish.]	
[*Rule.* Forgive, and you will be forgiven (Luke 6:37).]	*Case.* They do not know what they are doing.	[*Case.* Praying for someone who engages in negative actions (e.g., abuses you) is a form of kindness.]	[*Case.* Loving one's enemies is a form of kindness.]
Case. **We forgive every one** who is indebted to us.	*Result.* Father, forgive them (23:34).	*Result.* Pray for those who abuse you (6:28).	*Result.* **Love your enemies** (6:35).
Result. Forgive us our sins (Luke 11:4).	[*Rule.* A person should pray to Father God to ask him to forgive people who do not know what they are doing.]		

---

cf. Charles H. Talbert, *Reading Luke: A Literary and Theological Commentary on the Third Gospel* (New York: Crossroad, 1982) 219-20; and Vernon K. Robbins, "The Crucifixion and the Speech of Jesus," *Forum* 4/1 (1988): 40.

[28]See Lanigan, "From Enthymeme to Abduction," 53, 58, 62.

Jesus' statement in 23:34 appears to be an act of forgiving those who have beaten, humiliated, and crucified him.[29] What Jesus actually does, however, is petition God to forgive them. Adopting the mode he instructs his followers to adopt in 11:2-4, he addresses God as Father and petitions God to forgive those who have wronged him. In other words, Jesus does not personally forgive them and then petition God to forgive him because he has forgiven them. The presupposition is that those who have abused and crucified Jesus need God's forgiveness, not simply Jesus' forgive ness.[30] Indeed, the formulators of this discourse may presuppose that Jesus does not need forgiveness, either because he never committed a sin or because, if he did, he petitioned God for forgiveness and God granted it. Jesus' petition to God to forgive those who have wronged him moves beyond the principle he articulates in the Lord's prayer to the principle of "praying for those who abuse you" (6:28), which in turn is an enact-ment of "loving your enemies" (6:35). Both praying for those who abuse you and loving your enemies occur in an enthymemic context that grounds the actions in the belief that God "is kind to the ungrateful and to the selfish" (6:35).

The enthymeme about forgiveness in the Lord's prayer, then, is part of a Lukan enthymemic network of reasoning about forgiving others and about petitioning God to forgive oneself and others. These topics are im-portant enough in the social, cultural, and ideological environment of the Gospel of Luke to be expressed in enthymemic form. Assertions about these topics rarely stand unsupported. Rather, rationales accompany the assertions. The rationales create enthymemic reasoning, and this reasoning both interconnects statements in different locations in the work and introduces new topics that branch out to other related topics of importance.

II. Ideological Subversion of a Social Enthymeme in Luke 11:5-8

After Jesus recites the Lord's prayer to his disciples, he asks the disciples a lengthy and complex rhetorical question beginning with "which one of you . . . ?" and anticipating the answer "no one" (Luke 11:5-7).[31] A

---

[29]Robbins, "The Crucifixion and the Speech of Jesus," 40.

[30]When Jesus forgives sins in Luke, either there is criticism that God alone forgives sin (5:21) or there is an expression of consternation (7:49).

[31]Bernard Brandon Scott, *Hear Then the Parable: A Commentary on the Parables of Jesus* (Minneapolis: Fortress, 1989) 87; and Robert C. Tannehill, *Luke* (Nashville: Abingdon, 1996) 189.

rhetorical question makes an assertion, and this question asserts that no one has a friend who will refuse to get up and give three loaves to him when he needs bread for another friend who has come on a journey— even if the request for bread is made at midnight when the person being requested is sleeping comfortably in bed with his family.

These assertions evoke two syllogisms, one in which conventions of hospitality and friendship intertwine, and another that focuses more directly on friendship.

Hospitality and Friendship	Friendship
[*Rule*. Social conventions of both hospitality and friendship require a host-friend to feed bread to a hungry guest-friend.] *Case*. A guest-friend arrives at midnight and the host-friend does not have any bread.	[*Rule*: A friend willingly gives of his possessions to another friend.]

Result/Case. At midnight the host-friend asks his sleeping-friend for bread for his hungry guest-friend.

Result. At midnight the sleeping-friend will give the host-friend bread for his hungry guest-friend.

These syllogisms exhibit social reasoning: principles that all people in the Mediterranean world, whatever their specific cultural tradition, know. The reasoning concerns both hospitality and friendship. On the one hand, the arrival of the traveling friend enacts conventions of hospitality that overlap with friendship. There are many nuances to hospitality conventions,[32] including the nuance that a host invites a guest into his home and attends to the needs of that guest for food and rest, even if the guest arrives at an inconvenient time. In addition, friends offer hospitality to one another. These conventions explain why, according to Plutarch, having too many friends can be a problem (Plutarch, *On Having Many Friends* 95C).[33] Both as a friend and as one who knows the conventions of hospitality, the host-friend welcomes the traveling-friend into his home and does what is necessary to meet his needs. On the other hand, the host-friend's need to give bread to his guest-friend enacts additional

---

[32]Bruce J. Malina, "Hospitality," in *The HarperCollins Bible Dictionary*, rev. ed., ed. Paul J. Achtemeier (San Francisco: HarperSanFrancisco, 1996) 440-41.

[33]Friends also offer hospitality to the friends of one's friends (Bruce J. Malina, *Windows on the World of Jesus: Time Travel to Ancient Judea* [Louisville KY: Westminster/John Knox, 1993] 48-49), but the sleeping friend is not asked to offer this act of kindness in Luke 11:5-7.

conventions of friendship. It was a cultural assumption in Mediterranean antiquity that "friends own everything in common."[34] When the host-friend goes to his sleeping-friend, the sleeping-friend is obligated to give the host-friend the bread he needs for his guest-friend. At this point, the result of the reasoning about hospitality becomes the case in the reasoning about friendship. The intersection of the reasoning creates a double-column of reasoning in the story that intersects where the host-friend asks his sleeping-friend for bread.

The argument in Luke 11:5-7 introduces an analogy between the acts of hospitality within friendship and the acts of Father God to humans. The argument is similar to Hermogenes' introduction of farmers' toil over the land and its crops as an analogy for teachers' education of their students. These verses, then, have an intriguing relation to the fifth step in Hermogenean elaboration: argument from analogy.[35] Their basic function is the assertion that just as no one has a friend who will refuse to give something needed, even under extreme circumstances, so also no one has a heavenly Father who will refuse one's requests, even under extreme circumstances. Thus, verses 5-7 present what host-friends do as an analogy to what God the Father does.[36]

Luke 11:8 appends a rationale in the form of an objection[37] to the argument from analogy in Luke 11:5-7. Since verse 7 uses the verb δίδωμι (give) once, verse 8 uses it twice, and the subject is asking, giving, and receiving bread, the argument from analogy and the objection clearly elaborate the first petition for communal benefaction in the Lord's prayer (11:3: "Give us this day our daily bread."). The analogy intertwines hospitality with friendship, but the objection delimits the focus to an issue of friendship: "Why does one friend, when asked, give bread to another friend, even when it is a severe imposition?" Social convention would suggest the rationale: "Because the one asked is a friend of the one who asks." Jesus' statement subverts customary social reasoning by emphatically replacing this rationale with: "Because of his shameless-ness" (ἀναίδεια). Thus Jesus' statement presents an ideological recon-

---

[34]Κοινὰ γὰρ τὰ τῶν φίλων: Epictetus, *Oresteia* 735; Plutarch, *How to Tell a Flatterer* 65A. See Scott, *Hear Then the Parable*, 90-91, for more examples.

[35]Hock and O'Neil, *The Progymnasmata*, 177.

[36]Some interpreters (e.g., Talbert, *Reading Luke*, 132-33) consider vv. 5-7 to be an argument from lesser (friend) to greater (heavenly Father), but this imposes 11:13 and 18:1-8 on these verses.

[37]ἀντιλέγειν: Hock and O'Neil, *The Progymnasmata*, 100-101.

figuration of conventional social reasoning. The emphatic manner in which the objection is introduced ("I tell you") evokes an authority for the saying that approximates the phenomenon Hermogenes describes as an authoritative judgment (κρίσις).[38] In addition, the strong objection in the saying produces an argument from the contrary, the fourth step in Hermogenean elaboration:[39] One friend gives bread to another friend when it is a severe imposition not because he is a friend but because of his shamelessness (ἀναίδεια).

A problem arises, however, because one can dispute whether the shamelessness is an attribute of the sleeping-friend or the host-friend. The "his" (αὐτοῦ) may refer to either person.[40] One aspect of the problem has been the mistranslation of ἀναίδεια as "importunity" or "persistence." This mistranslation results from imposing the persistence of the widow in Luke 18:1-8 onto the analogy and objection in 11:5-8. Recent investigations have shown that the meaning of ἀναίδεια is "shamelessness,"[41] but whether the αὐτοῦ in verse 8 refers to the sleeping friend's or the host-friend's shamelessness is still disputed. Bernard Brandon Scott, in a context of interpretation well-informed about the meaning of shamelessness, concludes that the shamelessness is an attribute of the sleeping-friend. This conclusion is the result of a misconstrual of verses 5-7 as a "how much more" argument,[42] a rhetorical misunderstanding of these verses that is widespread among interpreters. While the common topic of "the more and the less" (Aristotle, *Rhetoric* 2.23.4) emerges in the conclusion (v. 13), this common topic is not present in the earlier stages of the elaboration (vv. 5-8). Rather, as stated above, verses 5-7 present an argument from analogy and verse 8 replaces

---

[38]For discussion of the authoritative judgment in rhetorical elaboration, see the page references in the index to Mack and Robbins, *Patterns of Persuasion in the Gospels*, 228.

[39]It was conventional practice to include rationales in the argument from the contrary (see *Rhetorica ad Herenium* 4.43.57). The reason appears to be twofold. First, both the contrary and the rationale serve the function of clarifying the nature and scope of the chreia or theme. Second, articulating a series of rationales in both positive and negative formulations points to wider horizons of the chreia or theme available from the arguments from analogy, example, and authoritative judgment.

[40]Cf. Talbert, *Reading Luke*, 132-33; and Scott, *Hear Then the Parable*, 89-90.

[41]Kenneth E. Bailey, *Poet and Peasant: A Literary-Cultural Approach to the Parables in Luke* (Grand Rapids MI: Eerdmans, 1976) 125-27; David Catchpole, "Q and 'The Friend at Midnight,'" *JTS* 34 (1983): 407-24; Scott, *Hear Then the Parable*, 88-89; and Bruce J. Malina and Richard L. Rohrbaugh, *Social-Science Commentary on the Synoptic Gospels* (Minneapolis: Fortress, 1992) 350-51.

[42]Scott, *Hear Then the Parable*, 90.

the conventional social rationale for the action with an ideological rationale by using the common topic of the contrary or opposite (Aristotle, *Rhetoric* 2.23.1). The sleeping-friend gives bread "not" because of friendship but because of the petitioner's shamelessness. The rhetorical question asserts that a person should address God with a feeling of assurance that Father God, like a friend, will respond to a person's petitions. The objection replaces the conventional social rationale for the action with an ideological rationale based on the shamelessness of the one who asks.

Social conventions are known by all, but idiosyncratic ways of understanding may generate a particular ideology. When looked at from a social perspective, the important thing is that one friend be willing to provide for another friend's need. If one does not, the person is not a friend. But one's understanding of the reasons why one person gives to another can be ideological—grounded in a point of view held only by a particular group of people. The understanding in this objection does not appear to be basic social or cultural knowledge in the ancient Mediterranean world. In other words, no clear statement in Jewish or Greco-Roman literature declares that friends give to other friends because they shamelessly ask each other for things. Friends unhesitatingly ask each other for things, but people do not perceive this request as a shameless activity. Since friends return favors, their requests are not shameless; beggars, in contrast, are shameless because they look on another's table and beg with no plan or ability to return the favor (Sir 40:28-30). Thus, verse 8 articulates a particular deductive ideology about petitioning.

> [*Rule*. A sleeping-friend will give bread at midnight to a host-friend who is willing to petition shamelessly for a hungry guest-friend.]
> *Case*. A host-friend petitions his sleeping-friend shamelessly at midnight for bread for a hungry guest-friend.
> *Result*. At midnight the sleeping-friend will give the host-friend bread for his hungry guest-friend.

The key to the ideological reasoning appears to be the willingness of the host-friend to adopt a social role of being shameless on behalf of another person's need. As we have seen above, the petition in the Lord's prayer for one's own forgiveness raises the issue of the petitioner's relation to other people who also need forgiveness. The enthymemic network about forgiveness not only includes directives to forgive others and to pray for those who abuse you, but it also includes a portrayal of Jesus' petition for God to forgive people who are abusing him. One sees, then, an ideological texture in the discourse whereby one's relation to God is implicated in one's relation to the needs of other people. The objection in verse 8 extends this ideological texture through an interruption of conventional social reasoning. The host-friend receives the bread from his sleeping-friend because he has been willing to be shameless by his request on behalf of his guest-friend's needs. On the one hand, this shamelessness is akin to the boldness (παρρησία) of a cynic. On the other hand, there is an ideological shift of conventional cynic reasoning as well as conventional social reasoning when the person acts boldly on behalf of another person rather than simply for oneself. The host-friend is, indeed, maintaining his honor as he petitions his friend for the bread. But the ideological twist is that he maintains his honor in the context of an unconventional understanding of why the bread was given.

It will be important in future studies to pursue the ideological texture of shamelessness throughout Luke. While the word itself occurs nowhere else in the New Testament, the social mode of shamelessness certainly appears in the parable of the dishonest steward and its subsequent commentary (Luke 16:1-9) and may be an aspect of the woman's action in Luke 7:36-50. Several other sayings and episodes appear to participate in an ideology of shamelessness in this gospel.

Thus, Luke 11:5-8 embodies a combination of argument from analogy and from the contrary (objection). The argument from analogy (vv. 5-7) plus the objection (v. 8) address the topic of petitioning bread for others who need it, elaborating the first petition for communal benefaction, which on its own simply asks for daily bread for oneself. The first step in the elaboration introduces conventional social reasoning about hospitality and friendship as an analogy for the relation of petitioners to God the Father. The second step introduces ideological social reasoning that emphasizes the need for petitioners to ask shamelessly on behalf of the needs of others.

III. A Cultural Enthymeme as a Rationale for the Lord's Prayer in Luke 11:9-10

The argument from analogy and the objection in Luke 11:5-8 set up the enthymemic sentence[43] in verses 9-10. These verses provide a rationale (Hermogenean step 3) for all the petitions in the Lord's prayer. It is

---

[43]For a definition and discussion of the enthymemic sentence, see Kennedy, *Aristotle*, 297-98.

notable that Lukan discourse here presents both the objection (v. 8) and the rationale (vv. 9-10) as authoritative judgments. There is no appeal to Scripture for authoritative judgment, precedent, or example throughout this elaboration. Rather, this portion of Luke, like a number of other portions of kingdom wisdom in the New Testament, uses only other sayings of Jesus as authoritative judgments to elaborate the pronouncement that stands at the beginning of the elaboration. Verses 9-10 expand the vocabulary of giving with the topics of asking and giving and receiving, of seeking and finding, and of knocking and opening as they provide a rationale for praying in the manner that Jesus instructs in the opening verses. One of the most noticeable results of this configuration of topics is the association of asking, giving, and receiving with seeking. The presence of the seeking reveals an enthymemic network of reasoning that interrelates Luke 11:1-13 with 12:30-32.

Luke 11	Luke 12
Rule. Everyone who asks receives; **everyone who seeks finds**; to everyone who knocks, it will be opened (11:10).	[*Rule*. The Father's kingdom gives food, drink, and clothes, as well as other things.]
[*Case*. **It is your Father's good pleasure to give you the kingdom** (12:32).]	*Case*. **It is your Father's good pleasure to give you the kingdom** (12:32).
Result. Ask and [the Father's kingdom] will be given you; **seek, and you will find [the Father's kingdom]**; knock, and [the Father's kingdom] will be opened to you (11:9).	*Result*. **Seek the Father's kingdom** and food, drink, and clothes shall be yours as well (12:31).

The enthymemic sentence in Luke 11:9-10 contains the rule and result of its reasoning. The unexpressed case of the reasoning is located in Luke 12:32. That which a person asks for, seeks, and knocks upon to have opened is "the Father's kingdom." Thus, the unexpressed phrase throughout 11:9 is "the Father's kingdom," which people receive, find, and have opened to them. The enthymemic construction in Luke 12:31-32 contains the case, rather than the rule and the result if its reasoning. The result clarifies that one aspect of the benefactions of the kingdom is the needs of the body—food, drink, and clothes. The case expressed in 12:32 clarifies why simply asking, seeking, and knocking will be successful: "It is the Father's good pleasure to give you the kingdom" [if one only asks for it, seeks it, and knocks for it to be opened].

The case (minor premise) in the reasoning in these enthymemes is a Christian reconfiguration of widespread wisdom in Hellenistic culture. It is widely recognized that gods like to give benefits to humans. Thus it not only exists as an assertion but as a premise for enthymemic reasoning. The following enthymeme appears in Plutarch, *How to Tell a Flatterer* (63F).

> *Rule.* It is in the nature of the gods to take pleasure in being gracious and doing good.
> [*Case.* Something that is in a being's nature to do is done regularly without display that creates public knowledge of the action.]
> *Result.* The gods confer their benefits, for the most part, without our knowledge.

In this instance, the topic is the secrecy of the work of the gods. Christian discourse configures the rule in terms of God as Father giving his kingdom to people. Luke 11:9-10 reasons from this rule to a conclusion that people must engage in earnest and extended action to receive the Father's kingdom. Luke 12:31-32, in contrast, clarifies that one aspect of the benefits of God's gracious activity is the needs of the body—food, drink, and clothing.

The reasoning in Luke 11:9-10 presents a rationale for the entire act of praying the Lord's prayer. One addresses God as Father, because one hopes to receive the Father's kingdom. One addresses the Father's name as holy, because as a divine being he is able to confer extraordinary benefits on humans. One petitions God's kingdom to come, because asking God for his kingdom is one condition for receiving it. One petitions for daily bread, because one benefit God's kingdom brings is food, drink, and clothing for the body. One petitions for forgiveness, because the benefits of God's kingdom reach beyond bodily needs to the removal of one's sins. One petitions not to be led into testing where one may seek the kingdom and authority of the devil rather than the kingdom and authority of God (cf. 4:1-13). The rationale in Luke 11:9-10 explains that a condition for receiving these benefits is to ask, seek, and knock for God's kingdom and its benefits. These two verses, then, present the rationale for a Lord's prayer dominated by petitions.

The enthymemic rationale in Luke 11:9-10, then, is built on deductive reasoning related to widespread cultural reasoning about gods in ancient Mediterranean culture. The gods take pleasure in being gracious and giving benefits. The gods have the power to do beneficial things, and they delight in using this power. Lukan discourse configures this Mediterranean reasoning in terms of God as king whose kingdom brings basic benefits of bodily needs as well as forgiveness and protection from testing. Lukan discourse asserts that people must actively seek and petition God for the benefits of his kingdom. The implication is that God's people cannot be inactive and receive all the benefits. Rather, they must ask, seek, and knock to have the benefits come to them. When a person undertakes these actions, however, it is God's pleasure to give the benefits of God's kingdom.

While the passage of Luke 11:5-8 elaborates the petition for the Father to give daily bread (v. 3) through an argument from analogy, verses 9-10 provide the rationale for praying the entire prayer. The unexpressed premise in the enthymemic sentence in 11:9-10 exists in 12:32, clarifying that the petitioner is asking, seeking, and knocking for the Father's kingdom. The enthymemic network of reasoning that links 12:31-32 with 11:9-10 confirms that one benefit of the Father's kingdom is basic provisions for the body. There are, however, other benefits as well; an explanation of these leads us into the next steps in the elaboration.

IV. A Social-Cultural Enthymeme as a Theological Conclusion in Luke 11:13

After the rationale, two arguments from comparison emerge in the form of rhetorical questions in Luke 11:11-12. The verses begin like verses 5-7 and, like them, also expect the answer "no one." The difference is that the subject of the questions in verses 11-12 is "fathers" rather than "friends." Verse 8 suggests that friends sometimes do not act out of friendship but out of shamelessness. Therefore, relationships between friends function as an analogy but not a direct comparison to the relationship between God and humans. Verses 11-12 appeal to earthly fathers in comparison with a heavenly Father.

Luke 11:13 is a conclusion to the unit in the form of an if-(then) statement that uses the common topic of "the more and the less" (Aristotle, *Rhetoric* 2.23.4). Perpetuating the address to "you," which plays a prominent role throughout the elaboration, this verse gathers together the topics of asking and giving in a context where it refers to God as "heavenly Father" and compares God's giving with that of earthly fathers. This comparison produces the following syllogism.

> [*Rule.* Your heavenly Father is greater than earthly fathers.]
> *Case.* All fathers, even if they are evil, know how to give good gifts to their children.
> *Result.* How much more will the heavenly Father give **the Holy Spirit** to those who ask him.

The result in this syllogism leaps beyond the reasoning in the premises. If the reasoning remained within the boundaries of an inductive-deductive cycle, the conclusion would be that the heavenly Father gives "better gifts" to those who ask him. Instead, the enthymeme uses abductive reasoning which makes constructions that "sometimes succeed in binding us to the underlying reality they imagine by giving us an intellectual tool—a metaphor, a premise, an analogy, a category—with which to live, to arrange our experience, and to interpret our experiences so arranged."[44] As humans use abductive reasoning to create intellectual tools, they create openings that reach out beyond inductive-deductive circles of reasoning. In other words, humans remain inventive and creative as they organize and interpret their experiences. Abductive reasoning is

> the faculty of imagination, which comes to the rescue of sensation and logic by providing them with the intellectual means to see through experience and leap beyond empty syllogisms and tautologies to some creative representation of an underlying reality that might be grasped and reacted to, even if that imagined reality cannot be found, proved, or disproved by inductive or deductive rule-following.[45]

The reasoning in the conclusion in Luke 11:13, then, reveals another use of "abductive" reasoning to assist inductive-deductive reasoning. As the abductive reasoning leaps beyond inductive-deductive reasoning, it invites elaborative reasoning. We can see this reasoning if we display in three columns how the reasoning reaches out into a Lukan enthymemic network about giving.

Deductive	Abductive	Elaborative
[*Rule.* Your heavenly Father is greater than earthly fathers.]	[*Rule.* Your heavenly Father is greater than earthly fathers.]	A. Setting: 14:1-2
Case. All fathers, even if they are evil, know how to give good gifts to their children.		B. Challenge/Question: 14:3
		C. Response:
		(1) Introduction: 14:4a
		(2) Chreia: 14:4bc
Result. How much more will the heavenly Father give **better gifts** to those who ask him.	*Result.* How much more will the heavenly Father give **the Holy Spirit** to those who ask him (11:13)!	(3) Rationale: 14:5
	Case. All fathers, even if they are evil, know how to give good gifts to their children (11:13).	Amplification: 14:6, 7b
		(5) Analogy: 14:7a,c-10
		(7,4) *Judgment and Contrary*: All who exalt themselves will be lowered, and those who lower themselves will be exalted (14:11).

---

[44]Richard A. Shweder, *Thinking Through Cultures: Expeditions in Cultural Psychology* (Cambridge MA: Harvard University Press, 1991) 361; in Lanigan, "From Enthymeme to Abduction," 55.

[45]Shweder, *Thinking Through Cultures*, 361; in Lanigan, "From Enthymeme to Abduction," 55.

> [*Inference*. Fathers, if they have the Holy Spirit, will give greater gifts than earthly fathers regularly do.]
>
> [*Rule*. Give, and it will be given to you; good measure, pressed down, shaken together, running over, will be put into your lap (6:38).]
>
> *Analogy*. When you give a dinner or a banquet, do not invite your friends or your brothers or your kinsmen or your rich neighbors, lest they also invite you in return, and you be repaid. But when you give a feast, invite the poor, the maimed, the lame, the blind, and you will be blessed, because they cannot repay you. You will be repaid at the resurrection of the just (14:12-14).[46]
>
> *Example*. A man gave a great dinner and invited many. When those who were invited declined, he invited the poor, the crippled, the blind, and the lame, then sent his slave into the roads and lanes to compel others to come in until his house was filled (14:16-24).[47]
>
> *Another example in Luke*. Zaccheus, possessing the gift of salvation, gives half of his goods to the poor and fourfold to anyone he has defrauded (19:8-9).

The result of deductive reasoning simply would be that God gives "better gifts" than earthly fathers, but once again in this rhetorical reasoning the rhetor invites abductive reasoning (the faculty of imagination) as an "assistant" to deductive reasoning. As the rhetor uses abductive reasoning to reflect on the transcendent reality of God's giving, interaction occurs once again between deductive and inductive reasoning that produces an inversion between the minor premise and the result in the deductive reasoning. Through abductive reasoning, "by shock, question, puzzlement, surprise, and the like, the rhetor or inquirer *discovers similarity* between" the giving of earthly fathers (deductive case) and the giving of God the father (first part of deductive rule) "because of the *experience of consciousness* constituted in" the greatness of God the Father (last part of deductive rule).[48] In other words, the statement, "all fathers know how to give good gifts," functions as a statement about human relationships, where fathers give to their children. The presence of language about God evokes a sudden experience of the consciousness of God's giving, which leads to an awareness that our ability to give is decisively inferior to God's ability to give. This "discovery" produces an inversion of the

---

[46]See Willi Braun, *Feasting and Social Rhetoric in Luke 14*, SNTSMS 85 (Cambridge: Cambridge University Press, 1995) 164, 171-73.

[47]See Braun, *Feasting and Social Rhetoric in Luke 14*, 164, 174-75.

[48]Cf. Lanigan, "From Enthymeme to Abduction," 59.

deductive reasoning so that the premise "All fathers give good gifts" calls forth the insight that "the heavenly Father gives the Holy Spirit"! Once this result emerges in the abductive reasoning, an inference is nearby that the presence of the Holy Spirit within earthly fathers will enable them to give greater gifts than they usually do. Similar to the reasoning about forgiving, the result of the deductive reasoning about giving (How much more does God give good gifts) becomes a newly discovered because-motive that extends beyond inductive and deductive reasoning (abductive result: God gives the Holy Spirit!). The emergence of this new insight generates a new result that also extends beyond inductive-deductive reasoning (fathers, if they have the Holy Spirit, will give greater gifts than earthly fathers regularly do).[49]

In a context where a rhetor has generated the result that extends beyond inductive-deductive reasoning, the new insight reduces the importance of the result of the deductive reasoning and creates a major inference that invites elaboration. One may naturally find other places in the Gospel of Luke that elaborate various results of the abductive reasoning (that is, "greater" behaviors in humans produced by the Holy Spirit in them). Willi Braun's analysis of Luke 14 exhibits people (including Jesus) distributing benefactions in a manner "greater" than conventional human action. This elaboration of the abductive reasoning emphasizes that the presence of the Holy Spirit in humans can produce "greater" giving than most earthly persons enact. Luke 14:11 characterizes this mode of giving beyond conventional social practice as "lowering oneself and being exalted." Thus, one lowers oneself to give, much as one lowers oneself to be forgiven. Once again, giving and forgiving intertwine in the enthymemic texture of Luke. Luke 14:12-24 elaborates the lowering by giving boldly to the poor, maimed, lame, and blind; the story of Zaccheus (19:1-10) shows how "giving" brings "salvation"; and Luke 18:13-14 displays how asking forgiveness in a position of lowering oneself (rather than asking in a position one may consider to bolster one's request, that is, having forgiven the debt of another; 11:4) puts one in a position to receive forgiveness from God. Lowering oneself either to give or to ask for forgiveness brings exaltation in the enthymemic texture of the Gospel of Luke.

---

[49]Cf. Lanigan, "From Enthymeme to Abduction," 63.

V. Conclusion

Luke 11:1-13, then, contains both intriguing similarities with and intriguing differences from Hermogenes' elaboration of the chreia. After an introduction that evokes an image of Jesus as an authoritative speaker, Jesus recites an abbreviated form of the Lord's prayer to his disciples. Immediately after this recitation, Jesus presents an argument from analogy that depicts relationships among friends. Jesus then appends this analogy with an authoritative objection that asserts that a friend gives bread to his friend at midnight not because of friendship but because of the petitioner's willingness to ask shamelessly for another person's needs. After this parable, Jesus presents an enthymemic rationale for praying to God in the petitionary manner manifest in the Lord's prayer. After the rationale, Jesus presents two arguments from comparison with earthly fathers and a conclusion that summarizes how much more their heavenly Father is able to give than earthly fathers.

There can be no doubt, then, that the units in Luke 11:5-13 elaborate aspects of the Lord's prayer. But this elaboration differs in significant respects from Hermogenean elaboration. In Hermogenean elaboration, a well-articulated rationale occurs immediately after the chreia or maxim, then the argumentation moves on to the contrary, to analogy, to example, to authoritative judgment, and finally, to an exhortative conclusion. In Luke 11:1-13, the rationale occurs only after an initial argument from analogy with an objection. Then, after two arguments from comparison, the conclusion ends with an if-(then) statement that is enthymemic in nature. In Luke, enthymemic discourse occurs already in the recitation of the Lord's prayer, and it continues into the conclusion. In the Hermogenean elaboration, in contrast, enthymemic discourse has its primary function immediately after the recitation of the chreia or maxim. In addition, Luke 11:1-13 is part of a longer text, namely the entire Gospel of Luke. The enthymemes throughout the unit create an enthymemic network that extends into various portions of the gospel. An enthymeme in the prayer itself creates a dynamic interaction between forgiving and giving. Then a surprise emerges in the conclusion of the elaboration when Jesus says the heavenly Father gives the Holy Spirit. At this point, the elaboration moves decisively beyond inductive-deductive reasoning characteristic of conventional social, cultural, and ideological reasoning into a mode of abductive reasoning that generates special ways of thinking and acting.

Does the conclusion to the elaboration in Luke 11:13 imply that people should petition God to send the Holy Spirit upon them? The answer probably is no. The Father gives the Holy Spirit as an addition when people petition for those things itemized in the Lord's prayer, but with this conclusion the topics for debate become fully theological. The issue is not what ordinary friends or fathers do, but what God does when people petition God in the manner Jesus teaches in the Lord's prayer. Enthymemic social, cultural, and ideological reasoning moves into theological reasoning as the elaboration reaches its conclusion. The topic is the heavenly Father's giving of the Holy Spirit in contexts where people pray the prayer Jesus taught his disciples. The authoritative placing of the recitation of the prayer on Jesus' lips at the beginning of the elaboration produces a context in which theological discussion will inevitably move into Christological discussion. God not only gives the Holy Spirit; God's son (10:21-22) has revealed special wisdom about the Father's kingdom. Through rhetorical elaboration, enthymemic reasoning configures social, cultural, and ideological topics into topics that inhabit the sacred texture of the text.[50] These topics interweave theology and Christology in a manner that creates not only a new social, cultural, and ideological world, but also a new theological and Christological world for the reader.

---

[50]Robbins, *Exploring the Texture of Texts*, 120-31.

Two Lords "at the Right Hand"?
The Psalms and an Intertextual Reading
of Peter's Pentecost Speech (Acts 2:14-36)

David P. Moessner

At the end of Luke's first volume Jesus "opens" the apostles' "mind(s) [νοῦς] to comprehend the Scriptures," claiming that "all that stands written *about me* in the law of Moses and the prophets and *the Psalms* must be fulfilled" (24:44-45). He goes on to explain more specifically what "stands written" and has been or will be "fulfilled" *about him*, when he declares, "Thus it stands written that the Christ must suffer and rise from the dead on the third day, and in his name, beginning from Jerusalem, a change of mind (μετάνοια) leading to the release of sins must be proclaimed to all the nations, these things of which you are witnesses" (24:46-48). Given the fact that the first five chapters of Luke's second volume contain fifteen citations from thirteen different psalms[1] and very few citations appear after that point, it is intriguing that Jesus now adds the *Psalms* to his second postresurrection assertion that "all the Scriptures" "speak" or "stand written" "about me" (cf. 24:25-27). It would also appear significant that only after the risen "Christ" "has

---

[1]The LXX numeration is used. The Hebrew number, when different, is given in parentheses: Ps 2:1-2 = Acts 4:25-26; Ps 15(16):8-11 = Acts 2:25-28; Ps 15(16):10 = Acts 2:31; Ps 17(18):4 = Acts 2:24; Ps 19(20):6 = Acts 2:36; Ps 68(69):26 = Acts 1:20; Ps 77(78):8 = Acts 2:40; Ps 88(89):4 = Acts 2:30; Ps 108(109):8 = Acts 1:20; Ps 108(109):16 = Acts 2:37; Ps 109(110):1 = Acts 2:34-35; Ps 114(116):3 = Acts 2:24; Ps 117(118):22 = Acts 4:11; Ps 131(132):11 = Acts 2:30; Ps 145(146):6 = Acts 4:24; cf. Ps 40(41):10 = Acts 1:16. These fifteen citations from the Psalms *establish the identity* of this Jesus who was rejected by his own people and given the most humiliating death that his nation could mete out, namely, execution by "hanging on a tree" (Acts 5:30, 10:39 paraphrase Deut 21:21 and Acts 2:23 alludes to it through the verb προσπήγνυμι, "affixing to wood."). Rather than "a rebellious son of Israel" who deserved its severest punishment, Jesus is the suffering righteous anointed servant whom the psalmist David prophesied and anticipated through his own career of righteous suffering as an "anointed servant." It is no accident, then, that most of the thirteen psalms are psalms of individual lament in which David is a suffering figure, and that six of these (Pss 17; 68; 77; 88; 108; 131) explicitly describe David as "servant" (παῖς/δοῦλος). Five of these psalms (Pss 2; 17; 19; 88; 131), mention a χριστός figure. According to Luke, then, the first Jewish believers in *Messiah* Jesus are going back to their Scriptures with new lenses and focusing upon an anointed sufferer that David himself had already *foreseen* and *preprofiled*.

opened the *mind*" of those gathered in the upper room does he articulate a "change of *mind*" regarding the suffering and risen Christ and incorporates this new orientation into the heart of "all that stands written about me." A new comprehension of the Scriptures is to be proclaimed by Messiah's witnesses to Israel and all the nations!

Professor Joe Tyson in his many scholarly articles and books and particularly in his *Images of Judaism in Luke-Acts* has "opened" up new vistas for understanding the relationship between the author of the Lukan writings and ancient Judaism and has thus—especially for the many younger scholars and colleagues fortunate enough to have worked directly with him—opened the mind to all sorts of new possibilities of comprehension. It is in gratitude to his collegial approach to knowledge and to his inspiration of only the best of the mind that the following intertextual reading of the Psalms and Acts 2 is offered.

My thesis is that Luke provides a luminous "opening" of this new understanding of the Scriptures on the day of Pentecost in the apostles' "opening" proclamation "beginning in Jerusalem." Moreover, two psalms (Pss 15 LXX and 109 LXX)[2] interpret each other by arguing that David already prophesied, even as he anticipated in his own career, a *suffering and risen* Christ, and these psalms affirm that the prophecy of Joel (Acts 2:17-21) is already being fulfilled in the *proclamation* of the gathered *witnesses* to *Israel* and *all the nations*. In particular, the referent of "my Lord" from the well-known Psalm 110 (Hebrew; 109 LXX; see Acts 2:34-35) is the same "Lord" whom David "keeps seeing before me continually in my presence" as cited from Psalm 15 and for whom, as God's "holy one," David prophesies resurrection from the dead (Acts 2:25-28).

I

We can establish the main divisions of the rhetorical thrust of Peter's Pentecost speech (Acts 2:14b-36) through his direct, threefold address of his audience: "men and women of Judea" (2:14); "you men and women who are Israelites" (2:22); "men and women, brothers and sisters" (2:29). It is also apparent that each section includes an explicit quotation of Scripture along with an introductory formula of its authority:

---

[2]Since the psalm citations and the Joel quotation follow more closely the LXX, numeration hereafter will be from the LXX. For a study on the Psalms of the LXX, see Joachim Schaper, *Eschatology in the Greek Psalter*, WUNT 76 (Tübingen: J. C. B. Mohr [P. Siebeck], 1995).

1. Acts 2:14-21—Joel 3:1-5 (in vv. 17-21): "rather this is that which is/has been spoken [perf.] through the prophet Joel. . . . God says";[3]
2. Acts 2:22-28—Psalm 15:8-11b (in vv. 25b-28): "for David says [pres.] concerning him";[4]
3. Acts 2:29-36—Psalm 109:1 (in vv. 34b-35): "but he [David] himself says [pres.]."

This symmetry appears to be broken in the third section when Peter states that David, "seeing in advance, *spoke* [aorist] about the resurrection of the Christ" (2:31). What follows, however, is a paraphrase of three phrases from the previous citation (Ps 15) which contrasts David's fate with the one who is of "the fruit of his loins" (2:30). We shall argue below that this paraphrase clarifies any doubt about the referents of the Psalm 15 quotation. Thus, Psalm 109 can be applied without confusion to the resurrection and exaltation of Jesus, and, in the larger strategy of the speech, can support the contention that this same Jesus whom they crucified (2:36b) "is pouring out that which you yourselves are seeing and hearing" (2:33c).

II

What roles then do the three explicit citations play in Peter's speech? Each quotation "opens up" the whole of the Scriptures to display the fulfillment of the three central components that Jesus has enunciated as the essence of "all that stands written" (Luke 24:44). Each citation singles out a different component of the three, but all three quotations overlap in their reaffirmation of each other and hence of all three aspects of fulfillment in Jesus of Nazareth, whom "God (has) established as Lord and Christ" (Acts 2:36b).

If this notion of the Scriptures' function can be grounded in the exegesis of Peter's speech, then, we obtain the following outline when we also consider both the opening setting and closing response of the audience.

---

[3]Neither "in the last days" nor "God says" occurs in any extant Joel text. It is not clear whether Luke is attributing these words to Peter or to Joel.

[4]The αὐτόν must refer to "Jesus of Nazareth" (Acts 2:22) rather than "death." See below.

Acts 2:1-41

Setting.   *2:1-13* "Residents" of Jerusalem and "visitors" "from every nation under heaven" are confused and marvel at Galileans speaking the "mighty acts of God" in their native language

1. 2:14-21 The "pouring out of the Spirit" upon "all flesh" is fulfilling the "proclamation to all the nations" of a "change of mind leading to the release of sins" as the Scriptures (*the prophet Joel*) declare

Joel 3   v. 17c—Prophesying (men and women)
         v. 17d—Visions and dreams (young and old)
         v. 19a,b—Wonders and signs (heaven and earth)
         vv. 19b-20—Cosmic impact to the day of the Lord (all space and time)

2. 2:22-28 Jesus' of Nazareth signs, crucifixion, and resurrection already inaugurated the end days of salvation as the Scriptures (*David in Ps 15*) declare

         v. 22—Mighty works, wonders, and signs attested by God
         v. 23—Affixing of Jesus by the Israelites *as plan of God*
         v. 24—Loosing/freeing from pangs/cords of death by God

Psalm 15   vv. 25-28—David (Ps 15:8-11b) speaks prophetically about Jesus of Nazareth, God's holy one, as suffering and as never decomposing in the grave

3. 2:29-36 As exalted "Lord and Christ" at God's "right hand," Jesus is "pouring out the Spirit" of the "proclamation of a change of mind leading to the forgiveness of sins" as the Scriptures (*David in Ps 109*) declare

         vv. 29-31—The prophet David saw and spoke of the resurrection and the enthronement of the Christ
         v. 32—God did raise up Jesus, of which the apostles are witnesses
         v. 33—Jesus has in fact been exalted and has received the promise of the Father and thus is the one who is pouring out what the audience is seeing and hearing

Psalm 109   vv. 34-35—David himself speaks of Jesus as the enthroned Lord who reigns over "enemies" (Ps 109:1)
         v. 36—Therefore, God has established the Jesus whom Israel crucified as both Lord and Messiah

Response.   *2:37-41* Through a "change of mind . . . leading to the release of sins" the "promise" of the Spirit is fulfilled for Israel and for "those afar"

The headings of each of the three divisions demonstrate the progression of Peter's main argument.

1. *Acts 2:14-21.* The speech opens with Peter's explanation of how it is that the gathered followers of Jesus really were not "drunk" in *speaking* all those international languages (2:7-12). Rather it is "God" (v. 17a), *speaking* through the *prophet* Joel (Joel 3:1-5), who is explaining

the pouring out of the Spirit in the end days; indeed, this, the longest Scripture citation in the New Testament, explains the *fulfillment* of the *proclamation* of "the mighty acts of God" that is taking place among the Pentecost celebrants "from every nation of those under heaven." As many have observed, this Joel citation not only explains the present "sound of a rush of mighty wind . . . and tongues as of fire"; it also becomes a lens for viewing much of the Acts plot, with its "sons *and* daughters prophesying, its youth seeing visions and its senior citizens dreaming dreams" (2:17 = Joel 3:1). Throughout each larger division of Acts, both major characters (like Peter, Stephen, or Paul) and minor figures (like Ananias, Cornelius, or Agabus) see visions and dream dreams,[5] and both *men* (like the "twelve" disciples of John the Baptist in Ephesus) and *women* (like the four daughters of Philip in Caesarea) prophesy.[6] Or again, Joel's depiction of "male servants and female servants" who "prophesy" (2:18 = Joel 3:2) adumbrates the gathered messianists as "servants" who "prophesy" (4:23-31, esp. v. 29).

The thrust of the Joel citation, however, within the larger rhetorical strategy of the speech emphasizes the *beginning* of the fulfillment of the *proclamation* which focuses upon the significance of the suffering, risen Christ for Israel and the nations:

a. The fact that "Jews" "from every nation" understand in their own tongue the content of the "prophesying" of the "sons and daughters" of Israel signals "amazement" about something most unusual (Acts 2:12a). Peter explains this speech as the "fulfillment" "of the end days" ("*This* is that *spoken . . . in the end days*," 2:16-17a).

b. "Prophesying" as *proclaiming* the "mighty acts of God" in Messiah Jesus and his witnesses is not only heightened within the setting of many languages and by the use of the verb (προφητεύω) with "sons and daughters" in Joel 3:1 (Acts 2:17); the activity of "prophesying" is also cited in Joel 3:2 (2:18) where male and female servants are said to "prophesy" upon receiving the Spirit "in those days"—although no

---

[5]See, e.g., Acts 7:55-56; 9:10-16 (11-12); 10:3-7, 10-16; 11:28. The "signs and wonders" from Joel introduce the "mighty acts of God" which God works through Jesus. See Robert B. Sloan, " 'Signs and Wonders': A Rhetorical Clue to the Pentecost Discourse," in *Steadfast Purpose: Essays on Acts in Honor of Henry Jackson Flanders, Jr.*, ed. Naymond H. Keathley (Waco TX: Baylor University, 1990) 145-62; in a similar vein, Daniel J. Treier, "The Fulfillment of Joel 2:28-32: A Multiple-Lens Approach," *JETS* 40 (1997): 13-26.

[6]See, e.g., Acts 19:6-7; 21:8-9.

known text of Joel includes the repeated verb. The effect is to form an inclusio of "prophesying" between Acts 2:17c and 2:18b as an interpretive framing for the significance of "visions" and "dreams."

c. The Joel citation ends with the claim that *"everyone* who calls upon the name of the Lord (κύριος) shall be *saved*," an inclusio with the opening verse of God's ("my") "Spirit upon *all flesh*" (Acts 2:17b, 21). The use of "Lord" is artfully ambiguous. Does "Lord" refer primarily to the "Lord God" (2:20—"the great and splendid day of the Lord"; 2:34—*"The Lord* said to my Lord"; 2:39b—"whomever the Lord our God calls"; cf. 1:24) or to the "Lord" Jesus (2:34—"my Lord"; 2:36—"both Lord and Christ"; cf. 1:6, 21—"Lord Jesus")? Moreover, to whom does David refer as "the Lord" who is continually in his presence (2:15 = Ps 15:8)? Or which Lord is "adding daily to the whole group of those *being saved*" (2:47)? In light of the fact that the main actor at Pentecost is "at the right hand of God" (θεός) pouring out God's Spirit and is identified as "Lord and Christ" Jesus, we cannot simply conclude that the "name of the Lord" of 2:21 is the name of the Lord God. On the contrary, one could perhaps build a stronger case for the Lord Jesus, since it is into *his name* that the audience is being baptized and is being promised the forgiveness of sins *and salvation*! (2:38, 40). Whatever the primary referent, it is clear that the Joel text heralds the beginning of the fulfillment of the proclamation of eschatological *salvation* of "God's" mighty acts, "in the name of the Lord" who is "pouring forth my Spirit."

d. As the audience response reveals ("their heart was stabbed [Ps 108:16!] . . . what shall we do?" [Acts 2:37]), the thrust of the hearing of the "mighty acts of God" *together with* the content of Peter's speech leads to a radical "change of mind" or understanding of the events of Jesus, particularly the audience's involvement in his death (cf. "this one you executed" [2:23b]; "this Jesus whom you crucified" [2:36b]). This new "mindset" or orientation moves furthermore to a "release of sins," "being baptized into the name of the Messiah Jesus," and a reception of "the gift of the Holy Spirit," all of which can be described as "being saved" (2:38, 40b). In other words, the beginning of the fulfillment of the *proclamation* which opens the Scriptures to Israel and all the nations has as its *noetic* core the mighty acts of God in the suffering and risen Christ according to the threefold delineation by Jesus of "all that stands written about *me*" (that is, as "the Christ"; Luke 24:44-48).

2. *Acts 2:22-28.* Peter now expounds the message of those many tongues of "the mighty acts of God," and in doing so he cites the second

longest scriptural passage in Acts and the third longest of the New Testament. If his immediate purpose in "opening up" the Scriptures is the same as in the first section, then the citation will answer the questions posed by the audience in light of the inexplicable sights and sounds that demand "explanation" (2:16: "this [speaking] is that spoken" [it is *not* drunken babbling, 2:15a]). In fact, Peter's words now thrust a question right back to the audience: How could *they* have executed "Jesus of Nazareth" who had been attested by God in their very midst through God's own actions of "powerful deeds and wonders and signs through him" (2:22-24)? If Joel is explaining *wonders* and *signs* in the wind, fire, and strange speech of Jesus' Galilean followers, then Psalm 15 would explain how the Jerusalem audience, representing every nation under heaven, put to death the one who exhibited such self-evident God-attested *wonders* and *signs*! Or, in other words, Psalm 15:8-11 would clarify the "determined plan and foreknowledge of God" which led to their "handing over" Jesus to the "lawless" Romans for execution (2:23) *as well as* to God's raising him up by "loosing the pangs of death" (2:24a = Pss 17:4; 114:3!).

The conventional exegesis of this lengthy citation, however, regards Psalm 15:8-11 as an explanation *only* of the resurrection. This citation is viewed as some obscure text which Christians allegedly mined from the Scriptures in order to find proof for the resurrection or as a text which simply makes one point, namely that Messiah's resurrection was already foretold by David, or both. David's famous line, "Nor will you let your holy one see decomposition" (Acts 2:27b = Ps 15:10b), is thought—wittingly or unwittingly—to foretell the resurrection of Jesus.[7] According to

---

[7]See, e.g., Jacques Dupont, *The Salvation of the Gentiles: Essays on the Acts of the Apostles* (New York: Paulist, 1979) 103-28; Ernst Haenchen, *The Acts of the Apostles* (Philadelphia: Westminster, 1971) 179-82; Luke T. Johnson, *The Acts of the Apostles*, Sacra Pagina 5 (Collegeville MN: Liturgical, 1992) 48-55; Donald Juel, "Social Dimensions of Exegesis: The Use of Psalm 16 in Acts 2," *CBQ* 43 (1981): 543-86; Gerhard Krodel, *Acts* (Minneapolis: Augsburg, 1986) 83-89; I. Howard Marshall, *The Acts of the Apostles* (Grand Rapids MI: Eerdmans, 1980) 73-81; Robert C. Tannehill, *The Narrative Unity of Luke-Acts: A Literary Interpretation*, 2 vols. (Philadelphia and Minneapolis: Fortress, 1986, 1990) 2:26-42; William H. Bellinger, Jr., "The Psalms and Acts: Reading and Rereading," in *Steadfast Purpose*, 127-43, esp. 128-36. For a traditiohistorical approach, see Hendrikus W. Boers, "Psalm 16 and the historical origin of the Christian faith," *ZNW* 60 (1969): 105-10. Boers comes to the interesting conclusion that, before it became a commentary on the resurrection experiences (that is, conventional interpretation), Ps 15(16) was used to interpret the *death* of Jesus. For the view that Ps 15 LXX in the ethos of the Hellenistic era brings out the fuller eschatological implications of Ps 16 (MT), see

this usual explanation, the purpose of citing Psalm 15:8-11, *therefore*, is to build a basis upon which to call the people to repentance by establishing at least some participation in the guilt of Messiah's death (2:38a). Everyone in and around Jerusalem had seen or heard of the mighty works of Jesus and it should have been obvious that none other than God's power was doing this; yet they killed him! David's oration perforce is proof! Jesus obviously fills the bill through his resurrection, and, accordingly, the audience's response of remorse at the end of the speech makes sense (2:37).

But the *therefore* of the conventional reading of Acts 2:25-28 (Ps 15:8-11) is not so transparent. How can a cryptic reference to "no decomposition in the tomb" possibly argue that the Jewish people in part or even as a whole must *share the blame* for executing Jesus and consequently stand in need of the "release of their sins" (2:37-38)? Why cite this long quotation in which David, the speaker, refers to *seeing* (imperf.) a certain "Lord" *before him continually* (Ps 15:8a = Acts 2:25)—at his (that is, David's) *"right hand* in order that he might not be shaken" (15:8b)? Why include the detail about his great joy in the presence of this Lord (Ps 15:9ab = Acts 2:26ab) *before* David goes on to *add yet another fact* (Ps 15:9c = Acts 2:26c): "more than that also, my flesh shall dwell in hope because you will not abandon my life in Hades"? The distinct impression is that David is undergoing a longer period of duress in which his conscious awareness of this "Lord" "continually at his right hand" provides a source of considerable strength and prevents him from succumbing to his opposition ("being shaken"). During this indefinite period of "pressure," he comes to the realization that even when he does finally succumb to death, even then in Hades "his life" "will dwell [fut.] in hope" because "you" will not abandon him to that fate (Ps 15:9c-10a = Acts 2:26c-27a). A critical question obviously looms: Who is this "you" (Ps 15:10-11 = Acts 2:27-28)? Is this "you" the "Lord" mentioned two verses previously, or is this change of person to *direct* address referring now to someone else, to "God" perhaps?

Curiously, many contemporary commentators place much emphasis, and rightly so, on the programmatic function of the Joel text, and yet tend to ignore this second longest citation altogether. But would it not make more "sense" in the rhetoric of the speech to interpret Peter as

---

Armin Schmitt, "Ps 16,8-11 als Zeugnis der Auferstehung in der Apg," *BZ* 17 (1973): 229-48.

expatiating upon "the determined plan and foreknowledge of God," *remembering Jesus' words* (Luke 24:46), *how it is that "the Psalms are written about me," namely that "the Christ must suffer and on the third day rise from the dead"* (v. 46)?

This "opening" of the "plan of God" as the distinct purpose of the Psalm 15 citation is transfigured when we place the quoted verses in the context of the entire psalm. Psalm 15 LXX diverges greatly from its counterpart in the Hebrew text, Psalm 16, which is a song of trust. The many differences in Psalm 15 become telling and "transform" the psalm into the *psalm of the suffering righteous*, and thereby present a very different context for verses 8-11. The LXX version[8] with my own translation follows. The verses cited in Peter's speech are printed in italics.

Psalm 15

¹ Στηλογραφία τῷ Δαυίδ.
Φύλαξόν με, κύριε, ὅτι ἐπὶ σοὶ ἤλπισα. ²εἶπα τῷ κυρίῳ Κύριός μου εἶ σύ, ὅτι τῶν ἀγαθῶν μου οὐ χρείαν ἔχεις. ³τοῖς ἁγίοις τοῖς ἐν τῇ γῇ αὐτοῦ ἐθαυμάστωσεν πάντα τὰ θελήματα αὐτοῦ ἐν αὐτοῖς. ⁴ἐπληθύνθησαν αἱ ἀσθένειαι αὐτῶν, μετὰ ταῦτα ἐτάξυναν· οὐ μὴ συναγάγω τὰς συναγωγὰς αὐτῶν ἐξ αἱμάτων οὐδὲ μὴ μνησθῶ τῶν ὀνομάτων αὐτῶν διὰ χειλέων μου. ⁵κύριος ἡ μερὶς τῆς κληρονομίας μου καὶ τοῦ ποτηρίου μου· σὺ εἶ ὁ ἀποκαθιστῶν τὴν κληρονομίαν μου ἐμοί. ⁶σχοινία ἐπέπεσάν μοι ἐν τοῖς κρατίστοις· καὶ γὰρ ἡ κληρονομία μου κρατίστη μοί ἐστιν. ⁷εὐλογήσω τὸν κύριον τὸν συνετίσαντά με· ἔτι δὲ καὶ ἕως νυκτὸς ἐπαίδευσάν με οἱ νεφροί μου. ⁸προωρώμην τὸν κύριον ἐνώπιόν μου διὰ παντός, ὅτι ἐκ δεξιῶν μού ἐστιν, ἵνα μὴ σαλευθῶ. ⁹διὰ τοῦτο ηὐφράνθη ἡ καρδία μου, καὶ ἠγαλλιάσατο ἡ γλῶσσά μου, ἔτι δὲ καὶ ἡ σάρξ μου κατασκηνώσει ἐπ' ἐλπίδι, ¹⁰ὅτι οὐκ ἐγκαταλείψεις τὴν ψυχήν μου εἰς ᾅδην οὐδὲ δώσεις τὸν ὅσιόν σου ἰδεῖν διαφθοράν. ¹¹ἐγνώρισάς μοι ὁδοὺς ζωῆς· πληρώσεις με εὐφροσύνης μετὰ τοῦ προσώπου σου, τερπνότητες ἐν τῇ δεξιᾷ σου εἰς τέλος.

¹ A Writing of David.
Keep me, O Lord, for I have hoped in you. ²I said to the Lord, you are **my Lord**; for you have no need of my goodness. ³On behalf of the saints who are in his land, he has magnified all his pleasure in them. ⁴Their weaknesses (illnesses/bodily afflictions) have been multiplied; afterward they hastened. I will certainly not assemble their bloody meetings, neither will I make mention of their names with my lips. ⁵The Lord is the portion of my inheritance and of my cup: you are the one who restores my inheritance to me. ⁶The measuring lines have fallen to me in the best places; yes, I have a most excellent inheritance. ⁷I will bless the Lord who has instructed me; my kidneys (loins) too have chastened me even till the night. ⁸*I kept seeing the Lord before me continually in my presence; for he is at **my right hand**, that I should not be shaken,* ⁹*Therefore my heart rejoiced and my tongue exulted; **more than that also**, my flesh shall rest (dwell) in hope.* ¹⁰*because you will not abandon my life in Hades, neither will you allow your holy one to see decomposition.* ¹¹You have made known to me the ways of (that lead to) life; you will fill me with joy with your presence; at **your right hand** there are delights for ever.

---

[8]*Septuaginta*, ed. Alfred Rahlfs (Stuttgart: Deutsche Bibelgesellschaft, repr. 1979; ¹1935).

The major divergences with Psalm 16 (MT) are as follows.

a. *Psalm 16:3*. *David* has "delight in the saints" "who are in the land." In Psalm 15:3 the *Lord* is said to "magnify all his delights/desires" "in/with the saints that are in his [the Lord's] land."

b. *Psalm 16:4*. David declares that *if* these same saints in whom he delights should "run after another [god]," then "their sorrows will multiply." If that should happen, David vows to distance himself from them decisively by refusing to participate in their idolatrous rituals and by refusing even to utter their names: "I [David] will not pour their drink offerings of blood; nor will I take their names on my lips." Psalm 15:4, on the other hand, presents the very opposite picture. Now the "saints" in whom "the Lord has magnified all his delights" are described as bearing "illness" or some sort of "physical afflictions." Now instead of describing apostates from the God of Israel, David depicts a group of embattled, persecuted saints whose "gatherings," rather than rituals, are dripping with "blood" and who have to flee for their lives. And instead of distancing himself from any association, David claims fundamental solidarity with them. He will "distance" himself from them *physically* only in order that they may not be exposed to further danger. He emphatically will not attempt to reassemble them, nor will he dare mention any of their names lest their identities be divulged!

c. *Psalm 16:5*. In accordance with the first two differences, David continues to affirm his unfailing trust in Yahweh. The Lord Yahweh is David's very "inheritance" and "cup." Yahweh shall uphold David's "lot" (cf. 16:6). In Psalm 15:5, however, the Lord (κύριος) who is David's "inheritance and cup" must "*restore* my inheritance to me." David's inheritance/heritage has either been taken from him or is in grave danger. The Lord will have to secure it back for him, and David affirms his unequivocal trust that the Lord will do just that (cf. 15:6).

d. *Psalm 16:7*. Because the David of Psalm 16:1-6 expresses only confidence in Yahweh's goodness and faithfulness to him, David proceeds to extol this Lord as one who gives him counsel (during the day) and who ensures that David's own "loins" or passions continue to teach him during the night. For the David of Psalm 15:7, by contrast, the night spares none of the discipline that he has received from the Lord through this great ordeal; his own loins (or lit. "kidneys") wreak their own form of chastening upon him during the night! We have, in other words, a self-affirmed expression of great pressure not unlike the depiction of the saints under duress in 15:4.

e. *Psalm 16:8.* When we come to the first verse quoted by Peter in Acts 2:25, the contexts of the psalm's two versions could hardly be more disparate. The David of Psalm 16 avers that he "has set" the Lord Yahweh "before me always." Moreover, "because he is at my right hand, I shall not be shaken." "It is for this reason," David continues, "my heart is glad and my glory rejoices; also my flesh shall rest in hope; for you will not leave my life/soul in Sheol nor will you give/allow your holy one to see decomposition" (vv. 9-11). Verses 8-10 reaffirm both Lord Yahweh's steadfast faithfulness to David and David's unfailing loyalty to Yahweh. Whatever trials or conflicts may lie "behind" or be presumed by such songs of trust (16:1), what rings through nearly every verse of the Hebrew version is the ebullient confidence David has in Yahweh's "goodness" and in his own "good lot" with Yahweh (16:2). Not even Sheol will be able to hold David's "life." Rather, Yahweh ("you") "will show" David "the way of life"; indeed, at Lord Yahweh's ("your") *"right hand"* are the very "pleasures" of life "forever" (16:10-11).

The David of Psalm 15, on the other hand, continues to speak out of great suffering (v. 8). Instead of speaking of his own resolve to be loyal to Lord Yahweh ("I have set Yahweh always before me"), David allows that during this whole time of great distress, he "kept seeing before me the Lord continually in my presence." "Because of" (ὅτι) this presence "at my right hand," David can rejoice and be assured that he will not die before his time and that the Lord would continue to protect him from his enemies. Beyond even this period of persecution—but precisely because of the Lord's presence through it—David also realizes that someday even in death "you" will not "abandon" him (15:8-10). *Because it has been through this term of persecution* that "the Lord has instructed" (aor.) David (15:7) and that "you have divulged" (aor.) to David "the ways of [that lead to] life," David knows that someday he will experience (fut.) the "delights" of life "forever" at "your" own "right hand" (15:11).

In sum, the David who speaks through Peter in Acts 2:25-28 is *a suffering righteous figure who is in solidarity with other saints under great persecution.* The Lord takes great delight in them because of their faithfulness in the midst of intense opposition. With the reference within the larger context of David's need for the Lord to *restore* his inheritance (Ps 15:5), this psalm could possibly reflect the time of rebellion by David's own son, Absalom. In any event, as we know from the Davidic narratives, most of the opposition the biblical writers describe is internal, within David's own *house*, a house divided, Israelite against Israelite! In short, in this psalm and curiously in most of the other twelve psalms cited in the opening of Acts, David's enemies are from his own people of Israel, the very people for whom David is king, their anointed, their *christ* (χριστός).[9]

Now let us see how this profile of David from Psalm 15 affects the argument of Peter's speech through the first two sections, Acts 2:14-28.

a. Peter's introductory formulation asserts that David in Psalm 15 "speaks" (pres.) "concerning him" (that is, "Jesus of Nazareth," Acts 2:22). The Jesus Peter has just described is, despite obvious signs of God's presence through him, nevertheless "handed over" to "lawless folk" for execution by his own people and whom "God raised up" (2:22-24a). Peter describes these events, moreover, as "the determined will and foreknowledge of God" (2:23a).

b. If the "Lord" who is at David's "right hand" "continually" during David's tenure of persecution is the "Lord Messiah Jesus" (cf. Acts 2:36), then David is proclaiming a solidarity with him as he (David) suffers (Ps 15:8-11). It follows, then, that the Lord Messiah's presence with him keeps David from being "shaken" by his enemies. David's great joy (Ps 15:9 = Acts 2:26), then, is his realization both that God's will for him is to reign precisely in the midst of his enemies and that he will fulfill God's purposes for him (cf. 13:36!).

c. If "your holy one" (Ps 15:10b = Acts 2:27b) is the same "Lord Messiah Jesus" of David's experience, then David realizes that the Lord Messiah Jesus himself will be given over to Sheol, not unlike the fate of entering Sheol (death) that awaits him. David's new insight ("more than that also")—that "you" will not abandon him(self) to this death—therefore, is predicated on the nondecomposition or resurrection from the dead *of the Lord Messiah Jesus* by "you."

d. If "b" and "c" above are correct, then David's statement ("you have made known to me the ways/paths of [leading to] life"; Ps 15:11ab = Acts 2:28ab) refers to his whole experience of solidarity in his suffering with the Lord Messiah Jesus. This experience includes the assurance to David that, because this same "Lord" who is "at his right hand" will be

---

[9]See, e.g., Pss 2:2; 17(18):50; 19(20):6; 88(89):38, 51; 131(132):10, 17; cf. n. 1 above. For the use of Ps 2 in interpreting the suffering and death of Jesus in Luke-Acts, see Wim J. C. Weren, "Psalm 2 in Luke-Acts: An Intertextual Study," in *Intertextuality in Biblical Writings: Essays in Honour of Bas van Iersel*, ed. Sipike Draisma (Kampen, Netherlands: J. H. Kok, 1989) 189-203.

raised up from the dead, he himself will someday experience life with
"*you*." Or restated, David's new knowledge of what constitutes "the paths
of life" (Acts 2:28a) is revealed precisely through his solidarity in
suffering with the Lord Messiah Jesus and David's foreknowledge of the
Lord Messiah Jesus' nondecomposition in Sheol. The leap is not great in
arguing also that Peter (Luke!) thinks of David as conceiving of life
beyond Sheol as life with this Lord Messiah Jesus, as well as with the
"*you*" (that is, the "Lord God"). We recall that the final line of Psalm
15:11 (and of the entire psalm), "at *your* right hand are delights forever"
(v. 11c), is left out by Peter. Is there a meaningful reason for this
omission?

To sum up, strong evidence now suggests that David is proclaiming in
advance the "determined will and foreknowledge of God" (Ps 15:8-11ab)
that is focused in the suffering (death) and raising up of Jesus of
Nazareth whom God—precisely through this whole will and foreknowledge—has established as "Lord and Christ" (cf. 2:36). That would also
mean that David, like Jesus' witnesses through their many languages at
Pentecost, is proclaiming the "mighty acts of God" in the suffering and
risen Messiah by prophesying "all that stands written" about this *Christ*!
Does the third movement of Peter's rhetorical strategy support these
conclusions? Our contention is that Peter's quote of Psalm 109 is
indispensable to his interpretation of Psalm 15 and integrates the three
citations into a harmonious proclamation of the noetic core of (all) the
Scriptures.

3. *Acts 2:29-36.* Peter moves in this third and final section of the
speech to return full circle to the clarifying thrust of the Joel text in order
to relate Jesus of Nazareth more precisely to that "pouring out of my
Spirit" ("this, that you yourselves are seeing and hearing!" 2:33). In
doing so, he pulls together the threads of his argument (marked by
"therefore" or "it follows that"—οὖν, vv. 30, 33) to sew up the final
conclusion of verse 36: "*therefore* let the whole house of Israel *know
with certainty* that . . . " (ἀσφαλῶς οὖν γινωσκέτω . . . ὅτι . . .).
Whatever else Psalm 109:1 (2:34b-35) accomplishes, it appears to clinch
the climax of Peter's address.

a. *Verses 29-32.*

(1) Peter begins by stating the obvious: David is still dead and his
tomb is "living" proof (Acts 2:29)!

(2) But with "his tomb in our midst," it is patently obvious that neither
line of the Semitic parallelism of Psalm 15:10 could as yet be described

as true for David. Did David misspeak? Not according to Peter's *new* hermeneutic—"it follows therefore" (οὖν) that David was a "prophet" (Acts 2:30a). In other words, Peter continues (2:30-31) by arguing that David knew that he was not the "holy one" of whom he spoke in Psalm 15:10! "Knowing that God had sworn an oath to him that from his *loins* one would sit upon his throne" (2:30b), *and further*, "seeing in advance [προιδών (aor.), v. 31a] he *spoke* about the resurrection of the Messiah" (ὁ χριστός; 2:31a). Peter thus clarifies any confusion by identifying "*your* holy one" with the Lord Messiah whom David "kept seeing" in Psalm 15. The aorist participle of προοράω—by stating a fact or summarizing an extended period of time as a whole—sums up David's ongoing experience of "seeing" this "Lord" who is "at his right hand" (προορώμην [imperf.], Ps 15:8 [Acts 2:25]). That προιδών refers directly back to David's experience and Peter's citation of Psalm 15:8-11 is clear because Peter continues to refer to his quotation by paraphrasing two phrases and by applying them as "proof" of "the Christ's resurrection" (v. 31b): οὔτε ἐγκατελείφθη εἰς ᾅδην (corr. Ps 15:10a); οὔτε ἡ σὰρξ αὐτοῦ εἶδεν διαφθοράν (corr. Ps 15:9b, 10b). Both lines of Psalm 15:10 must now refer to Messiah Jesus. And, by using "flesh" from Psalm 15:9b, Peter not only makes it clear that David's flesh is still "decomposing" in death, but also places David's prophetic hope squarely in his earthly or physical experience of seeing this "Lord" at his "right hand."

(3) It is curious that Peter uses the term "the Messiah" since χριστός occurs neither in Psalm 15 nor in his speech thus far. In fact, Acts 2:31a is the first use of χριστός in the book of Acts. But the reasons for his use of this designation are anything but obscure. Peter had had his "mind opened" by Jesus so that he could "comprehend" that the Psalms are written about Jesus as "the Christ" (Luke 24:45-47). What is more, Peter alludes (2:30) to psalms which characterize David as the Lord's anointed[10] whose offspring will "sit upon his throne" "forever" (Ps 131:11; 88:4); it is toward this "throne" that Peter's argument is moving (see vv. 33-35 below).

(4) Peter continues his argument (Acts 2:32) by stating that "this Jesus God raised." *Ergo*, Jesus is the one whom David foresaw as "not decomposing"; he is "the Christ" whom David "saw" in advance as experienc-

---

[10]David is χριστός in Pss 88(89):38, 51; 131(132):10, 17.

ing "resurrection" from Hades; he is "the Lord" whom David kept seeing at David's own "right hand." Moreover, Peter ties Jesus' mandate of "witness" to this fulfillment of Psalm 15. Or again, the Psalms through David are proclaiming in advance that "the Christ must . . . rise from the dead. . . . these things of which you are witnesses" (Luke 24:46-47).

b. *Verses 33-35.*

(1) Peter comes full circle to his opening explanation by drawing the conclusion (οὖν, Acts 2:33a) that Jesus is "exalted at the right hand of God" and "has poured out that which you are seeing and hearing" (v. 33). But Peter has Joel state that "God" "is pouring out *my* Spirit" (2:17); by what inference can Peter claim that Jesus is doing this, and how can he argue that Jesus' resurrection as the Christ is tantamount to being "exalted [ὑψωθείς] at the right hand of God"? The answer again goes back to Psalm 15 but now with the illumination or "enriching" interpretation of Psalm 109: "For [γάρ] David did not . . . he himself says . . . " (Ps 109:1).

Psalm 109[11]
(The quotation in Acts 2:34b-35 is found in verse 1.)

¹ Τῷ Δαυίδ ψαλμός.
Εἶπεν ὁ κύριος τῷ κυρίῳ μου Κάθου ἐκ δεξιῶν μου,
ἕως ἂν θῶ τοὺς ἐχθρούς σου ὑποπόδιον τῶν ποδῶν σου,
²ῥάβδον δυνάμεώς σου ἐξαποστελεῖ κύριος ἐκ Σιών,
καὶ κατακυρίευε ἐν μέσῳ τῶν ἐχθρῶν σου.
³μετὰ σοῦ ἡ ἀρχὴ ἐν ἡμέρᾳ τῆς δυνάμεώς σου
ἐν ταῖς λαμπρότησιν τῶν ἁγίων·
ἐκ γαστρὸς πρὸ ἑωσφόρου ἐξεγέννησά σε.
⁴ὤμοσεν κύριος καὶ οὐ μεταμεληθήσεται,
Σὺ εἶ ἱερεὺς εἰς τὸν αἰῶνα κατὰ τὴν τάξιν Μελχισέδεκ
⁵κύριος ἐκ δεξιῶν σου συνέθλασεν ἐν ἡμέρᾳ ὀργῆς
    αὐτοῦ βασιλεῖς·
⁶κρινεῖ ἐν τοῖς ἔθνεσιν, πληρώσει πτώματα,
συνθλάσει κεφαλὰς ἐπὶ γῆς πολλῶν.
⁷ἐκ χειμάρρου ἐν ὁδῷ πίεται·
διὰ τοῦτο ὑψώσει κεφαλήν.

(2) Psalm 109 enriches Psalm 15 in the following ways.

(a) Since David obviously did not "ascend into the heavens" (Acts 2:34a; cf. v. 29b), it is also evident that David himself in another psalm

---

[11]*Septuaginta,* ed. Alfred Rahlfs.

refers to one who in the future will be "exalted at the right hand of the Lord" (cf. ὑψόω in Ps 109:7) and thus will meet both criteria of Psalm 15:10 ("neither be abandoned in Hades" nor "see decomposition" in the tomb).

(b) Since David refers to this "exalted" one as "my Lord," it follows that he cannot wittingly or unwittingly be prophesying about himself.

(c) It is also now evident that David in his experience (Ps 109:1) speaks of two distinct "lords": "my Lord" and "the Lord." Further, "the Lord" of Psalm 109:1 commands "my Lord" to sit "at his right hand" to wield the kind of dominion that can only be ascribed to the "Lord God" (Ps 109:2; cf. 109:5-7).

(d) Psalms 15 and 109 both speak about a "lord" enabling either David (Ps 15) or "my Lord" (Ps 109) to rule in the midst of their enemies. It is not much of a leap for Peter or the early believers to identify David's experience of "my Lord" of Psalm 109 who rules in the midst of enemies with "the Lord who is before me continually at my right hand" of Psalm 15 who enables David "not to be shaken" by his enemies. In fact, the ambiguity of the referent for the "Lord at your right hand" of Psalm 109:5 (κύριος ἐκ δεξιῶν σου) could well invite such an identification. Is this "Lord" the "Lord God" at "my Lord's right hand" (that is, David is still addressing "my Lord" as he does in Psalm 109:2-3)? Or is the "Lord God" of Psalm 109:4 still speaking to David (v. 5) so that "the Lord at your [David's] right hand" (Ps 109:5) must be the "my Lord" of Psalm 109:1? Either way, the parallel of "Lords" enabling David/"my Lord" to rule is remarkable. Psalm 109 is thus identifying the "Lord" whom David both "sees be*fore*" him and "*fore*sees" as "being exalted at the right hand."[12]

(e) Unlike the more general reference to the "people" of "my Lord's" or the king's dominion in Psalm 110:3 (MT), Psalm 109:3a like Psalm 15:3-4, places David's/"my Lord's" rule over enemies in the midst of the solidarity of "the saints."

(f) Unlike Psalm 110:3b (MT), David in Psalm 109:3b "begets" "my lord" (σε) "from the womb"; the "my Lord" of Psalm 109:1 is David's own "offspring!" Peter's "therefore" of Acts 2:33a now makes perfect sense. The "my Lord" of Psalm 109 who is David's Lord in Psalm 15 is also from David's loins, and *therefore* is "the Christ." David not only

---

[12]προοράω can bear both senses in Greek literature. Peter in Acts 2:31, then, is capitalizing on this double sense as he refers to his quotation of Ps 15:8 (Acts 2:25).

"foresaw the resurrection of the Christ" (Acts 2:31), he also foresaw the enthronement of this same Christ, David's Lord. "For David himself says, 'The Lord said to my Lord, "Sit at my right hand"'" (Acts 2:34b).[13]

(g) Psalm 109 describes more fully what David means in Psalm 15:11c when he declares as a finale: "at *your* right hand are delights forever." Peter stops just short of quoting this climax in Acts 2:25-28 because Psalm 109 develops this "right hand" with respect to the "Lord" and "Christ" of Psalm 15. The "delights" at the Lord God's "right hand" are nothing less than the enthroned Lord and Christ whom David experienced in advance at his own "right hand." David "begets" this Lord and Christ, refers to him as "my Lord," and even addresses him in Psalm 109:2-3 if not also in 109:5-7. Hence, it is certainly true that "everyone who calls upon the name of [this] Lord"—the one who "has received the promised Holy Spirit from the Father" (Acts 2:33)—"shall be saved" (Joel 3:5 = Acts 2:21).

c. *Verse 36.*

Peter hardly needs to state the obvious in his final "therefore." There can be no other (ἀσφαλῶς!) than Jesus of Nazareth whom "God established as both Lord and Christ"[14]—"this Jesus whom you yourselves crucified."

To sum up the role of the Psalm 109 citation. The "my Lord" (Ps 109:1 = Acts 2:34b) who is now seated at the right hand is the same Lord who had been revealed to David during his time of great trials and opposition from his own people (Ps 15:8-10 = Acts 2:25-27). The "paths which lead to life" (Ps 15:11b = Acts 2:28a) lead to God's right hand![15] We can now see that Psalm 109 not only interprets Psalm 15 but also that Psalm 15 illuminates Psalm 109. The paths that lead to life are

---

[13]Cf. Jesus' posing of this conundrum to the scribes of the Sadducees in Luke 20:41-44 par: "David therefore calls him 'Lord,' how can he be his son?"

[14]Cf. Ps 19(20):6: "The Lord (κύριος) has saved (ἔσωσε) his Christ" (τὸν χριστὸν αὐτοῦ).

[15]Ps 109 develops the scenario of Ps 15 by describing David's foreseeing of his exalted Lord. Ps 109 functions as a kind of prophetic lullaby in which David sees that one day the one whom he "begets" will not only *not* be shaken by his enemies, but will also triumph over Sheol itself to reign in perpetuity. The use of second person pronouns in every verse except vv. 6-7 argues for the continuity of referent of the "you" being "my Lord" throughout. The "Lord at *your* right hand" in v. 5 would then be the Lord God at "my Lord's" right hand so that a parallel of "right hands" and reigning over "enemies" between Pss 15 and 109 would be formed: as the "Lord" (=my Lord) of Ps 15 is to David, so the Lord God of Ps 109 is to "my Lord."

essentially, quintessentially, the paths of David's suffering which anticipate "my Lord's" own suffering at the hands of his (and David's!) own people. But this path continues to the "right hand" of the Lord God where the exalted "my Lord" "has poured out this that you yourselves are seeing and hearing" (Acts 2:33). David could "not be shaken" because he foresaw that one day his Lord, God's holy one, would be seated at God's right hand where "there are delights forever."

III

It is time to summarize our conclusions. Psalms 15 and 109 are used by Peter to expound "the determined plan and foreknowledge of God" (Acts 2:23) which is the focus of the proclamation of the "mighty acts of God" in the tongues of "every nation under heaven" as clarified by Joel 3. Peter is identifying the career of Jesus of Nazareth directly from "all that stands written," from the Psalms of David, they—as the chosen *witnesses*—are now reading with new eyes, that is to say, the Psalms "opened" by the risen Lord and Messiah himself (Luke 24:44-46). In this "opening" of "all the Scriptures," Psalm 15 forms the critical hinge by linking the "pouring out of my [God's] Spirit" of "the last days" to the "Lord exalted at the right hand" of God such that "everyone who calls upon the name of the Lord" and is "baptized into the name of Jesus (the) Christ" "shall be saved." Thus all three citations unfold the essence of all that stands written and open up the *mind* of the "house of Israel" to "change their *mind* . . . and receive the gift of the Holy Spirit. For this promise is for you and your children and to all those far away" (Acts 2:38-39a).

Part III

**Jews, Judaism,
and Anti-Judaism
in the Lukan Writings
and Scholarship**

Redemptive Anti-Semitism:
The De-Judaization of the New Testament in the Third Reich

Susannah Heschel

What is the relationship between Jesus and Judaism? Was Jesus a Jew, teaching conventional Jewish ideas of the first century, or did he denounce Judaism and intend to found a new religion? Such questions have stood at the center of New Testament scholarship ever since the quest for the historical Jesus was begun by Lessing's publication of Reimarus's *Fragments*. While Jewish historians during the nineteenth century expressed sharp criticism of the limited and distorted representations of Judaism in Christian scholarship, few New Testament scholars took their criticisms seriously. Only in the most recent decades, since World War II, have Christian scholars of the New Testament attempted a serious engagement with the history of Judaism and a critical disengagement from the traditions of anti-Judaism that permeated their field for many generations.

The work of Joseph B. Tyson stands at the center of the efforts to disengage the New Testament from anti-Judaism. Trained by W. D. Davies, one of the pioneers in the reconsideration of Paul's relation to rabbinic Judaism, Tyson set himself to the scholarly task of examining the images of Judaism contained in Luke-Acts. By incorporating the insights of the most sophisticated contemporary schools of literary theory, Tyson opens the texts of Luke-Acts to a multilayered analysis of its representations of Jews and Judaism. The questions he poses are not the simple ones of how we read the New Testament today, but are the far more complex questions of how the text constructs an implied reader and creates images of Judaism for his or her consumption. In Tyson's work, the fictive quality of the narrative's "Judaism" is placed at the center and recognized for its imaginative power. By acknowledging the text's strategies in creating and shaping that Judaism, Tyson opens the door to a new kind of scholarship on the history of Christian views of Judaism, one that is not bound by theological determinism nor by a naïve historical positivism.

The freshness of Tyson's approach, particularly its sympathetic and theologically unbiased presentation of Judaism, stands in sharp relief when considered against the background of New Testament scholarship as it developed in Germany during the past two hundred years. Tyson himself is acutely aware of this contrast and has therefore become deeply involved in the study of the anti-Semitic roots of Lukan scholarship. Dr. Tyson is currently researching a book which will demonstrate the prevalence of anti-Semitism in German Lukan scholarship over the last two hundred years. In this study, I wish to engage in a similar examination of the anti-Semitic tendencies in German New Testament scholarship, limiting myself to an examination of scholars who worked in Germany during the Nazi era.

Despite the efforts of Jewish scholars, beginning in the nineteenth century, to engage New Testament historians in the shared enterprise of reconstructing second temple Judaism, Christian scholarship in Germany continued a tradition of anti-Judaism that held itself oblivious to Jewish historiography. German liberal Protestantism, in particular, developed theological models and historical-critical methods that led, I have argued elsewhere, to an anti-Judaism intrinsic to its affirmation of the nonsupernatural, historical figure of Jesus. When combined with a growing German nationalism and *völkisch* tendencies within the church, many renowned New Testament scholars easily fell victim to an enthusiastic embrace of National Socialism and an effort to synthesize Christianity with it. Calling themselves the *Deutsche Christen*, or Aryan Christians, this group of Protestant theologians developed theological rationales in support of Hitler and, in particular, his anti-Semitism. Among its most vocal leaders were several professors and instructors of New Testament, including Johannes Leipoldt, Walter Grundmann, Georg Bertram, Gerhard Delling, Karl Euler, Rudolf Meyer, and Herbert Preisker. They became leading figures in an anti-Semitic propaganda institute founded in 1939, the "Institute for the Study and Eradication of Jewish Influence on German Religious Life," which was headquartered in Eisenach. The Institute produced de-Judaized liturgical materials and theological literature which argued that Judaism was a dangerous and degenerate religion and that Jesus was its greatest opponent.

The combination of racial theory and religion in Germany, beginning in the nineteenth century and blossoming during the early decades of the twentieth, led to the creation of Aryan Christianity. This phenomenon, which Saul Friedländer has described as "redemptive anti-Semitism," was born, he writes, "from the fear of racial degeneration and the religious belief in redemption."[1] It advocated Germany's liberation from the Jews and from Jewish influences. An authentic Germany would be free of all Jewish accretions, those that had entered via modernity and those that had entered via Christianity. If the contemporary savior was Hitler, his mission was that of Christ. The redemption of Christianity itself was at stake, and could only be accomplished by purging Jesus of all Jewish associations and reconstructing him as he allegedly really was, an Aryan.

The implementation of Aryan Christianity within the institutional Protestant church was the goal of the pro-Nazi German Christian Movement, described by Doris Bergen. The Movement reached its zenith with the 1939 establishment of the anti-Semitic research institute mentioned above. Several of the major figures within the Institute had met as Gerhard Kittel's students, and had worked under him at the University of Tübingen during the early 1930s on the *Theological Dictionary of the New Testament*. Based on church archives, it is possible to reconstruct the establishment, activities, membership, funding and theology of the Institute, and to trace the postwar careers of its leaders within the church and the faculties of theological schools. Until now, the very existence of the Institute, from 1939 to 1945, was barely known, as a result of postwar efforts to hide all of the church's pro-Nazi activities.

The significance of the Institute lies in its efforts to identify Christianity with National Socialist anti-Semitism by arguing that Jesus was an Aryan who sought the destruction of Judaism. Its members proclaimed: "We know that the Jews want the annihilation [*Vernichtung*] of Germany."[2] "Jesus had taken up a fight against Judaism in all sharpness and had fallen as victim to [his fight]."[3] Once aware of the deportations and murders, they continued to justify the treatment of the Jews, on Christian grounds. In 1942, Walter Grundmann, professor of New Testament at the University of Jena and academic director of the Institute, declared:

---

[1]Saul Friedländer, *Nazi Germany and the Jews* (New York: HarperCollins, 1997) 87.
[2]Walter Grundmann, "Das Heil kommt von den Juden: Eine Schicksalsfrage an die Christen deutscher Nation," *Deutsche Frömmigkeit* 9 (Sept 1938): 1.
[3]Georg Bertram, *Denkschrift* betr. Aufgaben eines theologischen Forschungs-Instituts zu Thüringen 6 May 1945, 1; Landeskirchenarchiv Thüringen (hereinafter abbreviated LKA Thüringen), A921.

A healthy *Volk* must and will reject the Jews in every form. This fact is justified before history and through history. If someone is upset about Germany's treatment of the Jews, Germany has the historical justification and historical authorization for the fight against the Jews on its side![4]

Of the several research institutes in Nazi Germany, this one had the largest membership of academics and was the most productive in terms of publications. That it was run by theologians is highly significant. Academic expertise about Judaism resided within the domain of Protestant theological faculties, particularly among New Testament scholars with some training in postbiblical Hebrew and Greek Jewish sources. It is worth noting that many of the scholars who trained in early Judaism during the 1920s became active members in the Institute: Paul Fiebig, Hugo Odeberg, Georg Bertram, and Georg Beer, among others.

The efforts of these theologians to synthesize Christianity with National Socialism was motivated by political opportunism, to be sure, but also by an internal crisis within liberal Protestant theology that welcomed Nazi racial theory as its solution. The crisis arose in the late nineteenth century, as liberal Protestant New Testament scholars sought to define the historical figure of Jesus and identify Christianity with the faith *of* Jesus, not the faith *about* Jesus. The discovery that the historical Jesus was a Jew whose teachings were identical to those of other rabbis of his day led to the problem of determining the uniqueness of Jesus and the boundary between liberal Protestantism and liberal Judaism, as Uriel Tal has delineated.[5] The discovery of this problem motivated many Protestant theologians to embrace racial theory: while the content of Jesus' message may have been identical to that of Judaism, Jesus' uniqueness could be assured on racial grounds. Thus, serious theological debates about whether Jesus was a Jew or an Aryan began long before Hitler came to power. What was innovative about the Institute was its goal of revising radically Christian doctrine and liturgy as practiced in churches throughout the Reich, and bringing them into accord with racial anti-Semitism.

The theologians' embrace of National Socialism was an unrequited affection. Hitler showed little interest in church affairs after 1934, and the

---

[4]Walter Grundmann and Karl Friedrich Euler, Foreword to *Das religiöse Gesicht des Judentums: Entstehung und Art* (Leipzig: Wigand, 1942).

[5]Uriel Tal, *Christians and Jews in Germany* (Ithaca NY: Cornell University Press, 1975).

hopes of theologians for positions of power and influence within the regime met with disappointment. When Reich Bishop Ludwig Müller delivered the eulogy in Eisenach at the funeral of Thuringian Bishop Sasse on 31 August 1942, he voiced the situation: "When Bishop Sasse was consecrated as bishop eight years ago in this church, it was absolutely obvious that the higher representatives of the Party and the State would take part. Today there is hardly a brownshirt to be seen in the church."[6] Much historiography presents the Protestant church as the persecuted victim of the Nazi regime, as argued by Kurt Meier and John Conway, among others, or as theologically intact, thanks to the rigors of the German theological method, as argued by Trutz Rendtorff.[7] Such claims have to be revised radically in light of the control attained by members of the German Christian movement within most of the regional churches in Germany and within the university theological faculties. If the church experienced persecution, that persecution came primarily in the form of the regime's lack of interest in church affairs. For example, unpublished archival documents show that in 1935 the official representative of the theological faculties submitted several formal petitions requesting membership in the SS for theology students and pastors; the petitions were rejected by Heinrich Himmler.[8] Other evidence reveals that in 1936, when Nazi Party officials ordered the swastika removed from church altars and the mastheads of church newspapers, numerous church officials protested, claiming that the swastika on the altar was a source of profound inspiration to churchgoers.[9] During those years, church leaders would have defined persecution very differently from the way the term is used by some church historians today.

---

[6]Berlin Document Center (hereinafter abbreviated BDC), Sasse materials.

[7]Kurt Meier, *Kreuz und Hakenkreuz. Die evangelische Kirche im Dritten Reich* (Munich: Deutschen Taschenbuch Verlag, 1992); John S. Conway, *The Nazi Persecution of the Churches. 1933–1945* (New York: Basic Books, 1968); and Trutz Rendtorff, "Des Wissenschaftsverständnis der protestantischen Universitätstheologie im Dritten Reich," in *Theologische Fakultäten im Nationalsozialismus*, ed. Leonore Siegele-Wenschkewitz and Carsten Nicolaisen (Göttingen: Vandenhoeck & Ruprecht, 1993) 19-44.

[8]The exchange, between Hans Schmidt, president of the Fakultatentages der evangelisch-theologischen Fakultäten Deutschlands, the umbrella organization representing the seventeen Protestant theological faculties in Germany, and Heinrich Himmler, head of the SS, can be found in the Universitätsarchiv, Jena (hereinafter abbreviated UJ) Bestand J. Nr. 292, in Universitätsarchiv Heidelberg H 1/055, and in Universitätsarchiv Giessen, B6, Band 1.

[9]BDC: Schumacher Collection on Church Affairs, T580, R. 42; also in Bundesarchiv, Koblenz BA R43II/150 Fiche #3.

I. Origins of the Institute

In order to enhance the role of the church within National Socialism, the League for German Christianity (*Bund für deutsches Christentum*) was organized by Berlin church superintendent Herbert Propp and met on 26 January 1938 to plan a massive show of church support for the regime.[10] The renewed centrality of government anti-Jewish measures that began in late 1937 provided a focus. The group decided that a thorough de-Judaization of the church would be part of Hitler's "world struggle against world Jewry" (*Weltkampf gegen das Weltjudentum*). Hugo Pich, a church superintendent in Thuringia, prepared the report during the summer of 1938:

> The *Führer* of our *Volk* has now been called to lead an international fight against world Jewry. . . . In order to lead the National Socialist German struggle against world Jewry, the quick and thorough implementation of the de-Judaization of the Christian church is of high and essential significance. Only when the de-Judaization of the Christian church is completed can the German people join in carrying out the fight of the *Führer* within its Christian membership and within its religious beliefs, and can the divine commission of the German *Volk* assist in its fulfillment.[11]

Pich proposed that the work be carried out by a special office within the church that would supervise the de-Judaization process.

Shortly after the *Kristallnacht* pogrom in November of 1938, church headquarters in Berlin circulated Pich's proposal to the regional churches and received favorable responses. To give the plan a broad backing of support, the Godesberg Declaration was formulated in the spring of 1939, signed by representatives of eleven regional churches, and adopted as official church policy. It stated that National Socialism carried forward the work of Martin Luther and would lead the German people to a true understanding of Christian faith.[12] The centerpiece of the Declaration was the statement: "What is the relation between Judaism and Christianity? Is Christianity derived from Judaism and is it its continuation and com-

---

[10]Letters to Grundmann from Hempel; letter to Grundmann from Propp, 5 Feb 1938; LKA Thüringen, DC III 2 f.

[11]Hugo Pich, Superintendent in Schneidemühl, "Entjudung von Kirche und Christentum: Die praktische Durchführung;" LKA Thüringen, A921.

[12]Evangelisches Zentral Archiv, Berlin (hereinafter abbreviated EZA), fols. 7/4166 and 7/4167. The Godesberg Declaration was printed in the *Gesetzblatt der deutschen evangelischen Kirche* 5 (6 Apr 1939) 1.

pletion, or does Christianity stand in opposition to Judaism? We answer this question: Christianity is the unbridgeable religious opposition to Judaism." The Declaration was printed in the official *Gesetzblatt* of the German Protestant Church with an addendum stating the church's intention to implement the Declaration by establishing the Institute for the Study and Eradication of Jewish Influence on the Church Life of the German *Volk*.[13]

Bishop Martin Sasse of Thuringia, an early member of the Nazi Party (he joined in January of 1930), supported the proposal energetically and called for the establishment of the Institute at the University of Jena, in Thuringia, where the theological faculty was dominated by members of the German Christian movement. However, Karl Astel, rector of the university, professor of medicine, and an ardent Nazi, opposed any expansion of the theological faculty, so no formal linkage was made. Eventually, the Institute was housed in Eisenach at the church's training seminary, which was independent of the university but run by members of its faculty as well as local ministers who were leaders within the German Christian movement. Grand opening ceremonies took place on Saturday afternoon, 6 May 1939, in the old, historic Wartburg castle in which Martin Luther had once taken refuge. Quartets by Mozart and Schubert, telegrams of congratulations, and learned speeches filled the program. Julius Streicher had hoped to attend, but was prevented by recent surgery; his telegram declared: "Verspreche mir von Ihrer Arbeit viel Gutes für unser Feld."[14] The audience was welcomed by the Institute's nominal director, Siegfried Leffler, one of the original founders of the German Christian movement who was then serving in the Thuringian Ministry of Education. The president of the German Protestant Church, Friedrich Werner, also attended and welcomed the Institute with the hope that it would distance itself from theological special-interest groups and bring honor to German theological scholarship.[15] Grundmann, the academic director of the Institute, had served since 1936 as professor of New Testament and *Völkish* Theology at the University of Jena. His address at the Institute's opening, "The De-

---

[13]Other provisions of the addendum, including founding a central office in the church to fight against the misuse of religion for political goals, were not carried out.

[14]Nordelbisches Kirchenarchiv, Kiel. Repertorium des Archivs der Bekennenden Kirche Schleswig-Holstein, Signatur 51; Neue Nummer 292.

[15]EZA, fol. 7/4166. Werner joined the NSDAP on 1 Jan 1931, membership 411,184; BDC, Werner materials.

Judaization of the Religious Life as the Task of German Theology and Church," set forth his aspirations: "The elimination of Jewish influence on German life is the urgent and fundamental question of the present German religious situation." Theological scholarship had made apparent the "deformation of New Testament ideas into Old Testament preconceptions, so that now angry recognition of the Jewishness in the Old Testament and in parts of the New Testament has arisen, obstructing access to the Bible for innumerable German people."[16] Six thousand copies of Grundmann's lecture were printed and distributed through the German Christian movement's publishing house which was run by Heinz Dungs, an Institute member.[17]

Membership in the Institute was open and became large, even larger than published records indicate. More than fifty professors of theology at universities throughout the Reich joined, including many distinguished figures, as well as dozens of instructors and graduate students.[18] The Institute also listed about one hundred pastors and bishops as members. Most members were young, having studied theology in the late 1920s and 1930s, too young to have fought during WWI, and had shown their Nazi sympathies through early membership in the Nazi Party (NSDAP), the German Christian Movement, or the Storm Troopers (SA). Many were trained in the field of New Testament and assumed that they were experts in what they called "late Judaism"—a term used by scholars to designate Judaism during the centuries just before the advent of Christianity. Numerous pastors, religion teachers, and lay people also joined. The Institute established at least one branch, in Rumania in 1942, and built an alliance with faculty and students in Scandinavia, led by Hugo Odeberg, a distinguished scholar of Judaica at the University of Lund. In 1941 Grundmann and Wolf Meyer-Erlach formed a working group, *Germanentum und Christentum*, which brought Scandinavian theologians and writers to participate in two annual conferences in Germany.[19] Odeberg

---

[16]Walter Grundmann, *Die Entjudung des religiösen Lebens als Aufgabe deutscher Theologie und Kirche* (Weimar: Verlag Deutsche Christen, 1939) 9, 10.

[17]EZA, fol. 7/4166.

[18]Letter from Brauer to Finanzabteilung bei der Deutschen evangelischen Kirche, 19 May 1942; EZA 1/C3/174.

[19]Archiv des Auswärtiges Amt Inland I-D 3/4, Signatur R98796: Überwachung von Arbeitstagungen der Arbeitsgemeinschaft "Germanentum und Christentum" und ihrer Leiter Professor Wolf Meyer-Erlach und Professor Grundmann, Verweigerung von Reisesichtvermerken, 1942–1944.

took the initiative among the Scandinavians, inviting thirty academics, students, and writers from Sweden, Norway, and Denmark to lecture at the conferences, which were held in Weissenfels and in Eisenach. Impressed by the high quality of scholarship practiced by Institute members, Odeberg sent seven Scandinavian students to Jena to write doctoral dissertations under Grundmann.

Because its publications generated income and because its members were employed by churches and universities, the financial needs of the Institute were minimal. Indeed, in 1943, the only year for which its accounts are extant, the Institute had surplus income.[20] The Institute did not pay expenses for participants in its conferences; pastors who attended were reimbursed for travel expenses by their regional churches, since the conferences were considered to be work related.[21] Still, the Institute received funds which the national church headquarters in Berlin collected from the regional churches.

II. Work of the Institute

Of all the so-called research institutes that flourished during the Nazi era, the Eisenach De-Judaization Institute (*Entjudungsinstitut*), as it was informally called during its heyday, proved the most prolific and had the largest membership. Its members were divided into working groups and rapidly produced publications. The Institute's de-Judaized version of the New Testament, *Die Botschaft Gottes*, first appeared in 1940 and eventually sold around 250,000 copies, including a small, abridged version.

A de-Judaized hymnal, *Grosser Gott Wir Loben Dich*, which also appeared in 1940, was a commercial success. In 1941, a catechism, *Deutsche mit Gott: Ein deutsches Glaubensbuch*, was published to summarize the Institute's theological principles. All were sold to churches throughout the Reich, in small towns and villages as well as cities. Each eliminated Hebrew words, references to the Old Testament, and any links between Jesus and Judaism. For example, the hymnal expunged words such as "amen," "hallelujah," "Hosanna," and "Zebaoth," while the New Testament eliminated Jesus' descent from David, and the catechism proclaimed:

---

[20]LKA Thüringen, DC III 2 a.

[21]In some cases the church of Thuringia reimbursed, e.g., for five pastors from Austria; LKA Thüringen, DC III 2 a.

Jesus of Nazareth in the Galilee demonstrates in his message and behavior a spirit which is opposed in every way to that of Judaism. The fight between him and the Jews became so bitter that it led to his crucifixion. So Jesus cannot have been a Jew. Until today the Jews persecute Jesus and all who follow him with unreconcilable hatred. By contrast, Aryans in particular can find answers in him to their ultimate questions. So he became the savior of the Germans.[22]

The Institute's publications were not the first efforts to produce de-Judaized Christian liturgical materials. For example, Bishop Weidemann of Bremen issued a de-Judaized New Testament, composed with the assistance of the noted theologian Emanuel Hirsch.[23] Reich Bishop Ludwig Müller issued a "germanized" version of the sermon on the mount in 1936 to eliminate what he considered inappropriate Jewish moral teachings.[24] Yet those publications were generally limited to local church usage, whereas the Institute's publications were in far more wide-spread use; 100,000 copies of both the *Die Botschaft Gottes* and *Grosser Gott Wir Loben Dich* were printed in the first edition to meet the demands of prepublication orders from parish churches throughout the Reich.[25]

In addition to its liturgical materials, the Institute sponsored conferences and published books and articles delineating its view of Christian theology and history. The conferences were held in town halls and universities throughout the Reich. These conferences opened and closed with hymns, prayers, and the Nazi salute and attracted as few as thirty or as many as six hundred participants. Most of its publications emphasized the degeneration of Judaism after the eighth century BCE, which supposedly reached its nadir during the second temple period; Judaism's final and utter destruction was the mission of Jesus. The degeneracy of Judaism served to explain why God sent Jesus and why the Jews failed to recognize him as divine; it also served to highlight the extraordinary nature of Jesus' own religious personality in contrast to the Jews.

---

[22]Walter Grundmann et al., eds., *Deutsche mit Gott: Ein deutsches Glaubensbuch* (Weimar: Verlag Deutsche Christen, 1941) 46.

[23]Reijo E. Heinonen, *Anpassung und Identität: Theologie und Kirchenpolitik der Bremer Deutschen Christen 1933–1945* (Göttingen: Vandenhoeck & Ruprecht, 1978).

[24]Ludwig Müller, *Deutsche Gotteswort* (Weimar: Verlag Deutsche Christen, 1936). See also Müller's defense of the project, "Warum ich die Bergpredigt 'verdeutschte,' " *Briefe an Deutsche Christen* 5.8 (15 Apr 1936) 82.

[25]LKA Thüringen, C VI, 2.

At one of the Institute's first conferences (July 1939), Heinz Eisenhuth, professor of systematic theology at the University of Jena, explained "The Meaning of the Bible for Faith." He argued that Luther's translation of the Bible had transmitted the meaning of the gospel to the German people, but new historical-critical scholarship would refine Luther's understanding. The tie of Christians in Germany to the Bible was not legalistic, but ethical: "*Völkish* ethics also need an inner religious foundation." The Old Testament, however, was the expression of a racially foreign soul and a non-Christian religion.[26] Jewish influence had infiltrated Germany not only through the Old Testament, but also through secularization processes. Spinoza was one such nefarious Jewish influence, explained Martin Redeker, professor of systematic theology at the University of Kiel. He argued:

> Just as the Jew does not know and see the living God and his will, but only the Torah, the law and its development in the Talmud, so for Spinoza nature is not a living reality. Rather, he sees only rigid natural laws and seeks to explain them. Natural law takes the place of divine law for him. Jews lack the awe before nature that Germans have, and the sense of being bound up with nature; [the Jew] stands cold in relation to nature. The German experiences God as being in the background of all events and affecting all events; for the Jew there isn't this view of faith behind the superficiality of life and history, for him there is only the visible, material world.[27]

Exposing the dangers which the Jews posed to German society continued to be a major theme at Institute-sponsored conferences. At a meeting held in July 1941, the writer Wilhelm Kotzde-Kottenrodt argued that Jews had eliminated God from the world ("Jude hat die Welt entgottet"); they are unable to understand the higher thoughts of Nordics, that the world is filled with God. The Old Testament itself is an unreliable document, since Jews have used and distorted it to their own purposes through the centuries.[28]

The Institute's publications tried to prove that the Jews had always been threatening and aggressive. The Maccabees were cited as an example, as were the Hasmoneans generally and the Zealots. Judaism continued to be violent and dangerous; Jesus' goal was clear: to save the

---

[26]Report of Tagung held 6-7 July 1939 in Thüringen; EZA 1/C3/174.
[27]EZA 1/C3/174.
[28]Wilhelm Kotzde-Kottenrodt, "Eine Deutsche Gottes- und Lebenskunde," lecture delivered at Institute-sponsored conference on the Wartburg, 19 July 1941. Text in LKA Thüringen.

world and fight against Judaism.[29] Subtle perversions of society characterize Judaism; Bertram argued that, from Philo to the present day, Jewish
assimilation had the goal of decomposing a society and then taking
control over it.[30]

In their discussions of how to de-Judaize Christianity, Institute members debated how to define Judaism. Eisenhuth argued that the entire Old
Testament, including the prophetic literature, should be eliminated, while
the New Testament should be purged of all texts except the four
gospels—Paul being considered a Jewish theologian. Heinz Hunger, a
pastor who served as business director of the Institute, argued that de-
Judaization consisted of removing the *Gestalt* of the Jew ("Entjudung
heisse nur Ausmerzung der Gestalt des Juden."). Friedrich Wienecke, one
of the German Christian leaders in Berlin, identified Jewishness with
Pharisaism, in which depravity is religiously embellished; that is, the
stock market is transformed into religion—the Jewish Trick. Wienecke
was supported by Redeker and Grundmann. Redeker emphasized the
materialist influence of the Jews on German society, even on some major
theological figures, such as Karl Barth.[31]

The Institute's proposal to purge everything Jewish from Christianity
was perceived by many as radical and illegitimate. Grundmann defended
his proposals by arguing that, "just as people couldn't imagine Christianity without the Pope during the time of Luther, so, too, they can't imagine
salvation without the Old Testament."[32] De-Judaizing Christianity was
simply a continuation of the Reformation.

The problem of removing "Judaism" from Christianity was theologically complex. According to Grundmann, the very concept of God is
radically different in Judaism and Christianity: "The Jewish concept of
God is fundamentally determined through the *Vergeltungsgedanken*: God

---

[29]Walter Grundmann, *Gestalt und Sinn der Bergrede Jesu*, Schriften zur Nationalkirche Nr. 10 (Weimar: Verlag Deutsche Christen, 1939).

[30]Georg Bertram, "Philo und die jüdische Propaganda in der antiken Welt," in *Christentum und Judentum: Studien zur Erforschung ihres gegenseitigen Verhältnisses*,
Sitzungsberichte der ersten Arbeitstagung des Institutes zur Erforschung des jüdischen Einflusses auf das deutsche kirchliche Leben vom 1. bis 3. März 1940 in Wittenberg, hrsg.
Walter Grundmann (Leipzig: Wigand, 1940) 79-106.

[31]Report by Wieneke on Tagung in Thuringen 6-7 July, 12 July 1939; EKA Akten
betreffend Institut zur Erforschung und Beseitigung des jüdischen Einflusses auf das
kirchliche Leben. Bestand: 7/4166 vom April 1939 bis März 1941 und 7/4167 vom April
1941 bis Dezember 1959.

[32]Grundmann, *Die Entjudung des religiösen Lebens*, 17.

is the Judge who repays men. But Jesus sees God as One who forgives, in order to generate commmunity."[33] The distinction is not an accident; Jesus undertook a fight against Jahwe as a tribal God and against Judaism.[34] In the sermon on the mount, he argues, Jesus expresses a sense of community between God and human beings, and elsewhere Jesus addresses God in intimate terms, as "Abba," father, rather than the Hebrew term, "Jahwe." Grundmann devoted a book to discussing the ethical implications of that relationship.[35] He concluded that Jesus introduced a new understanding of God and of divine expectations for human beings which entailed a situational ethic that overrode commandments. Jesus' authority was rooted in himself, rather than in the Bible, and it was insignificant that Jesus cited the prophets and psalms of the Old Testament, because "so much more that is in the Old Testament was not cited by Jesus."[36] Rather than being bound by the Old Testament's laws and commandments, which represent a Jewish outlook, Christians are to follow Jesus' example and make moral decisions by listening to the religiosity of their own hearts. This religiosity transcends commandments, even those prohibiting murder. He wrote:

> With the proclamation of the kingdom of God as present, a new experience of God and a new understanding of God were linked. Internally, it had nothing to do with Judaism, but meant the dissolution of the Jewish religious world, that alone should be recognizable from the fact that the Jews brought Jesus Christ to the cross.[37]

III. Jesus as Aryan

The German Christians liked to claim that their mission was not to create a new Christianity, but to provide a Christianity appropriate to the German people. They argued that, since Christian missionaries in other parts of the world had not hesitated to synthesize elements intrinsic to the native culture with Christian beliefs and liturgies, native Germanic

---

[33]Walter Grundmann, *Die Bergrede Jesu*, Schriften zur Nationalkirche Nr. 10 (Weimar: Verlag Deutsche Christen, 1939) 16.

[34]Walter Grundmann, *Der Gott Jesu Christi* (Weimar: Verlag Deutsche Christen, n.d.). Delivered at conference in 1936.

[35]Walter Grundmann, *Die Gotteskindschaft in der Geschichte Jesu und ihre religions-geschichtlichen Voraussetzungen* (Weimar: Verlag Deutsche Christen, 1938).

[36]Walter Grundmann, *Jesus der Galiläer und das Judentum* (Leipzig: Wigand, 1940) 143.

[37]Grundmann, *Die Gotteskindschaft in der Geschichte Jesu*, 162.

expressions should be similarly included in German Christianity. It is striking, however, how they defined those native Germanic expressions: "German" was equated with the elimination of everything "Jewish." While purging Hebrew words from the liturgy or Scriptures was a fairly easy task, the greater problem was what to do with gospel accounts describing Jesus as a Jew. What role could there be for a Jewish savior in a religion of German Christianity? Opening his address to the Institute's conference in March 1941, Grundmann declared: "Our *Volk*, which stands above all else in a struggle against the satanic powers of world Jewry for the order and life of this world, dismisses Jesus, because it cannot struggle against the Jews and open its heart to the king of the Jews."[38]

That assumption was false, other scholars argued. Jesus was not a Jew at all, but the great enemy of the Jews, in fact, an Aryan. The idea of an Aryan Jesus had been proposed during the nineteenth century by a number of German philosophers and scholars. J. G. Fichte, in his *Addresses to the German Nation*, suggested that Jesus may not have been of Jewish origin, based on the omission of his genealogy in the Gospel of John.[39] The rise of racial theory in the nineteenth century provided a new vocabulary, allowing scholars such as Ernest Renan to distinguish between a Semitic Old Testament and an Aryan New Testament.[40] Renan sought to prove that Christianity was not semitic in origin because Jesus came from northern Galilee, rather than Judea;[41] Jesus' Galilean origin was a common motif in the 1860s and 1870s in German lives of Jesus.[42] Friedrich Delitzsch added the further suggestion that Galilee had been resettled after the Assyrian conquest by Babylonians of mixed Aryan descent.[43] Paul de Lagarde, one of Germany's great Semitic scholars,

---

[38]Walter Grundmann, "Das Messiasproblem," in *Germanentum, Christentum und Judentum*, 381.

[39]Fritz Medicus, ed., *J. G. Fichte Werke*, vol. 4 (Leipzig: Verlag von Felix Meiner) 105: "Es bleibt auch bei diesem Evangelisten immer zweifelhaft, ob Jesus aus jüdischem Stamme sei, oder, falls er es doch etwa wäre, wie es mit seiner Abstammung sich eigentlich verhalte." See also *Addresses to the German Nation*, trans. R. F. Jones and G. H. Turnbull (Chicago: Open Court, 1922) 68-69.

[40]Ernest Renan, *Essai psychologique sur Jesus Christ* (Paris: La Connaissance, 1921) 55-57.

[41]Ernest Renan, *La Vie de Jesus* (Paris: Calman-Levy, 1863).

[42]See, e.g., Theodor Keim, *Geschichte Jesu von Nazara* (Zürich: Orell, Füßli & Co., 1867).

[43]Friedrich Delitzsch, *Die grosse Täusching: Kritische Betrachtungen zu den alttesta-*

rejected Christianity's understanding of Jesus as an "intolerable distortion."[44] Jesus was no Jew, but a rebel against Judaism who deliberately called himself a Son of man to escape any association with the Jews. In another kind of approach, Edmond Picard argued in 1899 that Jesus must have been an Aryan because of his antipathy to capitalism, the tool of the Jews.[45] Houston Stewart Chamberlain gave widespread popularity to the idea that Jesus was racially Aryan. German professors of Protestant theology in the 1910s and 1920s found themselves debating the issue, granting the claim even greater legitimacy.[46] Ernst Lohmeyer developed the theory of a two-site origin of early Christianity: Galilee, where a universalistic, Son of man eschatology prevailed, and Jerusalem, dominated by nationalistic, Jewish eschatology.[47] Rudolf Otto had made a similar claim, based on his phenomenological observations of Jewish and Christian religiosity.[48]

In his 1940 study of Jesus, *Jesus der Galiläer und das Judentum*, Grundmann concluded that because Jesus rejected the Jewish title of "Messiah" in favor of the title "Son of man," he must have been of Galilean origin, and was therefore "with the greatest probability" not a Jew, but a member of one of the foreign peoples living in the region, among whom were also Aryans. Although Grundmann declared Jesus an Aryan, the troubling problem remained to account for those Jewish concepts and texts which the New Testament attributed to Jesus. The explanation was simple: the image and message of Jesus had been falsified by the early Jewish Christians, who presented Jesus as "the fulfiller of the law and the new teacher of law, only sent to the house of Israel."[49] Furthermore, the Jews expected a messiah who would be their

---

mentlichen Berichten über Israels Eindringen in Kanaan, die Gottesoffenbarun vom Sinai und die Wirksamkeit der Propheten (Stuttgart: Deutsche Verlagsanstalt, 1920).

[44]Fritz Stern, *The Politics of Cultural Despair: A Study in the Rise of German Ideology* (Berkeley: University of California Press, 1961) 41. See also Paul de Lagarde, "Die Religion der Zukunft," in *Schriften für deutsche Volk*, 2 vols. (Munich: Lehmanns, 1934) 1:262; cited by Alan T. Davies, "The Aryan Christ: A Motif in Christian Anti-Semitism," *JES* 12 (1975): 569-79.

[45]Edmond Picard, *L'Aryano-Semitisme* (Brussels: Lacomblez, 1899).

[46]Houston S. Chamberlain, *Die Grundlagen des neunzehnten Jahrhunderts* (Munich: Bruckmann, 1902).

[47]Ernst Lohmeyer, *Galiläa und Jerusalem* (Göttingen: Vandenhoeck & Ruprecht, 1936).

[48]Rudolf Otto, *Reich Gottes und Menschensohn: Ein Religionsgeschichtlicher Versuch* (München: Beck, 1933).

[49]Walter Grundmann, "Des Problem des hellistischen Christentums innerhalb der Jeru-

ruler, whereas Jesus' message was to be a servant of God and the community.[50] Johannes Hempel, professor of Old Testament at the University of Berlin and one of the early organizers of the Institute, argued that Jesus' monotheism broke with the Old Testament's henotheism, and that it similarly universalized the promise of salvation.[51]

The Institute took the argument a step further by seeking its recognition within the institutional church. Grundmann argued that Jewish motifs in the New Testament represented falsifications of the original text and were introduced by early Jewish Christians as a distortion of the tradition, in order "to make Christianity serve the purposes of Judaism."[52] German New Testament scholars were considered the finest in the world, and so could emend the biblical text to remove Jewish elements. Nonetheless, although students trained by Gerhard Kittel, Grundmann, Bertram, and other leaders of the Institute were considered experts on Judaism, their work shows only a limited awareness of the Hebrew Jewish sources from antiquity and a very narrow reading of Greek Jewish sources.

The eradication of Jewish influences from Christianity was viewed, in other words, as a restoration of the original message of Jesus and a recovery of his historical personage. Not the Aryan Jesus, but the Jewish Jesus was the falsification, and the sophistication of modern theology's historical-critical methods finally enabled that recognition and the reformation of church life it engendered. Far from being a threat to religious faith, National Socialism was viewed as a great opportunity for the revival of true Christianity.[53]

IV. The Theological Faculty at the University of Jena

Most of the theological faculties at German universities included professors who supported the German Christian movement, or who even were members of the Institute. These professors inevitably brought their anti-Jewish viewpoints to their scholarship and teaching. In some cases, such professors dominated and controlled the kind of theological education provided. The situation at the University of Jena was highly

---

salemer Urgemeinde," *ZNW* 38 (1939): 26.

[50]Grundmann, *Jesus der Galiläer und das Judentum*, 57-58.

[51]Johannes Hempel, "Der synoptische Jesus und das Alte Testament," *ZAW* 56 (1938): 1-34.

[52]See Friedrich Schenke, *Das Christentum im ersten Jahrhundert völkisch gesehen* (Weimar: Verlag Deutsche Christen, 1940).

[53]Grundmann, *Der Gott Jesu Christi*, 7 and passim.

politicized, and the theologians were no exception. The theological faculty at Jena strove to create, in the words of Professor Meyer-Erlach, "a stronghold of National Socialism."[54] To that end, only Nazi supporters were appointed professors, student dissertations had to comply with Nazi racial theory, and "Jewish" topics such as Hebrew language were eliminated.

Several other theological faculties had also abolished the study of Hebrew or made Old Testament studies optional. In 1938 Grundmann urged eliminating the study of Hebrew from the curriculum at the University of Jena because, he argued, the early Christians had read the Greek Bible and because the Greek text of the Old Testament is older than the extant Hebrew manuscripts; the decision to make Hebrew study optional was announced by Dean Eisenhuth, on 1 April 1939.[55]

Both Grundmann and Eisenhuth were appointed to the faculty in 1936. According to the recommendation written by Meyer-Erlach, who was then serving as rector of the university, Eisenhuth was "unquestionably a reliable Party member, who, out of deepest convictions stands true to the *Führer* and to the Movement and with greatest earnestness works to bring a decisive recognition of National Socialism to his discipline."[56] Similarly, Meyer-Erlach recommended Grundmann as a longtime member of the NSDAP who expressed his loyalty to National Socialism in his theological scholarship, which "will be pathbreaking for a National Socialist perspective in the field of theology."[57] On 17 December 1937, Eisenhuth was appointed tenured professor, on orders signed by Hitler. Identical orders making Grundmann a tenured professor were signed by Hitler on 5 October 1938.

During the Nazi era (1933–1945), thirty-six students submitted doctoral dissertations in theology at Jena. The students' dissertations frequently treated topics concerning Christianity's relationship to National Socialism; the faculty evaluated their work on political grounds. Ten were rejected, always on grounds that they had not paid sufficient attention to issues of race. Several of the students and faculty were active members of the Institute (twelve dissertations were written under

---

[54]Meyer-Erlach to Thüringen Minister für Volksbildung (hereinafter abbreviated TMV) re. Eisenhuth's appointment, 6 Mar 1937. UJ D, No 603.

[55]Memorandum dated May 1938 to Reichsministerium für die kirchliche Angelegenheiten; LKA Thüringen, DC: Hochschulangelegenheiten, 1937–1940.

[56]Meyer-Erlach to TMV 6 Mar 1937; UJ.

[57]Meyer-Erlach to TMV 23 Oct 1937; UJ.

Grundmann) and used the Jena faculty to promote their anti-Semitism. For example, although one student was an active member of the NSDAP since 1931, his dissertation, "Notwendiger Christ," claimed that Jesus' ideas must be understood within an Old Testament context. It was rejected. Meyer-Erlach explained: "The theologian lacks the understanding of National Socialism, that the racial question is the fundamental question for everything." On the other hand, the 1941 dissertation on "Praexistenz und Unsterblichkeit" received a mixed review from Grundmann:

> The author observes correctly that Judaism took over its ideas about the preexistence and immortality of the human soul from other perspectives and religions. This, however, did not lead him to the fundamental observation of the spiritual unproductivity of Judaism. . . . Judaism represents a level of human spirituality that has been left behind . . . and which has degenerate effects on higher perspectives.[58]

A third student, although himself a member of the Institute as well as of the NSDAP, had to make revisions in his 1942 dissertation, "Die Wandlung der katholischen Kirche in ihrer Stellung zur Judenfrage seit der franzosischen Revolution," because he gave too much credit to the Roman Catholics for developing anti-Semitism, thereby unfairly denying adequate credit to the Protestants.

The situation at Jena was not exceptional, although its small size and the dominance of leading figures from the Institute made it particularly problematic, and it can be said to have fulfilled Meyer-Erlach's goal of creating a "stronghold of National Socialism." Through their academic work, Institute members were able to transform their anti-Semitism into respectable teachings of Christian theology. Through theological faculties the anti-Semitic Christian theology of the Nazi era was transmitted to the next generation of ministers and theologians.

V. The Final Years

The distinguished church historian Kurt Meier has argued that the Institute was established as a defense of Christianity against Nazism.[59] There is, however, no evidence that the churches were in any danger of being dissolved by the regime, nor does Meier's claim explain the enormous

---

[58]Promotionsakten der Theologischen Fakultät, 1939–1941, Bestand J No. 90.
[59]Meier, *Kreuz und Hakenkreuz*, 164.

enthusiasm with which Institute members set about their tasks of de-Judaizing Christianity. On the contrary, Institute members seem to have been committed sincerely to the work they were undertaking. An exchange of letters between Grundmann and Institute member H. J. Thilo, written in November 1942, makes clear Grundmann's commitment to an Aryan Christianity: "I cannot go back to the old church . . . thus there remains nothing else but to go humbly into the corner and take up other work as a German literature scholar or historian."[60] Grundmann was disappointed over the failure of the German Christian movement to achieve its hoped-for recognition by the regime, but he had confidence that at least the Institute had broad popular support among German soldiers. In 1942, he wrote to another Institute member, Gerhard Delling, who was serving as a military chaplain, and articulated his awareness that his Christian support for National Socialism was an unrequited affection.[61]

In the fall of 1943, Grundmann was drafted and then replaced as director of the Institute by Georg Bertram. Even as growing numbers of Germans came to believe that they would not win the war, and as Goebbels's total war propaganda lost its ability to convince the skeptical, Carl Schneider, a member of the Institute and professor at the University of Konigsberg, called for an even more radical de-Judaization of Christian theology, redefining early Christianity as itself an anti-Semitic movement. Bertram sent a report to Institute members in March 1944, in which he described his goals:

"This war is the fight of the Jews against Europe." This sentence contains a truth, which is over and over confirmed by the research work of the Institute. However this work serves not only as a head-on attack, but also as a strengthening of the inner front to attack and defend against all clandestine Judaism and Jewish essence which has seeped into occidental culture during the course of the centuries.[62]

In the summer of 1944, Church Superintendent Hugo Pich, whose 1938 report had served as the basis for establishing the Institute, sent a proposal to church officials for a more thorough de-Judaization of the Scriptures, entitled "The Jew Saul and his Proclamation of Christ." Pich

---

[60]LKA Thüringen, Nachlass Grundmann, NG 44, vol. 2; *Briefe* Aug 1942–Apr 1943, 18 Nov 1942.

[61]LKA Thüringen, NG 44, vol. 2, 5 Nov 1942.

[62]Report on March 1944 Tagung, held in Predigerseminar in Thüringen, signed by Georg Bertram; LKA Thüringen, Akten des Landeskirchenrats der Evangelisch-Lutherischen Kirche in Thüringen über Entjudung der Kirche, 1939–1947; fol. A, no. 921.

called for a thorough overhaul of the Pauline epistles, arguing that they were infected with Jewish notions that had contaminated Christianity. By this time, both church and Institute officials were unsympathetic, given the war conditions.[63] Moreover, as one German Christian church official argued, Pich's proposal regarding the Pauline epistles would imply that for so many centuries the church had been held hostage by a Jew: "I consider Pich's statements totally misguided and moreover an insult to our *Volk*, whom one indirectly insults by saying that in its miserable narrowness and lack of instinct for 1500 years it was duped into servility by some stinking Jew."[64]

It is noteworthy that, even at the end of the war, Institute members did not give up their efforts. In May of 1945, as Thuringia fell under Allied occupation, Bertram petitioned the Thuringian church, now run by former members of the Confessing Church, to retain the Institute, on the grounds that its work was "neither politically determined, nor expressed politically." Rather, its goal was to demonstrate scientifically that "Jesus had taken up a fight against Judaism in all sharpness and had fallen as victim to [his fight]."[65] The Church Council of Thuringia met with Bertram on 24 May 1945 to decide whether the Institute should be retained as a research center. According to the minutes of the meeting, Pastor von Nitzsch thanked Bertram for his work but stated that such a worldwide project could not be supported by the small church of Thuringia. Church Consul Büchner stated the importance of retaining the Institute, especially since the theological library at the University of Jena had been damaged during bombings. Moritz Mitzenheim, soon to become bishop of Thuringia, urged dissolution of the Institute, but retention of its

---

[63]Sievers to Pich, 15 Aug 1944, re. "Der Weg zur entjudeten deutschen Reichskirche in der Glaubensgefolgschaft Jesu": "nachdem der totale Krieg in schärfster Form eingesetzt hat, wir nur einen Gedanken haben dürfen, wie wir unserem Vaterland in diesem Schicksalskampf dienen und helfen können. Ich muss es sowohl persönlich, als auch als Vorsitzender der Arbeitsgemeinschaft evangelischer Kirchenleiter und als stellvertretender Leiter des Instituts zur Erforschung . . . ablehnen, mich jetzt mit der Neugestaltung der Kirche zu befassen und ich möchte auch Ihnen dringend empfehlen, diese Sache jetzt when zu lessen."

[64]Bishop Walther Schultz to President Ronck, 2 Aug 1944 re. Pich's Denkschrift, *Der Jude Schaul*; LKA Thüringen, Personalia: Leffler, Grundmann: Institut 1938–1944.

[65]Georg Bertram, *Denkschrift* betr. Aufgaben eines theologischen Forschungs-Instituts zu Eisenach 6 May 1945, 1; LKA Thüringen, Bestand A921: Akten des Landeskirchenrats der Evangelisch-Lutherischen Kirche in Thüringen über Entjudung der Kirche, 1939–1947.

property. Church Consul Phieler wanted the Institute retained, but with its goals changed to a historical study of the Luther Bible and its effects on German culture and the Protestant people. On 31 May 1945, Phieler wrote to Bertram with the decision that the Institute would not be reopened. Bertram was thanked for his service, but rejected for future work within the Thuringian church.[66] He returned to Giessen.[67]

In the fall of 1945, Grundmann returned from a Russian prisoner-of-war camp and appealed to church officials to maintain the Institute, arguing that, since non-German scholars had arrived at the same conclusions, the work of the Institute could not be seen as merely reflecting "tendencies of the era" (*Zeittendenzen*), but was the result of serious scholarship that should be continued.[68] He explained that the Institute's research had concluded that Jesus was independent of the Old Testament and stood in opposition to the Judaism of his day. Moreover, he wrote, the Institute's goal had been a defense of Christianity against National Socialism: "The National Socialist system led the fight against Christianity with all legal means at its disposal."[69] In the eyes of the Nazis, he continued: "Christianity is of Jewish origin, is Judaism for Aryans and must therefore be rooted out. As spiritual Judaism it poisons the German soul."[70] The Institute, Grundmann concluded, was a defense of the church.

But Grundmann's argument produced no effect and his proposal to maintain the Institute was rejected in January of 1946. One church official, who shortly thereafter was appointed to the professorship in practical theology at the University of Jena once held by Meyer-Erlach, wrote that he regretted the curtailment of Grundmann's scholarship, which he respected, but that the church could not retain the Institute.[71] The Institute was closed, the extensive library of the Institute was incorporated into the Thuringian ministerial training seminar (*Predigerseminar*), and the liturgical materials it had published were no longer used. Readings from the Old Testament were reintroduced into church

---

[66]LKA Thüringen, A 921.

[67]The University of Giessen was closed by American military forces in 1945 because of its Nazi sympathies. In 1955, Bertram was reinstated as instructor in Old Testament. He was also given an instructorship in Hebrew at the University of Frankfurt. Bertram died in 1979.

[68]12 Dec 1945; LKA Thüringen, DC III 2 a.

[69]12 Dec 1945; LKA Thüringen, DC III 2 a.

[70]12 Dec 1945; LKA Thüringen, DC III 2 a.

[71]Hertzsch to Grundmann 14 Jan 1946, LKA Thüringen, DC III 2 a.

services after the war. No official condemnation of the Institute's anti-Semitism was ever issued by the Thuringian church. Most Institute members continued their careers unhampered after the war. Grundmann, Meyer-Erlach, and Eisenhuth lost their professorships at the University of Jena because of their early membership in the NSDAP, but all were given positions of distinction within the postwar church.[72] Jena replaced them with other Institute members, Herbert Preisker and Rudolf Meyer. Other Institute professors and instructors retained their academic positions: Hempel, Bertram, Hartmut Schmoekel, and Carl Schneider, among others. Georg Bertram moved from Giessen to Frankfurt, Gerhard Delling left Leipzig for Greifswald, Rudi Paret left Heidelberg for Bonn and then Tübingen. Martin Redeker remained at Kiel, Johannes Leipoldt at Leipzig, Wilhelm Koepp at Greifswald, Fritz Wilke and Gustav Entz at Vienna. Karl Georg Kuhn, one of the most notorious figures, lost his position at Tübingen, but moved on to Mainz and then Heidelberg.

Grundmann's return to the church came as a result of support from state officials. In January of 1946, state officials in Thuringia had refused Grundmann's request for support in securing a church position.[73] Less than a year later, however, they reversed their position. In the fall of 1946, the state urged Grundmann's retention by the church on the grounds that he had waged a "manly struggle" *against* National Socialist ideology. Testimony came from Grundmann's erstwhile colleagues, Eisenhuth and Meyer-Erlach, who declared that Grundmann had been persecuted by anti-Christian Nazi officials. His early membership in the NSDAP was dismissed as the error of an "unworldly" theologian who realized his error soon after 1933. His value as an internationally recognized scholar was cited by pointing to his membership in the distinguished Society of New Testament Studies (SNTS), which had offered him membership in 1938. Like so many other leaders of the German Christians, Grundmann emerged from the denazification process relatively

---

[72]Letter from Thüringen Landesamt für Volksbildung, 13 Sept 1945, signed Wolf, Landesdirektor: "Wir entlassen Sie daher auf Grund #2 der Verordnung über die Reinigung der öffentlichen Verwaltung von Nazi-Elementen mit sofortiger Wirkung aus dem öffentlichen Dienst." LKA Thuringen, DC III 2 a.

Grundmann, who had joined the NSDAP in Dec 1930, protested the loss of his professorship in a letter to the new rector, claiming that he had not been a perpetrator, but rather the victim of a struggle by the Nazi party against his work and his person.

[73]Thüringisches Hauptstaatsarchiv, Weimar, Personalakte Walter Grundmann.

unscrutinized. Yet Grundmann's Nazi-era activities were known to East German officials. As late as 1990, an East German secret police (Stasi) document lists his name among Nazi supporters and war criminals who had eluded responsibility by receiving a church position.[74] Gerhard Besier suggests that the information was used by the Stasi to control Grundmann.[75]

Few Institute members ever expressed any public repentance for their Nazi-era activities. In the later years of their lives, both Meyer-Erlach and Grundmann continued to present themselves as persecuted victims of the Nazi regime. Meyer-Erlach claimed that "despite threats and temptations" he had never abandoned the church and that he had "fought the Party" in his writings. Further, he claimed to have been mocked by regime officials because his name, Meyer, sounded Jewish and because he had once attended a synagogue service in Wurzburg in 1929, which had led Nazi officials to mock him as *"der Synagoge-Meyer."*[76] He was no anti-Semite, he further stated, since he retained his Jewish family physician until November 1933, and once permitted a Jewish doctor to operate on two of his children. By contrast, Grundmann's postwar defenses do not even mention anti-Semitism, and in his 1969 unpublished autobiography he barely acknowledges that he erred during the Third Reich: "We attempted to pose the questions raised by the period and not to avoid them. I admit that in so doing we made [big—this word is crossed out in the manuscript] mistakes."[77] While most of the materials pertaining to Grundmann's denazification remain closed, he writes in his autobiography that he had stood in real danger of Nazi retribution as the result of his writings criticizing Rosenberg.[78] Their claims were effective; in

---

[74]Gerhard Besier and Stephan Wolf, eds., *Pfarrer, Christen und Katholiken: Das Ministerium für Staatssicherheit der ehemaligen DDR und die Kirchen,* 2nd ed. (Neukirchen-Vluyn: Neukirchener, 1992) document 133, 653.

[75]Besier and Wolf, *Pfarrer, Christen und Katholiken,* document 133, 653.

[76]Wolf Meyer-Erlach, "Verfolgung durch die Partei," 12 June 1945; UJ Bestand J. no. 92: Promotionsakten, 1941–1947. Regarding his name: Gaudozentenbundsführer to Reichsamtsleitung des NSD-Dozentenbundes Dr. Redenz, Munich, 8 Aug 1938; UJ D, 2031: Wolf Meyer-Erlach Akten. An unsigned report to the Gestapo describes Meyer-Erlach's attendance at the synagogue and refers to him as *der Synagoge-Meyer.* "Meyer-Erlach: Beruchtigt durch seine Einweihungsrede der Synagoge der jüdischen Gemeinde Heidingsfeld bei Wurzburg 1929, führender Kopf der Deutschen-Christen. Poseur- und Schauspieler-natur mit starkem hysterischen Einschlag. Sehr starkes Geltungsbedürfnis."

[77]Grundmann, "Erkenntnis und Wahrheit," 44-45; LKA Thüringen.

[78]Grundmann, "Erkenntnis und Wahrheit," 44-45; LKA Thüringen.

January 1962, Meyer-Erlach, then living in Hessen, received the Federal Republic of Germany's *Verdienstkreuz*, First Class.[79] In meetings with church officials of Thuringia in late 1945, to clear himself of any Nazi suspicions, Grundmann insisted that his fundamental commitment to Christ had never wavered during the Nazi years. Church leaders asked him to express an acceptance of the Barmen Declaration as a sign that he accepted the ultimate sovereignty of Christ, rather than of political leadership; Grundmann agreed.

In the postwar years, Grundmann was appointed rector of the seminary in Thuringia that trained religion teachers and church organists. He taught at the ministerial seminary in Leipzig and held the powerful position of advisor to the Protestant publishing house of the German Democratic Republic. He continued to publish extensively and his commentaries on the synoptic gospels became highly regarded reference works in the postwar theological communities of East and West Germany. Shortly before his death in 1976, he was appointed *Kirchenrat* of Thuringia, an honorary position that indicates the esteem with which he was regarded by the postwar church in East Germany.

VI. Church Opposition to the Institute

The Institute was not without its critics within the church. A "church struggle" developed for control of the church between two Protestant factions, the German Christian movement and the Confessing Church. Members of the Confessing Church came from a more conservative theological tradition that objected to alterations in the biblical text, liturgy, and catechism, although many were sympathetic to the Hitler regime. Their opposition to the Institute and its theology was rooted in its radical changes of traditional Christian teachings, and was not directed primarily against its anti-Semitism. Indeed, Wolfgang Gerlach has documented the failure of the Confessing Church to take a stand in support of Jews, except those Jews who had converted to Christianity. He has also exposed theological anti-Judaism in the writings of many Confessing Church theologians.[80] For example, the Godesberg Declaration of April 1939, which

---

[79]Personal correspondence, Az: OK 123-032-05 (H 89/61); Bundespräsidialamt Bonn, Ordenskanzlei. The commendation mentions his establishment of a home in 1952 for East European refugee girls and his organization since 1956 of 5,000 Christmas and Easter packages for shipment to Germans living in the Soviet zone.

[80]Wolfgang Gerlach, *Als die Zeugen Schwiegen: Bekennende Kirche und die Juden*

created the Institute, evoked Confessing Church hostility and resulted in a counterdeclaration, issued on 31 May 1939, and signed by leading Confessing Church bishops, including Theophil Wurm (Württemberg), Hans Meiser (Bavaria), and August Marahrens (Hannover):

> In the realm of faith there exists the sharp opposition between the message of Jesus Christ and his apostles and the Jewish religion of legalism and political messianic hope, which is already emphatically fought against in the Old Testament. In the realm of the *völkish* life an earnest and responsible racial politics is required for the preservation of the purity of our people.[81]

In the argument of this statement, elimination of the Old Testament is unnecessary because it is not a Jewish book, but an anti-Jewish book. According to the statement, racial policies are acceptable and necessary, according to the statement, and Christianity stands in opposition to Judaism, as the Godesberg Declaration had also formulated.

Opposition to the Institute's publications also came from some of Grundmann's colleagues in the field of New Testament who sided with the Confessing Church. For example, Grundmann's 1940 study of Jesus' racial background, *Jesus der Galiläer und das Judentum*, which argued that Jesus could not have been a Jew, was reviewed negatively by Hans von Soden, professor of New Testament and Church History at the University of Marburg and an active member of the Confessing Church.[82] Yet von Soden simply argued that the racial question was theologically irrelevant, and criticized Grundmann for his sloppy scholarship; he did not fault Grundmann's negative presentation of Judaism.[83]

Most striking in the Confessing Church opposition to German Christian measures is the negative attitude toward Judaism shared by both sides. For example, in a pamphlet issued by the Confessing Church in 1939 to repudiate the Institute, von Soden distinguishes between the historical phenomenon of Judaism, which formed the basis of early Chris-

---

(Berlin: Institut Kirche und Judentum, 1987).

[81]EZA, 1/A4/170.

[82]Together with his colleague Rudolf Bultmann, von Soden was active in formulating the "Marburg Report" of Sept 1933, which opposed application of the Aryan paragraph in the realm of the church. See E. Dinkler and E. Dinkler von Schubert, eds., *Theologie und Kirche im Wirken Hans von Sodens. Briefe und Dokumente aus der Zeit des Kirchenkampfes 1933–1945*, vol. 2 (Göttingen: Vandenhoeck & Ruprecht, 1984).

[83]Hans von Soden, review of *Jesus der Galiläer und das Judentum, Deutsches Pfarrerblatt: Bundesblatt der deutschevangelischen Pfarrervereine und des Bundes der preussischen Pfarrervereine* 46.13/14 (5 Apr 1942) 49.

tianity, and a spiritual "Jewishness," which fails to understand religion because it "confuses outward and inward." This "Jewishness," he writes, "shudders before every Hebrew word in the liturgy or hymnal, but has itself fallen victim to the Jewish-anti-Christian spirit."[84] The German Christian movement is infected with this "Jewishness," according to von Soden, illustrated by the de-Judaization efforts called for in the Godesberg Declaration. Trying to de-Judaize Christianity by banning the Old Testament and rewriting the hymnal and New Testament actually "threatens a spiritual Judaization" of the church, according to von Soden. While von Soden, along with the majority of Confessing Church members, vigorously opposed German Christian measures, they agreed with the basic assumption that Judaization represents a real threat to Christianity. The difference between the two groups laid in their definition of what constitutes Judaization. For von Soden, the threat comes not from the Old Testament, Hebrew words, and other elements within traditional Christian theology, but from what he saw as an antispiritual, materialistic theology promoted by Grundmann and his German Christian colleagues.

The response of the Confessing Church represents a tradition that does not repudiate anti-Semitism, but redefines it. Judaism is a recognizable religion that can be debated, opposed, or accepted. Jewishness, however, was seen as an evil that potentially can afflict all people, even Christians, and must therefore be opposed with the strongest means available. Just as German anti-Semitism toward the end of the nineteenth century considered the greatest danger to be assimilated Jews, because they could inflict a nefarious influence before they were ever recognized as Jews, Jewishness could infiltrate Christian theology and poison it. The great danger of modern Christian anti-Judaism was not its opposition to the religion of Judaism, nor to Jews—Jews and Judaism were not the problem, and were even at times viewed with respect and concern during the Nazi era—but rather the imaginary danger associated with the loosely defined but far more threatening concept of "Jewishness."

VII. Historiographical Observations

The history of the Institute calls into question aspects of the historiography concerning developments within the Protestant church during the Third Reich. The relatively few studies of the German Christians have

---

[84]Hans Freiherr von Soden, "Die Godesberger Erklarung," n.d., [private archive], University of Marburg.

not examined its effective exploitation of anti-Semitism after 1938 to gain adherents and win support from the Nazi regime. Through the Institute the German Christians achieved an effective structure for disseminating its theology and avoiding disintegration after the onset of the war. Moreover, the German Christians cannot be considered an insignificant movement within the church, considering the support it won through the Institute from professors of theology at prominent German universities and the large number of orders placed for its liturgical materials by churches throughout the Reich. Its effectiveness is also shown by the individuals who at first kept themselves at a distance from the German Christians, such as Werner, but who eventually became supporters of the Institute.

How should the Institute's relation to the Nazi regime be evaluated? On the one hand, viewing the Institute primarily as a creation of Nazi anti-Semitic ideology would sever its links to pre-1933 theological tendencies and would not explain why church members found its theology respectable. On the other hand, without the Third Reich and its intensification of anti-Jewish policies after 1938, German Christian leaders might well have developed a different ideology; they clearly realized anti-Semitism would be politically advantageous. The Institute made effective use of traditional Christian anti-Judaism to support Nazi policy by offering theologians for the service of the regime. Institute membership included not only a few well-known theologians, but a large number, in all fields of theology, at universities throughout the Reich. Finally, it is significant that Institute associates continued to work within the churches and university theological faculties after 1945. Many records of the churches' denazification proceedings remain closed to scholars, but they would be important for establishing the degree to which the Institute's theology was viewed as acceptable even after the Third Reich collapsed.

The conventional treatment of the German Christians as a marginal phenomenon within the German churches is called into question by the accomplishments of the Institute. The popular and academic publications, the extent of their distribution to churches throughout the Reich, and the representation of its membership from the ranks of university faculties and church hierachies, all indicate a higher level of influence attained by the German Christians than has been recognized. Finally, the Institute's theology should be analyzed as a phenomenon parallel to Nazism itself; that is, the Institute's theology had roots within the history of German anti-Semitism and Christian theological anti-Judaism, taken to radical extremes out of both genuine conviction and quest for political power.

The Institute undertook within Christianity the goals of National Socialism: as the Nazi regime was creating an Aryan Germany, the Institute
was creating an Aryan Christianity.

VIII. Conclusion

Scholars in several fields have articulated their conviction that the
Holocaust calls into question the basic frame of reference of their fields.
Edith Wyschogrod writes that "the meaning of self, time, and language
are all affected by mass death. . . . We are in the grip of immense
experiential changes which both create and reflect new philosophical
perspectives."[85] No other field has been challenged as severely by the
Holocaust as that of Christian theology and biblical studies. Held
responsible as the major source for anti-Semitism, its moral legitimacy
is called into question. Not only its specific teachings about Jews and
Judaism, beginning in the New Testament, but one or another of its
modes of thinking—apocalyptic, gnostic, redemptive—is interrogated as
the mode by which Nazism structured its ideology. Church historians
studying the Nazi period rarely attempt to exempt the church from
responsibility for the Holocaust. Concluding that church members were
persecuted victims of National Socialism along with the Jews, as Kurt
Meier argues, or were independent wellsprings of theological purity, as
Trutz Rendtorff argues,[86] is possible only when disconfirming data in the
holdings of certain archives are ignored, a problem that has plagued the
field of church history until recently, particularly in Germany. Few
church historians, for example, have investigated the holdings of the
Berlin Document Center, which contains membership information for the
NSDAP and related organizations. As a result, no conclusions can be
drawn regarding the membership of ministers and theologians in the Nazi
Party in relation to other professional groups.

The theological problem is whether the German Christian movement
is a product of Christianity, or of Christianity gone awry. The experience
of the churches in Nazi Germany makes clear that no mechanism exists
within Christian theology that is capable of excluding Nazi excesses as

---

[85]Edith Wyschogrod, *Spirit in Ashes: Hegel, Heidegger, and Man-Made Mass Death*
(New Haven: Yale University Press, 1985) ix.

[86]Trutz Rendtorff, "Des Wissenschaftsverständnis der protestantischen Universitäts-
theologie im Dritten Reich," in *Theologische Fakultäten im Nationalsozialismus*, ed.
Leonore Siegele-Wenschkewitz and Carsten Nicolaisen (Göttingen: Vandenhoeck &
Ruprecht, 1993) 19-44.

unchristian. The story of the Institute calls into question whether German Protestant theology has an intrinsic moral commitment and self-judgment, because it is likely that Grundmann's efforts would have been praised had the Nazis won the war; the sympathetic judgment of several contemporary church historians makes that clear. I would argue that Christian inhibitions against violent atrocities were eroded when four conditions were met: the institutional church gave its approval; the actions and beliefs were routinized by citing older, well-known theological anti-Judaism; the Jews were presented as a moral danger to Christians; and a theological appeal to so-called higher authority, values, or spirituality was formulated. The German Christian movement's emergence out of liberal Protestantism is crucial; it presented itself as a modern, scientific theological movement, not as a religious faith rooted in the supernatural; it was a religion that affirmed society, its political structures, and its intellectual discourse.

In his critique of Emil Durkheim's claim that "man is a moral being only because he lives in society," Zygmunt Bauman has argued for the social production of immoral behavior. Morality, Bauman writes, "may manifest itself in insubordination towards socially upheld principles, and in an action openly defying social solidarity and consensus."[87] Morality is not the product of society, but is presocial, Bauman argues, and it is something that society manipulates and exploits. If responsibility, as Emmanuel Levinas argues, is the essential structure of subjectivity, morality is the primary structure of intersubjective relation, and its creation is presocial, Bauman argues. Morality is not a product of society, but is something that society manipulates and exploits. So, too, with theology. While it claims to be the creator and upholder of morality, morality is both prior to and independent of theology. The Institute functioned as the religious justification for the social production of Nazi anti-Semitism. What the German Christian movement created was a theology able to manipulate and exploit morality.

---

[87]Zygmunt Bauman, *Modernity and the Holocaust* (Ithaca NY: Cornell University Press, 1989) 177.

Freedom and Responsibility in Scripture Interpretation, with Application to Luke

Robert C. Tannehill

The journal *Semeia* has recently devoted two volumes to the issue of textual determinacy or indeterminacy.[1] The leading question, as stated by Robert Culley, was "to what extent and in what manner do texts determine and control their interpretation and to what extent and in what manner is meaning determined by factors lying outside the text in the reading process?"[2] Both the recent emphasis on reading as an active process and an increased willingness to accept multiple readings of the same text lead to this question. There is increasing recognition that, in reading, we are doing something more than absorbing, in pristine fashion, information encoded in the text. In reading we are actively responding to the text's codes, which otherwise remain mute. This recognition need not lead to the extreme view that we can make whatever we want of a text, which would imply that we are communicating only with ourselves. It does imply, however, that we have some freedom, and with it some responsibility, for our interpretive responses to a text. This is true even when we take account of the text's early historical and social context.

The issue becomes important for the conflict between those who approach Scripture with a hermeneutics of suspicion, determined to expose its inadequate ideologies, and those who, in some sense, attribute authority to Scripture in their religious and ethical life. When the first group tells the second group that the real purpose of the text is to promote an oppressive ideology, and makes this point from a position of academic prestige, the pressure of academic authority is being brought to bear on those who read Scripture differently.[3] I do not wish to defend naive readings of Scripture or simple-minded theologies, and I recognize that growth often comes through an appropriate challenge from helpful

---

[1]See *Semeia* 62 (1993): and *Semeia* 71 (1995), edited by Robert C. Culley and Robert B. Robinson.

[2]Robert C. Culley, "Introduction," *Semeia* 62 (1993): vii.

[3]Daniel Patte has written sensitively about this issue. See *Ethics of Biblical Interpretation: A Reevaluation* (Louisville KY: Westminster/John Knox, 1995) 73-107.

teachers who share with their students alternative perspectives. I realize that naive readings often ignore valuable parts of the text and neglect important issues. One can also make the valid point that the Bible has been used to oppress people and that some of its content makes that possible. We should not, however, move from this valid point to the implication that some biblical texts are inherently texts of oppression, if their true significance is recognized, without considering the various kinds of indeterminacy in the texts, which offer us some freedom to find good in texts that could be oppressive.

To be sure, there probably are cases in which we must reject the message of the text if we are to affirm human good for the modern world.[4] I believe it is possible to find biblical warrant for this critical reading of the Bible. When approached in a particular way, the Bible can be self-policing (see section VI below). The main argument of this article, however, asserts that the texts grant us more freedom than we commonly recognize, which we can and should use responsibly. In my understanding, to use this freedom responsibly means that we seek to find in sacred texts, whenever possible, a benefit for humanity (including the benefit of promoting harmony with God). In some cases the assumption that the text forces us to a negative conclusion about its significance is the result of insensitivity to the text's possibilities. The problem is not in pointing out that the text may have a negative significance, when used in a particular way, but in implying that this negative reading is the one true way to understand the text.

I. Gospel Stories as "Works of Art"

Literary studies of the Bible have moved away from aesthetic perspectives. It is useful to return to some of these perspectives for our discussion of freedom and responsibility in interpretation.

When I wrote *The Sword of His Mouth*, I borrowed from Ray L. Hart's discussion of imagination and the work of art.[5] The art object, Hart explains, is something less than the work of art. The art object is a work of imagination with designs on an answering imagination. It is designed

---

[4]For instance, I would not accept the prohibitions against women speaking in assemblies or having authority over men that we find in 1 Cor 14:34-35 and 1 Tim 2:11-14.

[5]Robert C. Tannehill, *The Sword of His Mouth: Forceful and Imaginative Language in Synoptic Sayings*, Semeia Supplements 1 (Philadelphia: Fortress; Missoula MT: Scholars Press, 1975) 21-28. See Ray L. Hart, *Unfinished Man and the Imagination* (New York: Herder and Herder, 1968).

to provoke an imaginative response, that is, a response in which the imagination of the viewer, which is often dormant, becomes awake and active. It is only through the answering imagination of the viewer that the art object functions as a work of art. Thus the art object seeks completion in the answering imagination of the viewer. Hart also explains that the imagination is the means by which the self can be transformed and grow. In the imagination new possibilities present themselves, and we become fascinated with them. When the imagination is dormant, we are stuck in our routines. It is doubtful that religious language can be transformative at a deep level unless it engages the imagination.

The component units of the synoptic gospels are mostly short and simple. Yet the pronouncement stories and aphorisms display an artful sense of literary form, and they are joined as parts of a larger art object, a gospel. The gospels and their parts are also rhetorical. While the New Critics wanted to draw a sharp line between literary art and rhetoric, it is not possible to do so. Gospel sayings and stories are designed to provoke commitment and action, but they often make their appeal through forceful and imaginative language designed to jolt the imagination, sacrificing clarity in the process. It is important to note that the command not to be anxious about food and clothing (Luke 12:22-31) uses an elaborate repetitive pattern built around two concrete images (ravens and lilies) and reinforced by strong contrast and strong diction. These observations supply the clue that the purpose of these words is not merely to guide behavior but to transform our imaginative perception of reality so that our behavior may change.[6] The imagination is the door through which a new perception of reality may enter, transforming our commitments, values, and actions.

A sensitive response follows the lines of provocation in the text. The imagination is not being aimlessly stimulated but is being led in a particular direction. The brevity and simplicity of many synoptic scenes contribute to this direction. Much remains unsaid in order to direct attention to what is said. What is said leads the hearer to construct an imaginative scene, and this imaginative scene is able to provoke imaginative thought on a particular issue or situation that is highlighted in the scene. Because the scene is briefly sketched, much is left to the hearer or reader. Jesus' words, as reported in the gospels, are often aphoristic, metaphorical, and hyperbolic, appealing to the imagination. Thereby his words gain trans-

---

[6]See Tannehill, *Sword of His Mouth*, 60-67.

formative power but renounce precise control. They are powerfully suggestive but ignore important details about application. Furthermore, any message for the hearer or reader is indirect. We are reading a story about other people and another time; Jesus is not talking directly to us. The reader must work out the right response in imaginative thought. Thus the reader has both freedom and responsibility.

II. Gaps

Any narrator will supply some features of the narrative world but not others. This selective presentation can be understood, in part, as a sign of the narrator's control of the story for rhetorical effect. Directing the hearer's attention toward certain things (and away from other things) gives the story a focus on certain issues and concerns. It would be a distraction, not a contribution to gospel interpretation, to speculate about Jesus' height. This is an example of a "blank," an omission because it is regarded as irrelevant. But there are also "gaps," omissions that are relevant to interpreting plot and characters.[7] Yet the narrative may withhold the information either temporarily—building suspense toward a future disclosure—or permanently. Biblical narrators are reliable narrators in the sense that their perspectives do not depart from a "truer" perspective, that of the implied author. Nevertheless, the narrator, charged with telling the truth as the implied author sees it, does not necessarily tell the whole truth. Significant ambiguities remain.[8]

The Lukan narrative is reticent about expressing characters' emotions and motivations. The depiction of Jesus weeping over Jerusalem (Luke 19:41) is a striking exception. Emotion and motivation are often relevant to understanding what is going on in a scene, and we may make assumptions about them when we interpret particular scenes, thereby filling some of the gaps. In doing so, we may be cooperating with the narrator, who assumed that the audience would contribute in this way. Yet we are going beyond the text, and it is possible that these gaps may be filled in a different way. We can interpret emotion and motivation in various ways

---

[7] On the distinction between "gaps" and "blanks," see Meir Sternberg, *The Poetics of Biblical Narrative*, Indiana Studies in Biblical Literature (Bloomington: Indiana University Press, 1985) 236. See also his more extensive discussion of "the relevance of absence" on pp. 235-63.

[8] Meir Sternberg's chapter on ambiguity is entitled "Between the Truth and the Whole Truth." See *Poetics of Biblical Narrative*, 230-63.

when reading the so-called "cleansing of the temple" scene in Luke 19:45-46.

In evaluating characters, we should remind ourselves how little we are told about them. Even the story of Peter, one of the more prominent Lukan characters, presents only a few incidents from his life story, and many of the characters appear only in one brief scene. We are left to wonder about their lives prior to the incident and their lives afterward. In particular, the possible effect of an encounter with Jesus on a person is a relevant gap in the narration of some scenes. In Luke 9:57-62 Jesus addresses three would-be followers with challenging words. How did they respond? We don't know whether to view these persons as hopelessly naive and shallow, or whether to assume that their encounter with Jesus changed them into radical disciples. Likewise, the discussion with the lawyer in Luke 10:25-37 ends simply with Jesus' words, "Go and do likewise." Did the lawyer accept Jesus' teaching and try to act like the Samaritan, or not? I think most modern readers are inclined to assume a negative response from the lawyer, but there is a gap at this crucial point. The text is indeterminate.

A gap with broader consequences concerns Jerusalem. The Lukan narrative highlights the rejection of Jesus in Jerusalem and the destruction of the city. In particular, there are four interconnected scenes that empha-size these events (Luke 13:31-35; 19:41-44; 21:20-24; 23:27-31). This emphasis suggests a tragic turn in the narrative after the great expecta-tions in the birth narrative.[9] In discussing the disciples in Mark, I once argued, appealing to Wolfgang Iser, that a negative trajectory in the story line invites the reader to ponder what went wrong and to imagine the better alternative that was missed.[10] The positive alternative need not be fully spelled out; it is the text's function to induce the reader to seek it. The positive possibility that Jerusalem missed when Jesus was rejected is not clearly defined in Luke. There are, to be sure, scriptural promises about the messianic king, which the Lukan narrative applies to Jesus, beginning at Luke 1:31-33. But how these promises were to be realized, if Jerusalem had not rejected its king, is not very clear, and whether and how they could still be realized for the Jewish people are also not very

---

[9]See Robert C. Tannehill, "Israel in Luke-Acts: A Tragic Story," *JBL* 104 (1985): 69-85.

[10]See Robert C. Tannehill, "The Disciples in Mark: The Function of a Narrative Role," *JR* 57 (1977): 395.

clear. We are left with some hints and considerable ambiguity. It may have been impossible for the author of Luke to fill this gap. The hints and ambiguity are left for the reader to ponder. Since the scriptural promises to the Jewish people are important in Luke, this is an important gap at a theological level.

There is also a gap in application. That is, the gospels do not tell us how they should be applied to later situations. We need to remember that the gospels are stories about other people at another time. Religious believers continue to assert their importance even for later centuries, but a story about the past can refer only indirectly to the present. There must be an interpretive decision that the story of the past applies to the present in a particular way. If we assert that the past applies to the present in some simple and unqualified way, we are the ones who have made that decision. The text does not require it. Even when Jesus uses general language ("Whoever wants to save his life will lose it," Luke 9:24), it may be significant that this language is used in addressing a particular group in a particular situation. The responsibility of appropriate application to other people at other times remains.

III. Reading Characters as "Open"

Many of the characters in synoptic scenes appear only in a single scene, or they are group characters who tend to play a set role repeatedly. It is possible to regard these as "flat" or "closed" characters—persons with few defining characteristics, no complexity, and with no potentiality for change. This way of reading is especially easy with a group such as the Pharisees, who regularly play the role of Jesus' opponents. Yet we should be wary of assuming that all Pharisees are incapable of sincere listening or positive change. I have argued elsewhere that there is no need to take Simon the Pharisee in Luke 7:36-50 as a closed character.[11] If we do so, it is not because the text requires it but because of the poverty of our imaginations.

Many characters appear in a single gospel scene. They may be allowed only one characterizing action or situation, sometimes with a bit of dialogue. That does not mean that we must think of them as having only the characteristic revealed in the scene or assume that they always act as described. We are given only a moment in a life history, a moment

---

[11]See Robert C. Tannehill, "Should We Love Simon the Pharisee? Hermeneutical Reflections on the Pharisees in Luke," *CurTM* 21 (1994): 424-33.

that poses an issue for reflection. The impression of the moment does not require us to conclude that these persons lack other possibilities or always behave in this way. If we wish, we can understand what is not said about these persons as a thick penumbra of possibilities, making them open characters. Although there has been a tendency to regard biblical characters—at least the minor ones—as flat and static, there is, fortunately, a willingness to question that conclusion now.[12] Whether characters are viewed as closed or open often tells us more about our reading than about the biblical text.

The freedom that the text gives us to regard many gospel characters as open or closed carries with it an ethical responsibility. There may not be an exact correspondence between our treatment of characters in an ancient story and our treatment of modern people whom we read about or meet in our daily affairs, but there is likely to be some overlap in our behavior. For reading stories is imaginative preparation for responding to people. Treating people as closed means refusing to believe in their possibilities. It is an ethical failure, a failure of love. (On the hermeneutical significance of the love commandments, see section VI below.)

Statements of Jesus and the outcome of events often imply evaluation of persons in a scene. In the scene of Jesus' visit with Martha and Mary (Luke 10:38-42), Jesus' concluding statement supports Mary against the criticism from her sister. We should, however, be cautious of the conclusions that we draw from such evaluation. The evaluation concerns Mary-at-this-moment and Martha-at-this-moment. The story indicates that, when Mary acts as she does in this scene and Martha reacts as she does, Jesus supports Mary. We cannot conclude that Martha is always a complainer nor that Mary is always a silent listener (nor that women should always be silent listeners because Mary was listening at this moment). All of these conclusions read more into the text than is there. This excessive interpretation of Mary's role is part of an interpretation of the passage as an oppressive text, designed to restrict the role of women in the church. This interpretation is supported by reconstructing a

---

[12]Commenting on a recent collection of essays on "Characterization in Biblical Literature," Robert Fowler writes, "Most of these authors want to break away from static or monolithic views of characters. Most want to crack characters open, to give them some wriggle room, to allow for fluidity and multiplicity in characterization." See "Characterizing Character in Biblical Narrative," *Semeia* 63 (1993): 97. See also David Gowler, *Host, Guest, Enemy, and Friend: Portraits of the Pharisees in Luke and Acts* (New York: Peter Lang, 1991) 77-176.

particular context for the story in the life of the early church.[13] (One of the ways in which multiple readings become possible is through placing the text in different social contexts; see section V below.) This construction is not necessary to make sense of the text, for the passage makes an excellent point without it (the passage defends the freedom of Mary—and others like her—to devote themselves to Jesus' way even if they neglect the expected social role of women). The proposed construction is not required by the text. To my mind it detracts from a text that could convey an important message. For this and other reasons, I decline to accept it.[14]

Stories affect their audience partly through a complex process of identification between hearers and story characters. Social roles are a factor in this identification process. Thus an ancient woman would have been more likely to see her situation reflected in the stories of women in Luke, while a person of high social standing and wealth would be more likely to recognize himself or herself in stories about such people. If social roles are significant factors in response to the gospels, reader-response criticism needs to be refined by taking account of the ancient social situation and by recognizing that the ancient audience would probably contain a variety of persons who would respond differently, partly because of their different social positions. Thus we must think of multiple kinds of reading (or hearing) of a gospel already in its early social context.[15] Furthermore, identification cannot be compelled, and even when it does take place, the hearer may recognize differences as well as similarities. Factors other than social roles may be important. The story allows for differences, because it does not speak directly about the hearers of the story but only about the characters within the story. What the story says about the characters remains a possibility but not a necessity for similar hearers. From this perspective, too, we see that there are multiple options in understanding the significance of a gospel story.

---

[13]For this interpretation, see Elisabeth Schüssler Fiorenza, "Theological Criteria and Historical Reconstruction: Martha and Mary, Luke 10:38-42," *Center for Hermeneutical Studies Protocol* 53 (1987): 1-12; and *But She Said: Feminist Practices of Biblical Interpretation* (Boston: Beacon, 1992) 52-76.

[14]For further discussion, see Robert C. Tannehill, *Luke*, Abingdon New Testament Commentaries (Nashville: Abingdon, 1996) 185-87, and Turid Karlsen Seim, *The Double Message: Patterns of Gender in Luke-Acts* (Nashville: Abingdon, 1994) 97-107, 112-14.

[15]For an experiment in such hearer-response criticism of Luke, see Robert C. Tannehill, " 'Cornelius' and 'Tabitha' Encounter Luke's Jesus," *Int* 48 (1994) 347-56.

IV. Drawing Connections

Narrative criticism and reader-response criticism have advocated reading the gospels as continuous narratives. The stories in Luke (or Luke-Acts) can communicate not only as individual scenes but as parts of a larger whole. Thus we may ask about connections between part and part (one part perhaps reinforcing another, or perhaps supplementing, balancing, or qualifying). We may also ask about connections between the part and the whole. (How does this part contribute to the whole, and how does it take on special meaning in light of the whole?) We may also ask about connections between the text and other texts, such as the Scripture of the early church and Judaism.

Readers seek meaning by drawing connections. An author can assume the reader's tendency to draw connections and seek to guide it, but the author cannot completely control this process. There are literary means of emphasizing certain connections, by comments of the narrator, by interpretive statements from characters to whom the implied author attributes authority, by repetition of themes, etc. Some connections are strongly emphasized in the text, and it will be a fault in reading if the reader misses them. But there are many possibilities of connections. In a lengthy and complex document, the possible connections among parts multiply, and the task of understanding how the parts form a whole becomes complex. When we consider the possible interrelations with the text's social world and important documents within that social world, the number of possibly significant connections becomes enormous. There is broad room for discussion as to which connections are supported by the text and important in interpretation. Different interpreters will demand different kinds and degrees of evidence in reaching conclusions. Consequently, interpreters will come to different conclusions, resulting in somewhat different readings of the text. The text allows this diversity.

For instance, some interpreters note similarities between Jesus' dialogue with a lawyer in Luke 10:25-37 and his dialogue with a rich ruler in Luke 18:18-23.[16] The two inquirers ask the same question about what they must do to inherit eternal life. Jesus replies with a counter-question which leads to citation of Scripture, providing a point of mutual agreement between Jesus and the inquirer. Then Jesus adds something

---

[16]See the essay by Tom Phillips in this volume.

that goes beyond the Scripture or its normal interpretation. There is, then, a certain connection between these two episodes. Is it a significant connection? In what sense? Is there a reason why a central Scripture text (the double love commandment and the Decalogue) is cited in each passage? A series of similarities may also highlight remaining differences. Is it significant that there is no indication of a negative response from the lawyer at the end of the first scene, as there is from the ruler at the end of the second (18:23)? Noting such similarities and differences entices us to further thought without providing any firm control of conclusions.

V. Contexts

Context is important in interpretation, both literary context and social-historical context. Literary studies should not ignore social-historical context, for literature always presupposes language codes and social codes that reflect the shared cultural knowledge of a social world. Knowledge of context can help to specify the significance of a text, to make it more determinate, and much biblical interpretation is an attempt to construct an appropriate context in order to make the significance of the text more specific. In the case of gospel literature, however, we may question the assumption of a single original context that we may recover in order to specify the text's significance. A gospel pericope is often useful in a number of possible contexts, and the content of the gospels is too complex to serve a single purpose or to speak to one narrowly defined context.[17] Even if we confine our consideration to the "authorial audience," that is, the audience that the author might have envisioned because it shared the author's time and general location, it is a mistake to think of context as single and limited. A gospel is suited to nourish faith over a broader time and space. Each gospel was undoubtedly read many times—to a variety of groups and to the same group over the changing years. It is hard to believe that the author of Luke—which has some literary pretensions—would not have anticipated this, and the other gospel writers may have as well. In subtle and not-so-subtle ways the context changed even in the early years. Much of the material could

---

[17]Elizabeth Struthers Malbon states the point more strongly. She says, "No text has just one context." See "Text and Contexts: Interpreting the Disciples in Mark," *Semeia* 62 (1993): 86.

accommodate this change because it was not designed for a single context in the first place.

The gospel material passed through a series of contexts before ever becoming part of our gospels, and it continues to bear the impression of those contexts. The gospel writers probably did not try to shape the material to a single purpose, and it would have been difficult for them to succeed if they had tried. It is a mistake, then, to overemphasize a particular reconstructed context. We reach a similar conclusion when we consider the early audiences. There would have been a variety of occasions for hearing each of the gospels, and the hearers on each occasion would vary, each bringing his or her social context to the understanding of the gospel. We should think, then, of the varied contexts within which the gospels and their component parts might meaningfully speak, and we should be cautious when we hear claims that a particular reconstructed context is the necessary key to understanding the text.

Consider, for instance, the Lukan story of Jesus' temptations (Luke 4:1-13). This story can be understood in different contexts, with somewhat different effects. It can be viewed only in its story context as a story about the personal struggle of Jesus as he was about to begin his mission. It can be viewed in the context of early Christological debates, perhaps as a reply to Jewish skeptics who thought that Jesus was being exalted in place of God. (Note the emphasis on Jesus submitting to the strict theocentric demands of Deuteronomy.[18]) It can also be viewed in the context of the early church's experience of Spirit-power. It then points to Jesus as a model for others who must conquer the temptation to use Spirit-power for the wrong purposes. We need not choose one of these contexts to the exclusion of the others, for it is likely that the story had all three of these functions (and perhaps others as well) within the experience of the early church.

VI. Varying Views of the Center of Scripture

When we consider Scripture as a whole, there is another layer of indeterminacy in interpretation. Scripture is a large library, with parts that are connected in complex ways. There is also tension, for the parts sometimes do not fit neatly together. If individuals and groups are to use this mass of material for inspiration and guidance, they must make judgments

---

[18]See Tannehill, *Luke*, 89-90.

about what in Scripture is central or most valuable. These judgments become guiding principles in interpretation. The material in Scripture that reinforces these judgments takes on special importance. Other passages are interpreted so that they correspond with these judgments, or, if that is impossible, they are reckoned to be unimportant or are openly rejected. This process of deciding what is central may operate in a naive way that ignores the historically conditioned character of biblical writings and their variety. But even sophisticated interpreters must make some judgment as to what is central if they study large portions of Scripture and look to Scripture for guidance.

These judgments vary. The center of Scripture is seen in the election of Israel, in the Mosaic revelation, in justification by faith rather than works, in the Christological interpretation of Old and New Testaments, or in particular creeds that become guides for the reading of Scripture. Scripture may provide some foundation for each of these approaches, but there are also difficulties with each of them.

There is another option for understanding what is central in Scripture. In discussing it, I do not wish to imply that this option should eliminate all the others. In fact, I doubt that it can stand by itself. It focuses on biblical commandments, and these commandments, I believe, rest on a perception of a foundational reality that makes them possible and necessary. Nevertheless, I want to suggest that the double love commandment may function as a hermeneutical principle. This approach may help us to deal with some urgent problems in the religious application of Scripture. It may help draw Jews and Christians closer together, since these commands are important to both.[19] And it may help us respond to one of the chief challenges to biblical authority today, the accusation that Scripture conveys an oppressive ideology, particularly through its androcentric perspective.

There is explicit discussion of the center of Jewish Scripture in the gospel pericope concerning the great commandments (Matt 22:34-40; Mark 12:28-34; Luke 10:25-37). St. Augustine made the suggestion long ago that the double love commandment should function as a hermeneutical principle in the interpretation of Scripture. This suggestion implies that the authoritative interpretation of Scripture emerges when we are

---

[19]The agreement in Luke 10:25-28 between Jesus and the lawyer who quotes the double love commandment may indicate a significant area of agreement that is still possible for Jews and Christians today.

able to show how it encourages love of God and neighbor.[20] If the commands to love God and neighbor are central to Scripture and central to a faithful life, then we should read Scripture from this perspective and use Scripture in ways that demonstrate such love. As with some of the hermeneutical principles mentioned above, this could be done in a naive way that reduces Scripture to a narrow and monotonous message and ignores all problems. But this need not be the result. How love of God and neighbor are to be shown will still be expressed differently in different parts of Scripture. And the interpreter must face squarely the challenge of those texts that seem not to promote love of God and neighbor—where God appears unlovable and where killing and oppression of neighbors seem acceptable. The interpreter who is committed to the double love commandment as an interpretive principle is then left with at least two options: (1) She or he may seek to show, through careful study of the text, that the passage need not be read in this oppressive way, for there are other options. These options may arise from the elements of indeterminacy discussed earlier in this article. The interpreter need not deny that the text can also be understood in an oppressive way. (2) She or he may decide that the text, because it does not encourage love of God or neighbor, has little or no value for life today, except, perhaps, as a negative example. It may be important for historical studies, but it is not a positive guide for faith and life in the contemporary world. Consistency in following the scriptural principle of love of God and neighbor may require us to say "No" to some passages of Scripture.

It is easy to read the Pharisees in the gospels as negative stereotypes, characters who are fully defined by negative traits and incapable of positive change. Stereotypes can have a function in teaching, but to regard another as simply a negative stereotype is a failure in love of neighbor. Do the gospel texts require us to reduce the Pharisees to negative stereotypes, if we are reading accurately? In another article, I asked this question concerning the Pharisees in Luke and recognized that the repeated introduction of Pharisees as opponents of Jesus, the protagonist

---

[20]See Saint Augustine, *On Christian Doctrine*, trans. D. W. Robertson, Jr. (New York: Liberal Arts Press, 1958) 30-31: "Whoever, therefore, thinks that he understands the divine Scriptures or any part of them so that it does not build the double love of God and of our neighbor does not understand it at all." Augustine then explains that an interpreter who finds this message in a passage where it was not the author's intention has reached the destination appropriate to Scripture even though he or she may be mistaken about the best road.

in the story, easily leads to negative stereotyping. Since there are some exceptions to this negative portrait, however, we need not view Jewish teachers as lacking potential for good. In particular, Simon the Pharisee, who appears in Luke 7:36-50, need not be viewed as a negative stereotype, for the story allows us to understand him as an open character, capable of change, particularly because the scene is open-ended. We do not know how Simon responds to Jesus' teaching.[21] If we are talking only about the potentialities of the text, we can admit that Simon can be read either as a stereotype or as an open character. If we are talking about how a Scripture passage should be used in religious formation, a commitment to love of God and neighbor will lead to the second of these options.

The choice to read Scripture as an invitation to love God and neighbor is a religious and ethical decision, as are other options for deciding what is central in Scripture. Scripture leaves us with some freedom in our decision, and we must take responsibility for the way we use that freedom. Our decision will help determine how we respond to other indeterminacies in the text—to the need for an imaginative response by the reader, to the gaps in the text, to the opportunity to read characters as open, to the various possibilities of drawing connections and reconstructing contexts. The interpreter is a responsible partner in a dialogue with the text and must ask whether and how it is possible to interpret this text so that human benefit flows from it.

---

[21]See Tannehill, "Should We Love Simon the Pharisee?" 424-33.

The God of Promises
and the Jews in Luke-Acts

Robert L. Brawley

Joseph Tyson's well-known interest in the treatment of the Jews in Luke-Acts is a corollary of his agony over twentieth-century anti-Semitism and his mortification over the Holocaust. In the company of people like Jack Sanders, John Gager, and Rosemary Reuther, Tyson detects the roots of Christian antipathy toward Jews in the New Testament.[1] In particular, he reads Luke-Acts ultimately as anti-Jewish.[2] Although I admire Tyson's fair-mindedness, I have suggested several difficulties with the reading of the rejection of "the Jews" in Luke-Acts: (1) it freezes in one image what Luke-Acts differentiates, (2) it presumes the separation of Christianity from Judaism whereas, at the end of Luke-Acts, Christianity is still a Jewish sect, (3) it misreads antagonism to the Lukan *Paul* as if it was opposition to *Christianity*, and (4) it misunderstands *Paul's* particular turn to Gentiles as if it was *Christianity's* rejection of Judaism.[3] Now I propose to fold two other ingredients into the batter—the characterization of God in relation to the Jews and the ethics of reading.

Readers construe characters by combining separate clues into holistic portraits, filling in gaps along the way. Readers build themes from the way clues reiterate, reinforce, redirect, or correct one another and construe characters from such thematization. Characterization develops sequentially, so that it, like all reading, progressively discovers what is true in the narrative world.[4] Consequently, my discussion takes a quick

---

[1]Jack T. Sanders, *The Jews in Luke-Acts* (Philadelphia: Fortress, 1987); John Gager, *The Origins of Anti-Semitism: The Attitudes towards Judaism in Pagan and Christian Antiquity* (Oxford: Oxford University Press, 1983); and Rosemary Reuther, *Faith and Fratricide* (New York: Seabury, 1974).

[2]Joseph B. Tyson, *The Death of Jesus in Luke-Acts* (Columbia: University of South Carolina Press, 1986) 29-47; "The Problem of Jewish Rejection in Acts," in *LAJP* (1988) 124-37; and *Images of Judaism in Luke-Acts* (Columbia: University of South Carolina Press, 1992).

[3]Robert L. Brawley, *Luke-Acts and the Jews: Conflict, Apology, and Conciliation*, SBLMS 23 (Atlanta: Scholars Press, 1987).

[4]On characterization, see Robert L. Brawley, *Centering on God: Method and Message in Luke-Acts*, LCBI (Louisville KY: Westminster/John Knox, 1990) 107-11; David B. Gowler, *Host, Guest, Enemy, and Friend: Portraits of the Pharisees in Luke and Acts*

excursion through Luke-Acts, although for the sake of space I summarize some patterns of thematization out of sequence.

God inhabits a cultural repertoire before entering Luke-Acts. This cultural repertoire is both essential and problematic. A God who does not exist prior to the world of Luke-Acts would hardly be God, but the cultural repertoire also contains norms that Luke-Acts revises. For example, God "does not dwell in sanctuaries made by human hands" (Acts 17:24). When the angel Gabriel appears to Zechariah in the temple, he alights at the point of contact between heaven and earth.[5] Therefore highly reliable, Gabriel characterizes God as one who promises a benevolent act— Elizabeth will bear a son. This benevolence will violate family privacy and produce joy for many (Luke 1:14).[6] The joy is for Israel's sake, because Elizabeth's son, John, will turn many Israelites to God (1:16). This lucid foreshadowing regarding joy over God's relation with Israel is foundational for characterizing God. Does the progressive discovery of what is true in the narrative world revise this view of God into its opposite?

In foreshadowing benevolence for Israel, Gabriel promises that John will be filled with the Holy Spirit. In *Centering on God*, I identified "Holy Spirit" as one of the clues out of which readers construe God's character. William Shepherd challenges my position and suggests that the Holy Spirit is an independent character, the onstage representative of a offstage God.[7] Is God indeed offstage? I think not for several reasons. (1) Shepherd superimposes an anachronistic cosmology onto Luke-Acts. In Luke-Acts the heavenly realm is the home base from which God acts *in heaven and on earth*. In Luke 10:21 Jesus not only characterizes God as Lord of heaven and earth but also speaks to God as an actor on the same stage. (2) When humans do not perceive that God is onstage, it is because God has hidden "these things" from the wise and intelligent. On the other hand, God has revealed "these things" to infants, who like Jesus know God as πατήρ (10:21-22). (3) Jesus claims that his exorcisms are

---

(New York: Peter Lang, 1991) 29-176; and John A. Darr, *On Character Building: The Reader and the Rhetoric of Characterization in Luke-Acts*, LCBI (Louisville KY: Westminster/John Knox, 1992) 42-47, 85-126.

[5] See Brawley, *Luke-Acts and the Jews*, 118-32.

[6] François Bovon, *Das Evangelium nach Lukas*, 3 vols., EKKNT (Zürich: Benziger, 1989) 1:55: "Seldom is the election of one person for the salvation of the community so clearly expressed."

[7] William H. Shepherd, Jr., *The Narrative Function of the Holy Spirit as a Character in Luke-Acts* (Atlanta: Scholars Press, 1994) 37-41, 255 and passim.

palpable evidence of God's rule in the earthly realm (ἐφ' ὑμᾶς; 11:20). Luke-Acts claims precisely that God is acting onstage. (4) "Holy Spirit" and "God" appear interchangeably. In one case, Gabriel informs Mary that the Holy Spirit will overshadow her (1:35), but in her retelling of the events, Mary says that "the Mighty One has done great things for me" (1:49). "Holy Spirit" is one of the clues which readers use to construe the character of God. Thus, as John the Baptist is filled with the Holy Spirit, he will be an agent of God's benevolent action on behalf of Israel (Luke 1:15-16).[8]

Anticipations of God's benevolence for Israel through Jesus are greater than those through John. Gabriel anticipates Jesus' rule by alluding to the Davidic covenant, in which God authorizes shepherding Israel— hardly tyrannical (Luke 1:33; 2 Kgs 7:7).[9] Further, the Magnificat, dominated by God and God's relation to Israel,[10] anticipates Jesus' birth as God's mercy for Israel in fidelity to the Abrahamic covenant (Luke 1:54-55). Zechariah anticipates that John the Baptist is part of the same benevolence of God for Israel—God's fidelity to promises made to David and to Abraham (1:68-75).[11] The Lukan God is preeminently the God of the Abrahamic covenant, a savior (1:47) who raises up a savior for God's people (1:68-69).

Simeon reiterates and therefore thematizes God's benevolence for Israel (Luke 2:32).[12] But his prediction of the fall and rising of many in

---

[8]Joseph A. Fitzmyer, *The Gospel according to Luke*, 2 vols., AB 28, 28A (Garden City NY: Doubleday, 1981, 1985) 1:326; and Gerhard Schneider, *Das Evangelium nach Lukas*, 2 vols., OTNT 3 (Gütersloh: Mohn, 1977) 1:46.

[9]Karl H. Rengstorf, *Das Evangelium nach Lukas: Übersetzt und erklärt* (Göttingen: Vandenhoeck & Ruprecht, 1978) 25; Fitzmyer, *The Gospel according to Luke*, 1:348; and Schneider, *Das Evangelium nach Lukas*, 1:50.

[10]Paul Bemile, *The Magnificat within the Context and Framework of Lukan Theology: An Exegetical Theological Study of Lk 1:46-55* (Frankfurt: Peter Lang, 1986) 134.

[11]Zechariah's song is aimed at Israel (Bovon, *Das Evangelium nach Lukas*, 104). See Vittorio Fusco, "Luke-Acts and the Future of Israel," *NovT* 38 (1996): 2; and Joachim Gnilka, "Der Hymnus des Zachariahs," *BZ* 6 (1962): 218-19. But Gnilka makes David and the exodus central (220, 222, 237) to the neglect of the Abrahamic covenant. Though Jose S. Croatto, "El 'benedictus' como memoria de la alianza (Estructura y teología de Lucas 1,68-79)," *RevistB* 47 (1985): 211, 214-16, centers on memory of the covenant, he also makes Sinai the focus.

[12]See David L. Tiede, " 'Glory to Thy People Israel': Luke-Acts and the Jews," in *LAJP* (1988) 21-34. Bart Koet, "Simeons Worte (Lk 2,29-32.34c-35) und Israels Geschick," in *The Four Gospels 1992: Festschrift Frans Neirynck*, 3 vols., ed. Frans van Segbroeck et al., BETL 100 (Leuven: Leuven University Press, 1992) 2:1553-57, shows how Simeon's canticle is a "disclosure" text indicating Jesus' task in God's salvation *for*

Israel qualifies how God's salvation is for Israel's glory. If the fall pertains to one group and the rising to another, a division among the people begins to revise normative definitions of Israel. But it is also possible to understand the fall and rising as subsequent experiences of one Israel on the way to God's salvation. This second reading is compelling for several reasons. (1) In the Isaianic context of "a light to Gentiles" (Isa 49:6), to which Simeon alludes (Luke 2:32), blessing follows the exile in the sequence of falling and rising. (2) The "many" in Luke 2:35 form one group whose thoughts will be revealed, and they correspond to the "many" in 2:34 who are destined for falling and rising. This correspondence implies that the "many" also form one group. (3) Simeon's forecast of the falling and rising of many in Israel stands in a context where he waits for the consolation of Israel. (4) Anna's address to those who await the redemption of Jerusalem reinforces Simeon's anticipation of glory for Israel (2:38).[13]

Nevertheless, John the Baptist revises normative definitions of Israel when he undercuts conventional notions of descent from Abraham. John substitutes the fruits of repentance for physical descent from Abraham (Luke 3:8).[14] Though salvation connotes benefit for Israel, John introduces God's wrath against Abraham's physical descendants who do not bear fruit and anticipates that the one who is coming will gather and sift the people (3:17).

An incident in Nazareth foreshadows Jesus' mission as beneficence (Luke 4:16-30). Though the incident is a case of gathering and sifting, it hardly reverses Jesus' promise to convey God's benefits. The subsequent exorcism in the synagogue in Capernaum bears out that those benefits are for Jewish people (4:31-34). Jesus proceeds to convey God's benevolence to Israel. He heals lepers, a paralytic, Jairus's daughter, another "daughter" whose flow of blood is stopped, an epileptic boy, a woman bent double (because she is a daughter of Abraham, 13:10-17),[15] and a blind

---

all people. On the significance for Israel, see Bovon, *Das Evangelium nach Lukas*, 145.
   [13]Koet, "Simeons Worte," 1557-67.
   [14]Jeffrey S. Siker, *Disinheriting the Jews: Abraham in Early Christian Controversy* (Louisville KY: Westminster/John Knox, 1991) 108-109. See Fitzmyer, *The Gospel according to Luke*, 1:468.
   [15]Robert F. O'Toole, "Some Exegetical Reflections on Luke 13,10-17," *Bib* 73 (1992): 84-107. O'Toole goes too far in making the woman a metaphor for all Israel. Joel Green, "Jesus and a Daughter of Abraham (Luke 13:10-17): Test Case for a Lucan Perspective on Jesus' Miracles," *CBQ* 51 (1989): 651, takes "daughter of Abraham" as designating a marginalized person but fails to hear overtones of the Abrahamic covenant. Turid

man. Jesus also raises a widow's son from the dead. He proclaims good news to the poor and characterizes God as father of Jewish people (6:36). To be sure, stereotyped Pharisees and lawyers oppose him (7:30).[16] In contrast, other stereotyped characters, including the populace at large and tax collectors, recognize God's justice for the people.

Robert Tannehill suggests that readers have an ethical responsibility not to vilify stereotyped antagonists, such as Simon the Pharisee (Luke 7:36-50), but to hold open the possibility that encounters with Jesus will change them.[17] This applies to the addressee of the parable of the good Samaritan (10:23-37) and the addressees of the parables in Luke 15. They are potential recipients of God's benefits through the teaching of Jesus.

Luke 11 characterizes God with multiple images of father and child.[18] Jesus proclaims that God acts benevolently toward those who appeal to God as God's children (11:1-13). His exorcisms are God's good gifts for God's children (11:14-20). But as part of a complex characterization of God, Jesus distinguishes stereotyped Pharisees and lawyers from God's children (11:42-52). On the one hand, God can cast into hell (12:5)—part of a forceful reiteration of God's judgment (12:13-56; cf. 13:5-9, 28). On the other hand, God's care extends to the point of counting the hairs on one's head (12:7)—part of a forceful reiteration of God's benevolence for Jesus' disciples, the little flock, that is also extended to all (12:32, 41, 58; cf. 13:8, 10-17).

The parable of the banquet dramatizes the type of crisis that the introduction to the parable of the lost sheep describes. The selective commensality that Jesus criticizes (Luke 14:12-13) contrasts with his own commensality with tax collectors and sinners (15:1-2). Further, the host of the banquet, who changes his social relationships to include outcasts,[19]

Karlsen Seim, *The Double Message: Patterns of Gender in Luke-Acts* (Nashville: Abingdon, 1994) 52-56, 251, takes the designation "daughter" to indicate Abrahamic progeny. See Dennis Hamm, "The Freeing of the Bent Woman," *JSNT* 31 (1987): 34-35.

[16]On the stereotyping of religious leaders in Luke-Acts as embodying self-righteousness as a "root character trait," see Mark Allan Powell, "The Religious Leaders in Luke: A Literary-Critical Study," *JBL* 109 (1990): 95.

[17]Robert C. Tannehill, "Should We Love Simon the Pharisee? Hermeneutical Reflections on the Pharisees in Luke," *CurTM* 21 (1994): 424-33, esp. 424: "Stereotyping, then, becomes an issue of how we read, and how we read becomes an ethical test." See also Tannehill's essay in this volume.

[18]Robert C. Tannehill, *The Narrative Unity of Luke-Acts: A Literary Interpretation*, 2 vols. (Philadelphia and Minneapolis: Fortress, 1986–1990) 1:238-39; and John Nolland, *Luke*, 3 vols., WBC (Dallas: Word, 1989–1993) 2:610, 613.

[19]See Willi Braun, *Feasting and Social Rhetoric in Luke 14*, SNTSMS 85 (Cambridge:

corresponds to Jesus who embraces tax collectors and sinners. The parables in Luke 15 thematize divine joy over repentance. Who do the parables anticipate as the repentant? The younger brother in essence forfeits what it means to be a Jew. Wasting the inheritance was forfeiting the heritage which the family traced back to the allotment of the land of Canaan as the Abrahamic heritage.[20] Consequently, he no longer expects to be a child of the Jewish family. But his father restores and expands his sonship. Thus, readers have an image of the inclusion of those who stand over against God's joyful beneficence in Jesus. Further, the parable suspends the resolution of the older son's demeanor toward his brother. At the end, the father implores him to join the celebration; the father's attitude toward his older son does not change in spite of the latter's objections to his younger brother. Do the opponents in 15:2 correspond to the older brother? Is it ethical for readers to fill in the gap only in terms of their refusal to become a part of God's joy?[21]

The next time God is explicitly characterized, however, God calls into question the value system of stereotyped, money-loving Pharisees (Luke 16:14-16). But what is the effect of Jesus' interchange with them? Does it characterize God as their eternal opponent? Or do readers have an obligation to consider their potential to change?

Luke 18:1-30 intersperses images of those who are estranged from God and those who are God's children. In the first incident, an unjust malefactor opposes the woman who appeals to the unjust judge. The woman before the judge has a counterpart in God's chosen ones who cry to God (18:7). In the parable of the Pharisee and the toll collector (18:9-14), the toll collector who cries to God reinforces the image of the woman in the previous pericope (18:1-8). Are those whom the parable addresses as self-confident permanently so? Or does the parable persuade them also to cry to God? The next episode urges the reception of God's

---

Cambridge University Press, 1995).

[20]See Karl H. Rengstorf, *Die Re-Investitur des verlorenen Sohnes in der Gleichniserzählung Jesu Luk. 15,11-32* (Köln: Westdeutscher Verlag, 1967) 22-24; and Kenneth E. Bailey, *Poet and Peasant: A Literary-Cultural Approach to the Parables of Luke* (Grand Rapids MI: Eerdmans, 1976) 167-68. The sheer Jewishness of the father and two sons speaks against Heikki Räisänen's allegory of the younger son as a *Gentile* believer of Acts and the older son as a Jewish Christian ("The Prodigal Gentile and His Jewish Christian Brother: Lk 15,11-32," in *The Four Gospels 1992*, 2:1617-36).

[21]On the open ending in contrast to the expected transformation of the older brother into a villain (so Vladimir Propp), see Petr Pokorný, "Saint Luke's Message about the Christian Relationship towards Israel," *Explorations* 11/2 (1997): 4.

rule as a little child (18:17)—presuming a transformation for every adult. The Lukan God is quick to be magnanimous to those who cry to God as God's children.

Jesus' entrance into Jerusalem leads up to one of the most negative characterizations of God in connection with the Jewish people (Luke 19:42-44). With antecedents in 13:35 and elaborations in 21:20-24, Jesus announces the devastation of Jerusalem and its populace as a consequence of the city's failure to recognize the things that make for peace.[22] The crowds on the descent from the Mount of Olives recognize Jesus as God's ἐπισκοπή ("visitation"). Who then does not recognize Jerusalem's ἐπισκοπή? It is possible for Jerusalem to stand synecdochically for Israel as a whole. The question of whether it does or not, and the question of the identity of those who have not recognized Jerusalem's ἐπισκοπή constitute gaps that can be filled only as there is further disclosure of what is true in the narrative world.

The parable of the wicked tenants (Luke 20:9-19) offers some of this disclosure. An influential interpretive tradition reads this parable as an allegory of early Christian history, and consequently deduces the passing of Israel's prerogatives to the Gentiles.[23] But the parable replicates Luke-Acts in miniature rather than early Christian history, and, at the end of Luke-Acts, the Jesus movement is still a Jewish sect (Acts 28:22). Further, the parable is in interplay with Isaiah 5:1-7. In Isaiah's song, the vineyard (Israel) is given up to destruction. Luke's parable revises Isaiah 5:1-7 so that the tenants rather than the vineyard are given up to destruction. The parable anticipates that the vineyard will bear fruit—a narrative theme beginning with John the Baptist—under other tenants. In the narrative world, the tenants who are destroyed correspond to the high priestly party (Luke 20:19), and the new tenants are the twelve.[24] In

---

[22]David P. Moessner, "Paul in Acts: Preacher of Eschatological Repentance to Israel," *NTS* 34 (1988): 97-98, construes these texts as judgment against a recalcitrant people who rejects God's prophet(s). Rengstorf, *Das Evangelium nach Lukas*, 220, 234, suggests that Jesus could make such a prediction on the basis of Jerusalem's past destruction and the practice of the Romans. Fitzmyer, *The Gospel according to Luke*, 2:1255: "Luke does not blame the destruction of Jerusalem on the death of Jesus."

[23]So Walter Schmithals, *Das Evangelium nach Lukas* (Zürich: Theologische Verlag, 1980) 193; Michel Hubaut, *La parabole des vignerons homicides* (Paris: Gabalda, 1976) 17; Sanders, *The Jews in Luke-Acts*, 32, 211-13; and Tyson, *Images of Judaism in Luke-Acts*, 74-88.

[24]For a detailed interpretation of the parable of the wicked tenants as a literary *mise en abyme*, see Robert L. Brawley, *Text to Text Pours Forth Speech: Voices of Scripture*

tandem with Jesus' lament over Jerusalem, this parable connotes that God judges recalcitrance among the Jewish priestly leadership with lethal consequences also for the populace. Is God thereby revoking God's fidelity to Israel?

Jesus' predictions in Luke 21:5-24 further disclose the destiny of Jerusalem. Who is the literary audience addressed as "you" in chapter 21? The pregnant women and nursing mothers, and perhaps also the nursing infants (21:23) apparently are members of the addressees. Jesus' prediction—in combination with the lament, the prophesy of the destruction of the temple, and the parable of the wicked tenants—enables readers to conclude that the destiny of Jerusalem hinges on the inability of Israel to bear fruit under the high priestly leadership. But the fulfillment of the time of the Gentiles places limits on the consequences, and in view of intertextual allusions to Ezekiel 39:23, 25-29 and Zechariah 12:3, the end of the time of the Gentiles anticipates God's mercy anew.[25] Further, should readers presume that the pregnant women and nursing mothers, and perhaps the nursing infants, are to be identified as those who did not recognize Jerusalem's ἐπισκοπή? This is unlikely for readers who next read that the addressees include those whose redemption is drawing near (Luke 21:28) and to whom God's kingdom is near (21:31).

At the last supper, Jesus predicts the fulfillment of the Passover in God's rule (Luke 22:16). This prediction can hardly be divorced from Israel's deliverance out of Egypt.[26] In the midst of the supper, Jesus characterizes God as his father and claims that God has assigned him a kingdom, which pointedly embraces the twelve tribes of Israel and which he in turn confers on the twelve (22:29-30). With this conferral, readers clarify further their understanding of the passing of the vineyard to other tenants. The twelve judge Israel with a mandate that derives from God through Jesus.

In the trial before Pilate, the people do align with Judas and the high priestly coterie against Jesus (Luke 23:13), but readers should hesitate to make these people representative of all Israel. Luke carefully distinguish-

---

in Luke-Acts (Bloomington: Indiana University Press, 1995) 27-41.

[25]Felix Flückiger, "Luk. 21,20-24 und die Zerstörung Jerusalems," *TZ* 28 (1972): 387-89; and Fusco, "Luke-Acts and the Future of Israel," 10-15.

[26]David P. Moessner, *Lord of the Banquet: The Literary and Theological Significance of the Lukan Travel Narrative* (Minneapolis: Fortress, 1989) 178-81.

es among Jewish crowds.[27] Luke allies the crowds at the trial with the high priestly party, who takes the lion's share of the guilt (23:4).[28]

In addition, Joseph of Arimathea, a member of the council, allies with Jesus. In awaiting God's reign (Luke 23:51), he is a concrete case of how God remembers the promises to the forebears and how God offers salvation for the glory of Israel. These themes of promise and salvation reach back to foreshadowings from Mary, Zechariah, Simeon, and Anna. As one who recognizes Jerusalem's ἐπισκοπή, Joseph is clearly an exception among the *council*.[29] But is he an exception among the *people*?

The two traveling to Emmaus reiterate the distinction between the people and the high priestly party (Luke 24:19-20). They also align themselves with Anna in expecting the redemption of Israel, though they are disenchanted. But when the risen Jesus overcomes their disenchantment, they become other concrete cases of those whom God saves for the glory of Israel.

Luke ends his gospel with the characterization of God as Jesus' father and as the one who sends what is promised in a fatherly fashion (Luke 24:49). At the beginning of Acts, God is again the God of promise. In Acts 1:4, however, Jesus calls God "the" father rather than "my" father and so broadens the characterization of God as father. In the narrative world, the father promises the Holy Spirit (Luke 11:13).[30] But memory of God's promises in the Abrahamic covenant lingers from the thematic development begun in Luke 1. Commentators often note that Luke begins and ends in the temple. More emphatically Luke begins and ends with the God of promises, but at the transition from Luke to Acts the father's promise is addressed to the eleven and those with them. Readers have strong warrant to ask: Are they exclusively the recipients of the promise?

---

[27]Paul S. Minear, "Jesus' Audiences according to Luke," *NovT* 16 (1974): 81-89. David L. Tiede, *Prophecy and History in Luke-Acts* (Philadelphia: Fortress, 1980) 105-18, shows that Luke takes pains to distinguish various roles of the people in the passion narrative.

[28]Jerome Kodell, "Luke's Use of *LAOS*, 'People,' Especially in the Jerusalem Narrative (Lk 19,28–24,53)," *CBQ* 31 (1969): 328-31, 341, 343. *Pace* Tyson, *The Death of Jesus in Luke-Acts*, 29-47.

[29]Powell, "The Religious Leaders in Luke," 94n.5, 97. As an ordinary priest, Zechariah is hardly a religious leader as Powell maintains.

[30]Tannehill, *The Narrative Unity of Luke-Acts*, 1:239, 2:12; and Rudolf Pesch, *Die Apostelgeschichte*, 2 vols., EKKNT 5 (Zürich: Benziger, 1986) 1:66.

In Acts 1:6-8, the apostles raise the question of the restoration of the kingdom to Israel. Both the inquiry and Jesus' answer focus on the time of the restoration. Some interpreters take Jesus' answer as Luke's compensation for the delay of the parousia.[31] In the narrative world, however, Jesus refers to waiting for the Spirit, and the coming of the Spirit is the restoration of the kingdom to Israel—that for which Anna, Cleopas and his companion, and Joseph of Arimathea have hoped. When the time of waiting for the Spirit is over, the kingdom is restored to Israel.[32] In keeping with the parable of the tenants, God gives the vineyard to others.

In Acts 2 Peter presents Jesus as the channel of God's benevolence specifically to Israelites (v. 22), even though he indicts them for the death of Jesus.[33] In honor/shame contests, the vindication of one party ordinarily means loss of honor for the other, but in Peter's case repentance and baptism make room for the competitors to participate in the honor.[34] Peter's basis for the offer to his ἀδελφοί is the promise (2:39). Though "promise" here is vague, astute readers may hear echoes of the promise to Abraham that appears as early as the Magnificat. Though repentance apparently is equivalent to calling on the name of Jesus, the promise is for everyone whom God calls (2:39). If "whom the Lord our God calls" qualifies "everyone," God excludes those who are

---

[31]Hans Conzelmann, *Acts of the Apostles: A Commentary on the Acts of the Apostles*, Hermeneia (Philadelphia: Fortress, 1987) 6-7; and Ernst Haenchen, *The Acts of the Apostles: A Commentary* (Philadelphia: Westminster, 1971) 142-43. Also Jürgen Roloff, *Die Apostelgeschichte: Übersetzt und erklärt*, NTD 5 (Göttingen: Vandenhoeck & Ruprecht, 1981) 23.

[32]See Robert C. Tannehill, "Israel in Luke-Acts: A Tragic Story," *JBL* 104 (1985): 76; C. K. Barrett, *A Critical and Exegetical Commentary on the Acts of the Apostles*, 2 vols. (Edinburgh: T.&T. Clark, 1994–) 1:77-78; Luke Timothy Johnson, *The Acts of the Apostles*, Sacra Pagina 5 (Collegeville MN: Liturgical, 1992) 38-39; and Gerhard Schneider, *Die Apostelgeschichte*, 2 vols., HTKNT (Freiburg: Herder, 1980–1982) 1:201. That the text presumes a stable identity for Israel and speaks of the restoration of the kingdom weighs against David Ravens's thesis that Israel must be restored (*Luke and the Restoration of Israel* [Sheffield: Sheffield Academic Press, 1995]).

[33]To entangle Israel in its entirety in the rejection and death of Jesus, as does Roloff, goes far beyond Peter's address to a definite audience (*Die Apostelgeschichte*, 63). On the other hand, the salvation Peter announces does go far beyond the audience as Acts 2:39 clearly indicates.

[34]Peter turns an originally negative challenge into a challenge to participate in the honor. See Bruce J. Malina and Jerome H. Neyrey, "Honor and Shame in Luke-Acts: Pivotal Values of the Mediterranean World," in *The Social World of Luke-Acts: Models for Interpretation* (Peabody MA: Hendrickson, 1991) 29-54; and Anne Etienne, "Lecture de l'événement de Pentecôte dans Actes 2,1-36," *Foi et vie* 80 (1981): 62-64.

not called. But if "everyone whom the Lord our God calls" is parallel to "all who are far away," God includes rather than excludes.

Peter explains the healing of a lame man at the temple as a *continuation* of God's benevolence to Israel through Jesus (Acts 3:1–4:22),[35] but he also indicts his audience for killing Jesus. The verdict, however, is not their guilt or innocence but God's vindication of Jesus. Peter calls on his audience to repent, and he offers them God's benevolence on the basis of a promise. Immediately this is God's promise of a prophet like Moses (3:22), but Acts 3:25 shows that the prophet like Moses is a part of the Abrahamic covenant. In fact, Acts 3:25 is momentous in disclosing several things that are true in the narrative world. (1) The content of the Abrahamic promise is the blessing of all the families of the earth. (2) The blessing of all the families of the earth is parallel to the restoration of all (3:21). (3) The healing of the lame man is a concrete case of God's promise to Abraham to bless all the families of the earth.[36] Even in the council, Peter's inclusion of his audience in salvation (ἡμᾶς; 4:12) makes it possible for the members of the council to become Jesus' allies. In spite of indicting the council for crucifying Jesus, Peter proclaims God's benevolence for the council and all the people of Israel as nothing less than salvation.[37]

Acts 4:25-28, however, reinforces antipathy between God and Jesus' opponents by employing Psalm 2:1-2 to explain the crucifixion. A figurative play on synonymous parallelism makes the "peoples" of Israel correspond to the Gentiles of the psalm who are God's opponents. But Acts 4:27 also uses the plural λαοί with respect to Israel. "The plural . . . enables Luke to involve *individual* Jews in the death of Jesus (such as the rulers), as he does individual Gentiles, without jeopardizing the special place of 'the people' as a religious designation for Israel."[38]

---

[35]Haenchen, *The Acts of the Apostles*, 205; Conzelmann, *Acts of the Apostles*, 28; Barrett, *The Acts of the Apostles*, 1:188, 195; and Johnson, *The Acts of the Apostles*, 67.

[36]Against Barrett, *The Acts of the Apostles*, 1:212, there is no covenant renewal and no new covenant. Against Johnson, *The Acts of the Apostles*, 70, σπέρμα implies the literal singular (Jesus) as a play on the collective "descendants." See a similar implicit play on the σπέρμα of David in Luke 1:32-33. See Barrett, *The Acts of the Apostles*, 1:191; Roloff, *Die Apostelgeschichte*, 78; and Pesch, *Die Apostelgeschichte*, 157-58.

[37]On salvation as benevolence, see Werner Foerster, "σωτηρία," in *TDNT* 7:967-68; and Frederick W. Danker, *Benefactor: Epigraphic Study of a Graeco-Roman and New Testament Semantic Field* (St. Louis: Clayton, 1982) 402-405. Schneider, *Die Apostelgeschichte*, 1:330: "Jesus is sent as the εὐλογῶν, as the giver of blessing, for Israel."

[38]Johnson, *The Acts of the Apostles*, 85.

As an encounter with opponents who align with the high priestly party, Stephen's speech centers on God (Acts 7:1-53).[39] God is a God who promised to give a heritage to Abraham's descendants. The speech also features Sinai and the temple. Stephen upholds Moses and the temple, but finds fault with people who disobeyed the revelation at Sinai and misconstrued the temple as God's residence in the house of Jacob alone (7:46).[40] The citation of Isaiah 66:1-2 is then not an attack on the temple but a proclamation of God's universality. Stephen's speech claims the Abrahamic heritage not only for Israel but for the whole earth.

In connection with Paul's call, Ananias's vision characterizes God as one who chooses Paul as a channel of God's benevolence (Acts 9:15).[41] A new element is that God aims benevolence toward Gentiles as well as toward Israel. Immediately, however, Paul preaches in synagogues in Damascus, and though Paul's opponents resist God's benevolence, their resistance may not be final. Paul himself is a resistant Jew who has ceased to resist.

By his association with Gentiles, Peter interprets his vision in terms of God's evaluation of human beings rather than foods (Acts 10:28). Consequently, readers must revise construals of God's preference for Jews in favor of a God who shows no partiality (10:34; 11:12). But readers cannot leave the Jews behind. For example, messianists in Antioch send relief to Jerusalem (11:27-30)—another case of God's benevolence for Jewish people, albeit Jewish messianists.

---

[39]Johnson, *The Acts of the Apostles*, 121; and Ravens, *Luke and the Restoration of Israel*, 59-71. Robert T. Anderson, "The Use of Hebrew Scripture in Stephen's Speech," in *Uncovering Ancient Stones: Essays in Honor of H. Neil Richardson*, ed. Lewis H. Hopfe (Winona Lake IN: Eisenbrauns, 1994) 212-13, makes Abraham, Moses, Solomon, David, and the temple dominant rather than God, and presumes a rejection of Jerusalem, monarchy, and the temple. Barrett, *The Acts of the Apostles*, 1:337-38, 373-74, catches the focus on God but claims also an attack on the temple. He bases an attack on the temple largely on associating χειροποίητος with idols. But it is also used by Philo to refer to the construction of the tabernacle under Moses (*Moses* 2.88, 168; cf. Josephus, *War* 1.419; *Ant.* 4.55).

[40]On God's transcendence of the temple in Acts 7, see Dennis D. Sylva, "The Meaning and Function of Acts 7:46-50," *JBL* 106 (1987): 262, 270-72. Jacques Dupont, "La structure oratoire du discours d'Étienne (Actes 7)," *Bib* 66 (1985): 159-60, notes that Stephen's use of Isa 66:1-2 reiterates Solomon's question at the dedication of the temple (1 Kgs 8:27; 2 Chr 6:18 LXX). See Francis D. Weinert, "Luke, Stephen, and the Temple in Luke-Acts," *BTB* 17 (1987): 88-90; and John J. Kilgallen, "The Function of Stephen's Speech (Acts 7,2-53)," *Bib* 70 (1989): 175-93.

[41]Johnson, *The Acts of the Apostles*, 167, emphasizes God as the main character.

Paul's address to the people in the synagogue in Pisidian Antioch as "Israelites and those who fear God" (Acts 13:16) places them in a positive relationship with God. Paul directly characterizes God as the God of "this people Israel," who with Paul share descent from "our forebears" (13:17). Paul's speech highlights God's benevolent acts on behalf of the people,[42] with Jesus as the epitome (13:23). Paul proclaims in a divine passive that God has sent salvation expressly to "the children of Abraham's race and to those among us who fear God" (13:26). In contrast to the misunderstanding of the Jerusalem leaders and people, God raised Jesus in fulfillment of the Davidic promises "for us children" (13:33), which in the thematic development of Luke-Acts is also fulfillment of the Abrahamic promises to "the children of Abraham's race and to those among us who fear God." God is unequivocally benevolent toward Israel.

On the other hand, against potential scoffers in the synagogue, Paul invokes Habakkuk 1:5 with a noteworthy twist. Whereas God's "work" in Habakkuk is judgment, in Paul's speech it is salvation. Further, Paul uses the text *to avert* disaster: "See that what was spoken in the prophets does not happen." Moreover, Habakkuk is a theodicy. In the face of judgment, Habakkuk "exults in God my savior" (Hab 3:18 LXX). So also Acts 13 is a theodicy that exults in the God who is benevolent to save.

But some Jews in Pisidian Antioch resist this benevolence. Although the text says that resisters judge *themselves* unworthy of eternal life (13:46), implicitly *God* also so judges them. Their opposition becomes the occasion for Paul and Barnabas to announce that they are turning to the Gentiles. Many interpreters detect here a reorientation of Christianity away from Jews to Gentiles. This is a point where I have resisted taking Paul and Barnabas as ciphers for Christianity. Rather, this incident gives a rationale for the inclusion of Gentiles in the Pauline mission.[43] But more crucially, how does God's character develop from this point forward?

In a debate over Gentiles in Acts 15, Peter makes their inclusion in his ministry God's choice. Because faith eliminates distinctions between

---

[42]Matthaus Buss, *Die Missionspredigt des Apostels Paulus im pisidischen Antiochien: Analyse von Apg 13,16-41 im Hinblick auf die literarische und thematische Einheit der Paulusrede* (Stuttgart: Katholisches Bibelwerk, 1980) 25, recognizes that God is the subject of the speech. See also Schneider, *Die Apostelgeschichte*, 2:131; and Johnson, *The Acts of the Apostles*, 236.

[43]See Pesch, *Die Apostelgeschichte*, 2:47; Barrett, *The Acts of the Apostles*, 1:657; and Johnson, *The Acts of the Apostles*, 241.

Jews and Gentiles in God's eyes, to make Gentile believers become proselytes is to defy God. Peter inverts readers' expectations by comparing believing Jews with believing Gentiles: as with Gentiles so also with Jews (15:7-11). But the inversion is temporary. James characterizes God as taking Gentiles under divine care in accord with Amos 9:11-12 LXX, and Amos confirms God's inclusion of the Gentiles in fulfillment of the Davidic promise. In contrast to Peter's inversion, God adds the Gentiles to the Jews: as with Jews so also with Gentiles.

The twofold characterization of God as benefactor and judge emerges with respect to Jews who oppose Paul in Corinth. As a sign of God's judgment, Paul acts out a ritual of degradation against them by shaking the dust from his clothes (Acts 18:6). But Paul's turn to Gentiles still includes going to Jews. In fact, as a sign of God's benevolence Crispus, the leader of the synagogue, immediately becomes a believer (18:8).

Apollos is a Jew who works with Ephesian Jews in Acts 19. When Paul baptizes Apollos's converts, he is God's agent of beneficence to them (19:5-6). Though Paul's work in the synagogue incurs the opposition of only some Jews (τινες; 19:9),[44] he moves to the hall of Tyrannus. Still both Jews and Gentiles receive God's beneficence in Paul's message and in concrete cases of healing.

Paul's summary of his ministry in his speech at Miletus reinforces the theme of God's impartial benevolence. Paul claims to have done what was beneficial for both Jews and Gentiles (Acts 20:20-21; see also 26:20). God's grace has two specific benefits: edification and the gift of *the* inheritance (ἡ κληρονομία; 20:32). Though clues are meager here, "inheritance" in the thematic development carries overtones of the Abrahamic covenant, which in 3:25 is God's promise to bless all the families of the earth.[45]

After Paul's arrest in Jerusalem, the high priest Ananias and his party portray Paul and his sect as a liability for the Jewish people rather than as an asset (Acts 24:5). In contrast to this portrait, Paul presents himself as faithful to the God of the forebears and as a benefactor to the nation (24:14-17). High priestly opponents appear again in 25:2 before Festus.

---

[44]Roloff, *Die Apostelgeschichte*, 283.

[45]On Abrahamic overtones of ἡ κληρονομία, see Werner Foerster, "κληρονόμος," in *TDNT* 3:781-85; and Lars Aejmelaeus, *Die Rezeption der Paulusbriefe in der Miletrede (Apg 20:18-35)* (Helsinki: Suomalainen Tiedeakatemia, 1987) 161-65.

On this occasion, Paul's denies that he is a liability to the Jews, but stops short of presenting himself positively as a benefactor.

Festus, however, redefines Paul's opponents as ἅπαν τὸ πλῆθος τῶν Ἰουδαίων (Acts 25:24). Some English Bible versions (e.g., JB, NRSV) translate πλῆθος as "community," implying the entire Jewish populace, but this translation ignores the progressive discovery of what is true in the narrative world. Festus specifies that the πλῆθος appealed to him both in Jerusalem and in Caesarea. So readers who have traversed the narrative know that he summarizes the opposition of the πλῆθος of the high priestly party. It should be translated accordingly "the entire group of Jews." Festus embellishes the magnitude of the opposition, but are readers not ethically obligated to avoid extending the opposition to the entire Jewish community?

Before Agrippa, Paul presents himself as a benefactor of the Jews because he advocates God's promise to the ancestors precisely for the twelve tribes of Israel. The raising of the dead in Acts 26:8 alludes to the resurrection of Jesus but also to the resurrection for the twelve tribes of Israel. Both cases fall under the canopy of the promise to the ancestors, which in the thematic development of the narrative is God's promise to bless all the families of the earth.[46] God is the God who made a promise to the forebears. This promise comes to fulfillment in the resurrection of both Jews and Gentiles.

When Paul meets with Jewish leaders in Rome, he claims that he has not been a liability to the Jewish people (Acts 28:17). His claim stands over against the opposition of "the Jews" (28:19). Readers know well that the opposition against Paul came from the high priestly crowd. In the ethics of reading, is it appropriate to take "the Jews" (v. 19) as representative of all Judaism?[47] Hardly! Paul presents himself as the representative of the hope of Israel (v. 20) and acts as an agent of God's benevolence toward the Jews who come to him.

---

[46]On recall of the Abrahamic promise from Luke 1, see Johnson, *The Acts of the Apostles*, 433.

[47]Daniel Marguerat, "The End of Acts (28.16-31) and the Rhetoric of Silence," in *Rhetoric and the New Testament: Essays from the 1992 Heidelberg Conference*, ed. Stanley E. Porter and Thomas H. Olbricht (Sheffield: Sheffield Academic Press, 1993) 87, suggests that Paul addresses specific Jews in Rome so that his speech is not his "last word to *Judaism*." Moessner, "Paul in Acts," 102, inverts Paul's declaration of innocence against "my nation" as a final *judgment* against the nation.

Does Paul cease being an agent of God's benevolence to Jews when he quotes Isaiah 6:9-10 (Acts 28:26-27)? The citation characterizes, first, the ancestors of Paul's guests and, second, Paul's guests themselves.[48] Paul joins voices with the Holy Spirit and with Isaiah to multiply the gravity of the hardening of those who hear the prophetic message—past and present.[49] But God also promises to heal the people. English Bible versions consistently translate ἰάσομαι (28:27) as if it is subjunctive: "I would heal them." Luke Timothy Johnson has correctly translated it "I shall heal them," but comments only that the indicative is odd.[50]

For readers who know the LXX, however, this oddity characterizes God as one who heals the Jewish people.[51] In Isaiah 6:10 LXX heart, ears, and eyes appear a second time in inverted order, accompanied by subjunctive verbs that are controlled by μήποτε. But because the subjunctive ἐπιστρέψωσιν moves beyond what is happening with eyes, ears, and heart, it is not controlled by μήποτε. In spite of the hardening, the sense is: "And should they turn, I will also heal them." That God heals the people is further played out in Isaiah 6:11-13 LXX. Where the Masoretic Text predicts judgment and vast emptiness in the land, the LXX says that those who are left behind *will multiply in the land*. Further, where the Masoretic Text says that, if a remnant remains in the land, it will be burned again like the stump of tree that has already been cut down, the LXX says: "And one-tenth shall still be in it [the land], and it [one-tenth or the land] will once again be for foraging like a terebinth[52] and like a nut when it falls from its husk" (6:13 LXX). As the second brackets show, the LXX contains some ambiguity. It is possible that either the one-tenth could be the object of enemy forays, or that the land could

---

[48]François Bovon, "'Schon hat der heilige Geist durch den Propheten Jesaja zu euren Vätern gesprochen' (Act 28:25)," *ZNW* 75 (1984): 227, takes ἀσύμφωνοι in Acts 28:25 in the sense that Paul (and the Spirit) disagree with the Jewish guests. But v. 24 distinguishes between those who believe and those who disbelieve. Paul obviously does not disagree with those who are convinced. Thus, ἀσύμφωνοι elaborates the division among Paul's guests.

[49]See Bovon, "Schon hat der heilige Geist," 227.

[50]Johnson, *The Acts of the Apostles*, 468, 472. Schneider, *Die Apostelgeschichte*, 2:419n.85, takes the future as replacing the subjunctive. So BDF §369 (3). Μήποτε controls the subjunctives ἴδωσιν, ἀκούσωσιν, and συνῶσιν, but not ἐπιστρέψωσιν and ἰάσομαι. On the independence of ἐπιστρέψωσιν and ἰάσομαι from μήποτε, see Bovon, "Schon hat der heilige Geist," 230.

[51]In agreement with my reading, see Koet, "Simeons Worte," 1554-55.

[52]On the terebinth kernel as a source for food, see Immanuel Löw, *Die Flora der Juden*, 4 vols. (Hildesheim: Georg Olms, 1967) 1:199.

once again be the source of foraging for the people. Two clues favor the land as a source for food. (1) The preceding promise that the remnant will multiply in the land implies a future recovery from devastation. (2) More definitively, the future indicative ἰάσομαι indicates that God reestablishes the proper relationship between the remnant and the land. According to the LXX, in spite of the people's failure to understand and perceive, should they turn, God, who alone is left to heal, promises to heal them.

But why should the context of Isaiah 6:1-13 come into view in Acts 28? There are two primary criteria for confirming allusions to precursor texts in successors—what Richard Hays has called volume and availability.[53] Allusions to Isaiah 6:9-10 in all the gospels and in Romans 11:8b confirm the availability of the text. But there is no explicit volume for Isaiah 6:13 LXX on the verbal plane. When, however, readers go beyond the verbal plane to consider setting and plot, uncanny correspondences come into view. Romans 11:8 alludes to Isaiah 6:9 just at the point where Paul appeals to a remnant in Israel, like those left behind who multiply in the land in Isaiah 6:12-13 LXX. Further, Paul's discourse plays out the plot of Isaiah 6:1-13 LXX: "A hardening has come upon a part of Israel until the full complement of the Gentiles comes in" (Rom 11:25). Something similar occurs to a lesser degree in John 12:40. On the one hand, the hardening explains the unbelief of Jesus' Jewish opponents. But immediately, John 12:42 reports that many, even among the authorities, believed in Jesus. Here also John plays out the plot of Isaiah 6:1-13, so that ὅμως μέντοι in John 12:42 should not be rendered "nevertheless," as if the belief of many goes against Isaiah 6:9-10, but "just so indeed," because the belief of many, in the face of the hardening of others, corresponds to Isaiah 6:9-10 LXX and its context. Similarly, Isaiah 6:9-10 comes into play in Acts 28 in a setting where those who were persuaded constitute a remnant among those who are hardened.[54] This is to say that, on the level of setting and plot, there are volume and availability for an allusion to Isaiah 6:1-13.

---

[53]Richard B. Hays, *Echoes of Scripture in the Letters of Paul* (New Haven CT: Yale University Press, 1989) 29-32, actually gives seven criteria, but only two are vital.

[54]On the correlation of the contexts of Isaiah and Acts 28, see Traugott Holtz, *Untersuchungen über die altestamentlichen Zitate bei Lukas* (Berlin: Akademie Verlag, 1968) 35-36.

Further, in Acts 28 what corresponds to the forebears' refusal to understand and perceive? Paul has attempted to persuade his Jewish guests about Jesus from Scripture. Some were persuaded; some were not. Thus, the citation from Isaiah 6:9-10 applies on the one hand to those who were not persuaded to respond to Paul's previous message about Jesus.[55] On the other hand, the citation also anticipates Paul's next message about God sending salvation to the Gentiles (Acts 28:28). Like the attempt to persuade his Jewish guests about Jesus, Paul's disclosure of God's sending of salvation to the Gentiles will encounter a failure to understand or perceive. The use of Isaiah 6:9-10, however, also anticipates that should the unpersuaded turn, God promises to heal them. As with Luke, so also Acts begins and ends with the God of promises.

Finally, even though Paul's use of Isaiah 6:9-10 makes an analogy between his audience and the forebears, I raise once again the question of whether ethical readers may take *Paul's words to certain Jews in Rome* as the message of Christianity to all Jews. The penultimate clue in the characterization of God in Luke-Acts is that God has sent (divine passive) God's salvation to the Gentiles. Does that mean the forfeiture of God's salvation for Jews? For readers who remember that Paul has shortly before claimed that his confinement was for the sake of the hope of Israel (Acts 28:20), the forfeiture of God's salvation for Jews will seem an unlikely outcome. Further, the antepenultimate clue in the characterization of God is that God will heal Jews, who do not understand or perceive, but who turn (28:27). The final clue is that Paul preaches God's rule to all (πάντας) who come to him.[56] In the ethics of reading, it is a serious matter for readers to ponder whether or not the "all" to whom Paul preached God's rule included Jews.

---

[55]The past nuance of the imperfect in Acts 28:24 is significant. Michael Wolter, "Israels Zukunft und die Parusierverzögerung bei Lukas," in *Eschatologie und Schöpfung: Festschrift für Erich Gräßer*, ed. Martin Evang et al. (Berlin: de Gruyter, 1997) 405-26, argues that, in light of the delay of the parousia, the hardening of unbelievers in Acts 28 is retrospective and applies literally to a generation of the past. On the future hope for Israel, see Fusco, "Luke-Acts and the Future of Israel," 1-17.

[56]Daniel Marguerat, " 'Et quand nous sommes entrés dans Rome': L'énigme de la fin du livre des Actes (28,16-31)," *RHPR* 73 (1993): 15-21, recognizes that the end of Acts suspends on the note that Paul receives all—contextually, Jews, pagans, and Christians—though he also argues for a reorientation of the history of salvation toward Gentiles. See also Gerhard Delling, "Das letzte Wort der Apostelgeschichte," *NovT* 15 (1973): 194.

Can Anything Bad Come out of Nazareth, or Did Luke Think That History Moved in a Line or in a Circle?

Jack T. Sanders

One of the issues that has occupied both Joseph Tyson—to whom I extend herewith my heartiest greetings on the occasion of this momentous occasion in his life—and me is the way in which Luke and Acts portray the Jews, both as a group and divided into different subgroups (leaders, Pharisees, etc.). In this essay I should like to clarify further the attitude of the author of Luke-Acts toward the Jews by responding to a vigorous attack on my position by a protégé of Martin Hengel, Helmut Merkel.[1]

Merkel, who writes that I have attacked "anti-Judaism" in Luke-Acts *mit unüberbietbarer Schärfe* (German for "fierceness that you can't beat with a stick"),[2] holds the view that there is no anti-Semitism—or anti-Judaism if you prefer—in Luke-Acts. In taking the "no-anti-Semitism-in-Luke-Acts" position Merkel, as he makes plain in his exemplary review of scholarship on the subject,[3] puts Michael J. Cook, Lloyd Gaston, Ernst Haenchen, Alfred Loisy, Robert Maddox, Franz Overbeck, Heikki Räisänen, Samuel Sandmel (in alphabetical order), and me into the "incorrect" box. I must say that this strikes me as a list of people with whom I am happy to keep company. I am reminded of Mark Twain's statement, which I once read somewhere, summarizing the relative merits of Heaven and Hell: "Heaven for climate and Hell for society."

In response I should like briefly to review Merkel's main arguments, with some discussion of his mistakes and omissions, and then to address the larger conceptual issues at which the above title hints. At the outset I should emphasize that there is no new evidence. The only evidence is the Gospel of Luke and the Acts of the Apostles, works with which we are all quite familiar. The argument lies in how one reads that evidence and, *most importantly*, in the reasons for reading it that way.

---

[1]Helmut Merkel, "Israel im lukanischen Werk," *NTS* 40 (1994): 371-98.
[2]Merkel, "Israel im lukanischen Werk," 380.
[3]Merkel, "Israel im lukanischen Werk," 371-82.

I. Review and Critique of Merkel's Main Arguments

Merkel's opening point, that "the Lukan Jesus-narrative . . . starts out with Jewish people who are described as manifesting exemplary piety,"[4] is a point that I wish to postpone until later because it is related to the larger issue that I want to bring up. Everyone, of course, sees what Merkel notes here.

Following discussions of Luke's redactional changes in Mark's narrative and of the Apostolic Decree (Acts 15)—discussions that seem not to have a major bearing on the issue under debate—Merkel turns to the all-important opening scene of Jesus' public ministry in Luke, his synagogue sermon in Nazareth (Luke 4:16-30),[5] and here he quite misreads the text. Accusing me of "biased exegesis," he proposes that all that is meant by the Lukan additions of the references to Elijah and Elisha in this narrative is that "God already thought of Gentiles in the Old Covenant, that he did not merely have the glory of Israel . . . in view." Such an interpretation, however, overlooks the fact that Luke has Jesus say here, "There were many widows in Israel in Elijah's days" (v. 25) when Elijah helped a Sidonian widow, and, "There were many lepers in Israel" (v. 27) when Elisha healed a Syrian leper. If Merkel (and others) cannot get the point of the Lukan version of this sermon, the (Lukan) synagogue audience certainly did. They attempted to lynch Jesus (vv. 28-29). Merkel's "*un*biased exegesis" entirely overlooks both the references to needy Israelites at the time of prophetic healing of foreigners and the attempted lynching. This overlooking is convenient at best, obscurantist at worst. How *un*biased is exegesis that overlooks the main points of a narrative? Merkel had just gone over a number of Lukan redactional changes (cf. immediately above); why did he suddenly become blind to redactional changes when noting them would have damaged his case?

Let us sketch this for ourselves as graphically as possible. In the episode under discussion Jesus reads from the Bible, "[The Lord] has sent me to proclaim release to captives, and sight to blind persons, to set the oppressed free"; then he explains that there were many widows in

---

[4]Merkel, "Israel im lukanischen Werk," 382. Cf. also my *The Jews in Luke-Acts* (London: SCM; Philadelphia: Fortress, 1987) 64-71, 159-62, 235-36, and the literature cited there.

[5]Merkel, "Israel im lukanischen Werk," 390.

Israel when Elijah helped a Sidonian widow and that there were many lepers in Israel when Elisha healed a Syrian leper; then his audience tries to lynch him. Why? Because he has said, in effect, that God's deliverance will go to Gentiles as well as to Jews? Nonsense! When the Lukan Jesus says that the hour of deliverance is at hand and then gives his Elijah/Elisha examples, he has pointedly told his audience that God's deliverance then and now is intended for Gentiles—non-Israelites. Luke correctly, therefore, portrays Jews as being irate at such a statement. Luke knows, so I would infer, that many Jews would not object to Gentile salvation but that most would object to the notion that God has rejected Jews. If that last sentence is an inference, the foregoing discussion is not. It is the only explanation of the episode that gives it coherence. Merkel has overlooked the main parts of the story: what Jesus says and how the Jewish crowds respond. We should, of course, prefer for Merkel to be correct and for the rejection of the Jews implied in the pericope not to be there; but alas! Such is not the case. It is hard to see how Merkel can escape his own label of biased exegesis here.

Incidentally, it seems impossible to find a commentary on Luke that does not label Luke 4:16-30 "programmatic." Everyone recognizes that this episode sets the scene for what is to come. Thus we already have information about how Luke wants us to read his work.

Merkel next takes note of Simeon's prophecy in Luke 2:34 that Jesus is "set for the fall and rise of many in Israel," and he proposes that the fall refers to "[the] leading circles,"[6] which he defines as Pharisees and scribes, over against whom is set "the Jewish people" as "friendly."[7] The notion that Luke's animus is against only the Jewish leaders is widespread, and one can read it in any number of places. Merkel, however, seems to overlook my fairly extensive discussion of the role of the Jewish people—as apart from their leaders—in Luke-Acts.[8] My proposal was that Luke wanted to show how the Jewish people slid from their warm embrace of Jesus and of early Christianity into a position, at the end of Acts, of general opposition and how this situation was somewhat prefigured at the end of the gospel. I cannot begin, of course, to repeat that discussion here, but we can note some key statements. When Merkel declares, "Only at Stephen's martyrdom do portions of the people appear,

---

[6]Merkel, "Israel im lukanischen Werk," 390.
[7]Merkel, "Israel im lukanischen Werk," 391-92.
[8]Sanders, *The Jews in Luke-Acts*, 37-83, 350-68.

together with the religious authorities, against the Christians (Acts 6:9-12)," he has plainly misread the text, which does not refer to any "portions."[9] The agitators "aroused *the people* and the elders and the scribes" (v. 12). Going forward in Acts, then, in 9:23 "*the Jews* conferred *together* about how to do away with" Paul; in 12:3 Herod's persecution is "pleasing to *the Jews*"; in 12:11 Peter says that the angel "rescued [him] from Herod's hand and from all the expectations of *the Jewish people* [τοῦ λαοῦ τῶν Ἰουδαίων]"; in 18:12 "*the Jews with one accord* rose up against Paul"; in 23:12 "*the Jews*" plot to ambush Paul; and in 25:24 Festus says that "*the entire multitude of the Jews*" has complained to him about Paul. In 21:27-36, further, it is "*all the crowd*" that apprehends Paul and "*the whole city*" and "a convergence of the people [τοῦ λαοῦ]" that drag him outside the temple. Finally, "*the multitude of the people*" calls for his death. Surely Merkel does not intend to propose that the entire multitude is one portion of the people, that the whole city is a second portion, and that the multitude of the people is a third?! The conclusion that Luke intended to give the impression that all the Jews opposed Christianity is inescapable when one looks at what he wrote. In addition to these explicit references, we should also note Luke's frequent use of subjectless third-person-plural verbs, which I discussed repeatedly in *The Jews in Luke-Acts*[10]—a usage that tends to increase the impression of Jewish opposition. (English translations normally render these subjectless verbs with "they" [did such and such]).

The section of Luke-Acts where these subjectless third-person verbs occur most pointedly is the passion narrative, but here Merkel prefers to ignore their presence altogether and to emphasize that the behavior of at least some of the Jewish people is favorable to Jesus.[11] What has been clear all along is that it is *not* clear what Luke has tried to do with the people (apart from designated individuals and groups) in the passion narrative, and I have elsewhere discussed the details at some length.[12] Since that scene does not contain Luke's final word on Jews, perhaps we can omit discussing it further here again.[13]

---

[9]Cf. Merkel, "Israel im lukanischen Werk," 393.

[10]Cf., e.g., 66.

[11]Merkel, "Israel im lukanischen Werk," 394.

[12]Cf. Sanders, *The Jews in Luke-Acts*, esp. 226-29.

[13]Another aspect of Luke's picture of Jews that Merkel discusses ("Israel im lukanischen Werk," 393-94) is that not all Jews in the cities that Paul visits oppose him and that not all opposition comes from Jews. That is correct, and I noted it earlier (cf.

Next, however, Merkel offers perhaps the most amazing interpretation of Acts 13:46 and 18:6 in print (Paul's blanket denunciations of Jews and statements of turning to Gentiles, recognized and emphasized by everyone since Dibelius fingered those two verses, along with Acts 28:28, as being geographically significant for Luke).[14] Merkel notes that, in both Acts 13:46 and 18:6, Luke says that the Jewish opponents blaspheme,[15] and he then connects this fact with Luke 12:10, where blasphemy against the Holy Spirit is the "unforgivable sin"; so, he concludes, Paul has to condemn the Jews of Antioch and Corinth because they have committed the unpardonable sin! Why did no one else ever think of this solution? Could it have something to do with the fact that Acts 13:46 and 18:6 make no mention of the Spirit? Or that Paul, in the first case at least, gives a rationale for his condemnation that has nothing to do with either blasphemy or the Spirit ("Since you reject him and judge yourselves unworthy of eternal life . . . ")? Or that Luke 12:10 speaks of God's refusal to forgive whereas Acts 18:6 speaks of blood guilt? Merkel and others of like persuasion, incidentally, need to consult Bauer-Aland for words on the root βλασφημ- because their interpretation of the term cannot be reconciled with the accepted meaning of the word.[16]

In this context we should also note a statement by Merkel about the Pauline mission with which we may agree completely: "Gentiles react no less brutally than Jews if they see their interests threatened by the proclamation of the gospel."[17] Given that he sees this, why does Merkel not raise the obvious question: If both Jews and Gentiles oppose the spread of Christianity, why does Luke condemn only Jews? The thinking of the "no-anti-Semitism-in-Luke-Acts" proponents seems impervious to this question. Let us pose it in another way: As the narrative of Acts progresses into the Gentile mission there are both acceptance and rejection of Christianity by both Jews and Gentiles; and Gentile rejection can be just as brutal as Jewish; so why are only Jews condemned? Why

---

The Jews in Luke-Acts, 75-78, 364-65). Let us for now just note the ambiguity of that evidence.

[14]Martin Dibelius, *Aufsätze zur Apostelgeschichte*, 4th ed., FRLANT, NF 42 (Göttingen: Vandenhoeck & Ruprecht, 1961) 129 (ET: *Studies in Luke-Acts* [London: SCM, 1956] 149-50).

[15]Merkel, "Israel im lukanischen Werk," 395.

[16]Walter Bauer, *Griechisch-deutsches Wörterbuch*, 6th ed., ed. Kurt Aland and Barbara Aland (Berlin and New York: Walter de Gruyter, 1988).

[17]Merkel, "Israel im lukanischen Werk," 394.

are they singled out at the end of Acts—*even after some of them*, on Merkel's terms,[18] *have accepted the gospel*—as being the people from whom Paul turns in order to take Christianity to Gentiles (Acts 28:28—where Merkel's blasphemy camouflage can't be used)? Why doesn't it work the other way? Since both Jews and Gentiles have both accepted and rejected the gospel, and since representatives of both groups have persecuted the Christian mission in some way, why doesn't Luke have Paul turn from Gentiles to Jews? Why not? Why do only Jews as a group incur guilt for rejecting the gospel? Why only they?

Finally Merkel cites, as proof of Luke's positive attitude toward Jews, the fact that there are positive statements about Jews in Luke-Acts. In spite of Merkel's patently false claim that I "hardly know what to make of Luke's positive statements about the Jews,"[19] in fact I discussed this issue at length in my book.[20] One wonders if Merkel actually read the book or merely thumbed it looking for statements with which he could disagree. But let us look at Merkel's use of the evidence here. First he discusses Paul's views on the ultimate salvation of the Jews (Rom 11).[21] While he never quite says so, it appears that he thinks that Luke must share Paul's views, since he observes that, while Luke never writes anything quite as direct as Romans 11:25-32, he does close Acts by saying that Paul received *all* who came to him. In the next paragraph, further, Merkel refers to the work of Andreas Lindemann who, according to Merkel, has shown it "likely" that Luke had read Romans.[22] Thus Merkel seems to want to make Luke hold Paul's views, although there is nothing in Acts to support such a desire. Now, it is an extremely dangerous procedure to assume that Luke thought something because we can show that Paul thought it; but let us now examine once again the way in which Luke closes Acts.

Of the Jews who came to Paul in his lodgings, "some were persuaded by what he said, but some disbelieved" (Acts 28:24). I am not convinced that Luke really means to say that some became Christians, but let me not belabor that point; so let us grant, for the sake of argument, that some

---

[18]Merkel, "Israel im lukanischen Werk," 393.

[19]Merkel, "Israel im lukanischen Werk," 381, where he again accuses me of being biased in my exegesis.

[20]Cf. Sanders, *The Jews in Luke-Acts*, 37-50, 350-53.

[21]Merkel, "Israel im lukanischen Werk," 396.

[22]Merkel, "Israel im lukanischen Werk," 397. Cf. Andreas Lindemann, *Paulus im ältesten Christentum*, BHT 58 (Tübingen: J. C. B. Mohr [Paul Siebeck], 1979) 169-71.

became Christians and that some did not. Immediately, then (v. 25), Luke accuses the audience of ἀσυμφονία (disharmony) and says that they were leaving, after Paul had said one last thing to them. That one last thing is the quotation of Isaiah 6:9-10 (Acts 28:26-27), used here as everywhere in the New Testament to condemn Jewish rejection of Christianity and to explain it as divinely prophesied. Then the Lukan Paul says, "Let it then be known to you that to the Gentiles has been sent this salvation of God; and they will hear" (v. 28); immediately after this, then, comes the statement (v. 30) about Paul's receiving all. What is one to make of this chain of statements?

Merkel argues that Paul's receiving all comers clearly shows that Paul continues to offer Christianity to Jews: "Individual conversions of Jews are therefore possible, afterward just as before."[23] That is not believable for two reasons. In the first place, Paul had just denounced all Jews merely because not all had been persuaded. (It is worth noting again that no comparable denunciation of Gentiles occurs, even though not all Gentiles had been persuaded, either.) Does Luke want his readers to think that Jews kept coming back to Paul after such an insult? If it strains credulity to believe that, then we need also to note that the statement about receiving all comers follows immediately on Paul's saying that "to the Gentiles has been sent this salvation of God; and they will hear." Since Paul condemned the divided Jews as they left, and since he then said that salvation was going to the Gentiles, isn't it the most logical conclusion that Luke intends for his readers to understand, by the immediately following statement that Paul received all comers, that those visitors were Gentiles? Of course one cannot prove that, but such an understanding gives more coherence to the text than the assumption that "all" still includes Jews. Merkel's assumption robs the conclusion of Acts of coherent sense.

As a further example of statements in Luke-Acts that are positive toward Jews, Merkel cites Luke 13:34-35, which he says allows for the hope "that the Jerusalemites, who refuse to be gathered by Jesus, pay homage to him at the parousia with the praise, 'Benedictus qui venit in nomine Domini.' "[24] Aside from being astounded by the realization that Merkel expects Jews in Jerusalem to speak Latin when Christ returns, we must also note that the basis for the hope that he finds in this passage is

---

[23]Merkel, "Israel im lukanischen Werk," 396; many others also hold this view.
[24]Merkel, "Israel im lukanischen Werk," 396-97.

quite thin. Surely, this saying pronounces judgment on Jerusalem. This was beautifully demonstrated by Jerome Neyrey over a decade ago in an article on Lukan judgment sayings, and he is worth quoting at some length:

> It is not Herod who will kill Jesus but characteristically Jerusalem. Jesus' statement contains an address to the guilty city (13:34a), a statement of its crimes (13:34b, 33) and a sentence-curse for those crimes (13:35). . . . The "house" spoken of in Luke is not simply the Temple, but the people as well. . . . [Thus] the sentence-curse in Lk. 13:35 should be understood as a judgment on the city for rejecting God and his agents.[25]

Neyrey is referring here only to the first sentence of verse 35, "Your house will be deserted for you"; but, given the obvious correctness of Neyrey's observation, how can Merkel then take the rest of the verse—"You will not see me until you say, 'Blessed,' " etc.—as offering a glimmer of hope? Does not the statement rather belong to the curse and mean that the Jerusalemites will never see Christ again, because they will never say that? If such is not what Luke 13:35 intends, then the entire passage (again) loses coherence and sense.

Merkel next offers the tired suggestion that, if Luke had not (like Paul) intended the eventual salvation of the Jews, he would have had Jesus answer the disciples' question at the beginning of Acts (1:6-7) differently.[26] They ask if Jesus "will at this time restore the kingdom to Israel." Since Jesus responds only cryptically ("It is not for you to know times and seasons") and does not specifically say, "Please understand, the Kingdom of God is not for Jews"—so reasons Merkel—we are to understand that Luke harbors hope for "a reinstatement of Israel." This is sheer nonsense. The fact is that Luke has not given Jesus an answer in harmony with the question. The question that the disciples put to Jesus

---

[25]Jerome H. Neyrey, "Jesus' Address to the Women of Jerusalem (Lk. 23,27-31)—A Prophetic Judgment Oracle," *NTS* 29 (1983): 79-80. Cf. already Rudolf Bultmann, *Die Geschichte der synoptischen Tradition*, 5th ed., FRLANT, NF 12 (Göttingen: Vandenhoeck & Ruprecht, 1961) 120-22: A "threat against Jerusalem," in which v. 35b is "probably to be understood from the connection with the myth of the divine Wisdom who, after she dwells on earth in vain . . . , takes her leave of the earth" (my translation; cf. ET: *The History of the Synoptic Tradition* [New York: Harper & Row, 1963] 114-15).

[26]Merkel, "Israel im lukanischen Werk," 397. So also Craig A. Evans, "Is Luke's View of the Jewish Rejection of Jesus Anti-Semitic?" in *Reimaging the Death of the Lukan Jesus*, ed. D. D. Sylva, BBB 73 (Frankfurt am Main: Anton Hain, 1990) 51.

is whether he will restore Jewish autonomy under a legitimate (Davidic) king, and Jesus' answer is that the timetable is in God's hands but that it is time to begin the worldwide mission. The answer does not comport with the question. But surely Merkel does not expect us to think that Luke endorses the notion of an eventual restoration of Jewish political autonomy under a Davidic king (reinstatement of Israel)!? Everything in Luke-Acts is against this notion. The entire central section of the gospel heightens expectation that the Kingdom of God is about to come, and then (19:11-27) Luke explains that Jesus must yet go away and return as royalty before the Kingdom comes, thus disappointing temporal and emphasizing divine or supernatural hopes for the Kingdom. Luke-Acts nowhere promotes or condones the notion that Jesus, God, or anyone else will ever "restore the kingdom to Israel." Luke apparently intends for his readers simply to understand that the disciples' question in Acts 1:6 is mistaken.[27] There is in any case no hope for Jewish salvation here.

In his conclusion Merkel reasons that Luke was actually pro-Jewish (on the basis of the presumed positive statements that I have just examined), but that therefore "he [had to] become anti-Jewish in some respects." This statement is hardly understandable. Merkel's preparation for it is this:

> Precisely because [Luke] saw Jesus so thoroughly in the Jewish context and no longer focused on what was new in Jesus' proclamations[, he was] no longer [able] to make the Jewish decision against Jesus understandable . . . and therefore [he had to] transpose it onto secondary conflicts . . . that carry an anti-Jewish stamp.[28]

We may of course agree that Luke did not understand Jesus, certainly not entirely, and that he did not understand the conflict that Jesus and his followers had with other Jews. To the degree that the conflicts that Luke does portray have anti-Jewish traits, then, they are Luke's portrayals. That was always my point, and the point that Haenchen, Loisy, Overbeck, and the others whom Merkel puts into the "incorrect" camp wanted to make. The connection between that and Merkel's concluding statement (above), however, continues to elude me, and it seems disharmonious

---

[27]For a somewhat different view, cf. Geza Vermes, *Jesus the Jew* (Philadelphia: Fortress, 1973) 51, who sees the disciples' question as a "survival of their [incorrect] political aspirations even in the 'post-Easter' period."

[28]Merkel, "Israel im lukanischen Werk," 397-98.

with the rest of Merkel's essay and with his ostensibly pro-Jewish statements in Luke-Acts that we have reviewed above.

In spite of his singling me out as the worst of the "incorrect" group, Merkel actually discusses the interpretive judgments that I earlier put forward only negligibly and my arguments not at all. He states early in his essay that none of the texts that I cite supports my judgments, and that Craig Evans has already shown that;[29] so it is necessary now to discuss Evans's essay briefly.[30]

In the first part of his essay Evans discusses the following passages in Luke-Acts: Luke 4:16-30 (Jesus' synagogue sermon); 10:30-35 (the good Samaritan); 14:15-24 (parable of the banquet); 19:11-27 (parable of the pounds, with the rich man who went into a far country and returned); Peter's speeches in Acts (chaps. 2–4); Acts 7:51-60 (Stephen); 13:16-51 (Antioch); and 28:17-31 (conclusion). Since we have reviewed about half of these here already, to go further into details now would prolong this essay beyond its assigned limits. Where Merkel and Evans have referred to the same passages, they have made the same point, so I would have no need to supplement my reply to Merkel. The more interesting part of Evans's essay, however, is the second part, where he seeks an answer to the question, "What were the attitudes and manners of expression of Jewish groups toward other Jewish and non-Jewish groups, with which there were serious disagreements?"[31] Many of the examples that Evans brings forward can hardly be relevant for comparison with Luke-Acts, since he reaches as far back as 1 Samuel and as far forward as the Babylonian Talmud.[32] He also includes a section on "Pauline Criticism of non-Christian Jews,"[33] the relevance of which is not entirely clear, since Paul, like Luke, wrote as a Christian. On the Dead Sea Scrolls,[34] of course, Evans is quite correct. Some of those documents, especially the *War Scroll* (which Evans neglects to mention), are well known for the viciousness with which they condemn everyone else. Evans's "point is that [the] hatred [that he finds in Jewish literature over a millennium or

---

[29]Merkel, "Israel im lukanischen Werk," 381.
[30]Evans, "Luke's View," 29-56, 174-83. In fact many of the points that Merkel makes in his paper were made already by Evans.
[31]Evans, "Luke's View," 38.
[32]Evans, "Luke's View," 38, 40-42.
[33]Evans, "Luke's View," 44-45.
[34]Evans, "Luke's View," 43-44.

more] is unmasked; subtle it is not."[35] Luke on "the Jews," thinks Evans, is mild by comparison.[36]

What can we make of this? Either Evans means that, although Luke has some harsh things to say about Jews in general, he is not as nasty as other Jews are capable of being; or he means that Luke, the Gentile writer, is not as nasty as Jews are capable of being. If he means the former, of course he is incorrect, because Luke was not a Jew. If he means the latter, then he should have considered, as comparators, other Gentile writers who criticized Jews. Let us, however, make the best of his attempt and agree that polemic at any time, including during the Hellenistic and early Roman periods, can be vicious. Evans's point would then be that Luke's attack on "the Jews" pales by comparison. We are surely taken somewhat aback by this morality of relativity. If I am less bad than someone else, am I then good? If I murder someone quickly, am I less a murderer than someone who murders by torture? Surely my more "humane" form of murder does not make me a philanthropist! But if not, then what help is it to introduce comparative polemic in defense of Luke's polemic? "Everyone else is doing it" is always the self-justification for everything from speeding on the highway to evading taxes to selling dope. Is that the morality to which Evans wants to hold the New Testament?

To be sure, this argument would not be taking place if Christianity had not triumphed and thus turned the empire, as well as successive Christian governments, against Jews. It is only the power that the New Testament's anti-Semitism finally gained that makes it significant. If Luke's view of Jewish rejection had become lost in the plethora of failed religious movements in the Roman Empire, no one would care today; it would be merely one more example of ancient religious and racial stereotyping. Such an insignificant position, however, would not make the theory of rejection disappear; it would just make it insignificant. Unfortunately, it did become significant, and that significance has had unfortunate consequences.[37] Mature Christians, as Norman Beck keeps reminding us, should openly reject the anti-Semitism in the New Testament, not pretend that it does not exist.[38]

---

[35]Evans, "Luke's View," 49.
[36]Evans, "Luke's View," 49.
[37]Cf. my discussion of Walter Eltester on this point in *The Jews in Luke-Acts*, 56-57.
[38]Norman A. Beck, *Mature Christianity in the 21st Century: The Recognition and*

Evans has one final point not also mentioned by Merkel, and that is that Luke uses the term "brethren" to address non-Christian Jews,[39] especially but not exclusively in Peter's speeches in the first part of Acts. Further, Luke "persists in calling non-Christian Jews 'brethren' right to the very end of the Book of Acts (28:21)."[40] Evans holds that such use of the term therefore means that Luke nourishes positive thoughts toward Jews. This is the exegesis of desperation, for Luke nowhere calls anyone "brethren"; rather, he uses this term in his speeches, where it provides a note of verisimilitude, nothing more. Evans's last example of this term occurs in what the Roman Jews say to Paul: No fellow Jews (brothers) who have come to Rome have said anything bad about Paul. What would Evans expect Luke to have his Jewish characters call one another, idiot(s)? What kind of writer would Luke have been if he had had the Roman Jews say to Paul, "None of the idiot Jews who have come here has said anything bad about you."? Or if he had had Peter begin his interpretation of Scripture in Acts 2:29 by saying, "Men, Idiots . . . "? Of course Luke uses "brethren" as a term of address in his speeches; that was the way—in his opinion, in any case—Jews talked to one another formally.[41] Luke's use of the term "brethren" in Jewish speech to other Jews says nothing about his own attitude toward Jews.

II. Conceptual Issues

Let us now turn to the larger issues here that the title of this essay implies. The first has to do with the rush of some New Testament scholars, like Merkel and Evans, to defend Luke-Acts against the charge of anti-Semitism. Let us quit quibbling over terms. The important thing is to see accurately the way in which Luke portrays the Jewish people generally. We have just seen that Merkel's and Evans's interpretations of the evidence in their attempts to discern positive statements about the Jewish people prove untenable on close scrutiny, and we are thus left with the general and overall impression of rejection and doom pronounced most particularly in Jesus' first address to Jews and in Paul's last—scenes that sandwich everything else between them and that

---

Repudiation of the Anti-Jewish Polemic of the New Testament, rev. ed. (New York: Crossroad; Philadelphia: American Interfaith Institute/World Alliance, 1994).

[39]Evans, "Luke's View," 53-55.

[40]Evans, "Luke's View," 54.

[41]Evans ("Luke's View," 54) adduces limited and late evidence that this was, indeed, a Jewish form of address.

therefore clearly give us the colors that Luke intended his readers to see everywhere in Luke-Acts.[42] But what seems to motivate modern scholarly defensiveness is this: Nearly all New Testament scholars have learned, since 1944, that anti-Semitism is bad, and therefore some cannot believe that it exists in the foundational documents of Christianity, which of course is good. A somewhat analogous attitude surfaced a few years ago when the press reported that an official of the government in Greece announced that Greece's financial problems were due to "Jews." When reporters asked him whether his statement were not anti-Semitic, he replied that it was not, that "Jews" was simply what one always called bankers and other financial manipulators. In other terms, anti-Semitism is an "incorrect" word, and so of course we cannot be anti-Semitic, whatever we may think of Jews. That is only an analogy; the defensiveness on the part of many New Testament scholars is rather that, because anti-Semitism is bad, it cannot be present in the New Testament.

Early in this century, as I became painfully aware when I was reading through much of the older literature on Luke-Acts in preparation for writing *The Jews in Luke-Acts*, New Testament scholars did not shy away from and twist the meaning of those statements in Luke-Acts that are hostile and defamatory toward Jews, as Helmut Merkel has done in his essay; they simply accepted, restated, and endorsed those views.[43] Let us bring into evidence Alfred Plummer's ICC commentary on Luke.[44]

On Luke 4:28, where it is said that Jesus' synagogue audience became enraged at his exegesis, Plummer (unlike Merkel) saw Luke's point exactly . . . and endorsed it!

> They see the point of His illustrations; He has been comparing them to those Jews who were judged less worthy of Divine benefits than the heathen. It is this that infuriates them, just as it infuriated the Jews at Jerusalem to be told by S. Paul that the heathen would receive the blessings which they despised (Acts xiii. 46, 50, xxii. 21, 22). *Yet to this day the position remains the same; and Gentiles enjoy the Divine privileges of which the Jews have*

---

[42]On this sandwiching effect, cf. again Eltester's remarks referred to above, n. 37.

[43]We eagerly await the appearance from University of South Carolina Press of Joseph Tyson's next book, which will chronicle attitudes toward Jews in scholarly literature on Luke-Acts since Baur. The book is expected in 1998.

[44]Alfred Plummer, *A Critical and Exegetical Commentary on the Gospel according to S. Luke*, 4th ed., ICC (Edinburgh: T.&T. Clark, 1910).

deprived themselves. . . . [The] early instances of God's special blessings being conferred upon heathen would have peculiar interest for Lk.[45]

Again, on Luke 19:14, where Luke adds to the parable of the pounds the narrative about Jesus' citizens who hated him and whom he then ordered executed, Plummer saw clearly that, "while the δοῦλοι [slaves] represent the disciples, the πολῖται [citizens] represent the Jews"; and then he added, "The Jews hated Jesus without cause, ἐμίσησάν με δωρεάν [they hated me without cause] (*Jn. xv. 25; Ps. lxviii. 5*),"[46] as if quoting John and the Psalms both clarified Luke and gave historical reality!

Finally, on Luke 23:25, where Pilate released Barabbas "but delivered Jesus to their will," Plummer wrote, "Both the repetition of τὸν διὰ στάσιν, κ.τ.λ. [the one . . . for insurrection, etc.] and the addition of τῷ θελήματι αὐτῶν [to their will] are peculiar to Lk." Thus again he understood the gospel correctly (unlike Merkel) and recognized that the emphasis on the Jewish motivation was Lukan, but again he endorsed Luke's emphasis by adding immediately, "The writer thus emphasizes the enormity of the transaction." And he then adduced supporting evidence: "In the *Gospel of Peter* Herod is present at this point and gives the sentence. He does not wash his hands, and the blame is transferred to him and the Jews. So also in the *Acta Pilati* (B. x.) it is the Jews who hastily execute the sentence, as soon as Pilate has pronounced it. Comp. Justin (*Try.* cviii.) ὃν σταυρωσάντων ἡμῶν [whom we crucified]."[47] (It is Trypho the Jew who is speaking in the last quotation.)

Where, we may wonder, would Plummer fit into Merkel's list of incorrect and correct interpreters of Luke (and Acts)? On the one hand, Plummer could see quite clearly how it was Luke's intent to show "the Jews" as the murderers of Jesus who rejected salvation for themselves. Since Merkel confusedly thinks that such was not Luke's intent, he would have to class Plummer as one of the incorrect. On the other hand, Plummer did not accuse Luke of anything bad—like anti-Semitism (a term that was hardly current in Plummer's day)—and so Merkel could not class him with Haenchen, the others, and me. What a puzzlement!

We thus see that New Testament scholars once upon a time had no difficulty seeing Luke's portrayal of the Jews for what it is, a condemna-

---

[45]Plummer, *S. Luke*, 128-29; emphasis added.
[46]Plummer, *S. Luke*, 440; emphasis added.
[47]Plummer, *S. Luke*, 527.

tion of them for rejecting the offer of salvation in Christ (for which God has rejected them) and for being Christ-killers. Now, however, New Testament scholars are divided into two camps: those who see Luke's intent accurately and condemn it; and those who cannot see it, refuse to see it, and grasp at straws to explain it away because they cannot agree with it and cannot bring themselves to condemn anything in the New Testament.

This (admittedly suspected) attitude on the part of some New Testament scholars goes beyond the case of anti-Semitism; it reaches to anything bad in the New Testament. Our profession finds it difficult to see that all in the New Testament does not meet our standards of morality, and the main case in point is slavery.

Slavery was and is a horrible institution, in spite of the fact that it existed in most societies worldwide until relatively recent times and still exists in some; yet the fact that it is condoned and even endorsed (1 Pet 2:18) in the New Testament is seldom emphasized. That slavery, however, is routine and accepted in the New Testament was clearly seen by Heinz-Dietrich Wendland in *RGG*[3]:

> In the New Testament slaves are assumed and accepted; therefore, never is the institution as such made into the problem or condemned as unjust (cf. 1 Cor 7:20ff.; Philemon; and the household codes). This is also true of some of Jesus' parables that simply assume the fact of slavery. . . . This is all the more noteworthy, since probably in the first congregations the number of slaves exceeded that of the slave holders to a considerable degree.[48]

Nowhere in the New Testament is slavery condemned; everywhere it is assumed. Yet New Testament scholars often have a blind side when it comes to New Testament endorsement of slavery; they are capable occasionally of noting its presence but are seldom willing to take up the problems posed by that presence. Luke's portrayal of "the Jews," it seems to me, falls into a similar category. We think that anti-Semitism should not be in the New Testament, and so we do our best to explain it away.

Finally, there is the matter of the Lukan view of history. Since the time of Conzelmann,[49] at least, we have all understood Luke to have had a strong view of historical development. He wrote as an historian and had

---

[48]Heinz-Dietrich Wendland, "Sklaverei und Christentum," in *RGG*[3] 6:101-2.

[49]Cf. Hans Conzelmann, *Die Mitte der Zeit: Studien zur Theologie des Lukas*, 2nd ed., BHT 17 (Tübingen: J. C. B. Mohr [Paul Siebeck], 1957); ET: *The Theology of St. Luke* (New York: Harper & Brothers, 1960).

a clearly laid-out notion of former time, present time, and future time. He showed historical progression from Jesus through the beginnings of the church and the inauguration of the Gentile mission to the promise of worldwide Christianity. Probably everyone reading this essay agrees with that general scheme. Yet Merkel and others seem now to propose that Luke held a static and unchanging view of history as far as Jews are concerned. In my study of Luke-Acts I came to realize that the narrative of Luke-Acts shows a progression, where the Jewish people are concerned, that justifies the harsh statements made in the speeches—beginning with Jesus' Nazareth sermon—about the two-sided Jewish rejection (that is, the Jews' rejection of Christ/Christianity and God's rejection of them). The gospel begins with a setting in a thoroughly Jewish matrix, and throughout the gospel the Jewish people remain on Jesus' side, except that the passion narrative begins to call this solidarity into question. Acts also begins in a thoroughly Jewish matrix, but the solidarity breaks down very quickly. Soon "all the people," as we noted above, begin to be the opponents of Christianity, and the term, "the Jews," begins to be used *in malam partem.* At the end of Acts, then, narrative and speech come together in the final departure of Paul's divided Jewish audience, at which time Paul delivers the supreme denunciation and turns toward Gentiles exclusively.[50] When Merkel lays emphasis, as we noted at the beginning, on the fact that "the Lukan Jesus-narrative . . . starts out with Jewish people who are described as manifesting exemplary piety," he implicitly denies this historical progression. If Merkel wants to keep Luke's portrayal of "the Jews" within a static and cyclical rather than within a dynamic and historical perspective, let us hope that he will do a better job of explaining how such a perspective coincides with Luke's general historical perspective.

---

[50]Cf. Sanders, *The Jews in Luke-Acts*, 81-83, 367-68. Tyson (*Images of Judaism in Luke-Acts* [Columbia: University of South Carolina Press, 1992] 188 and passim) has also seen the narrative progression but has continued to view the speeches as subordinate to the narrative. My explanation still seems to me to make the best sense of the tension between the speeches and narrative throughout much of Luke-Acts. Tyson, rather, refers frequently to "ambivalence" (e.g., *Images of Judaism in Luke-Acts*, 153).

Subtlety as a Literary Technique in Luke's Characterization of Jews and Judaism

Thomas E. Phillips

One of the burning issues within Lukan studies over the past decade and a half has been the Lukan assessment of Jews and Judaism. The Lukan characterization of the Jewish people, of their institutions, and of their apparent rejection of the Christian message, has prompted some prominent Lukan scholars to lament that the third gospel and Acts are "anti-Semitic."[1] Of course, given contemporary sensitivities, many persons within the scholarly community, including many of the contributors to this volume, have offered readings of the Lukan texts which seek either to negate or soften the force of this charge of anti-Semitism within the third gospel and Acts. Craig A. Evans, for example, has argued that the Lukan writings do not promote anti-Semitism *per se* even though they do contain a "narrow, nonecumenical approach to religion."[2] Robert Tannehill has sought to exonerate the Lukan writings even more fully from charges of anti-Semitism by appealing to the sense of tragedy with which they tell the story of Jewish rejection of the Christian message,[3] and Marilyn Salmon has attempted to read the Lukan texts within the social context of Israel's own (and obviously not anti-Semitic) tradition of prophetic self-criticism.[4] Jacob Jervell has suggested that the Lukan texts envisage a "divided Israel" and criticize only the portion of Israel (that is, unrepen-

---

[1]See, especially, Jack T. Sanders, "The Parable of the Pounds and Lucan Anti-Semitism," *TS* 42 (1981): 660-69; "The Jewish People in Luke-Acts," in *LAJP* (1988) 51-75; and "The Salvation of the Jews in Luke-Acts," in *Luke-Acts: New Perspectives from the Society of Biblical Literature*, ed. Charles H. Talbert (New York: Crossroad, 1984) 104-107.

[2]Craig A. Evans, "Is Luke's View of the Jewish Rejection of Jesus Anti-Semitism?" in *Reimaging the Death of the Lukan Jesus*, ed. Dennis D. Sylva, BBB 73 (Frankfurt am Main: Hain, 1990) 29-56 (quotation, 37).

[3]Robert C. Tannehill, "Israel in Luke-Acts: A Tragic Story," *JBL* 104 (1985): 69-85. In reply, however, Sanders, "The Jewish People in Luke-Acts," 75, argues that tragedy requires an innocent victim and the " 'Jews' are the villains, not the victims" in Luke and Acts.

[4]Marilyn Salmon, "Insider or Outsider? Luke's Relationship to Judaism," in *LAJP* (1988) 76-82.

tant Jews) who reject the Christian message. In his view, the new Israel into which believing Gentiles are incorporated is not criticized.[5]

Of course, with such an important and hotly debated Lukan issue at hand—and Sanders, Evans, Tannehill, Salmon and Jervell certainly do not exhaust the scope of scholarly readings focused upon the characterization of Jews and Judaism in the Lukan texts[6]—the pen of Joseph B. Tyson could not long be still. In several articles and ultimately in a monograph, Dr. Tyson formed and presented his reading of Jews and Judaism in the third gospel and Acts.[7] By employing the methodological tools of reader-response criticism, Dr. Tyson suggested that the third

---

[5]Jacob Jervell, "The Church of Jews and Godfearers," in *LAJP* (1988) 11-20, and *Luke and the People of God* (Minneapolis: Augsburg, 1972).

[6]Among the more recent readings of these issues are: David Ravens, *Luke and the Restoration of Israel*, JSNTSup 119 (Sheffield: Sheffield Academic Press, 1995); Jon A. Weatherly, *Jewish Responsibility for the Death of Jesus in Luke-Acts*, JSNTSup 106 (Sheffield: Sheffield Academic Press, 1994); Wolfgang Reinbold, *Der älteste Bericht über den Tod Jesu: Literarische Analyse und historische Kritik der Passionsdarstellungen der Evangelien*, BZNW 69 (New York: de Gruyter, 1994); Dennis D. Sylva, ed., *Reimaging the Death of the Lukan Jesus*, BBB 73 (Frankfurt am Main: Hain, 1990); David B. Gowler, *Host, Guest, Enemy, and Friend: Portraits of the Pharisees in Luke and Acts*, Emory Studies in Early Christianity 2 (New York: Peter Lang, 1991); Wolfgang Stegemann, *Zwischen Synagoge und Obrigkeit* (Göttingen: Vandenhoeck & Ruprecht, 1991); Anthony Saldarini, *Pharisees, Scribes and Sadducees* (Collegeville MN: Michael Glazier, 1988); Briggitte Kahl, *Armenevangelium und Heidenevangelium: 'Sola Scriptura' und die ökumenische Traditionsproblematik im lichte von Väterkonflikt und Väterkonsens bei Lukas* (Berlin: Evangelische Verlagsanstalt, 1987); James D. G. Dunn, ed., *Jews and Christians: The Parting of the Ways A.D. 70 to 135* (Tübingen: J. C. B. Mohr, 1992); Adele Reinhartz, "The New Testament and Anti-Judaism: A Literary-Critical Approach," *JES* 25 (1988): 524-37; and Mark Allan Powell, "The Religious Leaders in Luke: Literary-Critical Study," *JBL* 109 (1990): 93-110.

[7]Joseph B. Tyson, "Jews and Judaism in Luke-Acts: Reading as a Godfearer," *NTS* 41 (1995): 19-38; *Images of Judaism in Luke-Acts* (Columbia: University of South Carolina Press, 1992); "Torah and Prophets in Luke-Acts: Temporary or Permanent?" in *SBLSP* (1992): 539-48; "Authority in Acts," *Bible Today* 30 (1992): 279-83; "The Problem of Jewish Rejection in Luke-Acts," in *LAJP* (1988) 124-37; "The Emerging Church and the Problem of Authority," *Int* 42 (1988): 132-45; "Further Thoughts on *The Death of Jesus in Luke-Acts*," *Perkins Journal of Theology* 40 (April 1987): 48-50; "The Gentile Mission and the Authority of Scripture in Acts," *NTS* 33 (1987): 619-31; *The Death of Jesus in Luke-Acts* (Columbia: University of South Carolina Press, 1986); "The Jewish Public in Luke-Acts," *NTS* 30 (1984): 574-83; "Conflict as a Literary Theme in the Gospel of Luke," in *New Synoptic Studies*, ed. William R. Farmer (Macon GA: Mercer University Press, 1983) 303-27; "Acts 6:1-7 and Dietary Regulations in Early Christianity," *PerRS* 10 (1983): 145-61; "The Problem of Food in Acts," in *SBLSP* (1979): 69-86; "The Opposition to Jesus in the Gospel of Luke," *PerRS* 5 (1978): 144-50; and "The Lukan Version of the Trial of Jesus," *NovT* 3 (1959): 249-58.

gospel and Acts contain both positive and negative images of Judaism. Thus, "there is no need to reduce Luke-Acts to a single-minded point of view in regard to Jewish religious life and thought," even though the texts ultimately do promote the superiority of Christian faith over Judaism.[8]

In spite of the proliferation of differently nuanced readings (and I find Tyson's reading highly persuasive), nothing even approximating a scholarly consensus has emerged. In this essay honoring Joseph Tyson, I have no illusions of breaking what one reviewer described as the current "impasse on the question of Luke's view of Jews and Judaism."[9] Within the limitation of this space, I cannot defend a reading of the entire corpus. Rather I wish only to illustrate how subtlety is used as a literary technique for characterizing the Jews in some accounts within the third gospel. Specifically, I want to examine two passages within the third gospel (Luke 10:25-37; 18:18-30) in which Jewish religious leaders approach Jesus and inquire about eternal life. I believe that the subtle criticism of specific Jewish leaders within these accounts reflects a larger, more fundamental attitude of criticism toward Jews and Judaism on the part of the third gospel. More importantly, I believe that this subtle and indirect means of criticism was the most appropriate form of criticism available to accomplish at least one of the goals of the third gospel.

I. Synopsis of the Stories

On two occasions in the third gospel Jesus is encountered by a Jewish religious leader who asks him, "What must I do in order to inherit eternal life?" (10:25 and 18:18). The two stories bear striking formal similarities. Both stories follow the same plot structure. They begin with the respective Jewish leaders questioning Jesus about eternal life. In each case, the Lukan Jesus responds to that question by pointing to the very Jewish law which each leader believed himself to have obeyed scrupulously. After seeing Jesus point to the law, each leader offers a comment revealing a presumption of righteousness on his part. Then, in the climax of each story, Jesus undercuts that presumption of righteousness by confronting each leader with a demand from the law. In neither case is the religious

---

[8]Quotation from "Jews and Judaism in Luke-Acts," 38. Also see *Images of Judaism in Luke-Acts*.

[9]See Claudia Setzer, review of *Jewish Responsibility for the Death of Jesus in Luke-Acts*, by Jon A. Weatherly, *JBL* 115 (1996): 360-61.

leader able to comply with that demand—even though Jesus' demand is clearly rooted in the law. In both cases, the Lukan Jesus is not only highlighting the failure of the respective Jewish leaders to keep the law, but he is also attempting to reveal the absurdity of the premise underlying the religious leaders' original question, the absurdity of "doing" anything in order to "inherit" eternal life. In the depiction of the third gospel, this absurdity lies at the heart of Judaism—at least as practiced by the Jewish leadership. We will now examine each story in more detail.

II. Jesus Turns the Law on a Lawyer (Luke 10:25-37)

The parable (or example story[10]) of the so-called "good Samaritan" is introduced in the context of a controversy story[11] between Jesus and a Jewish expert on the law. This expert, a lawyer, asks Jesus what one must "do"[12] in order to "inherit" eternal life (v. 25). The Lukan Jesus answers, as he characteristically responds to all potentially entrapping questions, with his own question: "In the law, what is written? How do you read it?" (v. 26).[13] The lawyer then summarizes the law by quoting an amalgamation of Deuteronomy 6:5 and Leviticus 19:18 which requires one to love God and neighbor (v. 27).[14] Jesus shows apparent satisfaction

---

[10]On the importance of example stories within "L," that is, the materials unique to the third gospel, see Gerd Petzke, *Das Sondergut des Evangeliums nach Lukas* (Zürich: Theologischer Verlag, 1990) 108-109; and Gerhard Sellin, "Lukas as Gleichniserzähler," *ZNW* 65 (1974): 166-89, and *ZNW* 66 (1975): 19-60.

[11]I. Howard Marshall, *The Gospel of Luke*, NIGTC (Grand Rapids MI: Eerdmans, 1986) 439, claims that the lawyer is "friendly" to Jesus, but the use of ἐκπειράζω ("test") suggests otherwise. It is consistently used in Luke's gospel to indicate a "hostile attitude." See Joseph A. Fitzmyer, *The Gospel according to Luke*, 2 vols., AB 28, 28A (Garden City NY: Doubleday, 1981, 1985) 2:880; and Luke Timothy Johnson, *The Gospel of Luke*, Sacra Pagina 3 (Collegeville MN: Liturgical, 1991) 172. On 10:25-37 as a controversy dialogue, see John D. Crossan, "Parable and Example in the Teaching of Jesus," *NTS* 18 (1972): 285-307.

[12]On the importance of the lawyer's expectation that he could "do" something (aorist tense) in order to inherit eternal life, see Heinz Schürmann, *Das Lukasevangelium*, 3 vols., HTKNT (Freiburg: Herder, 1969–1994) 2:131-32.

[13]Note that the prepositional phrase Ἐν τῷ νόμῳ ("in the law") is placed at the beginning of the sentence for emphasis.

[14]Summarizing the demands of the law as love for God and love for neighbor was common among the Jews of Jesus' (and Luke's) day. See J. Ian H. McDonald, "Rhetorical Issue and Rhetorical Strategy in Luke 10:25-37 and Acts 10:11-18," in *Rhetoric and the New Testament* (Sheffield: Sheffield Academic Press, 1993) 63; Josef Schmid, *El Evangelio según san Lucas*, Comentario de Ratisbona al Neuvo Testamento 3 (Barcelona: Herder, 1981) 278-79; and John Nolland, *Luke*, 3 vols., WBC (Dallas: Word, 1989–1993) 2:580-83.

with the answer and tells the lawyer to do that and he will live (v. 28). The lawyer, however, will not let the issue drop and, in what the narrator characterizes as a vain attempt at self-justification, asks: "Who is my neighbor?" (v. 29).[15]

In reply to that question, the Lukan Jesus gives an "eloquent, though indirect, answer"[16] by telling the parable of the "good Samaritan" (vv. 30-35).[17] In the now familiar story, a Jewish priest and a Levite, who are traveling from Jerusalem to Jericho, pass by a wounded man without offering him aid, probably due to their fear that this "half-dead" man (v. 30) would have the audacity to die in their presence and leave them unfit for temple service.[18] Jesus' story then continues by relating how a Samaritan, in contrast to the priest and Levite and no doubt to the chagrin of the lawyer, cared for the wounded man and provided generously for his ongoing needs.[19]

Having finished the parable, the subtle Lukan Jesus is ready to entrap the lawyer who had sought to entrap him. Jesus asks the lawyer: "Which of these three appears to you to have become a neighbor to the one who fell among thieves?" (v. 36). Jesus' reframing of the lawyer's earlier

---

[15]John J. Kilgallen argues that the lawyer's real test began with this question and not the earlier question about inheriting eternal life. See "The Plan of the 'NOMIKOS' (Luke 10.25-37)," *NTS* 42 (1996): 615-19.

[16]C. E. B. Cranfield, "The Good Samaritan (Luke 10:25-37)," *TToday* 11 (1954): 368-70: "Jesus did not give the lawyer a direct answer, because his question was a bad question. Even a heathen ought to know who is his neighbor without being told. How much more a member of the people of God—and most of all one whose job it is to study and to teach the Law!"

[17]Critical scholars generally agree that the parable and its introduction were originally preserved separately and that Luke has placed them together in this context. See Nolland, *Luke*, 2:580, and Charles H. Talbert, *Reading Luke* (New York: Crossroad, 1992) 121. In contrast to the consensus, see William Richard Stegner, "The Parable of the Good Samaritan and Leviticus 18:5," in *The Living Text* (New York: University of America Press, 1985) 27-38; Birger Gerhardsson, *The Good Samaritan—The Good Shepherd* (Lund: Gleerup, 1958) 23-31; and Marshall, *The Gospel of Luke*, 445-46.

[18]See J. Mann, "Jesus and the Sadducean Priests, Luke 10:25-37," *JQR* ns 6 (1915): 415-22; J. Duncan Derrett, "Law in the New Testament: Fresh Light on the Parable of the Good Samaritan," *NTS* 11 (1964–1965): 22-37; and Fitzmyer, *The Gospel according to Luke*, 2:883.

On the possibility that the parable has origins in the Hellenistic synagogue's dissatisfaction with the Jerusalem temple, see Walter Schmithals, *Das Evangelium nach Lukas*, Züricher Bibelkommentare (Zürich: Theologischer Verlag, 1980) 127-28.

[19]The two denarii which the Samaritan left with the innkeeper would probably have provided for the wounded man's needs for over three weeks. See Douglas E. Oakman, "The Buying Power of Two Denarii," *Forum* 3 (1987): 33-38.

question ("Who is my neighbor?") has shown the inadequacy of the lawyer's question. The lawyer wanted to *define* neighbor (Who is my neighbor and consequently who is *not* my neighbor?); Jesus wanted to know who *became* a neighbor (Who behaved like a neighbor to the stranger and consequently did away with the distinction between neighbor and nonneighbor?).[20]

The Lukan Jesus has trapped the lawyer. For the lawyer to suggest that the priest and/or Levite became a neighbor to the injured man would fly in the face of simple human decency; but for him to acknowledge that the Samaritan proved himself to be a neighbor would indict the priest and Levite, the most prominent symbols of temple worship, for their failure to keep the law.[21] Even worse, to affirm the actions of the Samaritan would be to acknowledge that a Samaritan (who did not even worship on the right mountain [John 4:20]![22]) had done what the priest and Levite

---

[20]This shift of the central question under consideration has been pointed out by many interpreters, e.g., Schmithals, *Das Evangelium nach Lukas*, 128; E. Earle Ellis, *The Gospel of Luke*, NCB (Grand Rapids MI: Eerdmans, 1983) 160; Alois Stöger, *The Gospel according to Luke*, 2 vols. (London: Burns and Oats, 1969) 1:207; Johnson, *The Gospel of Luke*, 173; Talbert, *Reading Luke*, 122; Fitzmyer, *The Gospel according to Luke*, 2:884; Schürmann, *Das Lukasevangelium*, 2:147; Jacob Kremer, *Lukasevangelium*, Das Neue Echter Bibel 3 (Würzburg: Echter Verlag, 1988) 121; Marshall, *The Gospel of Luke*, 447; L. Paul Trudinger, "Once Again, Now, 'Who is my Neighbor?' " *EvQ* 37 (1976): 160-63; and Jan Lambrecht, "The Message of the Good Samaritan (Lk 10:25-37)," *LS* 5 (1974): 121-22.

[21]J. M. Furness, "Fresh Light on Luke 10:25-37," *ExpTim* 80 (1969): 182, suggests that this Lukan parable was intended to echo the story in 2 Chr 28:15ff and insists that "in its present Lukan setting, the Parable is by the way of an *argumentum ad hominem*. The Scribe is not answered by a brilliant story invented on the spur of the moment, but more brilliantly and devastatingly by a reference to a tale that the Lawyer already knew very well indeed. Tongue in cheek, Jesus sends the man away to reflect that the answer to his question is to be found in the texts on which he is supposed to be an authority." Also see F. Scott Spencer, "2 Chronicles 28:5-15 and the Parable of the Good Samaritan," *WTJ* 46 (1984): 317-49; and Frank H. Wilkinson, "Oded: Proto-Type of the Good Samaritan," *ExpTim* 69 (1957–1958): 94.

The connection between the parable and 2 Chr (the canonical status of which was probably an open question in the first century) is forced, but the story still has an *ad hominem* character because of its inferences about the inappropriateness of the lawyer's question and the apparent lack of understanding on the part of the self-justifying "expert" on the law.

[22]The contempt which first century Jews and Samaritans held for another is well documented. See, e.g., Klaus Haacker, "Samaritan," in *NIDNTT* (1978) 3:449-67, and John Bowman, "The Parable of the Good Samaritan," *ExpTim* 59 (1947–1948): 151-53.

would not do (love their neighbor) and what the lawyer for all his "self-justifying bluster"[23] had not even considered doing (become a neighbor).

Being squeezed between the obvious lunacy of asserting the neighborliness of the priest and/or Levite on the one hand and his own unwillingness to acknowledge the ethical superiority of any Samaritan on the other hand, the lawyer, who Luther called a "haughty hypocrite,"[24] attempted a slight of hand. He answered, "The one who gave mercy to him" (v. 37). He was unable to defend the actions of the priest and Levite, but also unwilling to dignify the actions of the Samaritan by even uttering the word "Samaritan."[25]

The "pulverizing indictment"[26] and "most scathing attack,"[27] which are implied by the Lukan characterization of this priest, Levite and lawyer, have not eluded interpreters. Commentators have suggested that this account "points out Judaism's failure"[28] and "rejects the proud separatistic nationalism of the Jews."[29] Indeed, in a discussion which begins with a lawyer inquiring about eternal life, the third gospel proceeds to demonstrate that none of the central figures in Jewish worship and religious life (the priest, the Levite, or the legal expert) was as close to eternal life as was the *Samaritan* who rejected both the authority of the Jewish legal experts and the legitimacy of priestly worship at the Jerusalem temple.[30] As Earle Ellis explains, "the despised Samaritan, who is anathema to all that Jewish legalism represents, is nearer than the Jew to a true fulfillment of the law."[31] The Lukan Jesus shows that a Samaritan

[23]Johnson, *The Gospel of Luke*, 176.

[24]See F. W. Farrar, *The Gospel according to St Luke: Maps, Notes and Introduction*, CBC (Cambridge: Cambridge University Press, 1910) 207.

[25]On the lawyer's unwillingness to utter the word "Samaritan," see Fitzmyer, *The Gospel according to Luke*, 2:883; William Arndt, *Luke* (St. Louis: Concordia, 1956) 291-92; Robert H. Stein, *Luke* (Nashville: Broadman, 1992) 318; and Eduard Schweizer, *The Good News according to Luke* (Atlanta: John Knox, 1984) 187.

[26]Peter Rhea Jones, "The Love Command in Parable: Luke 10:25-37," *PerRS* 6 (1979): 232.

[27]Mann, "Jesus and the Sadducean Priests," 46.

[28]Ellis, *The Gospel of Luke*, 159. Similarly, Farrar, *The Gospel according to St Luke*, 205.

[29]Arndt, *Luke*, 291. Similarly, Rafael Silva, "La Parábola del Buen Samaritano," *CB* 23 (1966): 234-40.

[30]Derrett, "Law in the New Testament," 22-37, is correct to emphasize that the primary reason for the enmity between the Jews and Samaritan was related to worship. He notes the importance of understanding that the Samaritans insisted that "the temple worship at Jerusalem was wrongheaded" (24).

[31]Ellis, *The Gospel of Luke*, 160.

understands the law more fully than the lawyer, the "recognized religious authority" of the synagogue,[32] and practices the law more fully than the priest and the Levite, the most prominent symbols of the temple cult and Jewish worship.[33] In showing the failures of these individuals (no doubt chosen for their immense symbolic value), Luke and the Lukan Jesus imply a strong criticism of both the temple and the synagogue, or at least the people most intimately associated with these core institutions of Jewish religious life. The specific basis for this criticism is, however, not clearly specified until the next time that Jesus encounters a Jewish leader who wishes to know what he must "do" in order to "inherit" eternal life.

III. Jesus Turns the Law on a Ruler (Luke 18:18-30)

Toward the end of Luke's travel narrative, Jesus is approached by another seemingly pious Jew, a synagogue "ruler" (ἄρχων).[34] Like the lawyer in the earlier story, the ruler asks Jesus: "What must I do in order to inherit eternal life?" (v. 18). The Lukan Jesus answers this question, as he answered the same question earlier, by pointing to the law.[35] In this case, however, rather than answering the question with another question as he had done with the lawyer, Jesus answers the question by volunteering a summary of the law. He quotes five of the ten commandments, omitting the first four commandments and the last commandment.[36] In providing this particular summary of the law, the subtle Lukan Jesus is preparing to entrap the ruler. The ruler, no doubt believing that his obedience to the law has been absolute, then claims to have kept "all of these" from his youth up (v. 21).[37] This presumption of righteousness, like the

---

[32]Marshall, *The Gospel of Luke*, 442. Schürmann, *Das Lukasevangelium*, 2:131, notes that it was "no accident" that Jesus' opponent in this controversy story is an expert in the law.

[33]On the symbolic value of the priest and Levite as leaders of the Jerusalem cult and the Jewish people, see Johnson, *The Gospel of Luke*, 173; Fitzmyer, *The Gospel according to Luke*, 2:883; Schürmann, *Das Lukasevangelium*, 2:144-45; and Gerhardsson, *The Good Samaritan*, 15.

[34]Although this "ruler" is not specifically identified as a ruler of the synagogue, this person was probably a synagogue ruler or a similar religious leader. See Acts 13:15; Luke 23:13, 35, and 24:20.

[35]On the Christological implications of Jesus' refusal to accept the designation "good" (v. 19), see Ulrich Luck, "Die Frage nach dem Guten," in *Studien zum Text und zur Ethik des Neuen Testaments* (Berlin: de Gruyter, 1986) 282-97.

[36]On the order of the commandments in Luke as compared to the order in Matthew and Mark, see C. E. Evans, *Saint Luke*, TPINTC (Philadelphia: Trinity Press International, 1990) 651.

[37]Frederick W. Danker, *Jesus and the New Age: A Commentary on St. Luke's Gospel*

lawyer's attempt to justify himself, is quickly undercut by Jesus' reply: "One you still lack" (v. 22). That which the ruler lacks is, of course, obedience to the tenth commandment which prohibits coveting—and which Jesus conveniently omitted in his original summary of the law. Note how the Lukan Jesus again communicates in an indirect though forceful manner. Jesus challenges the ruler, who claims to have kept all of the commandments from his youth up, to sell his goods and distribute the proceeds to the poor (v. 22). When faced with his own unwillingness to accept the prospect of impoverishment, the ruler becomes very sad (v. 23). The ruler's presumption of his own righteousness is shattered and he no doubt realizes that Jesus was correct. He did, in fact, still lack obedience to one commandment. He could not release his covetous grip on possessions. Thus the Lukan Jesus, capitalizing on the ruler's own knowledge of the law, undercut the ruler's presumption of righteousness in an indirect but forceful way (just as he had earlier undercut the lawyer's presumption of righteousness).

Although the claim that the ruler lacked obedience to one commandment, the tenth and unstated commandment, has found limited support among scholarly interpreters,[38] the majority of interpreters (and translations) do not concur with this reading. Rather, the majority reading has assumed that the ruler's *one* missing *"thing"* was (were) the *two acts* of selling his possessions *and* following Jesus. This majority reading, of course, faces the irony that the ruler, who lacked only *one thing*, is told to do *two things* (that is, to sell and to follow). The difficulty of this interpretation is well illustrated by C. E. Evans's defense of it. Assuming that Luke has used Mark as a source at this point, Evans explains that verse 22 is the

> climax, which Luke somewhat sharpens with *One thing you still lack* and *all that you have* for Mark's "You lack one thing" and "what you have." But

---

(Philadelphia: Fortress, 1988) 300, 305-306, classifies the ruler among "the righteous who need no repentance." This classification, although common, misses the force of the next verse.

[38]E.g., Craig A. Evans, *Luke*, NIBC 3 (Peabody MA: Hendrickson, 1990) 273, explains that "[a]lthough it does not explicitly say so, the passage suggests that the wealthy ruler had failed to keep the tenth commandment, the commandment not to covet (Exod 20:17; Deut 5:21)"; and Ellis, *The Gospel of Luke*, 218, asserts that "Jesus puts his finger on the one commandment, unmentioned before (20), that the young man failed to keep. He was covetous." Also see Charles M. Swezey, "Luke 18:18-30," *Int* 37 (1983): 69.

Jesus utters not one commandment but two, and it is not clear how they are related to each other, and to the original question and answer.[39]

The lack of clarity about which Evans complains dissipates when one recognizes two factors. First, the theme of commandments runs from verse 20 through verse 22:

[20] You know the commandments . . .
[21] . . . All these commandments . . .
[22] . . . One commandment you still lack.[40]

Second, the economic instructions (that is, to sell and give) are not in themselves what the ruler lacks,[41] but rather they serve to reveal which commandment the ruler has failed to observe, the tenth commandment against coveting. As soon as the ruler was faced with Jesus' call to unlimited generosity (selling all), the ruler knew which one commandment he lacked—even though the subtle Lukan Jesus never explicitly mentioned the tenth commandment.[42] (Only a history of misinterpretation has focused attention upon the *acts* of selling and giving, rather than upon the *commandment* against covetousness.[43])

---

[39]C. E. Evans, *Saint Luke*, 651-52. Similarly, Fitzmyer, *The Gospel according to Luke*, 2:1197, argues that Jesus tells the ruler that he lacks "one thing" and that Jesus then directs him to do "two things."

[40]Grammatically speaking, the antecedent of the pronouns ταῦτα (these) and ἕν (one) is ἐντολάς (commandments).

[41]In an interesting twist on the majority reading, B. Celada's "Distribución de los bienes y seguimiento de Jesús según Lucas 18:18-30," *CB* 26 (1969): 337-40, argues that the one thing which the ruler lacked was a willingness to distribute his goods among the poor as some wealthy persons did in Acts (2:44-45; 4:32, 34-37).

[42]Talbert, *Reading Luke*, 172, has correctly identified that the function of the instructions in 18:22 is to reveal the ruler's disobedience, but he has misidentified the commandment which the ruler refused to obey. In commenting on the instructions in verse 22, Talbert explains that "[f]rom this the ruler learned something about himself he did not formerly know. He learned that he was an idolater. . . . He did not really keep the first and greatest commandment."

[43]I suspect that this history of misinterpretation is due, in large measure, to a Matthean reading of Luke. Where Luke has "You still lack one [commandment]" (18:22), Matthew has "If you would be perfect, go, sell what you possess . . . " (19:21). Thus Matthew's economic instructions to the ruler do function as a *de facto* commandment rather than as a means of pointing to another (unspoken) commandment as they do in Luke. Matthew's interest at this point, to illustrate the greater demands of the "Christian" life, is less prominent in Luke's gospel which lays primary emphasis upon the ruler's unwillingness to fulfill even the commandments which he already acknowledges to be authoritative. A similar theme is sounded in the story of the rich man and Lazarus. The rich man's brothers were unwilling to listen to "Moses and the prophets" who could have

Sensing his own disobedience to God, the ruler became sorrowful, prompting Jesus to comment about the scene which has just transpired. He explains, "It is easier for a camel to pass through the eye of a needle than for a rich person to enter the kingdom of God" (v. 25).[44] Many interpreters have, of course, sought to blunt the force of this analogy, but in the final analysis, a camel simply cannot pass through the eye of a needle.[45] As Charles Swezey noted:

> No four-legged creature could thread the hole of an instrument so easily lost in a hay stack. The incongruity is compounded by the humorous addition of a hump. The image does not point to a difficult maneuver but to an impossible one.[46]

And precisely because the crowd of onlookers realized the impossibility of passing a camel through the eye of a needle, they desperately asked: "Then, who is able to be saved?" (v. 26). That is, if this rich and zealous religious leader cannot enter the kingdom of God, who can? Jesus enigmatically answered: "What is impossible for human beings is possible for God" (v. 27).

This enigmatic answer, understated in its elegance, is, of course, a proclamation that only God can save. In the narrative world of the third gospel, no person can enter the kingdom via his or her own resources. Acquiring salvation on one's own terms is an impossibility for any person whether that person is "very rich" (like this ruler) or very poor. According to a Lukan perspective, "when [and only when] a man who is in search of salvation becomes frighteningly aware that it is impossible for him to attain salvation of himself, he has learned the fundamental lesson on the way to salvation."[47]

In this enigmatic saying, therefore, lies the basis for the fundamental Lukan criticism of Judaism as it is presented in the third gospel. In the

---

shown them how to avoid the rich man's place of torments (16:19-31).

[44]For a comparison of the synoptic parallels to Luke 18:18-30, see Simon Légasse, "The Call of the Rich Man," in *Gospel Poverty: Essays in Biblical Theology* (Chicago: Franciscan Herald Press, 1977) 53-80.

[44]René Krüger, "El Precio Economico del Discipulado," *RevistB* 49 (1987): 193-207, suggests that 18:18-30 is a tightly structured chiasmus ("una bella estructura simétrica") which centers on the difficulty of entering the kingdom (v. 25).

[45]The once popular notion that this saying refers to a small gate within the walls of Jerusalem both lacks any historical support and ignores the literary context of this saying. That notion "has now largely been abandoned" by interpreters. See Nolland, *Luke*, 2:890.

[46]Swezey, "Luke 18:18-30," 68.

[47]Stöger, *The Gospel according to Luke*, 2:94.

narrative world of the third gospel, Judaism, or at least the Jews who practiced it, had never learned this fundamental lesson on the way to salvation. As they are characterized in the third gospel, the Jews cling to the futile hope of acquiring salvation by human efforts. The error of the ruler "was the fundamental error of his whole class."[48] From a Lukan perspective, the Jews had "a totally wrong conception of salvation."[49] In the Lukan portrayal, the Jews, at least as represented by their leaders,[50] mistakenly assume that the activities of religious life (particularly obedience to the law and participation in temple worship) produce eternal life; salvation comes by "doing." The outlook of the third gospel is fundamentally different. Salvation comes as an inheritance; "doing," as long as it is motivated by the desire to be deemed worthy of eternal life, brings only frustration.

This critical attitude toward what is perceived to be the Jewish motivation for worship and religious activity explains why the third gospel can be so stringent in its criticism of Jews and yet so accepting in its views about the ongoing significance of the primary institutions and expressions of Jewish religious life. The third gospel is not critical of the institutions and expressions of Jewish religious life *per se* (the third gospel does begin and end in the Jewish temple, and the Jewish law and prophets are the only scriptural authorities recognized by the third gospel!), but it maintains a fundamentally critical stance toward the dominant[51] motivation for that religiosity, that is, the desire to "do" something in order to "inherit" eternal life. According to the third gospel, the Jewish people characteristically (and mistakenly) pursue their religious endeavors (obey the law and participate in the temple cult) in order to inherit eternal life. Such endeavors, though noble in themselves, are, in the narrative world of the third gospel, counterproductive when undertaken for such (misguided) reasons. These endeavors, though not inappropriate in themselves, become encumbrances to attaining eternal life because they foster a false confidence in one's own ability to effect salvation. According to

---

[48]Farrar, *The Gospel according to St Luke*, 286.

[49]Arndt, *Luke*, 383.

[50]The Jewish leaders in the third gospel are characterized more negatively than the Jewish people in general. See Tyson, "The Jewish People in Luke-Acts," 574-83; and Powell, "The Religious Leaders in Luke," 93-110.

[51]The worship of a few *individual* Jews in the third gospel is not motivated by the desire to "do." These "righteous" Jewish exceptions live in expectation. Note the characterizations of Zacharias in Luke 1:5-80 and of Joseph in Luke 23:50-53.

the third gospel, "doing," even in the form of the most noble religious endeavors, is never a route to "inheriting." Jewish religious life, as presented in the third gospel, provided the Jews, or at least the Jewish leadership, with a false sense of accomplishment. The Jewish religious leader who should have been pleading, "God be merciful to me a sinner!" was prone to proclaim, "I thank God that I'm not like other people!" (Luke 18:9-14).

The fundamental criticism of Judaism maintained within the third gospel is, in theological terms, that the Jews had reversed the proper relationship between soteriology and worship. According to the third gospel, the Jews assumed that worship led to salvation. This put the cart before the horse. In the Christian theology of the third gospel, salvation precedes worship; and salvation itself is preceded by a realization of the absolute futility of "doing" as a means of "inheriting." Salvation, according to the third gospel, comes when one relies upon God for the impossible.

From a Lukan perspective, the Jews' misunderstanding of the relationship between worship and soteriology ultimately corrupted both their worship and their soteriology. Their soteriology was corrupted because they could never "do" enough worship stuff to "inherit" eternal life. As long as they accepted the premise that "doing" preceded "inheriting," they would forever be asking, "What *more* shall I do in order to inherit eternal life?" Their worship was corrupted because, from a Lukan perspective, true worship could not be founded upon human efforts and initiative.[52] Ironically, then, the Jewish leaders' zeal for worship betrayed them. The more zealously they practiced the forms—even appropriate forms—of worship, the more counterproductive their efforts became. Thus, in their zeal for pure worship, the priest and Levite had failed to obey the most basic of the commandments. And likewise, the lawyer and ruler, in spite of their (no doubt sincere) attempts to understand every nuance of the law, found themselves unable to obey even the most basic requirements of the law.

---

[52]Rob Wall, "Martha and Mary (Luke 10:38-42) in the Context of a Christian Deuteronomy," *JSNT* 35 (1989): 23-24, has also noted the irony in the parable of the good Samaritan that those who most diligently seek the promise of the law fail to attain it while the Samaritan, who stands outside the law, does attain it. Wall's conclusion is, however, based on an entirely different set of arguments.

IV. Conclusion

In this essay, I have suggested that two well-known controversy stories in the third gospel each function similarly. They use an introductory question about what must be done in order to inherit eternal life as an occasion to assault the underlying premise of that question, that is, that something—anything—can be "done" in order to "inherit" eternal life. I have suggested that, according to a Lukan perspective, the Jews of Jesus' time had reversed the proper relationship between soteriology and worship. For them, worship, taken up by human initiative, elicited salvation as a divine response. From a Lukan perspective, on the other hand, salvation, which came only upon the collapse of all human efforts, elicited worship as a human response.

I have also intimated that the criticisms of Jews and Judaism implicit within the third gospel (or at least these two accounts) are, in part, a subtle attempt at the transformation of the basis of Jewish religious life. The third gospel shows little interest in altering the forms of religious life (though as a practical matter that probably had already happened by the time Luke wrote). Rather the third gospel seeks to transform the basis of religious life. The third gospel envisages a religious life which begins with repentance and faith in Jesus Christ rather than a religious life based upon human initiative and accomplishment. Such a transformation of religious life could only be accomplished in a subtle manner. The character of the problem with the Jews, as portrayed in the third gospel, necessitated the use of subtlety. A direct call for a change in the basis of religious life would (and often did) meet with equally direct opposition. Only when the prevailing assumptions about the basis of religious life had, on their own terms, been undermined could this transformation occur. The Lukan Jesus accomplished this undermining activity by subtly entrapping these prominent Jewish leaders with the absurdity of their own assumptions. Only a subtle approach could hope to penetrate the accumulated pretenses of those who naively believed themselves already to have the best of motives. Only an indirect call could hope to produce the transformation of worship envisaged by the third gospel.

Believers
and Religious Leaders in Jerusalem:
Contrasting Portraits of Jews in Acts 1–7

Richard P. Thompson

Luke-Acts scholars have given more than a cursory glance to the Lukan portraits of the Jews in the Lukan corpus. Undoubtedly, the interest in these portraits has been provoked, at least in part, by the historical developments in the first half of the twentieth century, namely the Holocaust. To be sure, the anti-Semitism that many such scholars have identified in the Lukan gospel and Acts is most abominable in light of such holocaustic treatment of the Jewish people. Nonetheless, in no sense may one rightly assert that a scholarly consensus exists concerning the Lukan portrayals of the Jews.[1] A spectrum of conclusions concerning the Lukan attitudes toward the Jews has emerged out of these studies, with such conclusions ranging from anti-Semitism at one end of that spectrum to pro-Jewish attitudes at the other end.[2] The debate and dialogue continue with strong interest—and one of the prominent participants is Joseph Tyson, the honoree of this collection of essays. Tyson is one scholar (among others) who has insisted that, in order to assess the Lukan portraits of the Jews, one must not only appropriate *historical*-critical methods but also *literary*-critical methods in studying the Lukan corpus as *narrative* texts. That is to say, one must consider both "the images of the Jewish people and their religious life"[3] and the role or function of those images within the narratives of the third gospel and Acts.[4]

---

[1]See Joseph B. Tyson, ed., *Luke-Acts and the Jewish People: Eight Critical Perspectives* (Minneapolis: Augsburg, 1988), which usefully illustrates the lack of consensus concerning the Lukan portrait of the Jews.

[2]The conclusions at opposite ends of the spectrum may be seen in the respective works of Jack T. Sanders and Jacob Jervell. See, e.g., Jack T. Sanders, *The Jews in Luke-Acts* (Philadelphia: Fortress, 1987), and "The Jewish People in Luke-Acts," in *LAJP* (1988) 51-75; and Jacob Jervell, *Luke and the People of God: A New Look at Luke-Acts* (Minneapolis: Augsburg, 1972), and *The Theology of the Acts of the Apostles*, New Testament Theology (Cambridge: Cambridge University Press, 1996).

[3]Joseph B. Tyson, *Images of Judaism in Luke-Acts* (Columbia: University of South Carolina Press, 1992) 13.

[4]On the issues concerning the narrative unity of Luke-Acts, see, e.g., Mikeal C.

The difficulties associated with the critical assessment of the Lukan portraits of the Jews may well be created by the presence of *both* positive *and* negative images of the Jews in Luke-Acts, the presence of which Tyson has rightly noted.[5] In fact, Tyson is also correct in his suggestion that the examination of these Jewish pictures in the Lukan writings must also consider and account for the narrative role of the Jewish *believers*.[6] To date, however, his suggestion has not been given adequate consideration.[7] While attention has been given to the Lukan depiction of the Jewish public,[8] the Jewish religious leaders and the Pharisees,[9] and even to individual Jewish believers such as Peter and Paul,[10] little scholarly attention has been given to the narrative function of the Jewish believers in Jerusalem, particularly in the first seven chapters of the Acts narrative.[11] One would certainly agree, however, that the Lukan depiction of these Jewish believers must also be stirred into the simmering (and steaming) stew of Jewish images in Luke-Acts.

Parsons and Richard I. Pervo, *Rethinking the Unity of Luke and Acts* (Minneapolis: Fortress, 1993) 45-83.

[5]Tyson, *Images of Judaism in Luke-Acts*, 187-88.

[6]Tyson, "The Problem of Jewish Rejection in Acts," in *LAJP* (1988) 130-37, and *Images of Judaism in Luke-Acts*, 13.

[7]In response to this lack of attention, see my "Christian Community and Characterization in the Book of Acts: A Literary Study of the Lukan Concept of the Church" (Ph.D. diss., Southern Methodist University, 1996), for which Joseph Tyson served as advisor.

[8]E.g., Joseph B. Tyson, "The Jewish Public in Luke-Acts," *NTS* 30 (1984): 574-83.

[9]E.g., Jack T. Sanders, "The Pharisees in Luke-Acts," in *The Living Text: Essays in Honor of Ernest W. Saunders*, ed. Dennis E. Groh and Robert Jewett (Lanham MD: University Press of America, 1985) 141-88; and David B. Gowler, *Host, Guest, Enemy, and Friend: Portraits of the Pharisees in Luke and Acts*, Emory Studies in Early Christianity 2 (New York: Peter Lang, 1991).

[10]On the character of Peter, see, e.g., Robert L. Brawley, *Centering on God: Method and Message in Luke-Acts*, LCBI (Louisville KY: Westminster/John Knox, 1990) 139-47; David P. Moessner, " 'The Christ Must Suffer': New Light on the Jesus-Peter, Stephen, Paul Parallels in Luke-Acts," *NovT* 28 (1986): 220-56; and Wolfgang Dietrich, *Das Petrusbild der lukanischen Scriften*, BWANT 94 (Stuttgart: Kohlhammer, 1972).

[11]Attention has been given to isolated elements of these descriptions, such as the summary statements about the Jewish believers in Acts 2:41-47, 4:32-37, and 5:12-16. See, e.g., Alan C. Mitchell, "The Social Function of Friendship in Acts 2:44-47 and 4:32-37," *JBL* 111 (1992): 255-72; Gregory E. Sterling, " 'Athletes of Virtue': An Analysis of the Summaries in Acts (2:41-47; 4:32-35; 5:12-16)," *JBL* 113 (1994): 679-96; Maria Anicia Co, "The Major Summaries in Acts: Acts 2,42-47; 4,32-35; 5,12-16 Linguistic and Literary Relationship," *ETL* 68 (1992): 49-85; Henry J. Cadbury, "The Summaries in Acts," in *Beginnings*, 5:392-402; and Pierre Benoit, "Remarques sur les 'sommaires' de Actes 2. 42 à 5," in *Aux sources de la tradition chrétienne: Mélanges offerts à M. Maurice Goguel* (Paris: Delachaux et Niestlé, 1950) 1-10.

In this essay, I would like to explore an alternative reading[12] of the opening seven chapters of Acts, a reading that focuses on the role of the Jewish believers in those chapters. While this study cannot account for the entire Acts narrative or even for the entire cast of characters in those seven chapters, I want to examine the Lukan portrayals of two contrasting Jewish character groups found in Acts 1–7: the believers and the religious leaders. I would contend that this use of contrasting characters in the Acts narrative is consistent with both ancient and modern literary concerns, and is illuminative of potential objectives sought by reading this text.

I. Portraits of Characters in Greco-Roman Literature

Greco-Roman writings on the art of literary composition stress that the author is ultimately responsible for several important textual elements: the plot that provides consistency,[13] the descriptive details of the characters and their actions which enable that plot to come to life in the reader's mind,[14] and the creative means by which the reader's attention is held.[15] Such elements provided the criteria for what was included in the narrative. When the narrative is composed effectively, these elements may coax the reader imaginatively through the narrated events with interest and without boredom.[16] The reading process, then, was perceived as having a cumulative effect, so that the creative combination of episodic arrangement, literary patterns, character depictions, and descriptive allusions potentially escorts the reader to a point of final judgment and response.

While Greco-Roman discussions on composition emphasize the role of the text in the reading process, such discussions *also* include the recognition that the narrative text cannot and does not provide *all* infor-

---

[12]By "alternative reading," I mean that the potential for a variety of readings exists because of textual indeterminacies. However, the narrative must still guide such readings. See the essay by Robert C. Tannehill in this volume.

[13]See Aristotle, *Poetics* 7.1-10.

[14]The terms "reader" and "readers" are used here simply as a designation of those who engage the narrative text. I recognize, however, that the first-century recipients were probably members of a hearing audience.

[15]On the roles of emotion and interest created in the reader, see, e.g., Aristotle, *Poetics* 6.2; 9.11; 14.1-9; *Rhetoric* 2.5.14; and Longinus, *On the Sublime* 1.4; 7.3. Cf. Paul Woodruff, "Aristotle on *Mimêsis*," in *Essays on Aristotle's Poetics*, ed. Amélie Oksenberg Rorty (Princeton NJ: Princeton University Press, 1992) 86.

[16]See, e.g, Dionysius of Halicarnassus, *On the Style of Demosthenes* 45.

mation that the reader needs to imagine the narrative world and its characters.[17] Thus, as modern literary critics also stress, the reader must make
judgments that seek to account for what the text *does* and does *not* state
about actions and characters.[18] The characterization of a given narrative
refers *both* to the cumulative images of characters *and* to that part of the
reading process in which the reader constructs and reevaluates characters
in light of new information, scenes, and images. This process of character
building or characterization occurs, therefore, in the convergence of the
reader and the Acts text.[19]

The reader's role in characterization includes the construction and
evaluation of characters in the narrative—tasks that must account for the
narrative images as presented. The reader must assess both how certain
characters are presented and what function such depictions have in the
narrative's plot. In studying Greco-Roman literature, one finds character
portrayal to have been done in various ways. The typical way to present
a character is by implicit description, in which the narrative focuses on
the character's actions rather than on motives or attitudes.[20] Aristotle
insisted, for instance, that actions reveal one's ἦθος.[21] Ancient
historians used common literary *topoi* to describe a character's actions
with common social categories and ideals. Such descriptions in the beginning sections of an ancient narrative often provide the reader with images

---

[17]See, e.g., Dionysius, *Letter to Gnaeus Pompeius* 3, who states that Herodotus's work
is preferable to Thucydides' work because the latter lacks selectivity and thereby exhausts
the reader. See also Demetrius, *On Style* 4.222, who credits Theophrastus with the view
that some points "should be left to the comprehension and inference of the hearer, who
when he perceives what you have left unsaid becomes not only your hearer but your
witness."

[18]See Wolfgang Iser, *The Act of Reading: A Theory of Aesthetic Response* (Baltimore:
Johns Hopkins University Press, 1978) 163-231; and Meir Sternberg, *The Poetics of
Biblical Narrative: Ideological Literature and the Drama of Reading*, Indiana Studies in
Biblical Literature (Bloomington: Indiana University Press, 1985) 235-37.

[19]Cf. Wolfgang Iser, *The Implied Reader: Patterns of Communication in Prose Fiction
from Bunyan to Beckett* (Baltimore: Johns Hopkins University Press, 1974) 274-75; and
John A. Darr, *On Character Building: The Reader and the Rhetoric of Characterization
in Luke-Acts*, LCBI (Louisville KY: Westminster/John Knox, 1992) 59.

[20]See Aristotle, *Poetics* 6.5, 8, 21; 8.1; where the various forms of πράττω imply
that the characters of a tragedy are "actors" or "agents of action." Cf. Malcolm Heath,
"The Universality of Poetry in Aristotle's Poetics," *Classical Quarterly* 41 (1991): 389.
See also Thompson, "Christian Community and Characterization," 96-102.

[21]See, e.g., Aristotle, *Poetics* 6.7; 15.2. It is imperative, when one reads texts such as
Aristotle's *Poetics*, to make a distinction between "character" that is both reflected and
shaped by action and "character" as an actor.

that would potentially contribute to her evaluation of later scenes and characters.[22] Depicted action often includes speeches by one or more characters,[23] which provide implicit commentary or explanation on preceding narrative events and potentially guide the evolving judgments and understanding of the readers.[24] In other words, certain characters may function as reliable spokespersons for the narrator, who remains unseen behind her narrative composition but who subtly directs the reader's attention to certain details.

One must not conclude, because of the predominant use of implicit description in ancient characterization, that explicit or direct description of characters is absent from Greco-Roman literature. The narrator frequently strolls onto the narrative stage and addresses the reader directly about something central to the plot: a comment about certain actions, or the revelation of motives that are otherwise imperceptible to the reader.[25] In such explicit remarks—including summary statements and parenthetical remarks—the narrator shifts from *showing* the reader what happened to *telling* her what happened.[26] Such explicit descriptions become key elements of the narrative and provide the information necessary for the reader's evaluation of a character's actions and ἦθος.[27]

The Acts narrative, like other Greco-Roman literary texts, provides selected images and information from which its reader may imagine a particular narrative world. Whether implicit or explicit, these descriptions

---

[22]Peter Toohey, *Reading Epic: An Introduction to the Ancient Narratives* (New York: Routledge, 1992) 14.

[23]Cf. E. Auerbach, *Mimesis: The Representation of Reality in Western Literature* (Princeton NJ: Princeton University Press, 1953) 39.

[24]Speeches, then, would potentially assist the reader in the interpretation of subsequent narrative events. See Henry R. Immerwahr, *Form and Thought in Herodotus* (Cleveland: Western Reserve University Press, 1966); and Virginia J. Hunter, *Thucydides: The Artful Reporter* (Toronto: Hakkert, 1973), who stress the use of speeches to foreshadow narrative events in the histories of Herodotus and Thucydides. Cf. also Iser, *The Implied Reader*, 275, 288, and *The Act of Reading*, 112, whose emphasis on anticipation and retrospection is useful here.

[25]E.g., see how Thucydides comments directly about Pericles (*Peloponnesian War* 1.139.4; 1.277.3; 2.65.5-13) and Cleon (3.36.6; 4.21.3). Cf. Henry D. Westlake, *Individuals in Thucydides* (London: Cambridge University Press, 1968) 5-19.

[26]See Wayne C. Booth, *The Rhetoric of Fiction*, 2nd ed. (Chicago: University of Chicago Press, 1983) 3-20.

[27]See C. Garton, "Characterisation in Greek Tragedy," *JHS* 77 (1957): 249; and Simon Goldhill, "Character and Action, Representation and Reading: Greek Tragedy and its Critics," in *Characterization and Individuality in Greek Literature*, ed. Christopher Pelling (Oxford: Clarendon, 1990) 102.

present imaginative pictures of persons and scenes to be envisaged in the readers' minds. Thus, one is not surprised to find that such depictions of narrative characters in Greco-Roman literature were typically colored by common social categories and ideals.[28] Because characters were colored in this manner, the original recipients were able to share *both* the social conventions of the narrative world *and* also the evaluative framework by which those characters were depicted. The examination of the Lukan portraits of certain characters, therefore, requires that one must account for both the explicit and the implicit means by which those characters are presented in the narrative.

II. The Lukan Portrait of the Believers in Jerusalem

As we begin to examine the Lukan portrait of the believers in Jerusalem, we find immediately that the Acts narrative does not describe the followers of Jesus as a group that has separated itself from Judaism. Rather, the Lukan narrator describes these believers as faithful Jews who remained in Jerusalem (1:12)[29] and who obeyed the requirements of Jewish law. They prayed to the God of Judaism (1:14, 24-25; 2:42; 4:24-30; 6:6) and frequented the Jewish temple (2:1, 26; 3:1-26; 5:20-26).[30] Although the Jewish leaders challenged the apostles for their witness about the resurrection of Jesus (4:1-20) and for the apostles' subsequent disobedience of the orders given them by those leaders (5:27-32), Acts

---

[28]Christopher Gill, "The Question of Character and Personality in Greek Tragedy," *Poetics Today* 7 (1986): 251-73, esp. 269-71, who suggests that this means of characterization dominates the character portraits in history writing; and "The Character-Personality Distinction," in *Characterization and Individuality in Greek Literature*, 1-31.

[29]See, e.g., Walter Schmithals, *Die Apostelgeschichte des Lukas* (Zürich: Theologischer Verlag, 1982) 20-21; and Alfons Weiser, *Die Apostelgeschichte*, 2 vols., OTNT 5 (Würzburg: Echter, 1986) 1:82, who understand the importance of the Jerusalem location for the coming events as providing salvation-historical continuity with Israel.

[30]Although there is no consensus about the location of the Pentecost event, I understand ἐπὶ τὸ αὐτό ("in the same place"; Acts 2:1; cf. 1:15) and ὅλον τὸν οἶκον ("the whole house"; 2:3) to refer to the temple. Cf. Jacques Dupont, "L'union entre les premiers Chrétiens dans les Actes des Apôtres," in *Nouvelles études sur les Actes des Apôtres*, LD 118 (Paris: Éditions du Cerf, 1984) 304-308; Kirsopp Lake, "The Communism of Acts II. and IV.-V. and the Appointment of the Seven," in *Beginnings*, 5:140; and David John Williams, *Acts*, NIBC 5 (Peabody MA: Hendrickson, 1990) 39-40. *Contra* M.-É. Boismard and Arnaud Lamouille, *Les Actes des deux apôtres*, 3 vols., Ebib (Paris: Gabalda, 1990) 2:31-32; I. Howard Marshall, *The Acts of the Apostles* (Leicester: Inter-Varsity, 1980) 68; and Rudolf Pesch, *Die Apostelgeschichte*, 2 vols., EKKNT 5 (Zürich: Benziger, 1986) 1:103.

gives no indication that these believers did anything that would soil their spotless image as faithful Jews. Even the charges that some raised against Stephen—charges of contempt for the law and the temple that the narrator explicitly describes as both underhanded and false (6:11-14)[31]—fail to tarnish the blameless narrative image of these Jewish believers in Jerusalem.

This image of the believers in Jerusalem as faithful Jews is enhanced by the speeches of Peter (and the other apostles) that dominate these beginning chapters of Acts. These speeches (as mentioned in section I above) function as a means by which the Lukan narrator may implicitly comment on preceding narrative events.[32] These speeches in Acts 1–7 clearly focus on, among other things, the activity of God in the resurrection of Jesus and in the other extraordinary events that occurred (that is, the Pentecost event and the healing of the lame man). The God of the Jewish ancestors had promised a divine outpouring of the Spirit through the prophet Joel, and the Lukan narrator uses the speech of Peter (whom readers would recognize as a reliable character) to show that this same God had fulfilled that promise through Jesus (2:16-36). This fulfilled promise, however, is not limited to a "select" group such as the believers; for instance, the speech in chapter 2 concludes by stressing that God has acted on behalf of πᾶς οἶκος Ἰσραήλ ("the whole house of Israel"; 2:36).[33] Nonetheless, only those who repented or who "received" (cf. 1:8; 2:38) the gift of God belonged to the ones whom Luke describes both

---

[31]The similarities of the charges against Stephen (Acts 6:11-14) and later against Paul (21:20-21, 27-29; cf. 26:7-11) may suggest to the reader that these later charges are *also* underhanded and false.

[32]The Lukan speeches in Acts have generated significant attention. The classic discussions that compare the Acts speeches with those found in ancient historiography are by Henry J. Cadbury, "The Speeches in Acts," in *Beginnings*, 2:489-510; and Martin Dibelius, "The Speeches in Acts and Ancient Historiography," in *Studies in the Acts of the Apostles* (London: SCM, 1956) 138-85. Also see, e.g., Henry J. Cadbury, *The Making of Luke-Acts*, 2nd ed. (London: SPCK, 1958) 184-93; Eckhard Plümacher, *Lukas als hellenistischer Schriftsteller: Studien zur Apostelgeschichte*, SUNT (Göttingen: Vandenhoeck & Ruprecht, 1972) 38-72, and "Die Missionsreden der Apostelgeschichte und Dionys von Halikarnass," *NTS* 39 (1993): 161-77; Stanley E. Porter, "Thucydides 1.22.1 and Speeches in Acts: Is There a Thucydidean View?" *NovT* 32 (1990): 121-42; Eduard Schweizer, "Concerning the Speeches in Acts," in *Studies* (1966) 208-16; Robert C. Tannehill, "The Functions of Peter's Mission Speeches in the Narrative of Acts," *NTS* 37 (1991): 400-414; and Tyson, *Images of Judaism in Luke-Acts*, 103-109.

[33]Both Peter's speech in Acts 3:12-26 and the defense statement in 5:29-32 also affirm that the promise of God (that is, the God of the Jewish people) is offered to the Jewish people—to Israel.

specifically and explicitly as enjoying or as "being filled"[34] with the ful-filled promise of God (that is, the presence of the Holy Spirit). The pictorial résumé of these Jewish believers as portrayed by the Lukan narrator, therefore, is entirely impeccable. They were faithful to God and to Judaism.

The Lukan portrait of the believers in Jerusalem, in this sense, is sketched with distinctly Jewish markings. The large numbers of Jewish persons who were either "added" (προστίθημι; Acts 2:41; 5:14) to the believers or who belonged to the believers (4:4) are explicitly mentioned by Luke as indicative of two things: the blessing from the God of the Jewish people, and the continuity of the narrated events with Judaism.[35] However, the narrative is not limited to descriptions that are dependent solely on Jewish categories. Rather, the narrative offers other descriptions and allusions that assist its readers to fill in some of these sketchy outlines of the Lukan portrait of the believers. In particular, two additional communal descriptions will be examined here: the unanimity among the believers, and the dynamic of sharing and fellowship.

The first dominant image that the Lukan narrator uses in his depiction of these Jewish believers is that of unanimity and unity. Throughout this beginning section of the narrative, these believers are consistently described in terms of their unanimity and togetherness. In chapter 1, the narrative emphatically states not only that the apostles obediently returned to Jerusalem after Jesus' ascension but also that, along with others, "*these all* [οὗτοι πάντες] were constantly devoted *together* [ὁμοθυμαδόν] to prayer" (Acts 1:14).[36] The abundance of

---

[34]Note the use of the verb πίμπλημι in Acts 2:4 and 4:8, 31 to describe the "filling with the Holy Spirit," and the *contrasting* use of this same verb in 5:3 (Ananias) and 5:17 (high priest and others). I will return to this contrast a bit later.

[35]Paul Zingg, *Das Wachsen der Kirche: Beiträge zur Frage der lukanischen Redaktion und Theologie*, OBO (Göttingen: Vandenhoeck & Ruprecht, 1974) stresses that the growth in numbers implies that Jerusalem is swelling with believers. Cf. Wolfgang Reinhardt, "The Population Size of Jerusalem and the Numerical Growth of the Jerusalem Church," in *The Book of Acts in Its Palestinian Setting*, ed. Richard Bauckham, The Book of Acts in Its First Century Setting 4 (Grand Rapids MI: Eerdmans, 1995) 237-65, who defends the historical reliability of these figures; and Ernst Haenchen, *The Acts of the Apostles* (Philadelphia: Westminster, 1971) 184-85: "The question of whether such a mass-baptism was at that time possible in Jerusalem . . . is alien to the nature of the presentation."

[36]Of the eleven occurrences of the adverb ὁμοθυμαδόν in the NT, ten are found in Acts (1:14; 2:46; 4:24; 5:12; 7:57; 8:6; 12:20; 15:25; 18:12; 19:29). The first four occurrences, as well as 8:6 and 15:25, all describe positively the unanimity of the Jewish believers. However, three occurrences describe unanimous *opposition* against one or more

communal language in the narrative staging for the dramatic Pentecost event (2:1-4) depicts the gathered believers as unanimous in character when the extraordinary occurred.[37] This quality of unanimity would not be immediately obvious to its readers without this creative use of communal language.[38] The summary concluding chapter 2 continues the narrative trend by explicitly alluding to earlier images of the believers who were continually devoted *together*.[39] The picture of unanimity and togetherness, however, is now expanded as a result of the Pentecost event.[40] The picture in the summary section includes not only the apostles and others (1:12-14) or the 120 believers (1:15) but also the 3000 who were baptized (2:41).[41] Not only prayer but meeting "*together* [ὁμοθυμαδόν] in the temple" is expressly included in the Lukan depiction of the believers. Thus, these images of unanimity and togetherness are linked to the dramatic events of Pentecost and provide a portrait of these Jewish believers that colorfully blends together both divine activity and communal oneness.

This narrative blending of divine activity and corporate unity continues in the subsequent chapters of Acts. After the initial scene of opposition by Jewish leaders in Acts 4, Peter and John returned to τοὺς ἰδίους (literally "their own"; 4:23), an expression that refers to a gathering of unnamed believers who are described nonetheless as being almost like "family."[42] Even in the face of reported intimidation and

---

Christians. Cf. Hans W. Heidland, "ὁμοθυμαδόν," in *TDNT*, 5:185-86, who ignores the latter use.

[37]Note that, in the opening sentence, Καὶ ἐν τῷ συμπληροῦσθαι τὴν ἡμέραν τῆς πεντηκοστῆς ἦσαν πάντες ὁμοῦ ἐπὶ τὸ αὐτό (2:1), the communal language is stressed by the compound verb συμπληρόω, the word πάντες (see also 1:14), the adverb ὁμοῦ, and the phrase ἐπὶ τὸ αὐτό (which also is used with reference to the believers in 1:15; see n. 30 above).

[38]It is interesting to note that, in Acts 2:6, Luke uses the two verbs συνέρχομαι and συγχέω to describe the Jewish crowd's response to the Pentecost events: "they gathered *together*" and "they were confused *together*."

[39]In both Acts 1:15 and 2:42, the periphrastic construction ἦσαν προσκαρτεροῦντες is used along with the activity of prayer. In 2:42, however, other items are also included as part of their devoted activity.

[40]See Zingg, *Das Wachsen der Kirche*, 169; and Co, "The Major Summaries in Acts," 59, who both stress that δέ (Acts 2:42) links the summary to the preceding narrative events of Pentecost.

[41]Cf. Acts 2:44a for additional emphasis of unanimity: πάντες δὲ οἱ πιστεύοντες ἦσαν ἐπὶ τὸ αὐτό.

[42]On the use of this term for familial and compatriot relationships, see BAGD (1979) 370; LSJ (1940) 818; and Gerhard Schneider, *Die Apostelgeschichte*, 2 vols., HTKNT 5

opposition that have assembled together against them,[43] these believers *together* (ὁμοθυμαδόν) raised a *single* voice (φωνήν; 4:24) to God in prayer, which alludes again to earlier images of united believers (1:14; 2:42). Once again, their prayer resulted in divine blessing and presence that are reminiscent of the Pentecost images of unanimity and empowerment (4:31).[44] Grammatically linked (δέ) to this description is the first sentence of the subsequent narrative section, which depicts the believers as having "one heart and soul" (καρδία καὶ ψυχὴ μία; 4:32). The expression ψυχὴ μία borrows imagery from Greco-Roman friendship traditions to convey explicitly to the reader the communal relationship that united these believers.[45] Surprisingly, the Lukan narrator still uses these allusions in describing the believers after two scenes of internal problems: the Ananias and Sapphira incident in chapter 5,[46] and the controversy over the Hellenist widows in chapter 6 (see 6:5-6).[47] The narrator even describes the believers for the first time in Acts as ἡ ἐκκλησία (5:11), a Septuagintal term that refers to the assembly of God's people.[48]

(Freiburg: Herder, 1980, 1982) 1:356n.16.

[43]Note the use of the verb συνάγω to describe the *united* actions of the antagonists (Acts 4:5, 26, 27).

[44]See Jürgen Roloff, *Die Apostelgeschichte*, NTD 5 (Göttingen: Vandenhoeck & Ruprecht, 1981) 87, who notes that Pentecost was not repeated. *Contra* Jacques Dupont, "La prière des apôtres persécutés (Actes 4,23-31)," in *Études sur les Actes des Apôtres*, LD 45 (Paris: Éditions du Cerf, 1967) 522, who calls this "*la petite Pentecôte.*"

[45]The expression ψυχὴ μία is a proverb found in Greek literature, notably in the writings of Aristotle (*Nic. Ethics* 9.8.2), Plutarch (*On Brotherly Love* 478c), and Iamblichus (*Life of Pythagoras* 168; cf. Plato, *Republic* 5.462c). See Pieter W. van der Horst, "Hellenistic Parallels to Acts (Chapters 3 and 4)," *JSNT* 35 (1989): 46, for a list of additional references to Greek and Latin literature; also Jacques Dupont, "La communauté des biens aux premiers jours de l'Eglise (Actes 2,42.44-45; 4,32.34-35)," in *Études sur les Actes des Apôtres*, 513-14.

[46]See Acts 5:12: καὶ ἦσαν ὁμοθυμαδὸν ἅπαντες ἐν τῇ Στοᾷ Σολομῶν-τος. On the Ananias and Sapphira incident, see, e.g., Daniel Marguerat, "La mort d'Ananias et Saphira (Ac 5.1-11) dans la stratégie narrative de Luc," *NTS* 39 (1993): 209-26; Corina Combet-Galland, "Actes 4/32-5/11," *ETR* 52 (1977): 548-53; Philippe-H. Menoud, "La mort d'Ananias et de Saphira (Actes 5. 1-11)," in *Aux sources de la tradition chrétienne*, 146-54; and Thompson, "Christian Community and Characterization," 216-25.

[47]See Joseph B. Tyson, "Acts 6:1-7 and Dietary Regulations in Early Christianity," *PerRS* 10 (1983): 145-61, who sees this pericope as reflecting a fourfold literary pattern: peace, threat, resolution, restoration.

[48]Of the 103 occurrence of the noun ἡ ἐκκλησία in the LXX, as well as the twenty-two occurrences of the verb ἐκκλησιάζω, the dominant reference is to the assembly of the people of God (ὁ λαός), either in worship or as a nation (e.g., Deut 4:10, 23:9, 31:30; Judg 20:2; 2 Chr 30:2, 4, 13, 17, 23-25; Ezra 10:1, 8, 10, 14). The verb

Clearly, Luke is doing more than merely downplaying the internal problems facing the earliest believers in Jerusalem.[49] Rather, the Acts narrative presents the believers as united even when faced with opposition or conflict (whether internal or external). In the Lukan portrait of the believers in Jerusalem, this quality is directly linked to the God of the Jews, who blessed them with divine presence.

The second dominant image that the Lukan narrator uses in his depiction of these Jewish believers is the dynamic of sharing and fellowship. The uniqueness of this aspect of the Lukan characterization of the believers in Acts 1–7 is the narrator's use of explicit summary statements (2:42-47; 4:32-35; 5:12-16) to create a picture of their typical behavior.[50] That is to say, the Lukan narrator *tells* explicitly about the dynamic of sharing and fellowship rather than *shows* it implicitly by the characters' action. When one reads the Lukan summaries in the context of this Greco-Roman literary convention, therefore, what the narrator states or tells explicitly about the dynamic of sharing and fellowship among the Jerusalem believers becomes increasingly significant to that reading experience.

The dynamic of sharing and fellowship that Luke has included in the Acts narrative depicts the believers as an ideal community or utopia. More specifically, Luke's explicit description of the believers' typical activity is colored with concepts and ideals from Greco-Roman friendship traditions.[51] For instance, the narrator tells of the believers' devotion to ἡ κοινωνία (2:42), a term that was often used to describe the "partnership" between friends[52] and, as the articular form suggests, seems to refer here to the communal bond among the believers.[53] They had "all things

---

is also used with the noun ἡ συναγωγή (e.g., Lev 8:3, 4; Num 20:8, 10; Judg 20:1; 1 Kgs 12:21). See Karl L. Schmidt, "ἐκκλησία," in *TDNT*, 3:501-26; and Luke T. Johnson, *The Acts of the Apostles*, Sacra Pagina 5 (Collegeville MN: Liturgical, 1992) 89.

[49]Contra Schmithals, *Die Apostelgeschichte des Lukas*, 65.

[50]This idea of typical behavior is reflected by the shift from the aorist tense to the imperfect tense.

[51]Cf. esp. Mitchell, "The Social Function of Friendship," 255-72; Dupont, "La communauté des biens," 503-19, and "L'union entre les premiers Chrétiens," 296-318; Luke T. Johnson, *The Literary Function of Possessions in Luke-Acts*, SBLDS 39 (Missoula MT: Scholars Press, 1977) 1-5, and *Sharing Possessions: Mandate and Symbol of Faith*, OBT 9 (Philadelphia: Fortress, 1981) 119-27.

[52]See, e.g., Plato, *Republic* 4.449c; and Aristotle, *Nic. Ethics* 8.9.1-2, 9.8.2; *Politics* 2.1.8–2.2.9. Cf. Mitchell, "The Social Function of Friendship," 260-63.

[53]Cf. Dupont, "L'union entre les premiers Chrétiens," 298-99; and Johnson, *The Acts of the Apostles*, 58.

in common" (ἄπαντα κοινά; 2:44; 4:32).[54] They customarily provided for those in need (2:45; 4:32) by selling possessions and unselfishly giving the proceeds to meet any needs that arose (4:34-37; cf. 2:45).[55] As a result, the narrative presents the believers simply as having "no needy person . . . among them" (4:34). These expressions of goodwill or, in Luke's words, "grace" (χάρις) even extended *beyond* the believers to "all the [Jewish] people" in Jerusalem (ὅλον τὸν λαόν; 2:47; cf. 4:33).[56] The narrative description does not focus, as is often assumed, on the growing reputation of the believers in the eyes of the Jewish people.[57] Rather, in this context the participial phrase ἔχοντες χάριν πρὸς ὅλον τὸν λαόν places before the reader an image of ideal friendship that was expressed to *all* Jews, not merely to the believers (cf. 5:12-16).[58]

Scholarly discussions on these summary sections have frequently digressed to issues of primitive communism[59] or the historical plausibility of these ideal images.[60] However, the use of social concepts in the narrative characterization of persons or groups may suggest other functions.

---

[54]For the expression ἄπαντα κοινά or κοινὰ πάντα, see, e.g., Plato, *Critias* 110c; Aristotle, *Nic. Ethics* 8.1.4; Iamblichus, *Life of Pythagoras* 168; and Lucian, *On Salaried Posts* 19-20. For other references, see Dupont, "La communauté des biens," 505-9; and Plümacher, *Lukas als hellenistischer Schriftsteller*, 17-18.

[55]See John M. Cooper, "Aristotle on Friendship," in *Essays on Aristotle's Ethics*, 301-40, for a thorough examination of the role of unselfishness or *dis*interestness in Aristotle's understanding of εὔνοια in friendship.

[56]Luke uses ὁ λαός to refer to the Jewish people. See Tyson, "The Jewish Public in Luke-Acts," 574-83.

[57]Against the major English translations and most commentators on Acts (who usually ignore the issue), I understand ἔχοντες χάριν πρὸς ὅλον τὸν λαόν to present the believers as "having grace *toward* all the people" rather than "having the goodwill of all the people" (2:47, NRSV). See T. David Andersen, "The Meaning of EXONTEΣ XAPIN ΠPOΣ in Acts 2.47," *NTS* 34 (1988): 604-10.

[58]In the narrative summary of Acts 2:42-47, the believers are described consistently as *givers* of χάρις. To be sure, the believers may been seen to be depicted implicitly as recipients of χάρις as well, but this occurs within the context of the believers themselves, not some larger designation like ὁ λαός.

[59]See, e.g., Haenchen, *The Acts of the Apostles*, 233-35; Martin Hengel, *Property and Riches in the Early Church: Aspects of a Social History of Christianity* (Philadelphia: Fortress, 1974) 31-34; and Lake, "The Communism of Acts II. and IV.-V.," 5:140-51.

[60]See, e.g., S. Scott Bartchy, "Community of Goods in Acts: Idealization or Social Reality?" in *The Future of Early Christianity: Essays in Honor of Helmut Koester*, ed. Birger A. Pearson (Minneapolis: Fortress, 1991) 309-18; François Bovon, "Israel, die Kirche und die Völker im lukanischen Doppelwerk," *TLZ* 108 (1983): 403-14; and Brian Capper, "The Palestinian Cultural Context of Earliest Christian Community of Goods," in *The Book of Acts in Its Palestinian Setting*, 323-56.

As mentioned before (see section I above), characters in Greco-Roman literature were often colored in terms of common social categories or ideals. Thus, these explicit, ideal descriptions of the believers suggest that the Lukan narrator is portraying them in a *most* favorable way—as those who embody the ideals of Greco-Roman society.

The Lukan characterization of the Jewish believers, therefore, presents a positive portrait of a large group of Jews who fulfilled both the ideals of Judaism and, more broadly, the ideals of Greco-Roman society. These persons are depicted in Acts 1–7 consistently in a number of ways: (1) as faithful to the Jewish law and religious practices, (2) as those among whom the presence of the God of the Jews was found, (3) as those who were united together by that divine presence, and (4) as those who provided unselfishly for the needs of believers and others around them. While some of the narrative characterization may be categorized as *implicit* description, much of that characterization may be identified as *explicit* description which, although not complete, does more distinctly direct the reader's attention to potentially significant images within the plot of the Acts narrative.

III. The Lukan Portrait of the Religious Leaders in Jerusalem

Any consideration of the narrative depiction of a character is incomplete without due regard both for other character portrayals and for interaction between those characters in the narrative action. Such is the case in Acts 1–7. The believers do not stand alone. One finds the Jewish public, which is generally presented as responding favorably to the believers in the early chapters prior to the Stephen incident (cf. 2:37; 3:9-11; 4:21; 5:12-16). One also finds the religious leaders, who are surprisingly absent from the initial narrative action (especially if the extraordinary events of Pentecost occur at the temple; see section I above) but who assume increasingly active roles in the Acts narrative. How, then, does the Lukan narrator characterize these religious leaders?

One persistent Lukan image of the religious leaders in Jerusalem is as those who initiate conflict through their opposition of the believers. This image is evident in the first appearance of the religious leaders in Acts 4, immediately after Peter's explanation to the people (ὁ λαός) about the healing of the lame man. Since Peter's call for repentance (3:19-21; cf. 3:26) parallels his similar call after his explanation of the Pentecost event (2:38), the narrative creates a sense of anticipation that repentance and further action from God may result.[61] However, the mood quickly reverses as the narrator not only describes the ensuing arrest of Peter and John by the temple authorities but also provides the information necessary for the reader's evaluation of such actions: these leaders were greatly annoyed by the message of Jesus' resurrection (4:2; cf. 4:18).[62] While this information alone may not incriminate these antagonists, the narrative context given for this arrest scene, in which two Petrine speeches repeatedly identify *God* as the one who has raised Jesus from the dead (2:24, 32; 3:15, 26; cf. 2:36), suggests that these religious leaders were opposing a message that affirms the workings of God.[63] In ironic contrast to the believers, these Jewish leaders are described as *also* joining together (συναχθῆναι; 4:5; cf. 4:26, 27), albeit in opposition. The narrator inserts the response by Peter and John (4:19-20) to the "cease and desist" order—two apostles who are reliable characters by being faithful witnesses to God's working and those through whom the healing occurs.[64] This response functions as implicit commentary that further incriminates these leaders: their silencing order suggests that these Jewish leaders stood in opposition to the God of the Jewish people about whom the apostles served as witnesses.[65]

The initial picture of the religious leaders as opponents of the believers and of God is developed further in a second scene of opposition (Acts 5:17-42). The narrator begins the scene by explicitly giving the reader "inside information" about the motives of the high priest and Sadducees. These leaders were "filled with jealousy" (v. 17), presumably

---

[61]Note the affirmative response of the Jewish people that frames this pericope, as suggested both early in the scene (Acts 4:4) and at the end of the scene (4:21). See Christoph Zettner, *Amt, Gemeinde und kirchliche Einheit in der Apostelgeschichte des Lukas* (New York: Peter Lang, 1991) 261; also Beverly Roberts Gaventa, "Toward a Theology of Acts: Reading and Rereading," *Int* 42 (1988): 155, who stresses that both acceptance and hostility increase in these chapters.

[62]Cf. Tyson, *Images of Judaism in Luke-Acts*, 110, who sees the apostles being opposed as Jesus once was.

[63]See section I above, where I mention that speeches often function as implicit commentary for the narrator, who nonetheless remains behind the scenes.

[64]E.g., the use of σῴζω in Acts 2:47 and in Peter's explanation of the healing of the lame man (4:9, 12) links God's activity surrounding Pentecost to the healing event. See F. F. Bruce, *The Book of the Acts*, rev. ed., NICNT (Grand Rapids MI: Eerdmans, 1988) 78-79, 94-96; and Tannehill, "The Functions of Peter's Mission Speeches," 407.

[65]Cf. Richard I. Pervo, *Profit with Delight: The Literary Genre of the Acts of the Apostles* (Philadelphia: Fortress, 1987) 43: "Their [i.e., the apostles'] opponents are a pack of fascist clowns, reduced to silence with a few inspired words."

over the wonderful events surrounding the believers (vv. 12-16).[66] This negative information stands in contrast to the positive depiction of the believers in two distinct ways: (1) the believers have been "filled with the *Holy Spirit*," not jealousy,[67] and (2) the believers acted out of unselfish motives on behalf of others, not out of the jealousy which Greco-Roman texts often mention as spawning murderous impulses (cf. v. 33).[68] Nonetheless, while the religious leaders are presented as foolishly acting out their jealousy by arresting the apostles, an angel of the Lord released them and thereby affirmed that God was clearly on the apostles' side.[69] In the midst of the interrogation and "closed door" meeting in the subsequent narrative events, the warning by Gamaliel (vv. 38-39), one of the council members, functions all the more ironically.[70] That warning—that their opposition of the believers could make them θεομάχοι (that is, those who fight against God; v. 39)—states what the reader would undoubtedly see in the narrated events of Acts 1–5: "this work *is* of divine origin" (τὸ ἔργον τοῦτο . . . ἐκ θεοῦ ἐστιν; 5:38-39) and that the leaders' opposition of the believers is opposition of God. Here, the narrator surprisingly places information on the lips of an *unreliable* character—information to assist the reader in evaluating the actions of both the believers and their antagonists, the religious leaders.

One final scene must be included in this examination of the Lukan portrait of the religious leaders in Acts 1–7. The narrator makes it clear that charges against Stephen have so troubled the Jewish people and religious leaders that he was brought before the council, even though such accusations were products of connivance and deceit (6:11-14). The subsequent speech, however, focuses on God's activity on behalf of God's people rather than on the charges against Stephen (that is, that Stephen had spoken in opposition to the Jewish temple and law). The narrative mentions nothing about the audience's reaction to Stephen's

---

[66]The typical Lukan grammatical connection of narrative sections (δέ) links the "success" and growth imagery with the jealous reaction (Acts 5:17-18).

[67]Note that the same aorist passive indicative, ἐπλήσθησαν, is used to describe both the believers (Acts 2:4, 4:31) and the religious leaders (5:17).

[68]See Johnson, *The Acts of the Apostles*, 96; and William H. Shepherd, Jr., *The Narrative Function of the Holy Spirit as a Character in Luke-Acts*, SBLDS 147 (Atlanta: Scholars Press, 1994) 173n.65 for lists of references that mention the dangers of jealousy.

[69]Cf. Pervo, *Profit with Delight*, 21-23; Marguerat, "La mort d'Ananias et Saphira," 214-15; and Robert C. Tannehill, *The Narrative Unity of Luke-Acts: A Literary Interpretation*, 2 vols. (Philadelphia and Minneapolis: Fortress, 1986, 1990) 2:65.

[70]See the essay by John A. Darr in this volume.

speech until he accused them of, among other things, "opposing the Holy Spirit" like their ancestors (7:52) and failing to follow the law (7:53). Of course, the former description is consistent with the narrative depiction of the Jewish religious leaders, whose opposition of the believers may be also perceived as opposition of God (cf. 4:18-20; 5:29-32, 39).[71] The narrated response to such countercharges graphically appears as a violent "mob scene," as the fury of council members surpasses their earlier rage[72] against the apostles: they "gnashed their teeth" at the innocent Stephen, whom the narrator contrastingly describes as "filled with the Holy Spirit" (7:55); and they ironically united (ὁμοθυμαδόν; 7:57)[73] in stoning him to death (7:57-60).[74] The council's actions scatter the believers rather than bring them together. The downward narrative spiral of the leaders' actions—from threats to jealousy to rage to murder—culminates in an ironic scene of the leaders united in opposition of the very believers who were united by the presence of God earlier in the narrative.

The Acts narrative, therefore, presents negative images of the Jewish religious leaders. These persons are depicted consistently in Acts 1–7 in several ways: (1) as those who opposed the believers, (2) as those who were united together by that opposition, and (3) as those who were consumed with jealousy and rage that led finally to the murder of an innocent victim. The narrator has included both implicit and explicit descriptions to present these Jewish religious leaders in this manner. The question remains, however, how this presentation of these religious leaders may function in the Acts narrative.

IV. A Function of the Lukan Portraits
of Believers and Religious Leaders in Jerusalem

As the previous two sections of this study have shown, the portrait of the believers contrasts significantly with the portrait of the religious leaders

---

[71]The verb ἀντιπίπτω, referring here to the Jewish opposition against the Holy Spirit, appears in Num 27:14 to describes the rebellion of the congregation (τὴν συναγωγήν) against God. Cf. Shepherd, *The Narrative Function of the Holy Spirit*, 178.

[72]In Acts 5:33, Luke describes the response as διεπρίοντο καὶ ἐβούλοντο ἀνελεῖν αὐτούς. In 7:54, the intensifying response is described more intensively as διεπρίοντο ταῖς καρδίαις αὐτῶν καὶ ἔβρυχον τοὺς ὀδόντας ἐπ' αὐτόν.

[73]Note that the adverb (ὁμοθυμαδόν) is used earlier to describe the unanimity of the believers. Heidland, "ὁμοθυμαδόν," 185-86, however, ignores the Lukan description of these leaders as unanimous in their hostility.

[74]See n. 68 above.

in Acts 1–7. At the discretion of the creative activity of the Lukan author were narrative elements such as the plot, the cast of characters/actors, and the details by which the plot and those actors are described. However, while studies of Luke-Acts often explore the Lukan portrait of the Jewish religious leaders or, more generally, Lukan attitudes toward the Jews, such studies tend to ignore the role of the Jewish believers in the Acts narrative. When one does explore the role of Jewish believers, one finds that the believers and religious leaders in Jerusalem are presented in contrast to one another in the beginning chapters of Acts. These contrasts include the following:

1. The believers are presented as enjoying the presence of God; the religious leaders are never mentioned in terms of God's presence and they act like God's opponents.

2. The believers are presented as united together by that divine presence; the religious leaders are described as united together in jealousy and opposition.

3. The believers are presented as caring for the needs of others; the religious leaders are described as self-serving or as jealous of the positive events and scenes surrounding the believers.

4. The believers are presented as those who united the Jewish people together because of the fulfillment of God's promise to Israel—a fulfillment that has occurred in the midst of the believers; the religious leaders' response is described as increasingly divisive to the Jewish people, the historical people of God.

Is it mere coincidence that these two portraits of Jews are consistently presented in distinctly contrasting ways? I think not. The consistent use of contrasting images for these two Jewish groups suggests that the reader must consider the potential function of these contrasting portraits of Jews in the first seven chapters of the Acts narrative.

What, then, may one offer as a plausible explanation for this contrast in portrayals? If the portraits of the believers and religious leaders function in Acts to present the thesis and antithesis in the narrative, such as Dionysius identifies in the work of Demosthenes (*On the Style of Demosthenes* 21), then one may conclude that the contrast is between differing images of the people of God. The disparity of these portraits occurs on two related levels: the social level, including communal relations and social behavior; and the religious level, including God's blessing and presence. The contrast, which is actually created in the narrative plot by the Jewish leaders who *themselves* divide the Jewish people,[75] suggests that both the acceptance of God and the fulfillment of his promise are found in the believers and not *all* of Israel because of the religious leaders' actions. Although Israel identified itself as the people of God, these opening chapters of the Acts narrative portray the religious leaders specifically as violently opposing God and demonstrably contradicting their claim to be the people of God. These contrasting portraits of Jews, therefore, potentially function to assist the reader in identifying the Jewish believers, not the Jewish religious leaders, as embodying the ideals of the people who belong to God, ἡ ἐκκλησία. Such a vivid portrait of the believers may then provide the reader with essential images that would potentially contribute to her ongoing evaluation of subsequent scenes and characters (including other images of the believers) in Acts. While one may argue that the Lukan portrait of the religious leaders in Acts reflects anti-Jewish tendencies, the portrait of the Jewish believers in opposite, *positive* images suggests that the negative assessment of the Lukan characterization of the Jews (e.g., Lukan anti-Semitism) must be reevaluated.

---

[75]Whereas Jervell, *Luke and the People of God*, 41-74, and *The Theology of the Acts of the Apostles*, 34-43, refers to the people of God who were divided over the gospel, I would contend that the Lukan narrative focus is, more precisely, on the division that occurs *because* of the Jewish religious leaders' hostile reaction. This image of the "divided people of God," then, becomes something like an oxymoron for Luke, as he uses images of *unanimity* to depict the people of God (that is, those in whom the presence of God is found). The Lukan concept of God's people is incompatible with *division* among that people.

Contributors

Arthur J. Bellinzoni
   Professor of Religion, Wells College, Aurora, New York
C. Clifton Black
   Professor of New Testament, Perkins School of Theology, Southern Methodist University, Dallas, Texas
Darrell L. Bock
   Research Professor of New Testament Studies, Dallas Theological Seminary, Dallas, Texas
Robert L. Brawley
   Albert G. McGaw Professor of New Testament, McCormick Theological Seminary, Chicago, Illinois
John A. Darr
   Associate Professor of Theology, Department of Theology, Boston College, Chestnut Hill, Massachusetts
William R. Farmer
   Emeritus Professor of New Testament, Perkins School of Theology, Southern Methodist University, Dallas, Texas; Research Scholar, University of Dallas, Irving, Texas
Victor Paul Furnish
   University Distinguished Professor of New Testament, Perkins School of Theology, Southern Methodist University, Dallas, Texas
Susannah Heschel
   Eli Black Associate Professor of Jewish Studies, Department of Religion, Dartmouth College, Hanover, New Hampshire
David P. Moessner
   Professor of Biblical Theology, University of Dubuque Theological Seminary, Dubuque, Iowa
Mikeal C. Parsons
   Associate Professor of Religion, Department of Religion, Baylor University, Waco, Texas
David B. Peabody
   Professor of Religion and Chair of the Department of Religion and Philosophy, Nebraska Wesleyan University, Lincoln, Nebraska

Thomas E. Phillips
Assistant Professor, Division of Religion and Philosophy, Eastern Nazarene College, Quincy, Massachusetts

Vernon K. Robbins
Professor of New Testament and History of Religions, Department of Religion, Emory University, Atlanta, Georgia

Jack T. Sanders
Professor Emeritus, Religious Studies Department, University of Oregon, Eugene, Oregon

Philip L. Shuler
Professor of Religion, McMurry University, Abilene, Texas

Charles H. Talbert
Distinguished Professor of Religion, Department of Religion, Baylor University, Waco, Texas

Robert C. Tannehill
Academic Dean and Professor of New Testament, Methodist Theological School in Ohio, Delaware, Ohio

Richard P. Thompson
Associate Professor of Biblical Literature, Division of Religion and Philosophy, Olivet Nazarene University, Kankakee, Illinois

John T. Townsend
Professor of New Testament, Judaism, and Biblical Languages, Emeritus, Episcopal Divinity School, Cambridge, Massachusetts; Visiting Lecturer on Jewish Studies, Harvard Divinity School, Cambridge, Massachusetts

William O. Walker, Jr.
Professor of Religion and Dean of the Division of Humanities and Arts, Trinity University, San Antonio, Texas

Indexes

Index of Modern Authors

Index of Ancient Sources

Old Testament/Hebrew Scriptures
(EVV and LXX noted; Hebrew either noted or in parentheses)

New Testament

Apocrypha and Pseudepigrapha

Literary Studies in Luke-Acts.
Essays in Honor of Joseph B. Tyson.
edited by Richard P. Thompson and Thomas E. Phillips

Mercer University Press, Macon, Georgia 31210-3960.
Isbn 0-86554-563-4. Catalog and warehouse pick number: MUP/P185.
Text and interior designs and composition by Edmon L. Rowell, Jr.
Cover design by Mary Frances Burt.
Cover illustration ("The Good Samaritan [Luke 10:30-34]"):
    reproduction of a 19th century woodcut (by W. J. Linton)
    of an illustration by Jules Pelcoq (fl. 1866–1877).
Camera-ready pages composed on a Gateway2000
    via dos WordPerfect 5.1 and WordPerfect for Windows 5.1/5.2
    and printed on a LaserMaster 1000.
Text fonts: TimesNewRomanPS 11/13; ATECH Hebrew and Greek.
Display font: TimesNewRomanPS bf and bi.
Printed and bound by McNaughton & Gunn Inc., Saline MI 48176,
    via web-fed offset lithography on 50# Writers Natural
    and perfectbound into 10-pt. c1s stock
        (cover prints 4-color process and with lay-flat lamination).
[July 1998]

052898elr